"This timely and thought-provoking volume offers a compelling exploration of *wellbeing literacy* as a transformative capability for ed… n and beyond. By weaving together diverse voices across disciplin… s, the editors present a bold and clear framework for under… age and intentional communication shape personal … wellbeing. The book presents a compelling ca… ability to comprehend and compose wel… —with the intention of enhancing t… rld. As I read, I found myself not onl… ut also committed to cultivating this capab… our shared professional and educational spaces. It … resource for educators, policymakers, and wellbeing prac… ng to build more reflective, connected, and thriving communiti…

Dr Tayyab Rashid, *Research Affiliate The Human Flourishing Program, Harvard University*

"This book makes a timely and globally significant contribution to wellbeing science. With a clear framework on the language, knowledge, and skills needed for understanding and communicating wellbeing, it features diverse multidisciplinary and multicultural contributions from international scholars. Offering actionable insights, it showcases how wellbeing literacy can be fostered across educational and community contexts contributing to empowering individuals and communities to flourish. Bridging theory and practice, this volume is an invaluable resource for professionals, educators, policymakers, and researchers worldwide".

Professor Do Coyle, *Chair in Languages Education and Classroom Pedagogy, University of Edinburgh*

WELLBEING LITERACY

In this groundbreaking collection, editors Lindsay G. Oades, Narelle Lemon, Jacqui Francis, and Tim Lomas explore wellbeing literacy – the capability to understand and effectively use wellbeing language to enhance flourishing for oneself, others, and society. Drawing together international scholars across diverse disciplines, this volume examines how intentional communication about wellbeing serves as a critical mechanism for personal and collective thriving.

Moving beyond simplistic approaches to wellbeing, the contributors investigate how wellbeing literacy functions as a relational, contextual, and holistic capability that bridges individual experience with broader social systems. Chapters examine wellbeing literacy across different life domains, cultural contexts, and developmental stages, offering both theoretical frameworks and practical applications.

This pioneering work challenges readers to consider: How does wellbeing literacy manifest in various contexts? What role does it play in policy development? How might it serve as a lever for social change? Through multimodal and interdisciplinary perspectives, the collection illuminates the dynamic interplay between language, knowledge, and skills that enable flourishing across individual, communal, and systemic levels.

Essential reading for researchers, educators, and practitioners seeking innovative approaches to fostering wellbeing in an increasingly complex world.

Lindsay G. Oades, PhD, is a Professor of Wellbeing Science and Deputy Dean of the Faculty of Education, The University of Melbourne, Australia.

Narelle Lemon is a Professor of Education and a Vice Chancellor Professorial Research Fellow at Edith Cowan University, Australia and Creative Director of Explore & Create Co. She is an Interdisciplinary Scholar across arts, education, and positive psychology.

Jacqui Francis, PhD, is a Lecturer at the Centre for Wellbeing Science at the University of Melbourne, Australia, and Director for the Masters of Applied Positive Psychology. She has chapters co-authored in *Wellbeing and Resilience Education*, *The Handbook of Positive Psychology in Schools*, and *The International Handbook of Positive Education*.

Tim Lomas, PhD, is a Psychology Research Scientist in the Department of Epidemiology at the Harvard T.H. Chan School of Public Health, USA, and part of the Human Flourishing Program at Harvard University. His main research focus is exploring cross-cultural perspectives on wellbeing, especially concepts, and practices deemed "non-Western".

WELLBEING LITERACY

Theory and Practice Through Multidisciplinary and Transdisciplinary Lenses

Edited by Lindsay G. Oades, Narelle Lemon, Jacqui Francis, and Tim Lomas

Routledge
Taylor & Francis Group
LONDON AND NEW YORK

Designed cover image Cover artwork by Anastasia Theofanous

First published 2026
by Routledge
4 Park Square, Milton Park, Abingdon, Oxon OX14 4RN

and by Routledge
605 Third Avenue, New York, NY 10158

Routledge is an imprint of the Taylor & Francis Group, an informa business

British Library Cataloguing-in-Publication Data
A catalogue record for this book is available from the British Library

ISBN: 978-1-041-08209-5 (hbk)
ISBN: 978-1-041-08208-8 (pbk)
ISBN: 978-1-003-64429-3 (ebk)

DOI: 10.4324/9781003644293

Typeset in Galliard
by KnowledgeWorks Global Ltd.

CONTENTS

FIGURES

TABLES

CONTRIBUTORS' BIOGRAPHIES

Amanda Aitken works as a Project Officer for the Mental Health Council of Tasmania (MHCT), covering the Northern Tasmania region. She has educational qualifications in Commerce (marketing) and Counselling, along with experience in the health and community services sectors. In her role, Amanda has helped develop and implement the campaign by working with various stakeholders including community groups, neighbourhood houses, businesses, non-profit organisations, and government bodies. She adapts the campaign to suit each organisation's specific needs and gathers feedback on its effectiveness through qualitative group sessions. Amanda's combined background in marketing and counselling has been useful in her work connecting with different organisations and supporting mental health initiatives across the region.

Kelly-Ann Allen is an Associate Professor and educational and developmental psychologist at Monash University, a fellow of the College of Educational and Developmental Psychologists, and an honorary principal fellow of the University of Melbourne's Wellbeing Science Centre. A/Prof Allen's core work is in direct response to the widely reported global decline in belonging, particularly for students. Kelly-Ann is the editor-in-chief of the Educational and Developmental Psychologist.

Riccardo Amorati is a passionate educator and researcher currently working as a Senior Tutor in Italian Studies at The University of Melbourne. Following university studies in Italy, he completed his doctoral degree in Applied Linguistics in Australia. His research focuses primarily on the psychological factors that influence language learning (motivation, anxiety, wellbeing), gender-just language education, and innovative approaches to language teaching.

Wulan Aulia Azizah, SPd, MPd, is a lecturer in the Department of Primary Education at the Faculty of Education and Psychology, Universitas Negeri Semarang. Wulan's expertise area is in STEAM education in primary student, professional development, and instructional design for elementary students. Wulan has researched the implementation of STEAM education in elementary schools, and the development of STEAM education for and professional development of teachers for teaching science in elementary schools. Currently based in Semarang, Wulan is actively involved in teaching, research, and community service. In her leisure time, she enjoys exercise, traveling, and exploring new skill experience by volunteering in educational initiatives or attending creative class.

Lisa M. Baker has been a teacher, learner, and researcher in the early childhood field for over 35 years. She holds a Bachelor of Early Childhood Education, Masters of Applied Positive Psychology, Graduate Certification in Education Research and is undertaking a PhD at Melbourne University, Centre for Wellbeing Science, researching the application of wellbeing literacy. Having studied and taught in early education settings for 30 years, and raising her own children, Lisa has a breadth of early childhood knowledge, experience, and understanding of its critical time for development, learning, and wellbeing. Lisa advocates that wellbeing and meaningful relationships must be integral to early childhood environments, and that respect for the competency of children be prioritised in order that they flourish. Currently a Project Officer with the Research in Effective Education in Early Childhood (REEaCh) Centre at the University of Melbourne, Lisa has also been involved in Australia's national Early Years Strategy. Her presentations and publications, highlighting synergies between the fields of early childhood and wellbeing science, are grounded in literature and based on practice, combining theory, practice, and pedagogy.

Arnaldo Barone is a policy professional and researcher, amassing extensive experience across the government and education sectors. He is currently Principal Adviser at the Victorian Skills Authority, having previously worked as a Senior Lecturer at the Melbourne Centre for the Study of Higher Education, and Policy Director at the Victorian TAFE Association. Arnaldo has authored numerous higher and vocational education sector research papers and presented expert knowledge to government and parliamentary inquiries. Arnaldo's higher and vocational education knowledge is complemented by expertise in evolutionary economics, cultural economics, and history of economic thought. His doctoral thesis was awarded Best Dissertation by the History of Economic Thought Society of Australia.

Diane Bowles, Centre for Policy Development, Australia, is a wellbeing policy advisor dedicated to promoting public awareness and understanding of wellbeing science, government, economy, and literacy. She is currently working with the Centre for Policy Development's wellbeing government team, driving initiatives to improve decision-making for the advancement of wellbeing of individuals, communities, and the environment. As the co-convenor of the Wellbeing Economy Alliance Australia Hub, she fosters connections among stakeholders passionate about advancing wellbeing principles. Additionally, Diane spearheads the planning efforts for the Building Wellbeing Policy into Action conference. Her academic background includes a master's degree in Applied Positive Psychology from the University of Melbourne's Centre for Wellbeing Science, complementing her Bachelor of Arts in Political Science from Miami University. With over a decade of experience in international development, particularly in microfinance and poverty reduction, Diane brings a wealth of expertise to her advocacy work.

Bonnie Bozorg is a dedicated Clinical Psychologist affiliated with Shahid Beheshti University of Medical Sciences in Iran. Specialising in the treatment of mental disorders among university students, Mrs Bozorg is deeply committed to understanding and enhancing the factors that contribute to mental wellbeing. Her passion lies particularly in exploring the significance of belonging and engagement in fostering mental health across diverse populations. She focuses on the unique experiences of individuals from various races, genders, and national backgrounds, recognising that these elements play a crucial role in shaping one's mental health journey.

Emma L. Bradshaw is a Senior Research Fellow at the Institute for Positive Psychology and Education (IPPE) at the Australian Catholic University. She is the Deputy Lead for the Motivation and Behavior Program at IPPE, and a prominent researcher in the field of Self-Determination Theory (SDT). In her research, Emma uses a variety of both traditional and cutting-edge statistical methodologies to explore various aspects of SDT, with a special focus on goal contents theory (GCT). Her research in GCT has shed light on the role of intrinsic (e.g., growth, relationships, and community) and extrinsic (e.g., wealth, fame, and image) goals in supporting people's wellbeing as well as the social, contextual, and psychological conditions that promote positive values and the origins of striving to do good in the world. Emma was awarded the Dennis McInerney SELF PhD Award 2022 and nominated for ACU Vice-Chancellor's Award for Excellence During Doctoral Studies. She also serves as a review editor at *Frontiers in Psychology* and goals and values editor for the Centre for Self-Determination Theory.

Dr Emma Carlin is a Health Services Researcher based in Broome, Western Australia. Emma works with the University of Western Australia and Kimberley Aboriginal Medical Services. She has a strong interest in Aboriginal social and emotional wellbeing and mental health, and in research partnerships that are governed, informed, and responsive to the communities in which they serve.

Laura Cini has a background in health science, health promotion, and preventative health and has had numerous work roles in both government and not-for-profit organisations in Hobart. She has broad experience in community engagement, client management, project and program management, education, and training.

Professor Janet M. Clinton is an internationally recognised expert in Program Evaluation, Education and Assessment. She is a Professor of Evaluation and until previously the Deputy Dean at the Melbourne Faculty of Education, Director of the Centre for Program Evaluation and The Teacher Effectiveness Research Hub.

Rachel Colla, MPsych, MAPP, PhD, is a Lecturer and Education Innovation Leader at the Centre for Wellbeing Science at the University of Melbourne. Her work is dedicated to enabling wellbeing through education, leading change through the nexus of practice and research. Rachel has worked in education for over 20 years in diverse roles that have led to a deep appreciation of the complexity and hope for change within our education systems.

Berni Cooper, SFHEA, is the Associate Director, Wellbeing Strategy at the Queensland University of Technology (QUT). She is leading the implementation of a whole-of-university Health and Wellbeing Strategy co-developed with QUT students and staff. With a background in higher education and coaching, Berni's expertise spans student and staff development, curriculum design, and institutional change. Berni holds a master's in Applied Positive Psychology from the University of Melbourne, a Bachelor of Social Sciences (Hons) in Psychology from Waikato University, and a certificate in Tertiary Teaching.

Alex Couley is the Chief Leadership Officer at Richmond Fellowship Queensland and Adjunct Industry Research Fellow, Centre for Heritage and Culture at the University of Southern Queensland. He has over four decades of experience as a mental health clinician, delivering and managing services in both England and Australia. He has taught leadership practices in Australia, the USA, China, India, and Thailand. Alex has published on leadership, coaching, and mental health with some examples being, Manager as Coach: The Challenge in *Coaching in Professional Contexts*, Sage Press, Coach!

Simon Coulombe is an Associate Professor in the Department of Industrial Relations at Université Laval, Canada, where he holds the Relief Research Chair in Mental Health, Self-Management, and Work, powered by Beneva. He is a regular researcher at VITAM – Research Centre on Sustainable Health, the Cervo Brain Research Centre, and a member of the Centre d'études et d'interventions en santé mentale, the Centre for the Study of Democratic Citizenship and the Center for Public Policy Analysis.

Shannon Cowdrey-Fong is a Yawuru woman who works in the research team at Kimberley Aboriginal Medical Services. Shannon has a professional background in social and emotional wellbeing service delivery and clinical services. As a young woman Shannon is passionate about youth wellbeing and has been instrumental in the development of the LIYAN young mob.

Zaccariah Cox is a Nimanburru, Kija man from the Kimberley region of Western Australia. Zac is the senior manager for Social and Emotional Wellbeing and Mental Health at Kimberley Aboriginal Medical Services. He is active in social and emotional wellbeing research across the Kimberley and is passionate about supporting evidence based and culturally secure practice. His team is responsible for the delivery of the Kimberley Empowerment and Healing Program and LIYAN young mob.

Connie Digolis (GC-PUBHL, GAICD) is the CEO of the Mental Health Council of Tasmania (MHCT). Connie brings to her role a wealth of experience in population health and preventative health strategy, community sector management, advocacy, health promotion, and policy. Connie is a leading voice advocating for mental health system reform, providing solutions to support the mental health and wellbeing needs of all Tasmanians.

Elizabeth du Preez is an Associate Professor at Auckland University of Technology, Department of Psychology and Neuroscience. She has a longstanding international career as a researcher and psychological practitioner. As an activist scholar, her research focuses on the wellbeing of the LGBTIQ+ communities in Aotearoa/New Zealand through ensuring culturally safe and competent mental health practice.

Professor Pat Dudgeon is a Bardi woman with cultural ties to the Kimberley region. Professor Dudgeon's research and writings have made significant contributions to understanding and addressing the mental health challenges faced by Aboriginal and Torres Strait Islander communities in Australia. Professor Dudgeon is based at the University of Western Australia; she is highly regarded for her cultural sensitivity, inclusivity, and commitment to Aboriginal participatory action research approaches.

Dr Aylin Dulagil is a Coaching and Organisational Psychologist with experience in positive psychology, employee engagement, leadership development, talent management, and organisational development. Aylin is also an experienced coach and facilitator who has worked with a range of clients to set goals and achieve positive outcomes in areas including leadership development, career transition, and personal wellbeing enhancement.

Dr Kelly A. Ferber is a Psychological Researcher and Clinical Psychologist, who completed her PhD at the Institute for Positive Psychology and Education (IPPE) at the Australian Catholic University. Kelly has vast clinical experience with children and families, which is enriched by her passion for research in the area of Self-Determination Theory. Over the past decade, she has practiced in educational, healthcare, and private practice settings.

Dr Jacqui Francis, PhD, is a Lecturer at the Centre for Wellbeing Science (CWS) at the University of Melbourne (UoM). Jacqui is the Director for the Masters of Applied Positive Psychology. She leads undergraduate breadth subjects and masters level subjects at the CWS, and co-leads the CWS Wellbeing Literacy Research Stream team. Jacqui has recent articles published in the *International Journal of Environmental Research and Public Health*, and the *International Journal of Wellbeing*, and chapters co-authored in *Wellbeing and Resilience Education: COVID-19 and Its Impact on Education*, *The Handbook of Positive Psychology in Schools*, and *The International Handbook of Positive Education*. Jacqui has enjoyed presenting at national and international conferences, such as the International Positive Psychology Association World Congress in Canada and in Australia. Jacqui has a passion for wellbeing and has purpose-driven intention to find and share pathways to the language, knowledge, and skills of wellbeing, facilitating access equity, such that individuals and their communities can thrive.

Joël Gagnon, PhD, is currently a postdoctoral fellow at the Relief Research Chair in Mental Health, Self-Management, and Work at Université Laval. His research interests focus on the use of new technologies and self-management to improve service delivery in health and education. He co-authored the book *Déjouer la procrastination pour réussir et survivre à vos études: une méthode scientifique basée sur l'approche d'acceptation et d'engagement (ACT)* [*Thwarting procrastination to succeed and survive in your studies: A scientific method based on acceptance and commitment therapy (ACT)*], with the aim of fostering academic perseverance among post-secondary students through self-management.

Dr Jason Goopy is Lecturer and Coordinator of Secondary & Instrumental Music Education at Edith Cowan University, Australia. His interdisciplinary research investigates how music learning can support health and wellbeing by examining the nexus between music, education, and psychology. He is particularly interested in the power of arts-based research, such as narrative inquiry, share and tell interviews, and musical processes and products, to co-construct knowledge and privilege the perspectives and experiences of children and young people.

Dr Suzy Green is a Clinical and Coaching Psychologist and the CEO of The Positivity Institute. She is the co-editor of *Positive Psychology Coaching in Practice* and *Positive Psychology Coaching in the Workplace*. Suzy lectured in the Coaching Psychology Unit at the University of Sydney for ten years and is currently an Honorary Professor at UTS Business School, Sydney, and the University of East London. She is also an Honorary Fellow at the Centre for Wellbeing Science at the University of Melbourne, an Honorary Vice President of the International Society for Coaching Psychology, an Affiliate of the Institute for Well-Being at Cambridge University, and a member of the Scientific Advisory Board for Coach Hub.

John Hajek is a Professor of Italian Studies and director of the Research Unit for Multilingualism and Cross-cultural Communication (RUMACCC) at the University of Melbourne. Educated in Australia, Italy, and the UK, he is an experienced language teacher and linguist – with a wide range of research interests. He has published on different aspects of language education, including project-based learning as well as on wellbeing literacy.

Sharon Holmes was born and raised in a neighbourhood in Far Rockaway Queens, New York. She is one of eight children who grew a love for education because of her dad and his strong belief that education is the one thing that no one can take away from you. She strongly embraced this belief and has been pursuing her dream of becoming a high school English teacher. She obtained her associate's degree from Nassau Community College in Liberal Arts followed by a bachelor's degree in English from Queens College. She is currently finishing her last year at Brooklyn College's School of Education, where she will graduate with a Master of Arts in Secondary Education, all while being a New York City Police Officer for the past 12 years. She is eager to transition into her new career path.

Hanchao Hou, PhD, is currently a Postdoctoral Researcher at Tsinghua Shenzhen International School, Tsinghua University, and holds an Honorary Fellowship at the University of Melbourne. Dr Hou obtained his PhD from the Centre for Wellbeing Science, University of Melbourne. His research focuses on wellbeing literacy, positive psychology, and the application of AI in mental health. He has authored over ten publications in both Chinese and English journals and has presented his work at international conferences, with his research cited over 900 times on Google Scholar (h-index = 9).

Dr Lanxi Huang is a Research Project Officer at the Centre for Epidemiology and Biostatistics, Melbourne School of Population and Global Health, the University of Melbourne. Lanxi believes wellbeing is critical for human potential and thriving, and she aims to promote wellbeing for Culturally and Linguistically Diverse (CALD) communities in a people-centred, contextually responsive and systematic way. Lanxi's research interests include wellbeing literacy and language, intercultural experience and pathways, lay conceptualisation, international students and international education, natural language processing, AI, and digital wellbeing.

Dr Matthew Iasiello is a Post-Doctoral Researcher in the School of Biomedicine at the University of Adelaide and the Head of Data and Research Translation at Be Well Co. Matthew's research is focused on the most effective ways to promote mental wellbeing, and the relationship between mental wellbeing and psychological distress. Matthew is passionate about the development of high-quality wellbeing programs designed to improve mental wellbeing and integrating these interventions into real-world settings. Matthew has published in leading academic journals, is an editor of the *International Journal of Wellbeing*, and *Host of Researching Happy*, a podcast focused on mental wellbeing promotion and research.

Muhammad Nazil Iqdami, S.Pd.I., MEd, is a lecturer at the Faculty of Education and Psychology, Universitas Negeri Semarang, with over a decade of experience collaborating with a diverse range of Indonesian and international educators. Nazil's specialisation is in educational technology, and his expertise lies in instructional design, with a particular focus on technology integration to enhance teaching and learning methodologies.

Dr Margaret L. Kern is a Professor at the Centre for Wellbeing Science at the University of Melbourne's Faculty of Education. Her research is collaborative in nature and draws on a variety of methodologies to examine questions around who thrives in life and why, including understanding and measuring healthy functioning, identifying individual and social factors impacting life trajectories, and systems informed approaches to wellbeing. She has published 3 books, 1 handbook, and over 100 peer-reviewed articles and chapters. You can find out more about Professor Kern's work at www.peggykern.org.

Katherine Knutsen was born and raised in South Brooklyn, in a quintessential Brooklyn brownstone purchased by her Norwegian great-grandparents when they immigrated to New York City. Along with raising her two sons in their ancestral home, Katherine is a writer, poet, and steadfast advocate for the LGBTQIA2S+ community. She attended Hunter College, where she graduated Summa Cum Laude with a BA in English and Creative Writing.

Currently, she is performing at open mics all over her beloved city and completing her MA in English Education at Brooklyn College. She aspires to always be a teacher who writes, and a writer who teaches.

Riana Kolari, born and raised in Brooklyn, NY. She graduated with a BA in English, and is currently enrolled in a graduate program for English Education. Riana has a background in content and format editing at Brooklyn College for a literary magazine, *Stuck in the Library*. She's been working with children for three years and is currently working as a private tutor and teaching in a middle school as she finishes her education. She is also a published author for her first collection of poetry, Silent Chaos. Riana draws her strength from past experiences and determination for personal growth.

Professor Narelle Lemon is a Vice Chancellor Professoriate Research Fellow at Edith Cowan University, Perth, Australia. She is Lead of the Wellbeing and Education Research Community. Previous to moving to Perth in September 2023, Narelle was Associate Dean Education in the School of Social Sciences, Media, Film and Education at Swinburne University of Technology, Melbourne, and is best known for her work in Pedagogy of Belonging. Narelle is an interdisciplinary scholar across the fields of arts, education, and positive psychology. Her research expertise is in fostering wellbeing literacy in education and community contexts. Narelle focuses on capacity building in wellbeing and self-care of proactive action across diverse areas of evidence-based wellbeing science in order to flourish. Narelle is the series editor for *Wellbeing and Self-Care in Higher Education: Embracing Positive Solutions* (Routledge), which has garnered significant attention for highlighting the importance of self-care in academia. She is currently leading an international project called the "Citizen Wellbeing Scientist" capturing multimodal everyday actions of self-care (https://www.exploreandcreateco.com/citizen-wellbeing-scientist) and the Western Australian government-funded project in empowering women's wellbeing called SHESpeaks (https://www.shespeakswellbeing.com/). Narelle blogs, posts, grams, and podcasts as a part of her networked scholar practices.

Lu Li is an experienced NAATI certified translator proficient in Mandarin and English, with a proven track record of over seven years serving diverse clients. Her portfolio includes government bodies like the Government of South Australia, academic institutions like the University of Adelaide, and industry giants such as Google and Spotify, reflecting her adeptness in various fields. Beyond translation, Lu Li serves as a dedicated tutor and research assistant at the Department of Asian Studies, the University of Adelaide.

Tim Lomas, PhD, is a Psychology Research Scientist in the Department of Epidemiology at the Harvard T.H. Chan School of Public Health, and part of the Human Flourishing Program at Harvard University. Tim's main research focus is exploring cross-cultural perspectives on wellbeing, especially concepts and practices deemed "non-Western". Current projects include: assisting with the Global Flourishing Study, a longitudinal study of 240,000 people in 22 countries; helping lead the Global Wellbeing Initiative, a collaboration with Gallup to develop and analyse new items for their World Poll that reflect non-Western views of wellbeing; creating a lexicography and conceptual map of "untranslatable" words relating to wellbeing; and leading a project funded by the Templeton Foundation to look into Muslim perspectives on wellbeing. Before entering academia, Tim spent seven years as a professional musician, while also working part-time as a psychiatric nursing assistant. Tim completed his PhD at the University of Westminster in 2012, where his thesis focused on the impact of meditation on men's mental health (combining cognitive neuroscience, narrative, and ethnographic analysis). From 2013 to 2020 Tim was a lecturer in positive psychology at the University of East London. Since 2013, Tim has published over 100 papers and 12 books relating to wellbeing, involving topics/approaches including linguistics, semiotics, art, emotional dialectics, balance/harmony, systems theory, social theory, politics, gender, and Buddhism. His latest book, entitled *Happiness*, was published in 2023 by MIT Press as part of their Essential Knowledge series.

Daniel Loton (BPsych [Hons], GradCertTEd, PhD) is a Senior Lecturer in the Centre for Wellbeing Science and Co-Lead of the Centre's Education and Training Research Stream. Dan has two central themes in his research: enabling student success through educational development, especially for post-secondary education and non-traditional cohorts; and wellbeing, in education, parenting, and in relation to digital technology use. Dan has an interest in applied statistical research methods with extensive experience analysing very large datasets and application of causal modelling, and a passion for supporting researcher development.

Margo Lydon has influenced real-world reform in mental health and suicide prevention for over two decades. Margo is the Director of Workplace Mental Health Advisory, a boutique consultancy partnering with industry, organisations, and governments to help them navigate and respond to the complexity of workplace mental health, psychosocial safety, and wellbeing, delivering positive impact for people and business. Previously, Margo was the CEO of SuperFriend for 12 years.

Fatma Kusuma Mahanani, SPsi, MPsi, is a Lecturer and Psychologist at the Faculty of Education and Psychology, Universitas Negeri Semarang. She is dedicated to promoting the wellbeing of individuals within the Indonesian educational context, particularly focusing on students, teachers, and parents.

Her career philosophy centres around empowering individuals to thrive in their educational and professional endeavours. Fatma has developed Indonesian versions of measurement tools for quarter-life crisis, parental burnout assessment, and parenting self-efficacy.

Associate Professor Lisa McKay-Brown is the Associate Dean of Diversity and Inclusion at the Faculty of Education, University of Melbourne. Lisa has over 25 years of teaching and leadership experience in a wide range of education settings with a specific focus on the inclusion of students with disability. Internationally recognised for her research in the field of school attendance, she also serves on the Executive Board of the International Network for School Attendance.

John McNamara works as Mental Health Council of Tasmania (MHCT) Community Capacity Building Officer focusing on the development and implementation of the Take a minute campaign across Tasmania. John's professional experience has included contract management, a senior practitioner of a mental health psycho-social program and working as a quality assessor across a range of service including Alcohol and Other Drug/Mental Health/ Disability and Homelessness services. John has worked closely with stakeholders to conduct an environmental scan, provide information and training sessions on Take a minute and include feedback to researchers and the team at MHCT for the ongoing monitoring and improvement of Take a minute.

Dr Megan McPherson is a settler artist, educator, and researcher based at the Wilin Centre for Indigenous Art and Cultural Development at The University of Melbourne. Megan's overarching creative practice research emphasis is in printmaking, textiles, and installations. She publishes in the areas of academic identity, social media use, wellbeing, Indigenous knowledges and pedagogies, and studio pedagogies in the creative arts. She explores her focus in the intersections of pedagogical and material engagements in artistic, social and cultural productions using ethnographic, sociological, and creative practice methodologies to explore identity, subjectivities, affect, and agency.

D. J. Nemat-Nasser, who was born and raised in California, is a queer/nonbinary writer and musician based in Brooklyn. They will begin their career as a high school English teacher after completing their MSEd at Brooklyn College in 2025. D. J. received their BA in English with a dual concentration in Literature and Creative Writing from The City College of New York, where they were a recipient of the Julius & Betty Lewis Isaacs Scholarship. D. J. is also the videographer and photographer for Adverse Abstraction, an artist series that works to create a safe and nurturing space for all types of creators through monthly performances in New York City.

Linda Noble is an educator with over 30 years of professional experience across 7–12, adult and higher education. Linda has been recognised for excellence in teaching with awards that include Big Apple Award NYC Teacher 2023–2024; Brooklyn College, Long Island University and Butler-Cooley. As a Transformative Education Leadership alumnus, she is passionate about mindful self-care and wellbeing, especially translating evidence-based research into practice for everyday living. Dr Noble's research and practice of contemplative pedagogy is featured in publications by Routledge, Springer, Brill, Holistic Education Review, as well as in papers presented at local (New York), national, and international conferences.

Siti Nuzulia, SPsi, MSi, PhD, a lecturer in the Department of Psychology, Faculty of Education and Psychology, Universitas Negeri Semarang since 2005. Her area of expertise is occupational psychology. She wrote numerous research papers, one of which was titled "When the Dark Shines: The Role of Dark Personality Traits on Leadership Role Occupancy and Hiring Decisions in a Collectivistic Culture", and was published in *Social Psychological and Personality Science*. She now teaches research methodology, career development, and current issues in industrial and organisational psychology.

Professor Lindsay G. Oades, PhD is an internationally acclaimed wellbeing scientist, researcher, educator, and author. He is Deputy Dean of the Faculty of Education and Professor of Wellbeing Science. In 2013 he was awarded an Australian Government citation for outstanding contribution to student learning. In 2020 he was appointed as Associate Dean International, MGSE. As a sought after speaker, known to provoke thought, he has given keynote or invited presentations in 13 nations. With over 150 refereed journal articles and book chapters related to wellbeing, recovery, and coaching and 5 books with esteemed publishers including Cambridge University Press, Wiley-Blackwell, and SAGE, he is a scientific reviewer for the Australian Research Council. Lindsay has consulted to multiple organisations including the NSW Department of Education, NSW Mental Health Commission, Beyond Blue and the Australian Mental Health Commission. He is currently a non-executive Director of the Positive Education Schools Association and a former Director of Action of Happiness Australia, Reach Foundation and NEAMI National. Lindsay's multidisciplinary background spanning philosophy of science and ethics, clinical, coaching and positive psychology, business and public policy provides insights into the multidisciplinary area of wellbeing. He was previously a co-editor for the *International Journal of Wellbeing*, a scientific panel member at the Institute of Coaching (Harvard University), and a visiting researcher at Kings College London. Lindsay's current work involves understanding, measuring, and improving wellbeing literacy – how we communicate about and for wellbeing – as part of his new theory Thriveability Theory. Recently, Lindsay's work with UNESCO was published. UNESCO is part of the United Nations, influencing education policy in 130 member nations.

Kristen Orazi is an executive manager for Kimberley Aboriginal Medical Services overseeing the portfolio of Social and Emotional Wellbeing and Mental Health. Kristen has a background in social work and community development and her insightful contributions shape the strategic directions of mental health and social and emotional wellbeing service delivery across the Kimberley.

Tyler Pacheco is a postdoctoral fellow at Université Laval studying worker wellbeing and organisational interventions. Before the fellowship, he received his PhD in Social Psychology from Wilfrid Laurier University in 2024 and his honours BSc from the University of Toronto Mississauga in 2019. His PhD research on workers' wellbeing during pandemics and epidemics and, more specifically, the beginning of COVID-19, has garnered the attention of several news outlets (e.g., *The New York Times*). He has published five peer-reviewed articles (with two others in different stages of review), one book chapter, and one non-peer-reviewed article (dissertation). He has been awarded five competitive awards/scholarships (2020–2024).

Malgorzata Powietrzynska earned her PhD in Urban Education from the Graduate Center of the City University of New York. She provides support and coaching to faculty in a post-secondary adult learning environment. In addition, as an adjunct associate professor, she works with pre-service and in-service teachers enrolled in graduate level courses. A recipient of an Excellence in Teaching award, Malgorzata has been involved in collaborative research and publications focusing on emotions, mindfulness, and wellness in education. She also worked as a writing fellow with the education program at the Greater Good Science Center, UC Berkeley.

Kaitlin Rice is currently pursuing her master's degree after changing her career path to pursue a career in high-school education. After graduating from St. John's University with a bachelor's degree in English and Criminal Justice, Kaitlin worked in a law firm for several years before ultimately deciding a change was necessary in her life. Her call to be an educator came after a long struggle with finding herself and exploring what most fulfils her sense of belonging. Born and raised in New York City, she finds her strength in pushing past her comfort zone to explore unique perspectives and embrace the diverse city and people around her. Discovering more of herself along her educational journey has been particularly rewarding and her pursuit of becoming a teacher is a challenge she can't wait to begin.

Annalise Roache is a Positive Psychology Practitioner, coach, mentor, educator, and wellbeing researcher dedicated to facilitating personal growth and transformation. With a foundation in evidence-based practices, she specialises in empowering individuals and groups in personal and workplace settings through a solution-focused approach grounded in Positive psychology. As President of the New Zealand Association of Positive Psychology and co-author of the *Ethical Guidelines for Positive Psychology Practice* (2019, 2021), Annalise is committed to advancing ethical standards and best practices in the field. Her expertise extends to developing dynamic psycho-educational courses and online content, fostering knowledge sharing and active engagement in wellbeing practices.

Antonia Rubino is an Associate Professor in Italian Studies at the University of Sydney. She has research interests in multilingualism in migration contexts, educational linguistics, and language policy. She has conducted extensive research on different generations of Australian Italians, focusing on the intergenerational transmission of heritage languages and their educational and policy implications. She is a Fellow of the Australian Academy of the Humanities.

Laura E. Smith is a Research Fellow in the Assessment and Evaluation Research Centre at the University of Melbourne. She works in the field of teacher education and assessment, focusing primarily on research relating to the mental health and wellbeing of teachers and students. Laura has managed a wide range of research projects and evaluations across Australia in the disciplines of education, mental health, and wellbeing. Her areas of interest include teacher education research, education evaluation, wellbeing and mental health program evaluation, mixed-methods research, qualitative methods, and participatory methods of engagement. Laura holds a Master of Science in Behavioural and Social Sciences from Brown University and graduate qualifications in Psychology. In her PhD research, she is investigating the influence of dispositional factors on teachers' readiness to support student mental health and wellbeing.

Dr Kate Sollis, University of Tasmania and Centre for Policy Development, Australia, is a wellbeing researcher with an interest in conceptual issues around measurement, locally developed measurement tools, participatory approaches, policy impact, and human-nature connection. She is currently a Research Fellow at the University of Tasmania and a Consultant Policy Advisor with the Centre for Policy Development. Kate holds a PhD in Social Research, an MSc in Public Policy & Human Development, and a BSc in Statistics. She has previously held research positions at the ANU, the Australian Research Alliance for Children and Youth, and the Australian Bureau of Statistics.

Cass Spong is a Systems Informed Practitioner and Management Consultant working with individual leaders and complex organisations. She is an

Honorary Fellow at The Centre for Wellbeing Science at The University of Melbourne and an Adjunct Senior Industry Fellow with RMIT University FORWARD Centre for Future Skills and Workforce Transformation. Cass has over two decades of international consulting experience and in 2012 founded ENTHEOS Consulting, a systems-based organisational development consultancy which has partnered with large private corporates, public sector, universities, and not-for-profit organisations.

Antonella Strambi is a Lecturer in Academic Development in the Teaching Innovation Unit at the University of South Australia. In this role, she advises educators and educational leaders on pedagogical innovation and quality in learning design and teaching practice. She also provides professional development opportunities for teaching staff, and leads and manages the UniSA Teaching and Learning Grants portfolio. Prior to her appointment at UniSA. Antonella lectured in Italian language and Applied linguistics at Flinders University. Her research interests and expertise are in socio-emotional learning; the role of emotion communication, humour, and self-disclosure in rapport building; text analytics; and student and educator wellbeing.

Nick Sullivan, Mental Health Council of Tasmania Communications Manager, has over ten years' experience spanning corporate and community communications roles. Nick's ability to craft compelling narratives across diverse platforms, mediums, and audiences has been instrumental in develop the identity, personality, and story that has helped bring Take a minute to life as one of Tasmania's most impactful and recognisable mental wellbeing campaigns.

Sandra Surace's career journey is enriched by a unique blend of insights, with a focus on both individual and organisational wellbeing. Beginning as an Educator who made substantial contributions to workplace cultures and mental health awareness, her career evolved as she transitioned from schools into roles supporting organisational behaviour and wellbeing, integrating her background in Education with a Master in Applied Positive Psychology (MAPP) and Master in Counselling (MCouns). Her dedication shines through her passion for creating spaces where safety, personal wellbeing, and organisational success naturally intersect, fostering thriving environments for individuals and organisations alike. Sandra is Principal Consultant, Leadership and Organisational Behaviour for Fusion Safety Management.

Jessica A. Taylor is a Systems-Informed Wellbeing Strategist, Consultant, Practitioner, Curriculum Writer, and Researcher with expertise across the fields of education and wellbeing. As a senior wellbeing consultant for Geelong Grammar School's Institute of Positive Education, Jessica has collaborated with schools, organisations, and governments globally, including the

UAE Prime Minister's Office and the Singapore Ministry of Education, to assist them place wellbeing at the heart of their vision and practice. Jessica is currently completing her Doctorate with the Centre of Wellbeing Science at the University of Melbourne. Through her research she seeks to reframe responsibility for wellbeing away from a culture of self-governing individualism towards a systems-informed capability perspective.

Dr Joep van Agteren, the CEO of Be Well Co, a social enterprise focused on the promotion of mental wellbeing. Joep's PhD investigated ways to improve the way people with low mental wellbeing feel, i.e., looking at interventions to help people who "languish". His applied work has largely focused on translating scientific research on behaviour change and mental health into practical applications that people can use to improve the way they feel on a day-to-day basis. Joep also holds a title of Affiliate Senior Lecturer at the University of Australia and actively participates with NGO's and mental health commissions around Australia.

Dr Paige Williams is a Speaker, author, and PhD in Organizational Behaviour. Paige believes that leadership is the most potent leverage point in any system – team, family, or workplace – to create positive change. And that we each have a capacity to lead, exceptionally, that we are yet to realise. Her ambition is bold: to teach, inspire, and encourage you to have the confidence, clarity, and commitment to be the exceptional leader the world needs you to be. Using a potent blend of neuroscience, psychology, and her own extensive international business leadership experience, Paige helps leaders across business, government, NGOs, and education to lead themselves, their people, and the systems they work in, exceptionally.

FOREWORD

That I am the one writing this foreword – to a volume on wellbeing – says much about both the place wellbeing now holds in the broader field of education, as well as the domains to which the chapters in this book are making their contribution. I am new to the field of wellbeing science, with my own expertise lying in the fields of languages and literacies as a professor of education in these areas. Throughout the 1970s and 1980s, language rose to prominence as one of the most significant Australia curricular reforms, whether through its emphasis on spelling and grammar in the teaching of English, or the widespread expansion of languages other than English, particularly Asian languages. Similarly, in the UK, the 1970s Bullock Report, *A Language for Life*, had a lasting impact shaping educational approaches through to the 1980s. Literacy, while hard to imagine now, barely featured as a concept in educational policy with the ubiquity it has now until the 1990s, following the United Nation's *International Literacy Year* in 1990 and, in the case of Australia, the introduction of the Commonwealth Government's *Literacy for All* in 1996 – one of the most impactful education policy reforms to succeed Australia's 1987 *National Policy on Languages*.

The reason I sketch this brief history lesson is because, in the same way, we look back at the ubiquitous paring of languages with education in the 1970s and 1980s, and literacy with education in the 1990s and 2000s, wellbeing has now risen to the same level of prominence in the last 5–10 years: one that lies at the very core of how we understand the purpose of education. Education that is not simply knowledge and skills to "live" – or survive – but rather, as the authors of this book argue and demonstrate, the capability to flourish: the ability to thrive, and to do this across all domains of learning. As the authors in this book demonstrate, wellbeing literacy has applicability from second and foreign languages learning, through to the arts; from early childhood through to vocational training; and from workplace learning through to higher education. This volume demonstrates that wellbeing – conceived of as literacy – affords a conceptual framework that enables a notion as abstract as "being well" to be approached pedagogically in ways that are both meaningful and intentional. That is, the chapters, taken together, not simply offer iterations of what it means to flourish, but they go further to make the capability to achieve this both conceptually and empirically visible.

Part of me is not surprised to see this collocation of wellbeing with literacy, reflecting on the succession of "big ideas" that have shaped our understanding of what matters in education. I'm excited to see how this combination – of not simply "being literate", but literacy to thrive across all domains of learning and development – will continue to stretch and expand our understanding of education itself, as the kinds of work comprising this volume further impact our field.

Professor Russell Cross
The University of Melbourne

1

EMPOWERING CONVERSATIONS

Exploring the Potential of Wellbeing Literacy

Narelle Lemon, Lindsay G. Oades, and Jacqui Francis

Introduction

Wellbeing literacy refers to the capability of understanding and using wellbeing language effectively in various situations, aiming to enhance the wellbeing of oneself, others, and the world (Oades et al., 2021). Wellbeing literacy fosters the development of vocabulary around wellbeing, cultivating comprehension, contextual awareness, and purposefulness. By applying the language, knowledge, and skills of wellbeing, intentional communication for personal and communal wellness becomes feasible – a process that binds individuals, groups, and systems, including educational contexts, in the quest for flourishing (Oades et al., 2021, p. 327).

Wellbeing literacy involves understanding and using the language of wellbeing effectively across different situations, with the goal of enhancing the wellbeing of oneself, others, and the world (Oades et al., 2021). It's about building, maintaining, and safeguarding conditions that promote flourishing for individuals, groups, and systems. Wellbeing literacy encompasses the development of vocabulary related to wellbeing, fostering comprehension, context sensitivity, and intentionality. It serves as a broad term covering various aspects of wellbeing crucial for navigating present realities and creating opportunities in educational systems.

As a capability about *and* for wellbeing, wellbeing literacy is vital, enabling individuals to both understand and apply wellbeing concepts. The language, knowledge, and skills associated with wellbeing facilitate intentional communication, allowing individuals to convey and exchange ideas for personal and collective benefit. This intentional communication, guided by wellbeing

DOI: 10.4324/9781003644293-1

literacy, becomes a practical tool for reflecting on, repositioning, and reframing interactions, intentions, and experiences related to wellbeing.

Importantly, wellbeing literacy is relational, representing an ongoing process within the dynamic interplay between an individual and their environment. As Oades et al. (2021) emphasise, "individuals, groups, and systems … require this capability to flourish" (p. 327). In essence, wellbeing literacy is a practical and essential element for personal and collective thriving, underscoring the interconnectedness of individuals and their broader ecosystems. It goes beyond language proficiency, embodying a holistic approach necessary for building a flourishing society.

In this edited book collection, we bring together international researchers, scholars, and practitioners from varying contexts and disciplines to critique wellbeing literacy and consider this new area of wellbeing science in relation to how they view/understand the world. In doing we connect to intentionality, multimodal and interdisciplinary ways that wellbeing capabilities (the ability to *be* and *do*) facilitate flourishing. Language, knowledge, and language skills of wellbeing make it possible to intentionally communicate wellbeing for self and others. We aim to bring together scholars to consider wellbeing literacy through their disciplinary, interdisciplinary, and transdisciplinary lenses.

Introducing the Chapters

In this next section of the foreword, we introduce each chapter.

In this opening chapter, Oades, Lemon, and Francis establish the theoretical foundation for wellbeing literacy as a capability to comprehend and compose wellbeing language across contexts with the intention of improving wellbeing. They position wellbeing literacy at the intersection of wellbeing science and contemporary sociocultural views of literacy, emphasising that it's not merely about functional reading and writing but about how language actively constructs meaning and shapes wellbeing realities. The authors outline the five-component capability model of wellbeing literacy: vocabulary and knowledge about wellbeing, comprehension of multimodal wellbeing text, composition of multimodal wellbeing text, context awareness and adaptability, and intentionality for wellbeing. Drawing on constructivist and contextualist epistemological assumptions and the Capability Approach, they argue that wellbeing literacy empowers individuals to convert wellbeing opportunities into achievements across multiple contexts, disciplines, and cultures.

Hou examines wellbeing literacy measurement approaches, addressing challenges in capturing its multidimensional nature through both psychometric methods and AI technologies. The chapter advocates for contextually sensitive, culturally relevant assessment tools that balance precision with individual experience, concluding that improved measurement supports both individual wellbeing and broader societal health goals through more effective interventions.

Strambi and colleagues explore two distinct approaches to integrating wellbeing literacy within second language learning: a "Forward Planning" approach that explicitly embeds wellbeing activities into the curriculum and a "Looking Back" approach that cultivates wellbeing literacy through guided reflection on learning experiences. Through examining pilot studies in Australian universities, the research demonstrates how both approaches can enhance students' capacity to understand and communicate about wellbeing while highlighting the importance of contextual factors in determining their effectiveness.

In the chapter by Janet M. Clinton and Laura E. Smith, they argue for reconceptualising wellbeing literacy as a multidimensional and hierarchical construct, presenting a theoretical framework that integrates both wellbeing dimensions (cognitive, physical, psychological, and social) with literacy components (knowing, understanding, and communicating) in context-specific ways. Through developing a hypothetical validation framework for educational settings, the authors demonstrate how this structured approach enables more rigorous measurement and assessment of wellbeing literacy across different contexts, addressing current limitations in its conceptualisation and measurement.

This chapter explores how engaging with "untranslatable" words from different languages can develop wellbeing literacy by expanding our conceptual maps of emotions and providing insights into culturally specific wellbeing experiences that English may overlook. Lomas proposes that learning these words enhances emotional granularity and social-emotional development in educational settings, offering students new frameworks to articulate, understand, and experience wellbeing dimensions across diverse cultural perspectives.

This chapter advocates for the integration of wellbeing skills into vocational education and training systems, arguing that wellbeing literacy provides a theoretical foundation for how these skills can be effectively taught and acquired through language-based capability building. Daniel Loton, Matthew Iasiello, and Arnaldo Barone, through detailed analysis of competency-based training and vocational taxonomies, the authors demonstrate how wellbeing literacy could serve as a bridge between existing vocational frameworks and the implementation of evidence-based wellbeing interventions, while acknowledging that individual skills must be complemented by systemic environmental supports.

Central to Aboriginal and Torres Strait Islander wellbeing literacy is a broader conceptualisation that extends beyond traditional language-based capabilities to encompass lived experience, cultural knowledge, and community-led healing practices. Through examining the Kimberley Empowerment Healing and Leadership Program (KEHLP), Carlin and colleagues' research demonstrates how social and emotional wellbeing literacy must incorporate truth-telling, cultural narratives, and direct experiences of Country and community to effectively support Aboriginal and Torres Strait Islander peoples' holistic wellbeing.

Psychometric validation of the Well-Lit 6 scale across multiple studies demonstrates strong empirical evidence for measuring wellbeing literacy as a distinct construct, with consistent findings supporting its reliability, structural validity, and discriminant properties. Pacheco, Gagnon, and Coulombe illuminate the scale's robust performance across different contexts and populations, along with its incremental validity, indicates its effectiveness as a standardised tool for assessing individuals' capability to comprehend and communicate about wellbeing, though ongoing research continues to examine its test-retest reliability and measurement invariance properties.

Roache, Du Preez, and Oades examine wellbeing literacy through a social constructionist lens, highlighting how language not only describes but also actively constructs wellbeing realities, shaping what actions people believe are available to them. The authors emphasise that understanding lay concepts (everyday, non-expert beliefs) about wellbeing is essential to developing effective wellbeing literacy, as these concepts reveal how diverse populations conceptualise, articulate, and enact wellbeing within their specific cultural and social contexts.

Colla, Williams, and Oades' conception of storying practices intersect powerfully with wellbeing literacy, demonstrating how narrative and arts-based methods serve as fundamental capabilities for understanding and communicating about wellbeing across diverse cultural contexts. Through examining participatory narrative approaches like the Stories of Hope project, the authors reveal how storying methods enhance both the mechanics (vocabulary, comprehension, composition) and dynamics (context awareness, intentionality) of wellbeing literacy, while highlighting the crucial role of creating safe environments that enable these capabilities to emerge.

Baker's exploration of wellbeing literacy in early childhood demonstrates how this capability is fundamentally intertwined with children's developmental trajectory, arguing that the early years represent a crucial period for establishing wellbeing communication patterns and skills. Through examining how young children naturally develop language and literacy capabilities across multiple modes (visual, aural, sensory, gestural), the research reveals that wellbeing literacy can be intentionally fostered during these formative years to help children feel good, do good, and function well within their contexts.

Through an innovative duoethnographic approach, Francis and Couley reveal how the translation of wellbeing literacy research into community practice hinges on two critical elements: aligned values and goals and effective communication through storytelling. Their analysis demonstrates that successful implementation requires more than just technical knowledge transfer – it demands the intentional creation of shared understanding between researchers and practitioners through authentic dialogue and narrative exchange that supports both individual and collective wellbeing.

Through a rich tapestry of personal narratives from both educators and students, Noble and colleagues demonstrate how wellbeing literacy can be systematically developed within teacher education through intentional course design incorporating the five components of wellbeing literacy: vocabulary, multimodal comprehension, composition, context sensitivity, and intentionality. Their analysis of a Mindfulness in Teaching and Learning course reveals how contemplative pedagogy and collaborative learning experiences create transformative spaces where educators can develop not only their individual wellbeing capabilities but also the skills to foster communal wellbeing in their future classrooms.

Lemon and Huang's ethnographic dialogue reveals the critical need for a systematic approach to wellbeing literacy in higher education, where both top-down institutional frameworks and bottom-up grassroots initiatives must converge to create sustainable change. Through examining university contexts across different cultural perspectives, they demonstrate how wellbeing literacy can serve as a transformative capability that extends beyond individual interventions to create systemic change, arguing for an integrated approach that addresses wellbeing at individual (I), communal (We), and institutional (Us) levels while emphasising the importance of culturally sensitive and contextually appropriate communication strategies.

Li, Francis, and Oades' exploration of wellbeing literacy within social media contexts reveals a novel understanding of how digital environments can be leveraged for positive wellbeing outcomes. Through analysing eight core contextual characteristics of social media (physicality, accessibility, latency, interdependence, synchronicity, permanence, verifiability, and anonymity), they demonstrate how wellbeing literacy capabilities can transform potentially harmful digital spaces into opportunities for intentional wellbeing communication. Their research shows that when users are equipped with wellbeing literacy skills, they can navigate social media's unique attributes to create meaningful connections and foster positive wellbeing outcomes despite the platform's known challenges.

Through artistic practices like music, visual arts, and cultural expression, new dimensions of wellbeing literacy emerge that transcend traditional verbal communication. Lemon, Goopy, and McPherson demonstrate how these multimodal approaches – whether through photography, music education, or printmaking workshops – create powerful pathways for both experiencing and expressing wellbeing, revealing that artistic engagement itself can be an act of wellbeing while simultaneously building the capability to communicate about and for wellbeing across diverse contexts and cultures.

Lydon, Cooper, and Surace extend wellbeing literacy into the workplace domain by introducing "Workplace Wellbeing Literacy" (WWL), demonstrating how intentional language use and communication about wellbeing must operate across three distinct organisational levels: intrapersonal (individual worker), interpersonal (workgroup), and organisational (systems and policies). Through examining real-world vignettes, they reveal how WWL capabilities can transform traditional hazard-focused workplace approaches into more balanced frameworks that actively foster workplace wellbeing, arguing that this literacy is essential for creating sustainable, flourishing work environments.

Ferber and Bradshaw demonstrate how wellbeing literacy for parents should include understanding need-supportive parenting practices that foster children's basic psychological needs for autonomy, competence, and relatedness as defined by Self-Determination Theory. The authors emphasise that parental wellbeing literacy is fundamentally relational, requiring both knowledge of need-supportive environments and the intentional application of this knowledge through autonomy support, involvement, and structure that are adapted to each child's developmental stage and context.

Through exploring the intersection of wellbeing literacy and public policy, this chapter reveals how enhancing policymakers' capabilities to understand and communicate about wellbeing can transform traditional policy approaches into more effective wellbeing-focused frameworks. Bowles and Sollis demonstrate that when policymakers develop strong wellbeing literacy – through knowledge, comprehension, composition, context awareness, and intentionality – they can better design and implement policies that address root causes rather than symptoms, leading to more sustainable and equitable societal outcomes that foster both individual and collective flourishing.

Green, Dulagil, and Baker position wellbeing literacy (WBL) as an essential competency for evidence-based coaching (EBC), arguing that coaches must develop their own WBL capabilities to effectively facilitate wellbeing outcomes through intentional language use with clients. The authors demonstrate how the WBL model (vocabulary and knowledge, comprehension, composition, context awareness, and intentionality) aligns with coaching frameworks like GROW (Goal, Reality, Options, and Will), suggesting that coaching provides an ideal vehicle for developing sustainable wellbeing capabilities rather than merely implementing short-term interventions.

Allen, Bozorg, and Kern explore wellbeing literacy as fundamentally a social construct, proposing that it develops through collective interactions and is intrinsically linked to our fundamental need to belong. The authors argue that wellbeing literacy is shaped by social validation, learning mechanisms, cognitive processes, and epistemic foundations, all of which occur within broader social systems that both influence and are influenced by our sense of belonging and ultimately our wellbeing.

Through documenting the development and implementation of Tasmania's "Take a Minute" campaign, Iasiello and colleagues demonstrate how wellbeing literacy theory can be effectively translated into practical public health interventions. Their needs analysis reveals four critical themes for wellbeing literacy campaigns: focusing on wellbeing promotion rather than just illness prevention, allowing personal definitions of wellbeing, enabling decentralised public participation, and incorporating behaviour change principles around motivation, capability, and opportunity. This work importantly shows how wellbeing literacy initiatives must balance universal accessibility with personalised meaning-making to create sustainable community impact.

Nuzulia and colleagues offer critical insights into how wellbeing literacy manifests within specific cultural contexts through their examination of Javanese undergraduate students. Their research reveals that wellbeing literacy is deeply embedded in cultural values and spiritual practices, where traditional Javanese concepts like rukun (harmony) and suwung (inner peace) shape how individuals understand, express, and communicate about wellbeing. The study importantly demonstrates that wellbeing literacy cannot be understood through a purely Western lens, but must consider how cultural frameworks, including collectivist values, hierarchical social structures, and indirect communication patterns, fundamentally influence how people develop and express their capability to comprehend and compose language about wellbeing.

Taylor and Spong present the System of Wellbeing (SoW) as a regenerative, integrative framework for fostering environments that promote collective wellbeing beyond individual-based interventions. By emphasising regenerative capabilities – such as wellbeing literacy and systems awareness – and conditions like reciprocity, authentic relationships, shared higher purpose, and response-ability, the chapter illustrates how schools and organisations can transition from mechanistic models to thriving, interconnected systems that nurture long-term flourishing.

This chapter examines inclusive language as a crucial component of wellbeing literacy, highlighting how intentional, context-sensitive language affirms identity and addresses equality, non-discrimination, and equity. McKay-Brown aligns inclusive language with the five conditions of wellbeing literacy (vocabulary, comprehension, composition, context awareness, and intentionality), proposing an intersectional framework to enhance wellbeing outcomes. The author presents inclusive language guides as practical tools for operationalising wellbeing literacy while acknowledging that language alone cannot address systemic inequalities without deeper understanding of power dynamics and historical marginalisation.

Concluding Remarks

Wellbeing literacy offers a transformative lens through which we can navigate and enrich personal, educational, social, and professional contexts. As contributors to this collection have demonstrated, it encompasses the capability to intentionally communicate about and for wellbeing, enabling us to comprehend, compose, and act in ways that support flourishing at both individual and systemic levels. Wellbeing literacy invites an ongoing dialogue that builds connections between diverse fields and disciplines, making it a versatile and evolving concept with broad applicability.

One of the key insights from this volume is the power of language – spoken, written, visual, and embodied – to influence our experiences and understandings of wellbeing. From education and public policy to creative arts and digital spaces, wellbeing literacy emerges as a critical capability for fostering meaningful relationships, enhancing community resilience, and creating environments where people can thrive. The chapters have illustrated how wellbeing literacy can take different forms depending on cultural, organisational, and situational contexts, but its core elements remain consistent: vocabulary development, contextual awareness, intentionality, and the capacity to act for wellbeing.

Readers are encouraged to consider the dynamic role that wellbeing literacy can play in their own professional and personal lives. Whether as educators, policymakers, practitioners, or community members, we all have opportunities to enhance our capacity for wellbeing-focused communication. This collection invites you to reflect on how you understand, express, and cultivate wellbeing and to think critically about how these capabilities can be nurtured in diverse settings.

As you continue exploring the practical applications and theoretical advancements presented in these chapters, we hope you are inspired to contribute to the growing global conversation around wellbeing literacy. By embedding this capability in our daily interactions and systemic practices, we collectively move closer to creating environments where individuals, communities, and organisations can flourish. Let us embrace wellbeing literacy not just as a theoretical construct but as a lived practice – a pathway to intentional, inclusive, and flourishing futures.

Reference

Oades, L. G., Jarden, A., Hou, H., Ozturk, C., Williams, P., R. Slemp, G., & Huang, L. (2021). Wellbeing literacy: A capability model for wellbeing science and practice. *International Journal of Environmental Research and Public Health*, *18*(2), 719. https://doi.org/10.3390/ijerph18020719

2

WHAT IS THE THEORY UNDERPINNING WELLBEING LITERACY?

Lindsay G. Oades, Narelle Lemon, and Jacqui Francis

Introduction

Wellbeing literacy is defined as a capability to comprehend and compose wellbeing language, across contexts, with the intention of using such language to maintain or improve the wellbeing of oneself, others, or the world. This can be stated most simply as "*how we communicate about and for wellbeing*". In this chapter we explore the intellectual influences on the development of the capability model of wellbeing literacy. We then describe the five components of the capability model of wellbeing literacy, commenting on its potential applications to multiple contexts, and its need to be informed by multiple cultures and multiple disciplines, and hence the need also for multimethod investigations of its inherent knowledge claims.

The Role of Language and Literacy in Our Individual and Communal Lives

We live in and through language. Humans construct meanings in their experiences through language. These constructed meanings make language an important leverage point for people to influence their own wellbeing and the wellbeing of others. Language is not just a means of transmitting information; it also serves to actively construct meaning in experiences. Indeed, the Linguistic Relativity Theory (otherwise known as the Sapir–Whorf Hypotheses), proposes that the structure of a language influences the language speaker's cognition and how they view the world. Sapir and Whorf asserted that people are not often aware of the impact of these linguistic differences until they come across cultures different from their own.

DOI: 10.4324/9781003644293-2

Literacy, traditionally defined as the "ability to read and write", has evolved considerably since the 1970s. Sociocultural literacy theories emphasise how literacy practices are embedded within social and cultural contexts, highlighting the power dynamics inherent in language use. This perspective reconceptualises literacy beyond individual cognitive processes of reading and writing, viewing it instead as a social practice operating between people.

This evolved understanding of literacy fundamentally shapes our approach to wellbeing literacy. We adopt Keefe and Copeland's (2011) five core principles, which assert that:

1 Literacy acquisition is universally possible
2 Literacy represents both a human right and a fundamental human experience
3 Literacy extends beyond individual capacity, requiring and fostering relationships
4 Literacy enables communication and interaction, offering pathways to empowerment
5 Literacy development is a communal responsibility, encompassing all modes of meaning-making and information exchange.

Literacy is increasingly seen as important across areas of life, scholarly domains, and public discourse, intersecting in different ways, for example, academic literacy in education (Bassett & Macnaught, 2024), intergenerational literacy in family (Kennedy & Caspe, 2013), health literacy in communities (Belfrage et al., 2025), and AI literacy in the workplace (Goryachev, 2024). Despite literacy's established importance across domains, its specific role in wellbeing science remains unexplored. We introduce "wellbeing literacy" as a distinct concept that moves beyond the application of literacy to external contexts (such as health, workplace, or education). Instead, wellbeing literacy focuses on how language shapes and expands our internal capacity for experiencing wellbeing, while empowering individuals to engage in practices that enhance and sustain wellbeing for themselves and others.

Literacy, while rooted in education, has evolved into numerous specialised forms. These range from widely recognised variants such as digital literacy, financial literacy and health literacy to equally significant but less familiar such as critical literacy, futures literacy and transformational literacy. Originally associated with reading and writing, the term "literacy" covers a much broader spectrum of competencies and capabilities that enable individuals and communities to pursue meaningful lives, enhance freedom, and foster wellbeing in their pursuit of a better world.

Critical literacy examines how histories are constructed and reveals power dynamics embedded within sociocultural, environmental, and political systems. Through language, it challenges established power structures, fostering individual empowerment and agency. This approach encourages readers to examine both authors' ideological positions and their own beliefs, while embracing their contextual perspectives in the ongoing construction and reconstruction of knowledge, while critically evaluating their own lived experiences (Anderson & Irvine, 1993; Luke, 2000).

Transformational literacy is the capacity to be free from old ways of habitual thinking and patterns of the past (Berger et al., 2014). Through transformational literacy we engage in deep reflection and embrace emergent possibilities, thus allowing us to become more fully ourselves as we lean into co-creating the future we seek, by letting go of deep-rooted conceptions (Buchannan, 2017). The ability to transform moves beyond the notion of doing more of the same more effectively and more efficiently. Instead, its core aim is to repurpose systems and structures in line with ongoing evolutions, new ideas, desires, perceptions, and mindsets (Göpel, 2016).

Futures literacy is a capacity embracing imagination and anticipation, using the future as an anchor for alignment of perceptions, emergent reality, and aspirations (Miller, 2018). Futures literacy is an increasingly prominent literacy, supported by UNESCO, and fundamental to the sense-making needed to imagine, design, and create the future.

The pedagogy of literacy, in all its evolved forms, is often underpinned by approaches that involve sociocultural interaction and communication between people (Vygotsky, 1962), where meaning is made through democratic, experiential, and reflective engagement with language (Dewey, 1998), and where language use shapes personal and communal life perspectives (Kienpointner, 1996).

Diverse scholarly domains see diverse applications of literacy, which are related to but distinct from wellbeing literacy. Just a few examples include public health literacy, health literacy, mental health literacy, and emotional literacy. Both public health literacy and health literacy are concerned with assessing and applying information to prevent disease and promote health (Sørensen et al., 2012). Health literacy primarily relates to individuals within medical contexts, and their capability in meeting complex health needs (Sorensen et al., 2012). Whereas public health literacy focuses on community-level benefits (Freedman et al., 2009). Mental health literacy relates to the specific needs associated with preventing or reducing mental illness and promoting mental health (Jorm, 2015). Emotional literacy relates to effective and contextually appropriate identification, management, and expression of emotion (Waterhouse, 2019). Emotional literacy is informed by environmental opportunity and developmental potential (Zins, 2004), as well as conceptualisations of emotional intelligence (Mayer et al., 2016), and emotional competence (Buckley et al., 2003).

Constructivist Assumptions of Wellbeing Literacy

Language may be usefully understood from at least three perspectives. The first views language as a marker that reflects people's psychological status and individual differences. The second views language as a stimulus by which people's cognition, emotion, or behaviour can be passively influenced. The third view is that language is a resource that people use actively to construct their psychological and social realities. Wellbeing literacy is based on this third view of language. Humans construct wellbeing through language and their own lay concepts. Language provides insights into wellbeing experiences.

Drawing on constructivist epistemology and social constructivism, and key to wellbeing literacy, is the notion that meaning-making is socially constructed through language. Social constructivism proposes that the world is understood and perceived through language in culturally and time-bound ways. Perspectives are considered shaped and changed through dynamic discourse, where the world is understood by how it is represented through language, and socially determined phenomena direct where we focus our attention. Social constructivist discourse represents culturally meaningful sets of ideas used to make meaning of the world. Discourse is rooted in socially constructed power, influencing how people choose to act, as well as societal concepts of "normality". A social constructivist perspective embraces the notion that different people with different life experiences likely hold different perspectives, and reality is an individually constructed subjective phenomenon (Burr & Dick, 2017).

Contextualist Assumptions of Wellbeing Literacy

Contextualisation is fundamental to communicating about and for wellbeing and deeply tied to meaning-making. How different people in different circumstances conceptualise and communicate about wellbeing, in their preferred modalities varies. What is meaningful for one person may be different to another, or what is suitable in one life domain may not be suitable in another.

Pragmatics in Linguistics describes how implication and inference are derived from meaning gleaned beyond the literal text. For instance, taking turns in conversation, text organisation, deixis, and presupposition, point towards contextual elements that help the reader create meaning and understanding. Broadening to consider wider society, and the language that is used in dominant discourse, we see further instances where language holds meaning and power.

"Discourses" refer to how social groups think and talk about aspects of society, often determined by social institutions such as the media or education. Dominant discourses are often considered embedded in power relations, which shape societal knowledge and relationships (Barton et al., 2000; Burr, 2003; Gee, 1991; Raskin, 2012). A contextualist approach to wellbeing provides the opportunity to unveil and acknowledge existing wellbeing discourse in society. Recognising diverse definitions of wellbeing across the whole of society, and studying language use in context, helps create a more inclusive and representative understanding of wellbeing.

The assumptions of wellbeing literacy are consistent with Alexandrova's (2017) schema of (1) concept, (2) differential realisation of wellbeing, and

(3) context. That is, wellbeing, there may be a conception of wellbeing that pervades across contexts; however, it is realised differently by different people. Moreover, this realisation varies greatly by context and hence any utterance of the word wellbeing should be grounded in context. Similarly, wellbeing literacy is differentially constructed as a dynamic and evolving process that is socioculturally created and experienced. Communicating about and for wellbeing is therefore also seen as contextually bound and dynamic. Additionally, the multimodal nature of literacy provides pathways for more meaningful, contextually agile ways to communicate (Cope & Kalantzis, 2013).

Capability Assumptions of Wellbeing Literacy

In educational discourse, the terms *capability, capacity, competence, skill,* and *ability* are often used interchangeably, however, they are distinct concepts (von Tunzelmann, 2009). From the perspective of wellbeing literacy, and specifically the Capability Model of Wellbeing Literacy (outlined below), a *capability* is defined as the fluid, dynamic, and interwoven formation of skills, knowledge, opportunities, choices, and behaviours that emerge as a dialectic between a person and the environment (Nussbaum, 2011; Scheffler, 1985; Sen, 1993). For example, Aanya wishes to ride a bike. If Aanya has some ability to ride a bike, and the opportunity to ride a bike is present (e.g., there is a bike and a pathway), then you could say that Aanya has the capability to ride a bike. If Aanya chooses to ride, she has exercised the capability referred by Sen as functionings (realised capabilities), also sometimes referred to as achievements. This is distinctive from a capacity, which is seen as the limit of her ability. A competency is the demonstrable and measurable aspect of one's ability, but unlike the concept of a capability, is silent on whether the opportunity to ride a bike is present beyond that situation.

A capability can be summarised as what one is able to be and do. In terms of literacy, this becomes what people are able to be and do through language use. In terms of wellbeing literacy this becomes what people are able to be and do for wellbeing, through intentional wellbeing-related language use. Pioneered by economist Amyrta Sen (1993, 2001) and developed further by philosopher Martha Nussbaum (2011), the Capability Approach proposes that any effective conceptualisation of wellbeing must have genuine opportunities to experience wellbeing, as defined by the person. Such "self definition" is very consistent with the approach of wellbeing literacy, as it emphasises lay concepts and local language communities to construct wellbeing meanings.

The Five Component Capability Model of Wellbeing Literacy

The Capability Model of Wellbeing Literacy presents wellbeing literacy as a mediator or moderator of the wellbeing experience (Oades et al., 2021); a capability (or freedom in terms of a Sen conceptualisation of capability) that influences the experience of wellbeing (functioning or achievement). Wellbeing literacy allows individuals options of what to *do* with the environmental conditions that are available to them. Hence, the capability is closely related to the concept of agency. The higher the wellbeing literacy, the more options that are available to the individual to "convert" the wellbeing language opportunities in their internal or external environment into meaningful wellbeing language use achievements. Combined with a constructivist view of language, it follows that language use about and for wellbeing can have tangible effects on wellbeing itself.

The capability model of wellbeing literacy is a formal model with five necessary components as outlined in Table 2.1. A formal model is designed to be relevant across multiple contexts. It will however be realised differently in different concepts. For example, its applications will be different in relationships, families, schools, organisations, etc. For this reason, it does not provide a prior definition of wellbeing per se, rather it emphasises the examination of how language is used to construct wellbeing in different contexts. It does however assume that wellbeing is valuable. In this regard, like wellbeing, wellbeing literacy is a "thick concept" (Alexandrova, 2017), something we value and seek to examine at the same time.

Vocabulary and knowledge *about* wellbeing – Wellbeing Literacy involves the vocabulary and knowledge of wellbeing. The vocabulary and knowledge of wellbeing may relate to conceptualisations of wellbeing (such as different frameworks about wellbeing), operationalisation of wellbeing (such as

TABLE 2.1 The five component capability model of wellbeing literacy

Function	*Component*	*Description*
The *what* of language use	Vocabulary and knowledge *about* wellbeing	Words and basic facts about wellbeing (i.e., content that is signified).
The *how* of language use	Comprehension of multimodal text related to wellbeing	Reading, listening, viewing about and for wellbeing.
That *how* of language use	Composition of multimodal text related to wellbeing	Writing, speaking, creating about and for wellbeing.
The *where* and *who* of language use	Context awareness and adaptability	Awareness of differences across contexts and adapting the use of language to fit the relevant context.
The *why* of language use	Intentionality *for* wellbeing	Habit of intentionally using language to maintain or improve wellbeing of self or others.

components and measures of wellbeing), or different domains of wellbeing, such as emotional, psychological, or social wellbeing. Within wellbeing literacy, knowledge is relevant only as it is signified by language – language about wellbeing. The focus of this component of the model is vocabulary about wellbeing phenomena, which implies that there is something to know. We cannot meaningfully and intentionally utter the word "table" without having a concept or knowing of something that is a table.

Capability to comprehend multimodal text related to wellbeing – Wellbeing literacy comprehension is multimodal and involves reading, listening, and viewing (ACARA, 2020) about and for wellbeing. For instance, listening for wellbeing could involve intentionally listening to music to calm an overstimulated mind or to boost one's mood.

Capability to compose multimodal text related to wellbeing – Wellbeing Literacy composition is multimodal and involves writing, speaking, and creating (ACARA, 2020) about or for wellbeing. For instance, composition about and for wellbeing can be demonstrated in an art exhibit. For example, the created artworks themselves may represent the emotion and experience of belonging (compositions *about* wellbeing), while the exhibit itself may bring community and artists together, to interact and connect, sharing and discussing the artwork, while also nurturing a sense of community connection and belonging (hence the artwork and the exhibit have been created *for* wellbeing).

Context awareness and adaptability – Wellbeing Literacy requires that the language user is able to recognise different life situations, and responsively adapt their language use accordingly. For instance language use choices during in-person interactions, where meaning is simultaneously garnered via body language, facial expressions, and conversation tone, may be quite different to language use choices made during online communication.

Intentionality for wellbeing – Wellbeing Literacy involves the intentional belief, desire and awareness of language use for wellbeing (Malle & Knobe, 1997). The language user aims for wellbeing outcomes. For instance, autonomy, relationship, and competence-supportive environments provide enabling conditions for wellbeing in the workplace (Slemp et al., 2018). Providing leaders and employees with the vocabulary and knowledge about how to create wellbeing supportive conditions, increases capability (what they can be and do: Sen, 1993), to intentionally communicate about and for optimal workplace functioning.

Multiple Contexts, Multiple Disciplines, and Methodologies for Wellbeing Literacy

The capability model of wellbeing literacy emphasises that the literacy is multimodal; see Figure 2.1. In addition to the modes of language use, its applications are also relevant to multiple contexts, and it should be informed by lay concepts and multiple cultures. Moreover, it has been and needs to be

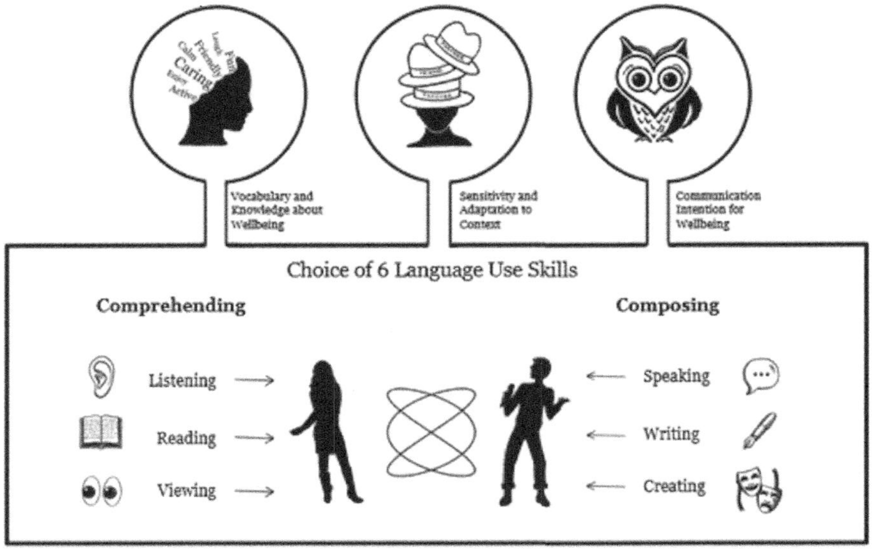

FIGURE 2.1 Visual representation of key components of the capability model of wellbeing literacy

informed by multiple disciplines, and multiple methodologies: quantitative, qualitative, and mixed methods.

Conclusion

Wellbeing is valued by humans. Wellbeing literacy examines how wellbeing can be facilitated by intentional language use in different contexts. This chapter has explored the theoretical influences and epistemological assumptions underpinning the capability model of wellbeing literacy. The model is presented deliberately as a formal model, affording it to be used in many contexts, consistent with its contextualist assumptions of language. Moreover, it requires and affords multimethod approaches to both its implementation and investigation.

References

Alexandrova, A. (2017). *A philosophy for the science of well-being*. Oxford University Press. https://doi.org/10.1163/17455243-01606005

Anderson, G. L., & Irvine, P. (1993). Informing critical literacy with ethnography. Critical literacy: Politics, praxis, and the postmodern, 81–104.

Australian Curriculum, Assessment and Reporting Authority (ACARA). (2020). General Capabilities. https://www.australiancurriculum.edu.au/f-10-curriculum/general-capabilities/

Barton, D., Hamilton, M., IvaniÚc, R., & Ivanič, R. (2000). *Situated literacies: Reading and writing in context*. Routledge.

Bassett, M., & Macnaught, L. (2024). Embedded approaches to academic literacy development: A systematic review of empirical research about impact. *Teaching in Higher Education*, 1–19. https://doi.org/10.1080/13562517.2024.2354280

Belfrage, S., Husted, M., Fraser, S., Patel, S., & Faulkner, J. (2025). A systematic review of the effectiveness of community-based interventions aimed at improving health literacy of parents/carers of children. *Perspectives in Public Health*, *145*(1), 25–31. https//doi.org/10.1177/17579139231180746

Berger, R., Woodfin, L., Plaut, S. N., & Dobbertin, C. B. (2014). *Transformational literacy: Making the common core shift with work that matters*. John Wiley & Sons.

Buchannan, A. (2017). Transformational literacy: The virtues that shape the self and the world in a single act. http://medium.com/benefit-mindset/transformational-literacy-efc32cdbbl15d

Buckley, M., Storino, M., & Saarni, C. (2003). Promoting emotional competence in children and adolescents: Implications for school psychologists. *School Psychology Quarterly*, *18*(2), 177–191. https://doi.org/10.1521/scpq.18.2.177.21855

Burr, V. (2003). *Social constructionism* (2nd ed.). Routledge.

Burr, V., & Dick, P. (2017). Social constructionism. In: B. Gough (Ed.), *The Palgrave handbook of critical social psychology*. Palgrave Macmillan. https://doi.org/10.1057/978-1-137-51018-1_4

Cope, B., & Kalantzis, M. (2013). "Multiliteracies": New literacies, new learning. In D. R. Cole & D. L. Pullen (Eds.), *Framing languages and literacies* (pp. 105–135). Routledge.

Dewey, J. (1998). *The essential Dewey: Pragmatism, education, democracy* (Vol. 1). Indiana University Press.

Freedman, D. A., Bess, K. D., Tucker, H. A., Boyd, D. L., Tuchman, A. M., & Wallston, K. A. (2009). Public health literacy defined. *American Journal of Preventive Medicine*, *36*(5), 446–451. http://doi.org/10.1016/j.amepre.2009.02.001

Gee, J. (1991). Socio-cultural approaches to literacy (literacies). *Annual Review of Applied Linguistics*, *12*, 31–48.

Göpel, M. (2016). *The great mindshift: How a new economic paradigm and sustainability transformations go hand in hand*. Springer Nature. https://library.oapen.org/bitstream/handle/20.500.12657/27799/1/1002206.pdf

Goryachev, A. (2024). Embracing AI Literacy: The key to thriving in the age of GenAI. *Forbes*. https://www.forbes.com/councils/forbescommunicationscouncil/2024/07/16/embracing-ai-literacy-the-key-to-thriving-in-the-age-of-genai/

Jorm, A. F. (2015). Why we need the concept of "Mental Health Literacy". *Health Communication*, *30*(12), 1166–1168. https://doi.org/10.1080/10410236.2015.1037423

Keefe, E. B., & Copeland, S. R. (2011). What is literacy? The power of a definition. *Research and Practice for Persons With Severe Disabilities*, *36*(3-4), 92–99.

Kennedy, J. L., & Caspe, M. (2013). An intergenerational approach to family literacy. In H. Kreider, M. Caspe, & D. Hiatt-Michael (Eds.), *Promising practices for engaging families in literacy*. Information Age Publishing.

Kienpointner, M. (1996). Whorf and Wittgenstein. Language, world view and argumentation. *Argumentation*, *10*, 475–494.

Luke, A. (2000). Critical literacy in Australia: A matter of context and standpoint. *Journal of Adolescent & Adult Literacy*, *43*(5), 448–461. Retrieved from http://www.jstor.org/stable/40017081

Malle, B. F., & Knobe, J. (1997). The folk concept of intentionality. *Journal of Experimental and Social Psychology*, *33*, 101–121. https://doi.org/10.1006/jesp.1996.1314

Mayer, J. D., Caruso, D. R., & Salovey, P. (2016). The ability model of emotional intelligence: Principles and updates. *Emotion Review*, 8, 1–11. https://doi.org/10.1177/1754073916639667

Miller, R. (2018). Introduction: Futures literacy: Transforming the future. In B. Miller (Ed.), *Transforming the future* (pp. 1–12). Routledge.

Nussbaum, M. C. (2011). *Creating capabilities: The human development approach.* Harvard University Press.

Oades, L. G., Jarden, A., Hou, H., Ozturk, C., Williams, P., R. Slemp, G., & Huang, L. (2021). Wellbeing literacy: A capability model for wellbeing science and practice. *International Journal of Environmental Research and Public Health*, *18*(2), 719. https://doi.org/10.3390/ijerph18020719

Raskin, J. D. (2012). Evolutionary constructivism and humanistic psychology. *Journal of Theoretical and Philosophical Psychology*, *32*(2), 119.

Scheffler, S. (1985). Agent-centred restrictions, rationality, and the virtues. *Mind*, *94*(375), 409–419.

Sen, A. K. (1993). Capability and wellbeing. In M. C. Nussbaum & A. K. Sen (Eds.), *The quality of life* (pp. 30–53). Clarendon Press.

Sen, A. K. (2001). *Development as freedom.* Oxford Paperbacks.

Slemp, G. R., Kern, M. L., & Patrick, K. J. et al. (2018). Leader autonomy support in the workplace: A meta-analytic review. *Motiv Emot*, *42*, 706–724. https://doi.org/10.1007/s11031-018-9698-y

Sørensen, K., Van den Broucke, S., Fullam, J., Doyle, G., Pelikan, J., & Slonska, Z. (HLS-EU) Consortium Health Literacy Project European (2012). Health literacy and public health: A systematic review and integration of definitions and models. *BMC Public Health*, *12*, 1–13.

von Tunzelmann, N. (2009). Competencies versus capabilities: A reassessment. *Economia Politica*, *26*(3), 435–464.

Vygotsky, L. S. (1962). Thought and word. In L. Vygotsky, E. Hanfmann, & G. Vakar (Eds.), *Thought and language* (pp. 119–153). MIT Press. https://doi.org/10.1037/11193-007

Waterhouse, A. (2019). *Emotional literacy.* Routledge.

Zins, J. E. (Ed.) (2004). *Building academic success on social and emotional learning: What does the research say?* Teachers College Press.

3

MEASURING WELLBEING LITERACY

Hanchao Hou

Introduction

Wellbeing literacy (WBL) refers to the mindful use of language about and for wellbeing (Oades et al., 2020). This emerging and interdisciplinary concept seeks to connect wellbeing science, positive psychology, education, and public health. WBL encompasses several components: a well-developed vocabulary and knowledge about wellbeing, the ability to comprehend and compose multimodal texts related to wellbeing, awareness of context, and the intentional use of language to foster wellbeing (Oades et al., 2021). As a teachable skill, WBL plays a crucial role in enhancing both individual and collective wellbeing. To effectively teach and evaluate WBL, reliable and valid measurement tools are essential, particularly for advancing research and practice in education and public health.

This chapter examines the current state of WBL measurement, highlighting the challenges and opportunities that exist in the field. We review existing measurement approaches, explore the implications of modern psychometric techniques, and assess how advanced technologies, such as large language models (LLMs),[1] could influence future WBL assessments. Additionally, we propose directions for future research and practice, emphasising the importance of developing measures that are contextually sensitive, culturally relevant, and empirically grounded. Ultimately, this chapter aims to help readers grasp the key issues surrounding WBL measurement, stimulate discussion and new ideas, and suggest possible pathways for advancing the measurement of WBL.

Current State of WBL Measurement

The field of WBL measurement remains in its early stages, with few tools specifically designed to measure it. The Well-Lit 6 is a parsimonious six-item

DOI: 10.4324/9781003644293-3

scale that assesses individuals' wellbeing knowledge, vocabulary, and skills to comprehend and compose language and to adjust language depending on context (Hou et al., 2021). This measure demonstrates good validity. To our knowledge, the Well-Lit 6 is the most widely recognised WBL tool grounded in the construct originally developed by Oades and colleagues (Oades & Johnston, 2017; Oades et al., 2020, 2021).

As interest in WBL grows within wellbeing science and public mental health communities, various tools, many with distinct operationalisations of WBL, have been developed to measure WBL. Chng et al. (2022) assessed WBL by examining participants' ability to identify 11 key wellbeing indicators in a study investigating and comparing the mental health literacy MHL and WBL of Australian adults. These indicators, drawn from the European Social Survey Wellbeing Module, included dimensions of social, psychological, and subjective wellbeing (Huppert & So, 2013). Example items from the measure include statements such as "feeling close to the community and people in the local area," "feeling that what you do in your life is valuable and worthwhile," and "feeling happy most of the time." While this method captures essential aspects of wellbeing knowledge and vocabulary, which form a foundational element of WBL, it falls short of measuring the broader, multidimensional aspects of WBL, such as communication of wellbeing.

Given tools for measuring WBL are still in their early stages and limited in number, examining related constructs such as positive MHL can offer valuable insights for assessing WBL. MHL initially focused on recognising and preventing *mental disorders* (Jorm, 2012; Jorm et al., 1997), distinguishing it from WBL. However, as MHL expanded to encompass knowledge and skills for promoting and maintaining *positive mental health*, the measures of positive MHL became more relevant to those of WBL (Kutcher et al., 2016; Mansfield et al., 2020). One such tool is the 10-item Mental Health Promoting Knowledge Scale (MHPK-10), a self-report measure that assesses understanding of key factors for achieving and maintaining mental health (Bjornsen et al., 2017). Sample items include statements such as "Handling stressful situations in a good manner," "Feeling that you belong in a community," and "Setting limits for what is OK for me." While these elements of self-awareness and knowledge of mental health overlap with WBL, the MHPK-10 also failed to encompass the communicative and language-based components that WBL aims to address.

Current WBL measurement tools are in the nascent stages of development, mirroring trends in related fields like health literacy, where a proliferation of instruments has emerged over decades (Tavousi et al., 2022). Tavousi et al.'s systematic review of health literacy measurement underscores the need for WBL research to adopt rigorous validation practices, ensuring comprehensive reporting of psychometric properties and alignment with study objectives. Furthermore, a multidimensional approach is needed, with each dimension measured by at least three items to ensure a more thorough and precise assessment (Spector, 1992). Such measures should encompass the full scope of WBL, addressing its components such as knowledge, language use, contextual sensitivity, and intentionality. Additionally, they must be adaptable to diverse cultural and demographic contexts.

Challenges and Considerations in WBL Measurement

Relationship between Conceptualisation and Measurement

WBL can be conceptualised at different levels of abstraction. At higher levels, the concepts cover broader cases and categories, but measuring them becomes more challenging due to fewer defining attributes. Conversely, at lower levels of abstraction, WBL is more specific and measurable, though this restricts its applicability across diverse contexts. For instance, defining WBL as "mindful language use about and for wellbeing" (Oades et al., 2020) provides a broad and flexible interpretation of WBL, though with less specific direction for developing measures. In contrast, defining WBL as "the capability of comprehending and composing wellbeing languages, across various contexts, that may be intentionally used to maintain or improve the wellbeing of oneself, others or the world" (Oades et al., 2021) provides a more concrete basis for measurement.

To measure WBL effectively in a specific context, researchers may operationalise the concept according to the needs of that context and develop corresponding tools, as demonstrated by Burns et al. (2024) and Chng et al. (2022). It suggests that multiple measures of WBL will likely emerge to address varying circumstances, such as family or workplace settings. For instance, An et al. (2023) introduced the concept of digital WBL. Although measurement tools for this particular adaptation of WBL are not yet available, it is expected to inspire the development of a new measure.

While the plurality of WBL measurements allows for capturing its complexity, it also presents challenges in ensuring coherence and comparability across different measures. However, the development of varied tools should not be discouraged, similar to what has been practised in related fields like health literacy and MHL. For instance, although many studies still rely on Nutbeam's (2000) early definition of health literacy, others have tailored the concept to particular contexts, such as health literacy for nursing professionals (Toronto, 2015).

The iterative process of moving between abstract conceptualisation and specific measurement is inevitable and necessary to advancing the field of WBL and its assessments. Meanwhile, an integrated, context-sensitive theoretical model of WBL is necessary to account for evolving definitions and to maintain consistency across the field. In developing new WBL measures, two key approaches are recommended to avoid proliferation: (1) clearly operationalise

WBL in each study to provide a solid foundation for future researchers to compare, refine, and build upon the results, and (2) validate different measures against one another to ensure they complement, rather than contradict or replicate, each other.

Strengthening the Validation of WBL

Discriminant and Incremental Validity

Given that WBL is an emerging concept, it is essential that the instruments used to measure it demonstrate both uniqueness and the capacity to offer insights beyond existing measures. Discriminant validity ensures that WBL measures capture information distinct from related measures, while incremental validity confirms that these measures explain additional variance in wellbeing outcomes beyond what current tools can account for (Haynes & Lench, 2003; Messick, 1995).

Although initial evaluations of WBL measures have shown promising results (Hou et al., 2021), further validation using additional variables – such as general literacy, health literacy, and MHL – is necessary. Since WBL is a domain-specific form of literacy that likely overlaps with general literacy, it is important to assess whether WBL measures add unique value beyond instruments like the National Assessment Program – Literacy and Numeracy (NAPLAN). Similarly, since studies suggest that mental health and wellbeing are often conflated (Burns et al., 2024), further research is needed to compare WBL measures with those of MHL. These evaluations are crucial for developing robust WBL measurement tools that offer unique insights into understanding and predicting wellbeing and mental health.

Cross-Cultural Validity

Cross-cultural validity ensures that a measurement instrument maintains equivalence in meaning and psychometric properties across cultural contexts (Sousa & Rojjanasrirat, 2011). This type of validation is crucial for WBL because cultural, socioeconomic, and demographic factors influence how individuals understand and express wellbeing (Diener et al., 2018). For instance, Oishi et al. (2013) found that individuals from collectivist cultures placed greater emphasis on social harmony and relational wellbeing, while those from individualist cultures prioritised personal achievement and self-expression. Such differences underscoring the necessity of culturally adapting WBL measurement tools to ensure their validity and relevance across diverse populations.

Recent studies highlight key strategies for adaptation, including translation-back translation procedures, cognitive interviews to assess item clarity, and pilot testing with target populations (Cruchinho et al., 2024; Sousa &

Rojjanasrirat, 2011). An example of cross-cultural validity can be found in Jia et al. (2024), who validated a Chinese version of the Well-Lit 6 scale, demonstrating its good cross-cultural validity. Future studies should also test the measurement invariance (Vandenberg & Lance, 2000) of WBL tools across diverse populations to ensure that the constructs are measured and interpreted consistently.

Methods Other Than Self-Reported Scales

Performance-Based Assessments

Performance-based assessments offer a valuable alternative to self-report measures of WBL, as they evaluate participants' skills and knowledge through standardised functional tasks rather than subjective perceptions (Moore et al., 2007). While self-report measures are easy to administer and relatively accurate, they are prone to reporting bias and social desirability concerns. In contrast, performance-based assessments are more objective, less influenced by personality traits, and provide a direct measure of individuals' ability to apply wellbeing knowledge in real-world situations (Goldenberg et al., 2006). These assessments are widely used in educational settings to track progress and facilitate learning (Coombe et al., 2020).

For WBL, performance-based tools could include multiple-choice questions, situational judgment tests, and multimodal materials like images to test participants' comprehension and application of wellbeing concepts. For example, a multiple-choice question could ask participants to identify research-backed strategies for enhancing happiness, such as volunteering, practising gratitude, or exercising, while including an incorrect option like excessive social media use. This assesses their understanding and practical application of wellbeing knowledge and strategies.

To improve the accuracy and comprehensiveness of WBL assessments, future research should integrate both objective and subjective measures. While studies in health literacy have yielded mixed results regarding the predictive power of these approaches (Kiechle et al., 2015), recent findings suggest that performance-based assessments may better predict outcomes like the ability to recognise misinformation and make informed health decisions (Schulz et al., 2021). However, objective measures may overlook the personal and contextual nuances of wellbeing experiences, so integrating both objective and subjective assessments remains crucial for capturing the full complexity of WBL.

Interview-Based Assessments

Interview-based measures play an important role in clinical practice because they provide idiosyncratic information about clients (Guy et al., 2008). An interview-based assessment tool of WBL could be used in personalised PPIs and coaching for individuals who have special needs, such as students facing challenges with self-reported or performance-based measure (Ciarrochi et al., 2022). Wolstencroft et al. (2010) proposed a three-step protocol for developing interview-based assessment tools, which can be adapted for WBL measurement. This protocol involves creating a coding framework based on an operational definition of WBL, followed by data collection through semi-structured interviews, and then analysing the data to identify key indicators of WBL development. Existing scales, such as Well-Lit 6, can be adapted into interview formats by directly mirroring scale items in the interview questions (Ventura et al., 2010). For example, the "Composing" dimension of WBL could be assessed with a question like, "Can you describe a time when you expressed your thoughts on wellbeing?" Responses can then be scored using a rubric ranging from 1 (vague or incomplete) to 5 (specific and contextually adaptive). A tailored approach could be used in the interview process, incorporating open-ended questions and follow-up prompts to explore responses in depth. This flexibility provides room for clarification and elaboration as needed, allowing the assessment to be adapted to specific contexts – such as schools or clinics – without compromising theoretical rigour.

The Role of AI Technologies in WBL Measurement

Recent advancements in artificial intelligence (AI) offer significant opportunities to improve the measurement of WBL in terms of scalability, efficiency, accuracy, and engagement. This chapter will explore how cutting-edge AI technologies, including LLMs, multimodal computing,[2] and gamification,[3] can enhance the measurement of WBL.

LLMs and Language-Based Assessment of WBL

LLMs, such as GPT-4, BERT, and LLaMA, hold great potential as transformative tools in measuring WBL. Previous research using traditional natural language processing (NLP) methods has demonstrated the effectiveness of using language-based methods to assess psychological constructs (Kjell et al., 2021). For example, it has been used in measuring wellbeing, screening for mental health problems (He et al., 2019), and identifying abilities that improve mental health (Zhang et al., 2019). Compared to rating scales, which reduce subjective experiences to numerical scores and often fail to reflect the complexity of human emotions and thoughts, language-based assessments can analyse natural language to capture the richness of real-life experiences (Kjell et al., 2024). The introduction of LLMs enhances these methods even further. LLMs streamline the process, making language-based assessments more accessible and user-friendly, even for researchers and practitioners who are unfamiliar with traditional NLP techniques. LLMs' ability to automatically process large volumes of data and interpret linguistic patterns makes them a powerful tool for assessing WBL on a broader scale.

LLMs could be used to assess individuals' WBL by analysing their written or spoken texts. WBL, as a capability of language use, is reflected in how individuals communicate their thoughts, feelings and beliefs related to wellbeing, and research suggests that those with higher WBL tend to use positive, precise, and constructive language. For instance, students engaged in positive education programs often show more strength-based, multidimensional, and relational narratives regarding wellbeing, as found by Waters and Higgins (2022). Similarly, flourishing individuals on social media tend to express empathy and concern for societal issues, use vocabularies emphasising positive emotions and a broad range of emojis, and cover topics from spirituality and health to practical matters like work and success (Cebral-Loureda et al., 2023). These linguistic patterns suggest that LLMs, which excel at processing such nuanced content, are well-positioned to assess WBL effectively.

LLMs are emerging as a scalable and efficient tool for educators and policymakers to dynamically track WBL and respond with targeted interventions without relying on traditional surveys that are time-consuming and limited in scope. In educational contexts, LLMs provide a tool for educators to track the change of knowledge, vocabularies and skills on wellbeing, by analysing their speaking language during class or their written language of positive education assignments. This enables educators to offer timely feedback and personalised learning pathways for each student to improve their WBL and ultimately wellbeing effectively.

LLMs also offer great potential for monitoring WBL across populations by analysing social media content. As individuals increasingly share their emotions and thoughts online, LLMs can identify language patterns, such as word choice and emotional tone, that reflect WBL, providing a dynamic and scalable way to assess WBL at both individual and community levels. This real-time analysis can also help shape more responsive public health strategies, fostering environments that support both individual and collective wellbeing.

Multimodal Computing

Multimodal computing methods present exciting opportunities for measuring multimodal WBL. Empirical studies have shown that combining verbal and nonverbal cues could improve the accuracy of affective state detection in assessing mental health (Liu et al., 2024). Since WBL extends beyond written language to encompass multimodal communication – incorporating images, sounds, and gestures – leveraging these diverse modalities can provide a more comprehensive understanding of WBL. For example, image recognition techniques can analyse an individual's visual representations of wellbeing or their reactions to visual stimuli related to wellbeing. Additionally, audio analysis can capture the emotional tone and stress levels in a person's voice, providing further insights into their wellbeing. Integrating these multimodal data sources through advanced computing methods offers a holistic view of WBL.

Gamification

Gamification, particularly when powered by AI, reframes traditional WBL assessments by embedding Likert-scale constructs into dynamic, scenario-based interactions. Central to this approach is designing scenarios that map in-game behaviours to the five-component WBL model. LLMs have been used to generate adaptive narratives and analyse user choices to align with psychological assessment frameworks (Yang et al., 2024). For instance, in a conflict-resolution scenario, LLMs evaluate participants' textual choices (e.g., empathetic dialogue) and decision pathways (e.g., collaborative solutions vs. self-focused strategies), which may correlate with "comprehension" and "intentionality" dimensions of WBL. While empirical validation is ongoing, this method shows promise in mitigating self-report biases by identifying disparities between claimed competencies (e.g., high self-rated "empathy") and in-game behaviours that mirror real-world competence (e.g., frequent dismissive responses). Moreover, it holds particular interest for adolescents, who are at a critical developmental stage for cultivating WBL.

The Considerations of Using AI in WBL Measurement

However, the ethical implications of AI in WBL measurement, including data privacy concerns, algorithmic biases, and the erosion of human agency, necessitate careful deliberation and ethical oversight. For example, sensitive personal data may be processed, necessitating robust data protection measures to safeguard users' privacy. Additionally, biases inherent in AI models – whether due to the data used to train them or societal inequalities – could affect the fairness and accuracy of assessments across different demographic groups. Therefore, it's crucial that future AI-based WBL measurement tools undergo thorough validation to ensure their cultural sensitivity and ethical integrity. AI holds promise in transforming WBL measurement by offering innovative approaches to analyse complex, multimodal data, but it must be employed carefully to avoid potential biases and privacy risks.

Practical Implications

Measuring WBL at the societal level has significant benefits for both public health and collective wellbeing. Drawing from Nutbeam's (2000) model,

WBL can be seen as a key outcome of positive education and other wellbeing-promoting programs, with its measurement helping to predict future trends in population wellbeing. Tools like the Well-Lit 6, which are efficient and easy to administer, provide valuable insights into the effectiveness of wellbeing initiatives and enable the continuous evaluation of these programs. For example, schools integrating Well-Lit 6 into social-emotional curricula can monitor students' knowledge and vocabulary related to wellbeing or utilise scenario-based tasks (e.g., resolving peer conflicts) to assess the composing and contextual sensitivity dimensions of WBL. This approach facilitates more targeted skill development for wellbeing and directly informs actionable improvements in wellbeing initiatives.

For practitioners, adopting a multidimensional and culturally adaptive approach to WBL measurement is essential. Educators and community health workers can integrate tools like Well-Lit 6 with scenario-based tasks to assess real-world application, while ensuring cultural relevance through localised adaptations. Looking ahead, embracing AI-driven assessments – though not yet fully realised – will be critical for analysing multimodal language use patterns, and practitioners should prepare to leverage these advancements as they emerge.

Furthermore, establishing national targets for WBL would be highly beneficial, just as the importance of national goals for health literacy (Nutbeam, 2009). Policymakers could use WBL data to assess the impact of educational and public health interventions, informing the development of more targeted strategies. By embedding WBL into public policy frameworks, regular monitoring would drive long-term improvements in wellbeing outcomes across communities.

In conclusion, the ongoing measurement of WBL is crucial for advancing both education and public health. With the use of efficient tools and the establishment of national goals, WBL has the potential to become a powerful metric for predicting and enhancing the overall wellbeing of populations, offering a clear pathway for improving collective wellbeing.

Conclusion

In conclusion, the development of WBL measures has made significant progress, offering a range of effective instruments while also revealing challenges. These challenges, however, should be viewed as opportunities for improvement. Measuring WBL is a critical step in understanding and fostering overall mental health and wellbeing. Employing diverse methods allows for a deeper understanding of individuals' knowledge, vocabularies, and skills related to wellbeing. Future research should remain focused on clarifying the conceptualisation and operationalisation of WBL, strengthening the validation of WBL measures, and leveraging new methods to measure WBL. These efforts will result in more reliable and validated measures of WBL. In turn, the accurate assessment of WBL will not only support individual wellbeing but also will contribute to broader public health and societal wellbeing goals. By advancing WBL measurement, we can better support positive education initiatives and public health strategies aimed at improving overall wellbeing.

Notes

1 Advanced AI systems trained on vast amounts of text data to process, generate, and analyse human-like language, enabling applications such as automated text evaluation and natural language understanding.
2 A computational approach that integrates multiple data sources (e.g., text, images, audio) to analyse complex human behaviours and interactions, providing a more comprehensive understanding of phenomena like wellbeing literacy.
3 The application of game-design elements, such as interactive scenarios, rewards, and challenges, to non-game contexts (e.g., assessments) to enhance engagement, motivation, and user participation.

References

An, N., Vesty, G., & Cheong, C. (2023). Defining digital wellbeing literacy in remote work integrated learning. *Australasian Journal of Information Systems*, *27*. https://doi.org/10.3127/ajis.v27i0.3969

Bjornsen, H. N., Eilertsen, M. E. B., Ringdal, R., Espnes, G. A., & Moksnes, U. K. (2017). Positive mental health literacy: Development and validation of a measure among Norwegian adolescents. *BMC Public Health*, *17*(1), 717. https://doi.org/10.1186/s12889-017-4733-6

Burns, R. A., Sargent, K., & Crisp, D. A. (2024). Mental health and wellbeing literacy: A cross-national comparison. *Applied Research in Quality of Life*. Advanced online publication. https://doi.org/10.1007/s11482-024-10330-z

Cebral-Loureda, M., Hernandez-Baqueiro, A., & Tames-Munoz, E. (2023). A text mining analysis of human flourishing on Twitter. *Scientific Reports*, *13*(1), 3403. https://doi.org/10.1038/s41598-023-30209-7

Chng, J., Burns, R., Murray, K., & Crisp, D. (2022). A community mental health and wellbeing literacy study among Australian adults. *Journal of Happiness and Health*, *2*(1), 12–30. https://doi.org/10.47602/johah.v2i1.13

Ciarrochi, J., Hayes, S. C., Oades, L. G., & Hofmann, S. G. (2022). Toward a unified framework for positive psychology interventions: Evidence-based processes of change in coaching, prevention, and training. *Frontiers in Psychology*, *12*, 809362. https://doi.org/10.3389/fpsyg.2021.809362

Coombe, C., Vafadar, H., & Mohebbi, H. (2020). Language assessment literacy: What do we need to learn, unlearn, and relearn? *Language Testing in Asia*, *10*(1), 1–16. https://doi.org/10.1186/s40468-020-00101-6

Cruchinho, P., López-Franco, M. D., Capelas, M. L., Almeida, S., Bennett, P. M., Miranda da Silva, M., Teixeira, G., Nunes, E., Lucas, P., & Gaspar, F. (2024). Translation, cross-cultural adaptation, and validation of measurement instruments: A practical guideline for novice researchers. *Journal of Multidisciplinary Healthcare*, *17*, 2701–2728. https://doi.org/10.2147/JMDH.S419714

Diener, E., Oishi, S., & Tay, L. (2018). Advances in subjective well-being research. *Nature Human Behaviour*, *2*(4), 253–260. https://doi.org/10.1038/s41562-018-0307-6

Goldenberg, I., Matheson, K., & Mantler, J. (2006). The assessment of emotional intelligence: A comparison of performance-based and self-report methodologies. *Journal of Personality Assessment*, *86*(1), 33–45. https://doi.org/10.1207/s15327752jpa8601_05

Guy, L. S., Poythress, N. G., Douglas, K. S., Skeem, J. L., & Edens, J. F. (2008). Correspondence between self-report and interview-based assessments of antisocial personality disorder. *Psychological Assessment*, *20*(1), 47–54. https://doi.org/10.1037/1040-3590.20.1.47

Haynes, S. N., & Lench, H. C. (2003). Incremental validity of new clinical assessment measures. *Psychological Assessment*, *15*(4), 456–466. https://doi.org/10.1037/1040-3590.15.4.456

He, Q., Veldkamp, B. P., Glas, C. A. W., & van den Berg, S. M. (2019). Combining text mining of long constructed responses and item-based measures: A hybrid test design to screen for posttraumatic stress disorder (PTSD). *Frontiers in Psychology*, *10*, 2358. https://doi.org/10.3389/fpsyg.2019.02358

Hou, H., Chin, T. C., Slemp, G. R., & Oades, L. G. (2021). Wellbeing literacy: Conceptualization, measurement, and preliminary empirical findings from students, parents and school staff. *International Journal of Environmental Research and Public Health*, *18*(4), 1485. https://doi.org/10.3390/ijerph18041485

Huppert, F. A., & So, T. T. (2013). Flourishing across Europe: Application of a new conceptual framework for defining well-being. *Social Indicators Research*, *110*(3), 837–861. https://doi.org/10.1007/s11205-011-9966-7

Jia, Z., Zheng, F., Wang, F., & Yang, G. (2024). Psychometric properties of the wellbeing literacy 6-item scale in Chinese military academy cadets. *Frontiers in Psychology*, *15*, 1293845. https://doi.org/10.3389/fpsyg.2024.1293845

Jorm, A. F. (2012). Mental health literacy: Empowering the community to take action for better mental health. *American Psychologist*, *67*(3), 231–243. https://doi.org/10.1037/a0025957

Jorm, A. F., Korten, A. E., Jacomb, P. A., Christensen, H., Rodgers, B., & Pollitt, P. (1997). "Mental health literacy": A survey of the public's ability to recognise mental disorders and their beliefs about the effectiveness of treatment. *Medical Journal of Australia*, *166*(4), 182–186. https://doi.org/10.5694/j.1326-5377.1997.tb140071.x

Kiechle, E. S., Bailey, S. C., Hedlund, L. A., Viera, A. J., & Sheridan, S. L. (2015). Different measures, different outcomes? A systematic review of performance-based versus self-reported measures of health literacy and numeracy. *Journal of General Internal Medicine*, *30*(10), 1538–1546. https://doi.org/10.1007/s11606-015-3288-4

Kjell, O., Daukantaitė, D., & Sikström, S. (2021). Computational language assessments of harmony in life — Not satisfaction with life or rating scales — Correlate with cooperative behaviors. *Frontiers in Psychology*, *12*. https://doi.org/10.3389/fpsyg.2021.601679

Kjell, O. N. E., Kjell, K., & Schwartz, H. A. (2024). Beyond rating scales: With targeted evaluation, large language models are poised for psychological assessment. *Psychiatry Research*, *333*, 115667. https://doi.org/10.1016/j.psychres.2023.115667

Kutcher, S., Wei, Y., & Coniglio, C. (2016). Mental health literacy. *The Canadian Journal of Psychiatry*, *61*(3), 154–158. https://doi.org/10.1177/0706743715616609

Liu, I., Zhong, Q., Liu, F., Xu, H., Chen, W., Zhu, X., Ma, Y., & Ni, S. (2024). Assessing mental health during Covid-19 lockdown: A smartphone-based multimodal emotion recognition approach. In *Proceedings of the Tenth International Symposium of Chinese CHI* (pp. 262–269). Association for Computing Machinery. https://doi.org/10.1145/3565698.3565795

Mansfield, R., Patalay, P., & Humphrey, N. (2020). A systematic literature review of existing conceptualisation and measurement of mental health literacy in adolescent research: Current challenges and inconsistencies. *BMC Public Health*, *20*(1), 607. https://doi.org/10.1186/s12889-020-08734-1

Messick, S. (1995). Validity of psychological assessment: Validation of inferences from persons' responses and performances as scientific inquiry into score meaning. *American Psychologist*, *50*(9), 741–749. https://doi.org/10.1037/0003-066X.50.9.741
Moore, D. J., Palmer, B. W., Patterson, T. L., & Jeste, D. V. (2007). A review of performance-based measures of functional living skills. *Journal of Psychiatric Research*, *41*(1-2), 97–118. https://doi.org/10.1016/j.jpsychires.2005.10.008
Nutbeam, D. (2000). Health literacy as a public health goal: A challenge for contemporary health education and communication strategies into the 21st century. *Health Promotion International*, *15*(3), 259–267. https://doi.org/10.1093/heapro/15.3.259
Nutbeam, D. (2009). Building health literacy in Australia. *Medical Journal of Australia*, *191*(10), 525–526. https://doi.org/10.5694/j.1326-5377.2009.tb03301.x
Oades, L. G., Jarden, A., Hou, H., Ozturk, C., Williams, P., Gavin, R. S., & Huang, L. (2021). Wellbeing literacy: A capability model for wellbeing science and practice. *International Journal of Environmental Research and Public Health*, *18*(2), 719. https://doi.org/10.3390/ijerph18020719
Oades, L. G., & Johnston, A. L. (2017). Wellbeing literacy: The necessary ingredient in positive education. *Psychology and Behavioral Science International Journal*, *3*(5), 555621. https://doi.org/10.19080/PBSIJ.2017.03.555621
Oades, L. G., Ozturk, C., Hou, H., & Slemp, G. R. (2020). Wellbeing literacy: A language-use capability relevant to wellbeing outcomes of positive psychology intervention. *The Journal of Positive Psychology*, *15*(5), 696–700. https://doi.org/10.1080/17439760.2020.1789711
Oishi, S., Graham, J., Kesebir, S., & Galinha, I. C. (2013). Concepts of happiness across time and cultures. *Personality and Social Psychology Bulletin*, *39*(5), 559–577. https://doi.org/10.1177/0146167213480042
Schulz, P. J., Pessina, A., Hartung, U., & Petrocchi, S. (2021). Effects of objective and subjective health literacy on patients' accurate judgment of health information and decision-making ability: Survey study. *Journal of Medical Internet Research*, *23*(1), e20457. https://doi.org/10.2196/20457
Sousa, V. D., & Rojjanasrirat, W. (2011). Translation, adaptation and validation of instruments or scales for use in cross-cultural health care research: A clear and user-friendly guideline. *Journal of Evaluation in Clinical Practice*, *17*(2), 268–274. https://doi.org/10.1111/j.1365-2753.2010.01434.x
Spector, P. E. (1992). *Summated rating scale construction: An introduction*. Sage.
Tavousi, M., Mohammadi, S., Sadighi, J., Zarei, F., Kermani, R. M., Rostami, R., & Montazeri, A. (2022). Measuring health literacy: A systematic review and bibliometric analysis of instruments from 1993 to 2021. *PLoS One*, *17*(7), e0271524. https://doi.org/10.1371/journal.pone.0271524
Toronto, C. E., & Weatherford, B. (2015). Health literacy education in health professions schools: An integrative review. *Journal of Nursing Education*, *54*(12), 669–676. https://doi.org/10.3928/01484834-20151110-02
Vandenberg, R. J., & Lance, C. E. (2000). A review and synthesis of the measurement invariance literature: Suggestions, practices, and recommendations for organizational research. *Organizational Research Methods*, *3*(1), 4–70. https://doi.org/10.1177/109442810031002
Ventura, J., Reise, S. P., Keefe, R. S. E., Baade, L. E., Gold, J. M., Green, M. F., Kern, R. S., Mesholam-Gately, R., Nuechterlein, K. H., Seidman, L. J., & Bilder, R. M. (2010). The cognitive assessment interview (CAI): Development and validation of an empirically derived, brief interview-based measure of cognition. *Schizophrenia Research*, *121*(1), 24–31. https://doi.org/10.1016/j.schres.2010.04.016
Waters, L., & Higgins, M. C. (2022). The impact of a teacher-based positive education intervention on student wellbeing literacy. *Journal of School and Educational Psychology*, *2*(1), 22–43. https://doi.org/10.47602/josep.v2i1.12

Wolstencroft, K., Oades, L. G., Caputi, P., & Andresen, R. (2010). Development of a structured interview schedule to assess stage of psychological recovery from enduring mental illness. *International Journal of Psychiatry in Clinical Practice*, *14*(3), 182–189. https://doi.org/10.3109/13651501003668552

Yang, Q., Wang, Z., Chen, H., Wang, S., Pu, Y., Gao, X., Huang, W., Song, S., & Huang, G. (2024). PsychoGAT: A novel psychological measurement paradigm through interactive fiction games with LLM agents. In *Proceedings of the 62nd Annual Meeting of the Association for Computational Linguistics (Volume 1: Long Papers)* (pp. 14470–14505). Association for Computational Linguistics. https://doi.org/10.18653/v1/2024.acl-long.779

Zhang, L., Zhu, G., Zhang, S., Zhan, X., Wang, J., Meng, W., Fang, X., & Wang, P. (2019). Assessment of career adaptability: Combining text mining and item response theory method. *IEEE Access*, *7*, 125893–125908. https://doi.org/10.1109/ACCESS.2019.2938777

4

FOSTERING WELLBEING LITERACY IN AND THROUGH SECOND LANGUAGE LEARNING

"Forward Planning" and "Looking Back" Approaches

Antonella Strambi, Riccardo Amorati, Antonia Rubino, and John Hajek

Introduction

In the contemporary landscape of education and learning design, the cultivation of wellbeing literacy has emerged as a critical component of holistic student development (Oades et al., 2021). Wellbeing literacy, defined as the capacity to understand, communicate, and effectively apply knowledge about wellbeing in one's own life (Oades, 2017), encompasses a diverse range of competencies. These extend from the fundamental skill of recognising and articulating emotions to the more complex application of strategies that promote mental health and personal growth, both for oneself and for others (Lemon et al., 2024). This chapter explores the integration of wellbeing literacy within the specific context of second language acquisition at the university level, arguing that the pedagogical environment of language learning classrooms offers a uniquely advantageous setting for fostering wellbeing literacy among students.

Language courses, by their very nature, prioritise the development of communicative competence in the target language. This inherent focus on communication creates a flexible pedagogical space that can readily accommodate content responsive to learners' individual needs and interests. Such flexibility allows educators to seamlessly introduce and integrate a focus on wellbeing literacy without compromising the core learning outcomes of the language curriculum. In effect, this integration enhances the richness of the learning experience while maintaining the integrity of established curricular objectives.

Furthermore, a significant synergy exists between the learning activities typically employed in language classrooms and those designed to promote wellbeing. Established practices within Positive Psychology (PP) coaching,

DOI: 10.4324/9781003644293-4

such as maintaining gratitude journals, nurturing interpersonal connections, and envisioning one's ideal future, find parallels in language learning activities (Strambi et al., 2017). Language learners are in fact frequently encouraged to share their thoughts, feelings, and aspirations – both present and future – as a means of practising linguistic and communicative skills. This natural overlap provides a fertile ground for integrating wellbeing literacy into language learning.

This chapter proposes two distinct pedagogical approaches to cultivating wellbeing literacy within second language courses; we have termed them "Forward Planning" and "Looking Back." The "Forward Planning" approach entails the intentional and explicit integration of wellbeing literacy components into the language curriculum from the outset. This proactive strategy ensures that wellbeing concepts are interwoven with language learning objectives, providing students with consistent exposure, practical application, and a clear understanding of wellbeing literacy as a learning goal.

In contrast, the "Looking Back" approach adopts a reflective perspective. Here, the wellbeing literacy aspect is revealed to students retrospectively through activities undertaken after the course concludes. This method allows students to recognise *a posteriori* the wellbeing strategies they have practised, often inadvertently, and to articulate their impact on both language development and personal wellbeing.

By presenting two distinct projects exemplifying these approaches, we aim to illustrate how language learning can serve as a conduit for enhancing wellbeing literacy. Examining these practical experiences will provide actionable insights for language educators seeking to enrich their courses and contribute to the holistic development of their students, ultimately fostering well-rounded and resilient graduates.

The FL2 Project and the "Forward Planning" Approach

Background

The integration of student wellbeing considerations and a focus on cognitive, affective, and social strategies within Second Language Learning and Teaching (SLL&T) are not a recent phenomenon. Historically, however, SLL&T research and practice have primarily concentrated on anxiety and motivation as key variables influencing the learning process, with connections to humanistic approaches and research into second language learning strategies traceable back to the 1970s (see, e.g., Dörnyei, 2009).

The FL2 Project (Strambi et al., 2017) builds on this solid tradition and explicitly draws upon the principles and strategies of PP to support students' psychological, emotional, and social wellbeing while simultaneously providing opportunities for language skill development. At its inception in 2015, the

FL2 Project represented a novel approach in Australia. Academic literature on similar interventions was scarce, and Australian language educators reported limited familiarity with PP (Strambi et al., 2017).

Over the past decade, however, interest in PP within the context of L2 education has grown significantly. A 2019 special issue of *The Modern Language Journal* focusing on emotion and affect included a scoping review by MacIntyre et al. (2019), which highlighted 33 projects incorporating L2 learning activities aligned with PP principles. Numerous presentations engaging with PP principles have been featured at international conferences, such as the International Association for the Psychology of Language Learning (IAPLL) conference and the Language Education and Emotions conference. Furthermore, online repositories of PP-informed L2 learning activities, such as *ELTandhappiness.com*, have emerged, further solidifying the integration of PP within language education. The FL2 Project is situated within this fertile landscape.

Project Design and Initial Pilot Implementation

The FL2 Project involved incorporating specific activities designed to foster students' wellbeing literacy into the L2 curriculum. The project team developed 24 learning activities in Italian and English, many adapted from evidence-based practices available on the Greater Good in Action website (Greater Good in Action, n.d.) at the University of Berkeley. Other activities were designed specifically for the project, drawing upon the PERMA model of wellbeing (Seligman, 2011) and established language pedagogy principles, including communicative language teaching and content-and-language-integrated learning (CLIL).

The FL2 Project approach offers a flexible framework: educators can select and adapt activities from a searchable online database, categorised by PERMA components, PP themes, language learning outcomes, and language proficiency levels, to suit their specific context and student needs. Crucially, these activities are intended for seamless integration within existing curricula and promote a holistic pedagogy centred on a positive learning environment. This includes fostering rapport, encouraging collaboration, celebrating achievements, and normalising mistakes. Educators are also encouraged to explicitly discuss the wellbeing benefits of each activity with their students and highlight links to language learning goals (see Strambi et al., 2017, for further details). A sample activity instruction sheet is reproduced in Figure 4.1.

The FL2 Project resources and approach were initially piloted with three cohorts of first-year beginner Italian students at Flinders University and The University of Sydney in Australia. At the end of the first semester, students completed an evaluation survey regarding their overall course experience and the usefulness and relevance of the FL2 Project activities. Interviews were also conducted with participating students at the end of the academic year, following the second semester of study.

FLOURISHING IN A SECOND LANGUAGE

FL2

Use your strengths

Talking about future plans

Knowing, using and developing one's strengths can be very beneficial. Which one of your strengths are you going to use today?

Instructions

[adapted from: http://ggia.berkeley.edu/practice/use_your_strengths]

Time required: 15 minutes + varied.

Type of activity: writing.

Preparation: If you are not sure what your strengths are, you may want to take the VIA survey: https://www.viacharacter.org/survey/account/register. Free registration is required, and the survey takes approximately 15 minutes. You may also want to complete the FL2 activity, "Your strengths".

Then, think about one of your personal strengths—for instance, creativity, perseverance, kindness, modesty, or curiosity. Consider how you could use this strength today in a new and different way. For example, if you choose the personal strength of perseverance, you might make a list of tasks that you have found challenging recently, then try to tackle each one of them. Or if you choose curiosity, you might attempt an activity that you've never tried before.

How to do it: Use the guide on the following page to describe the personal strength you plan to use today and how you are going to use it. Then, go ahead and do it—act on your strength as frequently as possible throughout the day. Repeat the steps above every day for a week. You may use the same personal strength across multiple days, or try using a new personal strength each day.

Extension [optional]: At the end of the week, write about the personal strengths that you focused on during the week and how you used them. Write in detail about what you did, how you felt, and what you learned from the experience.

Why do this?

This activity is adapted from one of the practices available at ggia.berkeley.edu

Greater Good in Action
Science-based Practices for a Meaningful Life

Greater Good in Action is a freely accessible online collection of the best research-based methods for a happier, more meaningful life. It is produced by the Greater Good Science Center at UC Berkeley. Here is more info on this activity from Greater Good in Action:

WHY YOU SHOULD TRY IT

Research suggests that thinking about personal strengths can increase our happiness and reduce depression. This exercise asks you to identify one of your personal strengths—a positive trait that contributes to your character, such as kindness or perseverance—and consider how you could use it in a new and different way. Recognising and exercising these strengths can make them stronger and better equip you to meet life's challenges.

EVIDENCE THAT IT WORKS

Seligman, M. E., Steen, T. A., Park, N., & Peterson, C. (2005). Positive psychology progress: Empirical validation of interventions. *American Psychologist, 60*(5), 410-421.

L2 Learning Objectives

Communication	Vocabulary	Grammar
• Talking about plans • [Optional: writing about past events]	• Everyday activities	• Definite articles • Verbs in the present tense • Modal verbs • [Optional: Verbs in the past tense]

FIGURE 4.1 Sample FL2 project activity (page 1)

At the end of Semester 1, although students' evaluations of their learning environment were overwhelmingly positive, scores relating specifically to the FL2 Project activities were slightly lower. Some students expressed uncertainty about the value added by these activities; a small number of mature-age students found the activities "juvenile," while others reported limited perceived benefit due to prior exposure to similar practices. These results were observed in one of the institutions that participated in the pilot implementation; it is possible that they may have been influenced by varying levels of educators' awareness and investment in the project. The teaching staff at this institution, while briefed on the project, were not part of the project team and may have had a limited understanding of its approach, potentially impacting their ability to convey its relevance to students. The small number of survey respondents (N = 12) also limited the reliability of these results.

Interview data collected at the end of the second semester indicated a greater appreciation for the FL2 Project activities as a valuable source of wellbeing literacy, suggesting that implementing these activities after students have developed foundational language skills might be more effective. Importantly, students' learning outcomes and academic results remained consistent with previous years, demonstrating that the activities did not negatively impact the core curriculum, which continued to address students' learning goals and expectations.

Second Pilot Implementation

A second pilot implementation was conducted in 2018 with beginner Spanish students to extend our evaluation of the FL2 Project resources. The FL2 Project approach and activities were implemented in two units: Spanish Studies 2 at The University of Western Australia and Introductory Spanish Part 2 at Flinders University. Both were second-semester, first-year courses. The overall FL2 Project approach and principles guided teaching and learning, mirroring the Italian pilots. Seven FL2 Project activities, translated into Spanish, were integrated into the curricula, selected based on their alignment with the units' syllabi and intended learning outcomes.

An evaluation survey was administered to gather student feedback on their experiences with the FL2 Project approach and activities. This survey included 22 Likert-scale statements assessing the usefulness and relevance of the activities and students' overall perceptions of their learning environment, as well as 10 open-ended questions focusing on the perceived value of the activities for language learning and overall wellbeing literacy. The data collection methods used in the Italian pilot implementation at the end of semesters 1 and 2, respectively, were thus combined into a single procedure for this second pilot, which only ran in semester 2.

The Spanish evaluation data supported and expanded upon the findings from the Italian pilot (Strambi et al., 2023), revealing similar results from a larger participant pool. Twenty-seven students completed the surveys, and their evaluations of the learning environment were overwhelmingly positive, particularly in the areas of positive emotions, relationships, and accomplishment, echoing the Italian evaluations. The emphasis on positive relationships in the classroom is particularly significant, considering the established importance of rapport and a sense of belonging for student satisfaction and subjective wellbeing (Baik et al., 2019). However, student evaluations of the seven PP-informed learning activities were more varied and nuanced. While a majority of participants believed that the FL2 Project activities contributed to both their L2 development and personal wellbeing, only a minority preferred them over standard language learning activities.

Analysis of the survey data also revealed that three out of five male respondents in the Spanish trial provided significantly less feedback, suggesting a potential lack of engagement within this cohort. This raises important questions regarding potential gender bias in student evaluations of wellbeing literacy-focused activities. Given that men are statistically less likely to seek help for mental health issues (Black Dog Institute, n.d.), this represents a crucial area for future research. Alternative strategies, such as action-oriented activities or gender-specific study groups, warrant exploration to ensure inclusivity and engagement for all students.

Students who found the FL2 Project activities useful and enjoyable commented that they provided variety, facilitated language practice, and expanded their vocabulary in the target language. This is an important outcome from a wellbeing literacy perspective, as it demonstrates that the activities provided opportunities for students to develop their "wellbeing vocabulary" in both their main and additional language. Many respondents also indicated that the activities encouraged personal reflection and a sense of perspective, prompting some to seek greater study-life balance and supporting positive emotions and social connections. These results, which are aligned with the Italian pilot data, suggest that, for most participants, the FL2 Project activities contributed to students' wellbeing literacy by introducing and reinforcing actionable strategies for enhancing their overall wellbeing. However, it must be recognised that not every student found that the specific focus on wellbeing provided by the FL2 Project activities responded to their individual needs.

The "I Am an Author" Project and the "Looking Back" Approach

Project Background

In contrast with the explicit focus of the "Forward Planning" approach, the "Looking Back" approach fosters wellbeing literacy by encouraging students to reflect retrospectively on the impact of learning activities on their overall wellbeing. To illustrate this approach, we discuss the "I am an author" project (Amorati & Hajek, 2025), designed for upper-intermediate/advanced language students, incorporating core principles of project-based learning and the Deep Approach to World Language Education (Tochon, 2014). Both methods emphasise meaningful learning experiences where students have agency and can personalise their learning. The Deep Approach positions students as central to the learning process and views language education as a form of social action with the potential to positively influence society and its members. While we anticipated that the project would have a positive impact on various aspects of student wellbeing, such as motivation, agency, autonomy, self-worth, and pride, wellbeing literacy was not an explicitly stated objective from the outset.

The "I am an author" project is integrated into a twelve-week, semester-long Italian course structured into weekly components focusing on culture, conversation, and language. The project is embedded within the language component, emphasising the development of writing skills while reinforcing students' knowledge of Italian grammatical structures. As part of the project, students undertake the motivating task of writing, illustrating, and self-publishing a short story in Italian. A selection of these stories is then made publicly available online to address the scarcity of accessible Italian reading materials for young children. This addresses a genuine community need, as maintaining language skills and promoting literacy within Italian diasporic communities, particularly in countries like Australia, present ongoing challenges (Amorati & Hajek, 2025).

Throughout the project, students receive in-class support through exposure to characteristic features of narrative writing in Italian via various reading and writing activities and instruction on relevant grammatical structures and textual conventions. Dedicated class time is also allocated for creative writing and brainstorming story ideas. At the end of the semester, students submit their self-published stories and a reflective evaluation of their experience in the project, their creative process, and the reception of their book by family and friends.

"I Am an Author" Project Evaluation

To systematically assess the project's influence on student wellbeing, participants (n = 21) completed a questionnaire based on Oxford's (2016) EMPATHICS model. EMPATHICS, developed as an alternative to PERMA for conceptualising wellbeing in second language learners, theorises that wellbeing arises from the dynamic interplay of various psychological dimensions: emotion and empathy, meaning and motivation, perseverance, agency and autonomy, time, hardiness and habits of mind, intelligences, character strengths, and self-factors. These interacting dimensions "help learners achieve high well-being and progress rapidly, develop proficiency, and relish the language learning experience" (Oxford, 2016, p. 10).

The questionnaire comprised 33 Likert scale items (e.g., "I enjoyed working on a project that I valued highly"; "Being the author of something that could be useful for others […] adds meaning to my life") and open-ended questions requiring more in-depth reflection and personal elaboration (e.g., "Did you experience any positive or negative emotions while working on the project?"; "Looking back now, how memorable is the experience of the book project?"; see Amorati & Hajek, 2025). These prompts provided students with the opportunity to recognise and articulate how their learning experiences impacted various components of their wellbeing.

While a comprehensive analysis of the study's results exceeds the scope of this chapter, the project's overwhelmingly positive reception warrants mention. Student responses revealed that the project enhanced their wellbeing by empowering them as authors and enabling them to make a positive contribution to the local Italian community. This experience fostered student ownership of their learning through an activity they found challenging, enriching, socially valuable, and memorable. Moreover, the project enhanced students' self-efficacy and self-concept, increased their intrinsic motivation to learn Italian, and fostered a stronger sense of belonging and achievement (see Amorati & Hajek, 2025, for a detailed account).

Incorporating a reflective component at the project's conclusion effectively prompted students to explicitly consider and articulate the project's impact on both their learning and their lives. This retrospective reflection was crucial for developing wellbeing literacy, as it required students to utilise appropriate language and terminology to describe their own wellbeing and evaluate how the project contributed to it (Oades et al., 2020). Through reflection, students identified specific project elements that fostered positive emotions, increased motivation, and enhanced their sense of autonomy and self-worth.

Discussion and Conclusion

In summary, both the "Forward Planning" and "Looking Back" approaches discussed above can contribute effectively to the development of university students' wellbeing literacy within language learning contexts. The key features of the two approaches are highlighted in Table 4.1.

Evaluation data from the FL2 Project pilot implementations demonstrated that an explicit "Forward Planning" approach, in which wellbeing literacy is intentionally embedded within the curriculum, can yield positive outcomes. By combining PP principles with established language pedagogy best practices, the FL2 Project supported elements of the PERMA model of wellbeing (Seligman, 2011) and equipped students with knowledge and strategies applicable beyond the course.

However, the "Forward Planning" approach also presents challenges that require careful consideration. Educators must clearly articulate the alignment

TABLE 4.1 Key features of "Forward Planning" and "Looking Back" approaches to wellbeing literacy in second language learning

Feature	*Forward Planning*	*Looking Back*
Focus and awareness	Explicit integration of wellbeing literacy	Implicit development of wellbeing literacy through reflection
Activity design	Requires design of specific wellbeing activities	Can utilise existing learning activities complemented by reflective components
Curriculum integration	Wellbeing interwoven with language objectives	Wellbeing reflected upon in relation to completed activities
Challenges	Ensuring relevance, avoiding over-exposure, catering to individual differences	Scaffolding reflection effectively, ensuring meaningful connections
Benefits	Directly addresses wellbeing, provides explicit strategies	Encourages deeper learning, connects learning to personal experience without changing existing curriculum

between wellbeing-focused activities and course learning outcomes to ensure students perceive their value and relevance. Some student comments in the FL2 Project pilot evaluations indicated a lack of clarity in this area despite educators' efforts. Furthermore, individual differences in the reception of explicit wellbeing literacy activities must be acknowledged. With increasing exposure to such interventions in primary and secondary education, future university students may be less receptive to similar practices in tertiary settings. Other individual student variables, such as mature age and gender, can also influence engagement. In cases where an explicit focus on wellbeing literacy may not be suitable, a "Looking Back" approach may be more appropriate.

The "Looking Back" approach offers the advantage that educators need not design entirely new activities. Instead, they can evaluate existing classroom practices to determine their implicit contribution to student wellbeing literacy through carefully designed reflective evaluations. Student reflections on the "I am an author" project, alongside collected data on its impact on student wellbeing, suggest that a "Looking Back" approach can effectively foster wellbeing literacy in second language classrooms. Based on our evaluation data, we offer two recommendations for implementing this approach.

First, educators should integrate reflective evaluations into teaching practices. Reflective thinking is a valuable component of language learning (see, e.g., Hammad Al-Rashidi & Aberash, 2024) and can significantly contribute to the development of wellbeing literacy. By articulating their feelings, thoughts, and the significance of their learning experiences, students learn to identify activities and actions that support their wellbeing both inside and outside the classroom. Integrating reflective practices such as journaling, end-of-project evaluations, and class discussions into the curriculum can deepen students' understanding of the connection between their learning experiences and personal wellbeing. As students reflect on these connections, they develop wellbeing literacy by cultivating the capacity to recognise and articulate how educational experiences contribute not only to intellectual growth but also to overall life satisfaction and personal development. However, to maximise the benefits of reflective thinking, careful scaffolding of reflective evaluations is essential. Without proper guidance, students may focus on superficial aspects of projects and miss more meaningful observations about their growth and the impact of their actions. Effective reflection should encourage critical evaluation of experiences, an understanding of the value of their work, and the connection of these insights to their sense of self and wellbeing. By avoiding generic prompts and providing structured guidance, educators can ensure that reflection becomes a powerful tool for learning and growth.

Second, educators should create real-world, impactful learning opportunities. Our study highlights that learning activities incorporating creative freedom, an appropriate level of challenge, and community involvement can significantly enhance student wellbeing. Providing opportunities for students to reflect on such activities can effectively promote wellbeing literacy. When students engage in meaningful projects with real-world impact, they develop an awareness of how their actions influence their own wellbeing and that of others, fostering a deeper understanding of wellbeing literacy.

Regardless of the chosen approach – "Forward Planning" or "Looking Back" – it is clear that both contribute valuable perspectives to the development of tertiary students' wellbeing literacy within the context of second language learning. While "Forward planning" offers a direct and structured approach to wellbeing literacy development, "Looking back" encourages deeper learning and personal connection through reflection. The most appropriate approach will depend on the specific context, learning objectives, and student characteristics. By incorporating these approaches thoughtfully and strategically, language educators can create enriching learning experiences that support students' holistic development and cultivate essential skills for navigating the complexities of life beyond the classroom.

Future research on fostering wellbeing literacy in second language contexts could benefit from incorporating a constructivist lens. While the studies discussed in this chapter focused on educator-designed activities, subsequent investigations might explore a more student-centred approach, acknowledging the dynamic and emergent nature of wellbeing literacy development. Specifically, research designs could be implemented that prioritise student experience and agency by allowing space for learner-generated content, exploring how wellbeing literacy skills are constructed organically within the classroom through interaction and negotiation of meaning. This approach would provide further insights into the contingent and evolving processes through which learners develop wellbeing literacy within the unique social and cultural context of the language classroom.

References

Amorati, R., & Hajek, J. (2025). Fostering well-being in the university L2 classroom: The "I am an author" project. *International Review of Applied Linguistics in Language Teaching. 63*(1), 655–684. https://doi.org/10.1515/iral-2023-0051.

Baik, C., Larcombe, W., & Brooker, A. (2019). *Enhancing student wellbeing*. Uni Student Wellbeing. https://unistudentwellbeing.edu.au

Black Dog Institute. (n.d.). *Facts & figures about mental health*. https://www.blackdoginstitute.org.au/docs/default-source/factsheets/facts_figures.pdf

Dörnyei, Z. (2009). *The psychology of second language acquisition*. Oxford University Press.

Greater Good in Action. (n.d.). University of California, Berkeley. https://ggia.berkeley.edu

Hammad Al-Rashidi, A., & Aberash, A. (2024). Reflective thinking and self-evaluation in language learning: Mirroring the impacts on Saudi Arabian EFL students' growth mindfulness, resilience, and academic well-being. *Asian-Pacific Journal of Second and Foreign Language Education, 9*(44), 1–24. https://doi.org/10.1186/s40862-024-00265-1

Lemon, N., Francis, J., & Baker, L. M. (2024). Well-being literacy in the academic landscape: Trioethnographic inquiry. *Journal of Educational Research and Practice, 33*(1), 27–48. https://doi.org/10.26522/brocked.v33i1.1120

MacIntyre, P. D., Gregersen, T., & Mercer, S. (2019). Language education and emotions. *The Modern Language Journal, 103*(2), 265–267. https://doi.org/10.1111/modl.12544

Oades, L. G. (2017). Wellbeing literacy: The missing link in positive education. In: M. White, G. Slemp, & A. Murray (Eds.), *Future directions in well-being*. Springer. https://doi.org/10.1007/978-3-319-56889-8_29.

Oades, L. G., Baker, L. M., Francis, J. J., & Taylor, J. A. (2021). Wellbeing literacy and positive education. In M. L. Kern & M. L. Wehmeyer (Eds.), *The Palgrave handbook of positive education* (pp. 325–343). Springer. https://doi.org/10.1007/978-3-030-64537-3_13

Oades, L. G., Ozturk, C., Hou, H., & Slemp, G. R. (2020). Wellbeing literacy: A language-use capability relevant to wellbeing outcomes of positive psychology intervention. *The Journal of Positive Psychology, 15*(5), 696–700. https://doi.org/10.1080/17439760.2020.1789711

Oxford, R. L. (2016). Toward a psychology of well-being for language learners: The "EMPATHICS" vision. In P. MacIntyre, T. Gregersen, & S. Mercer (Eds.), *Positive psychology in SLA* (pp. 10–88). Multilingual Matters. https://doi.org/10.21832/9781783095360-003

Seligman, M. E. P. (2011). *Flourish: A visionary new understanding of happiness and well-being*. Free Press.

Strambi, A., Gadd, A., Luzeckyj, A., Rubino, A., & Diaz Martinez, J. (2023). Flourishing in Spanish: A pilot implementation of a wellbeing-supportive approach to L2 teaching and learning. *Australian Review of Applied Linguistics*, 1–23. https://doi.org/10.1075/aral.21024.str

Strambi, A., Luzeckyj, A., & Rubino, A. (2017). Flourishing in a second language (FL2). *Australian Review of Applied Linguistics, 40*(2), 121–139. https://doi.org/10.1075/aral.40.2.03str

Tochon, F. V. (2014). *Help them learn a language deeply: François Victor Tochon's deep approach to world languages and cultures*. Deep University Press.

5

DECONSTRUCTING WELLBEING LITERACY

Rebuilding a Multidimensional Hierarchical Model

Janet M. Clinton and Laura E. Smith

Introduction

With the increasing use of the term "wellbeing literacy" in research, various sector campaigns, organisational initiatives and politically, the notion has garnered significant attention. Wellbeing literacy has emerged as a notable neologism in recent years, reflecting the growing emphasis on holistic health and personal development. The term has hence become popularised and engrained in everyday vernacular. This term combines the increasingly nuanced concept of "wellbeing" with the idea of "literacy" traditionally associated with reading and writing skills. As a neologism, wellbeing literacy encapsulates the ability to know, understand and apply information related to one's overall welling.

"Wellbeing literacy" presents several conceptual issues that warrant careful consideration. Primarily, it combines two inherently complex and multifaceted concepts – wellbeing and literacy – each subject to varied interpretations across different cultural, social, and academic contexts. This process risks oversimplifying the complex nature of wellbeing by suggesting it can be reduced to a set of learnable skills or knowledge. Moreover, framing wellbeing as a form of literacy may inadvertently undervalue the significance of lived experiences, intuitive understanding, and the myriad external factors that contribute to an individual's state of wellbeing in any context.

This chapter deconstructs and critically examines the conceptual limitations and potential drawbacks associated with the widespread adoption of this term. Also, questions are raised about the current conceptual nature of wellbeing literacy, and subsequently the capacity to build valid and acceptable contextually based measures.

DOI: 10.4324/9781003644293-5

Conceptualising Wellbeing

Wellbeing is a multidimensional concept relating to a spectrum of positive health and quality of life, encompassing both subjective and objective aspects of human experience. While rooted in Greek and Roman Stoicism, its meaning has experienced both semantic broadening and depletion in recent years, leading to challenges in definition and measurement across disciplines (Alexandrova, 2017; Curren et al., 2024; Sollis et al., 2024).

Two fundamental western philosophical approaches have shaped understanding: hedonistic (focusing on happiness and pleasure) and eudaimonic (emphasising virtue, meaning, and potential realisation) (Deci & Ryan, 2008). Most modern interpretations acknowledge both perspectives, recognising wellbeing as comprising subjective experiences like happiness alongside objective factors such as physical health. Subjective wellbeing encompasses an individual's overall life satisfaction and the balance of positive and negative emotions, while psychological wellbeing is seen as constituting one's potential and the pursuit of meaningful goals. Psychology has developed several theoretical frameworks, including Diener's Subjective Wellbeing Theory (Diener et al., 1999), Ryff's Six-Factor Model of Psychological Well-Being (Ryff, 1989; Ryff & Keyes, 1995), and Keyes' Mental Health Continuum Model (Keyes, 2002), that broadened the concept beyond its previous narrow focus on happiness and distress. These theories acknowledge the multidimensional nature of wellbeing and integrate both hedonic and eudaimonic constructs, reflecting a complex conceptualisation of the notion.

For some researchers in the fields of psychology and sociology, the concept of wellbeing has expanded to incorporate social, environmental, and spiritual aspects. Factors such as strong social connections, a sense of purpose, and a healthy relationship with the natural environment are now posited as components of wellbeing by many theorists (Lambert et al., 2020; Sollis et al., 2024). Cultural perspectives also vary significantly: Indigenous communities emphasise community connection, African and Middle Eastern countries focus on dignity and civic engagement, Western cultures prioritise autonomy, while Southeast Asian contexts place less emphasis on individual autonomy (Sollis et al., 2024).

Wellbeing is not a term exclusive to psychology, and the ways in which the term and its usage have evolved in other disciplines further illustrate the broad conceptualisations that exist. The fields of medicine, education, and economics provide useful examples of how wellbeing is understood and operationalised differently, each with their own implications for measurement, research, and policy. In medicine and public health wellbeing has evolved from functional health, physical and mental health, and the absence of disease to include psychological, social and emotional dimensions (see the biopsychosocial model; Bolton, 2022; Engel, 1980).

In education, the conceptualisation of wellbeing has been informed by positive psychology. For example, Seligman's PERMA model of wellbeing (e.g., Seligman, 2011; 2018), which emphasises the importance of positive emotions, engagement, relationships, meaning, and accomplishments, has been influential. This approach to wellbeing in education recognises that academic achievement alone is not sufficient for promoting overall wellbeing and that a holistic approach is needed to support students' psychological, social, and emotional development. Indeed, in education, there has been a shift away from earlier conceptualisations of wellbeing towards an idea of "lifelong flourishing" as a goal of education (Curren et al., 2024).

By contrast, in the field of economics wellbeing has conventionally been seen as access to resources for meeting basic needs, human capital and economic stability (World Health Organisation, 2022). Organisations like the Organisation for Economic Co-operation and Development (OECD) now incorporate broader factors including quality of life, social connections, and resources for future wellbeing (OECD, 2017).

Wellbeing is also often conflated with terms like flourishing and happiness in popular discourse (e.g., Stevens et al., 2020). This lack of consensus in scientific and public understanding creates measurement and practical application difficulties. The various interpretations across disciplines acknowledge wellbeing's multidimensional nature but add complexity to implementation. Further, the importance of considering cultural and contextual factors in both conceptualisation and measurement creates additional challenges for developing standardised approaches to assessment and application.

How Is Wellbeing Measured?

Wellbeing measurement approaches differ both across and within disciplines. To be useful in theory, research and practice, the concept of wellbeing must be objective and measurable (Alexandrova, 2017). Currently, there is a lack of consensus on the measurement approaches, constructs being measured, and conceptualisations of the latent concept (Cooke et al., 2016; Linton et al., 2016; Vander Weele et al., 2020). Understanding the importance and impact of wellbeing is complicated by this lack of consistency in how it is measured, and building concepts or constructs with wellbeing as a component is an inherently fraught exercise.

In some fields (e.g. economics), wellbeing has been measured using single constructs such as life satisfaction or macroeconomic indicators. Examples of single construct measures include the Satisfaction with Life Scale (SWLS), which measures an individual's self-reported satisfaction with their life, and the Subjective Happiness Scale (SHS), which is a single-item measure of an individual's perception of whether they are happy (Diener et al., 1985; Lyubomirsky & Lepper, 1999). In more recent years, as debates and research about what wellbeing is have continued, the measures and constructs have become broader.

Most contemporary measures of wellbeing include a multitude of different dimensions and constructs. For example, a 2016 systematic review found 196 different dimensions across 99 measures of wellbeing (Linton et al., 2016). Across multiple reviews, the most commonly included factors were life satisfaction, affect, meaning/purpose, and relationships, reflecting the commonly used theories underpinning measures of wellbeing (Cooke et al., 2016; Iasiello et al., 2024; Linton et al., 2016).

For the purposes of this chapter, we have developed a working model and theoretical framework of wellbeing (see Figure 5.1) that brings together

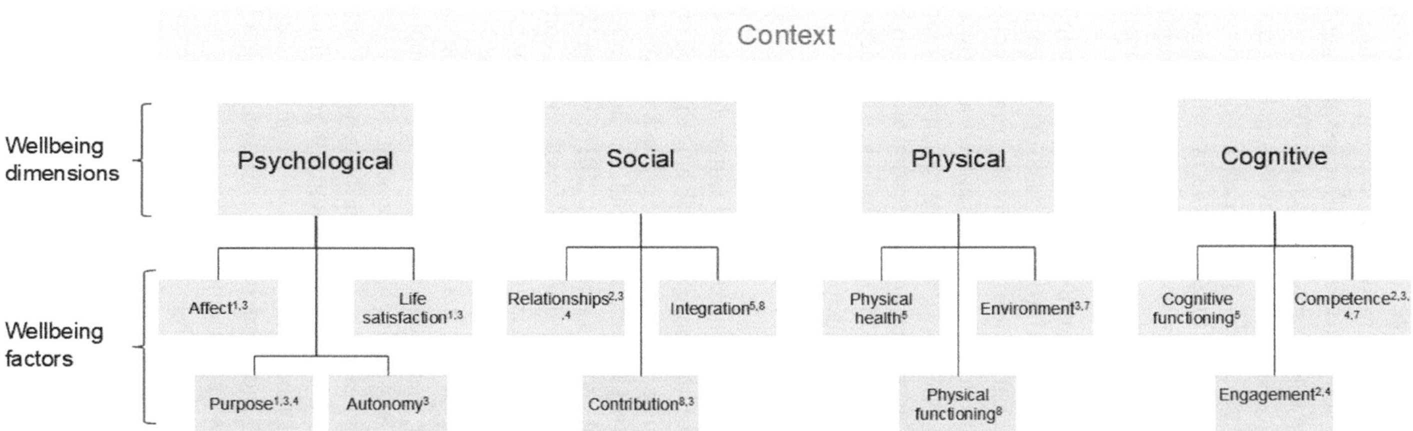

Legend:

1 Subjective wellbeing theory (Diener et al., 1999)

2 PERMA (Seligman, 2011)

3 Psychological wellbeing (Ryff, 1989; Ryff & Keyes, 1995)

4 PROSPER framework (Noble & McGrath, 2015)

5 Biopsychosocial model (Engel, 1980; Borrell-Carrió et al., 2004)

6 OECD framework for measuring wellbeing (OECD, 2020)

7 Human motivation theory (Maslow, 1943)

8 Self-determination theory (Deci & Ryan, 1985)

FIGURE 5.1 Working model of multidimensional concept of wellbeing.

accepted frameworks and definitions and draws from commonly used theories and findings from recent systematic reviews. These key dimensions and subfactors presented in the working model drawn from commonly used frameworks, theories, and models of wellbeing, including subjective wellbeing theory (Diener et al., 1999); PERMA (Seligman, 2011; 2018); psychological wellbeing (Ryff, 1989; Ryff & Keyes, 1995); PROSPER (Noble & McGrath, 2015); Self-determination Theory (Deci & Ryan, 1985); the biopsychosocial model (Borrell-Carrió et al., 2004; Engel, 1980); OECD framework for measuring wellbeing (OECD, 2020); and human motivation theory (Maslow, 1943; 1954).

This hierarchical model is not posited to represent a consensus view of wellbeing, but as an illustrative model that can be used for deconstructing the concept of wellbeing literacy; next we consider the concept of literacy.

The Meaning of Literacy

Literacy, originating from the Latin "literatus" (learned/lettered), has evolved from its initial definition of reading and writing ability to encompass broader concepts of knowledge and communication. The United Nations, for example, has positioned literacy as fundamental to lifelong learning, development, health, and democratic participation (United Nations, 2003).

The philosophical foundations of literacy extend beyond technical skills, representing an epistemological tool for accessing, processing, and transmitting knowledge. Historical western philosophical perspectives range from Plato's concerns about writing's impact on memory and wisdom to later celebrations of literacy as essential for rational thought and intellectual autonomy. Paulo Freire's critical pedagogy framed literacy as emancipatory, linking the ability to "read the word" with the capacity to "read the world" and challenge oppressive structures (Freire & Macedo, 2003).

Critical thinking and literacy are inherently connected, with Scriven (1987) noting that "literacy is a ghost that haunts the teaching of critical thinking and informal logic" (p. 93). This relationship has become more complex in the digital age, where multiple literacies – digital, media, and critical – interact with traditional textual literacy. The concept has expanded to include disciplinary literacy, an approach which "emphasises the specialised knowledge and abilities possessed by those who create, communicate, and use knowledge within each of the disciplines" (Shanahan & Shanahan, 2012, p. 7). This perspective acknowledges that literacy skills are both general and subject-specific, reflecting the specialised nature of different fields of knowledge.

Taking this idea further, UNESCO's contemporary definition describes literacy as "the ability to identify, understand, interpret, create, communicate and compute, using printed and written materials associated with varying contexts" (UNESCO Institute for Statistics, n.d., line 1). This broader understanding reflects literacy's role in modern society, where it functions as a continuum of skills essential for full participation in social, economic, and political life.

Similarly, the National Council of Teachers of English (NCTE, 2019) makes it clear that our definitions of literacy must continue to evolve. In their definition, the NCTE emphasise the shared sociocultural and communication practices that constitute literacy, and acknowledge that as these change, so must literacy. They state that to be literate, a person must "possess and intentionally apply a wide range of skills, competencies, and dispositions. [...] As in the past, they are inextricably linked with histories, narratives, life possibilities, and social trajectories of all individuals and groups" (NCTE, 2019, para 2).

These definitions underscore the complex, context-dependent nature of literacy. They suggest that our understanding of literacy must adapt to cultural, social, and technological changes. Just as the operationalisation of wellbeing varies across different settings, so does the nature and application of literacy. For practical purposes, literacy can be distilled into knowing, understanding, and communicating.

How Is Literacy Measured?

To measure formal literacy, teachers, educators, and researchers typically employ assessments that assess an individual's reading comprehension, writing skills, and basic understanding. These assessments often include tasks such as reading passages and answering questions about their content, and composing short essays or responses to prompts. The results are often scored against established benchmarks to determine literacy levels.

It is argued that measuring literacies involves assessing various skills that enable individuals to effectively engage with their environments and achieve personal and professional goals. It encompasses assessing a range of skills and competencies beyond basic reading and writing, including the ability to critically understand, interpret, and apply information across multiple contexts. These literacies may include digital, media, financial, and cultural literacies, among others. Diverse assessment tools, including formative assessments, performance tasks, and self-assessments, can provide a more holistic view of a learner's literacy capabilities. These measures should reflect both individual progress and the ability to engage in complex, multifaceted literacies that are essential in today's society.

Moreover, it is crucial to adhere to established norms of assessment development to ensure psychometrically sound literacy measurements in context.

This comprehensive approach ensures that literacy assessments are contextually relevant and methodologically sound, providing a more accurate and nuanced understanding of an individual's literacy capabilities in today's complex world. Literacy relating to wellbeing is no exception.

Wellbeing Literacy

It is acknowledged that wellbeing literacy is an emerging concept. The primary conceptualisation of wellbeing literacy was developed by Oades and colleagues, who define it as language use capability (including knowledge, comprehension, composition, contextual sensitivity, and intentionality) relating to and for wellbeing (Oades et al., 2021). This definition emphasises how understanding and using wellbeing-related language can promote wellbeing for oneself and others (Hou et al., 2021; Oades et al., 2021).

A contrasting definition by Chng et al. (2022), adapted from the Oades definition, focuses on knowledge of wellbeing indicators and behavioural changes for improvement. Unlike Oades' language-centred approach, this definition parallels traditional mental health literacy frameworks, which address knowledge, beliefs, and help-seeking behaviour (Jorm, 2015; Kutcher et al., 2016). The divergence between Oades' language-focused definition and Chng's knowledge-based approach reflects broader debates about how wellbeing literacy should be conceptualised and measured (Burns et al., 2024).

Given the multidimensional nature of wellbeing and a lack of a unified definition, and the complexity of literacy, measuring wellbeing literacy is a challenge. Hou et al. (2021) developed the Well-Lit 6 scale to assess wellbeing literacy. This measure includes six items: wellbeing-related vocabulary, knowledge, skills, comprehension, composition, and multi-modal communication, with intentionality assumed to underpin the scale. Developed from existing psychological questionnaires for use in education contexts, the short scale has shown incremental validity and provides empirical evidence for wellbeing literacy as a distinct construct. However, the complexity of wellbeing literacy poses challenges in applying the scale as a universal measure of the concept. The scale relies on respondents' self-reported knowledge, vocabulary, and skills, measuring perceptions of these factors rather than objective knowledge, vocabulary, or skill. Hou et al. (2021) acknowledge that further research is needed to develop a more comprehensive measure. This limitation underscores the ongoing challenges in conceptualising and measuring wellbeing literacy.

We argue that to address the call for a more comprehensive assessment system, the approach to understanding wellbeing literacy must be both multidimensional and hierarchical.

A Proposed Approach to Measuring Wellbeing Literacy

Wellbeing literacy remains largely conceptual, lacking a fully developed operational construct. To advance the field, we need to establish consensus on how to measure this concept and develop a more precise operational definition. This clarity will be essential for creating valid and meaningful assessments.

A construct of wellbeing literacy requires specificity such that the dimension can be defined from an operational sense and criteria and indicators are readily built. Doing so will help address the social desirability bias inherent in self-report measures and ameliorate potential limitations of existing tools that may arise (Paulhus, 1984).

Given the multidimensional nature of both wellbeing and literacy, a concept encompassing both might be considered multidimensional and hierarchical in nature, particularly when applied to various contexts. A multidimensional hierarchical model framework organises constructs into multiple levels where higher-order factors subsume lower-order factors. It allows for examining both broad and specific aspects of complex constructs while maintaining theoretical and statistical relationships between dimensions.

At the top of a hierarchy is the broad, overarching construct, which is then divided into several main dimensions or factors at the next level down. Each of these dimensions is further composed of more specific sub-dimensions or facets, which in turn may be broken down into even more granular elements or indicators. The model acknowledges that these various components are not independent but interact with and influence each other across levels. We argue that such a wellbeing literacy is such a complex construct, and as such requires the creation of a validation framework.

If we consider that wellbeing has four latent dimensions relating to cognitive, physical, psychological and social aspects, and literacy in essence, is knowing, understanding and applying, then wellbeing literacy, the construct, is a combination of these high-level dimensions in any particular context. In an effort to create an understanding, the figure below suggests a model that can form the basis of a measurement model.

Figure 5.2 shows the conceptualisation of wellbeing literacy. The wellbeing dimensions stay consistent, while the wellbeing factors are context-specific. The literacy constructs of knowing (K), understanding (U), and communicating (C) are nested underneath each context-specific wellbeing factor.

The understanding wellbeing literacy as a construct needs to be context-specific, hence, within any particular setting, the wellbeing factors and criteria might change. However, the dimensions of wellbeing and literacy would remain constant.

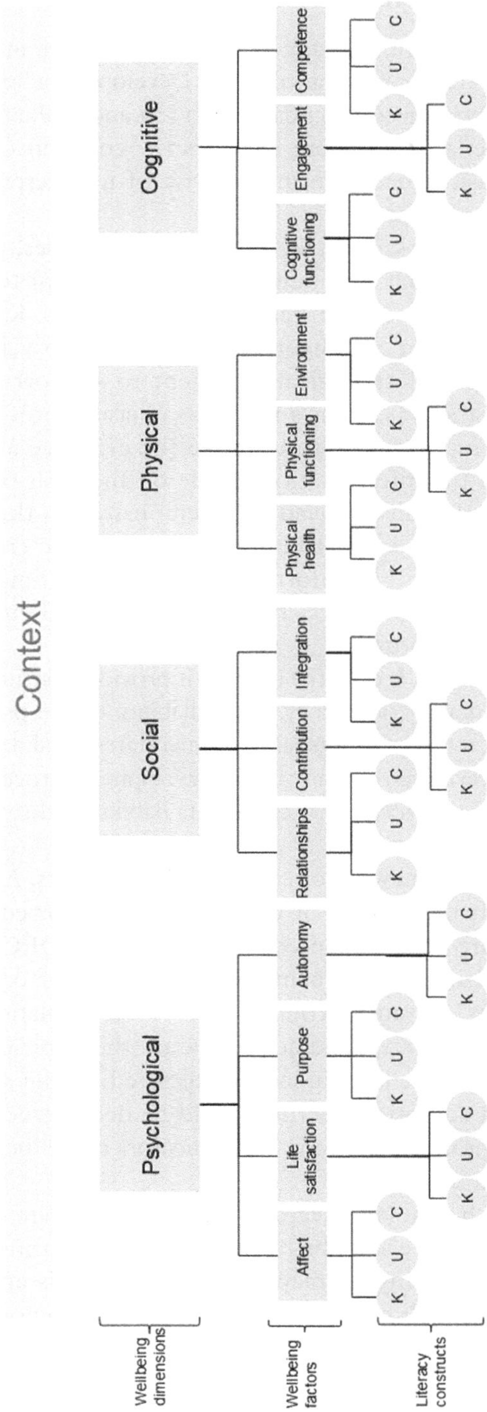

FIGURE 5.2 Conceptualisation of wellbeing literacy.

Hypothetical Validation Framework

To develop such a measure, we suggest that a validation framework must be created within the realms of that context. Developing a validation framework can lead to specific recommendations to test and evaluate claims against pre-established criteria. It therefore increases the confidence that the interpretations are robust, hence reducing the risk of misinterpretation leading to potential errors or failures.

A validation framework is a structured set of processes, guidelines, and criteria used to ensure that a particular system, model, or tool performs as intended and meets the required standards or objectives. Kane (2013), for example, has outlined an argument-based approach to validation, which emphasises building a clear, logical argument to support the interpretation and use of test scores. Kane's model emphasises how critical it is to go beyond collecting evidence, to organise the evidence around clear arguments to defend the interpretations made on the basis of the evidence. Validation frameworks can also lead to a demonstration that the interpretation adheres to quality standards, thus enhancing the credibility of the interpretations with users and informing better decision-making as well as assisting to optimise performance. Importantly, this will ensure its acceptability across various contexts.

A validation framework is essential because it provides a structured approach to ensuring the accuracy, consistency, and reliability of the processes. By systematically verifying inputs, outputs, and internal states, a validation framework helps identify and prevent errors early in the development process. Additionally, a robust validation framework enhances maintainability and scalability, making it easier to adapt to any context.

Currently no such framework or construct model exists. As such, we have developed a hypothetical model of wellbeing literacy for education. Based on existing literature (e.g. Noble & McGrath, 2015; OECD, 2017), this hypothetical model defines wellbeing in the context of education (using wellbeing constructs relevant to context such as self-regulation, sense of belonging, and sense of safety), and acknowledges the importance of culture and context. This example is designed to illustrate how the concept of wellbeing literacy in an educational setting could be deconstructed. Figure 5.3 describes, hypothetically, the criteria and indicators of wellbeing literacy in a school's educational setting.

Such an approach enables researchers and practitioners to examine the construct of different levels of abstraction, hence facilitating deeper analysis of the idea of wellbeing literacy. We argue that this approach is vital when considering complex human attributes and behaviours in different contexts.

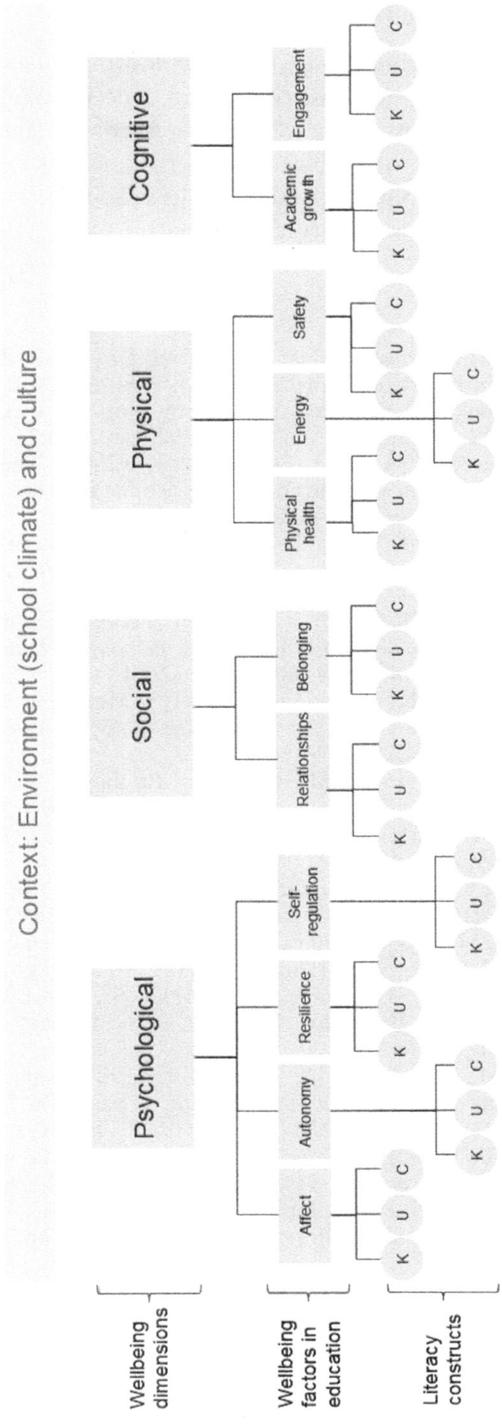

FIGURE 5.3 Hypothetical model of wellbeing literacy in education.

Conclusion and Recommendations

This chapter argues wellbeing literacy is both ***multidimensional and hierarchical*** in nature, given the nature of its constituent concepts. We have suggested that to build a detailed construct of wellbeing literacy applicable across various contexts, the development of a robust validation framework is necessary. Such a framework should be acceptable to the various stakeholders and participants of any program, measurement, or research.

References

Alexandrova, A. (2017). *A philosophy for the science of well-being*. Oxford University Press. (Online edition). https://doi.org/10.1093/oso/9780199300518.001.0001

Bolton, D. (2022). Looking forward to a decade of the biopsychosocial model. *BJPsych Bulletin*, *46*(4), 228–232. https://doi.org10.1192/bjb.2022.34

Borrell-Carrió, F., Suchman, A. L., & Epstein, R. M. (2004). The biopsychosocial model 25 years later: Principles, practice, and scientific inquiry. *Annals of Family Medicine*, *2*(6), 576–582. https://doi.org/10.1370/afm.245

Burns, R. A., Sargent, K., & Crisp, D. A. (2024). Mental health and wellbeing literacy: A cross-national comparison. *Applied Research Quality Life*. https://doi.org/10.1007/s11482-024-10330-z

Chng, J., Burns, R., Murray, K., & Crisp, D. (2022). A community mental health and wellbeing literacy study among Australian adults. *Journal of Happiness and Health*, *2*(1), 12–30. https://doi.org/10.47602/johah.v2i1.13

Cooke, P. J., Melchert, T. P., & Connor, K. (2016). Measuring well-being: A review of instruments. *The Counseling Psychologist*, *44*(5), 730–757. https://doi.org/10.1177/0011000016633507

Curren, R., Boniwell, I., Ryan, R. M., Oades, L., Brighouse, H., Unterhalter, E., Kristjánsson, K., de Ruyter, D., Macleod, C., Morris, I., & White, M. (2024). Finding consensus on well-being in education. *Theory and Research in Education*, *22*(2), 117–157. https://doi.org/10.1177/14778785241259852

Deci, E. L. & Ryan, R. M. (1985). *Intrinsic motivation and self-determination in human behavior*. Plenum. https://doi.org/10.1007/978-1-4899-2271-7

Deci, E. L., & Ryan, R. M. (2008). Hedonia, eudaimonia, and well-being: An introduction. *Journal of Happiness Studies*, *9*, 1–11. https://doi.org/10.1007/s10902-006-9018-1

Diener, E., Emmons, R. A., Larsen, R. J., & Griffin, S. The satisfaction with life scale. (1985). *Journal of Personality Assessment*, *49*(1). https://doi.org10.1207/s15327752jpa4901_13

Diener, E., Suh, E. M., Lucas, R. E., & Smith, H. L. (1999). Subjective well-being: Three decades of progress. *Psychological Bulletin*, *125*(2), 276–302. https://doi.org/10.1037/0033-2909.125.2.276

Engel, G. (1980). The clinical application of the biopsychosocial model. *American Journal of Psychiatry*, *137*(5), 535–544. https://doi.org/10.1176/ajp.137.5.535

Freire, P., & Macedo, D. (2003). Rethinking literacy: A dialogue. In A. Darder, M. Baltodano, & R. Torres (Eds.), *The critical pedagogy reader* (pp. 354–365). Routledge Falmer.

Hou, H., Chin, T.-C., Slemp, G. R., & Oades, L. G. (2021). Wellbeing literacy: Conceptualization, measurement, and preliminary empirical findings from students, parents and school staff. *International Journal of Environmental Research and Public Health*, *18*(4), Article 4. https://doi.org/10.3390/ijerph18041485

Iasiello, M., Ali, K., van Agteren, J., Kolovos, E., Kyrios, M., Kashdan, T. B., & Fassnacht, D. B. (2024). What's the difference between measures of wellbeing, quality of life, resilience, and coping? An umbrella review and concept map of 155 measures of positive mental health. *International Journal of Wellbeing*, *14*(2). https://doi.org/10.5502/ijw.v14i2.3621

Jorm, A. F. (2015). Why we need the concept of "mental health literacy. *Health Communication*, *30*(12), 1166–1168. https://doi.org/10.1080/10410236.2015.1037423

Kane, M. (2013). The argument-based approach to validation. *School Psychology Review*, *42*(4), 448–457. https://doi.org/10.1080/02796015.2013.12087465

Keyes, C. L. M. (2002). The mental health continuum: From languishing to flourishing in life. *Journal of Health and Social Behavior*, *43*(2), 207–222. https://doi.org/10.2307/3090197

Kutcher, S., Wei, Y., & Coniglio, C. (2016). Mental health literacy: Past, present, and future. *The Canadian Journal of Psychiatry*, *61*(3), 154–158. https://doi.org/10.1177/0706743715616609

Lambert, L., Lomas, T., van de Weijer, M. P., Passmore, H. A., Joshanloo, M., Harter, J., Ishikawa, Y., Lai, A., Kitagawa, T., Chen, D., Kawakami, T., Miyata, H., & Diener, E. (2020). Towards a greater global understanding of wellbeing: A proposal for a more inclusive measure. *International Journal of Wellbeing*, *10*(2). https://doi.org/10.5502/ijw.v10i2.1037

Linton, M. J., Dieppe, P., & Medina-Lara, A. (2016). Review of 99 self-report measures for assessing well-being in adults: Exploring dimensions of well-being and developments over time. *BMJ Open*, *6*(7), e010641. https://doi.org/10.1136/bmjopen-2015-010641

Lyubomirsky, S., & Lepper, H. S. (1999). A measure of subjective happiness: Preliminary reliability and construct validation. *Social Indicators Research*, *46*, 137–155. https://doi.org/10.1023/A:1006824100041

Maslow, A. H. (1943). A theory of human motivation. *Psychological Review*, *50*(4), 370–396. https://doi.org/10.1037/h0054346

Maslow, A. H. (1954). *Motivation and personality*. Harper and Row.

National Council of Teacher of English. (2019). Definition of Literacy in a Digital Age [Position Statement]. Retrieved from https://ncte.org/statement/nctes-definition-literacy-digital-age/

Noble, T., & McGrath, H. (2015) PROSPER: A new framework for positive education. *Psych Well-Being*, *5*. https://doi.org/10.1186/s13612-015-0030-2 https://doi.org/10.1186/s13612-015-0030-2

Oades, L. G., Jarden, A., Hou, H., Ozturk, C., Williams, P., R. Slemp, G., & Huang, L. (2021). Wellbeing literacy: A capability model for wellbeing science and practice. *International Journal of Environmental Research and Public Health*, *18*(2), 719. https://doi.org/10.3390/ijerph18020719

OECD. (2017). Students' well-being: What it is and how it can be measured. *PISA 2015 results (Volume III): Students' well-being*. OECD Publishing. https://doi.org/10.1787/9789264273856-6-en

OECD. (2020). *How's life? 2020*. OECD. https://doi.org/10.1787/9870c393-en

Paulhus, D. L. (1984). Two-component models of socially desirable responding. *Journal of Personality and Social Psychology*, *46*(3), 598–609. https://doi.org/10.1037/0022-3514.46.3.598

Ryff, C. D. (1989). Happiness is everything, or is it? Explorations on the meaning of psychological well-being. *Journal of Personality and Social Psychology*, *57*(6), 1069–1081. https://doi.org/10.1037/0022-3514.57.6.1069

Ryff, C. D., & Keyes, C. L. M. (1995). The structure of psychological well-being revisited. *Journal of Personality and Social Psychology*, *69*(4), 719–727. https://doi.org/10.1037/0022-3514.69.4.719

Scriven, M. (1987). Critical thinking and the concept of literacy. *Informal Logic IX*, *9*(2). https://doi.org/10.22329/il.v9i2.2665

Seligman, M. (2011). *Flourish: A visionary new understanding of happiness and well-being*. Simon & Schuster.
Seligman, M. (2018). PERMA and the building blocks of well-being. *The Journal of Positive Psychology*, *13*(4), 333–335. https://doi.org/10.1080/17439760.2018.1437466
Shanahan, T., & Shanahan, C. (2012). What is disciplinary literacy and why does it matter? *Topics in Language Disorders*, *32*(1). https://doi.org/10.1097/TLD.0b013e318244557a
Sollis, K., Biddle, N., Maulana, H., Yap, M., & Campbell, P. (2024). Measuring well-being across culture and context–are we getting it right? Evaluating the variation in wellbeing conceptualisations throughout the world. *Social Indicators Research*, *174*(1), 123–155. https://doi.org/10.1007/s11205-024-03382-z
Stevens, R., Petermans, A., Pohlmeyer, A., Cain, R., & Vanrie, J. (2020). Wellbeing, happiness and flourishing: Different views on a common goal. In A. Petermans & R. Cain (Eds.), *Design for wellbeing: An applied approach* (pp. 13–30). Routledge/Taylor & Francis Group.
UNESCO Institute for Statistics. (n.d.). *Literacy*. September 30, 2024, Retrieved from https://uis.unesco.org/node/3079547
United Nations. (2003). *literacy prerequisite for reaching global anti-poverty goals says secretary-general in literacy day message* [Press Release]. Retrieved from https://press.un.org/en/2003/sgsm8849.doc.htm
VanderWeele, T. J., Trudel-Fitzgerald, C., Allin, P., Farrelly, C., Fletcher, G., Frederick, D. E., Hall, J., Helliwell, J. F., Kim, E. S., Lauinger, W. A., Lee, M. T., Lyubomirsky, S., Margolis, S., McNeely, E., Messer, N., Tay, L., Viswanath, V., Węziak-Białowolska, D., & Kubzansky, L. D. (2020). Current recommendations on the selection of measures for well-being. *Preventive Medicine: An International Journal Devoted to Practice and Theory*, *133*, Article 106004. https://doi.org/10.1016/j.ypmed.2020.106004
World Health Organisation. (2022). Valuing Health for All: Rethinking and building a whole-of-society approach. *The WHO Council on the Economics of Health for All—Council Brief*, (3). Retrieved from https://cdn.who.int/media/docs/default-source/council-on-the-economics-of-health-for-all/who_councilbrief3.pdf

6

CULTIVATING WELLBEING LITERACY THROUGH UNTRANSLATABLE WORDS

Tim Lomas

Introduction

Language shapes how people perceive, experience, and understand the world, and even affects what constitutes reality itself (e.g., which phenomena are even noticed at all). A prominent metaphor with which to understand this power of language is cartography: language is a map we use to represent and navigate the world. Much therefore depends upon the nature of our map. Just as geographical maps vary in detail, accuracy, and overall quality, so do linguistic ones. A given person or culture, for example, might only have a vague representation of a particular area of experience, whereas another person or culture may have a much more fine-grained guide. This applies to anything from emotional experience and philosophical ideas to artistic pursuits and practical skills.

Crucially, however, our maps are not fixed but capable of refinement. We can learn to make them more detailed and accurate. From one perspective, this process is central to learning itself. In any educational arena, much of the process is about developing our linguistic cartography: carving up the conceptual terrain with more precision and learning the relevant terminology. This separates beginners from experts: the latter has a more detailed map, allowing them to understand the terrain with greater accuracy. This applies to every aspect of life, including, most relevantly here, wellbeing. Thus, at the heart of wellbeing literacy is developing better conceptual maps regarding flourishing.

There are numerous ways to refine our maps. This chapter focuses on one that has received relatively little attention but may be among the most powerful: engaging with 'untranslatable' words. Although a contested phenomenon, untranslatability usually refers to a word that lacks an *exact equivalent* in one's

DOI: 10.4324/9781003644293-6

own language (even while there may be similar terms). Key to understanding their significance is that different cultures have different maps. For myriad reasons, from climate and geography to values and traditions, languages conceptually "carve up" the world differently, varying in how they draw linguistic boundaries. Essentially, such words signify phenomena one's culture has overlooked or undervalued (perhaps because not common or salient enough to receive the distinction of its own label), but which another culture *has* noticed, valued, and named. By engaging with such words, we can refine our own maps, developing better literacy regarding wellbeing, indeed all areas of life.

This chapter discusses these ideas in three parts. First, it explores the idea of language as cartography. Second, it highlights the significance of untranslatable words. Third, it suggests engaging with such words promotes wellbeing literacy.

Language as Cartography

The idea that language offers a map of life has a long pedigree. It was utilised, for example, by de Saussure (1916), founder of structuralism (which recognises language as a system of signs), and subsequently by Korzybski (1933) and Peirce (1955). Harnessing this metaphor, this first section elucidates parallels between language and conventional cartography, allowing us to appreciate the significance of untranslatable words. First though, to clarify this suggestion that language maps the "world," let's elucidate the relationship between language and the world it purports to map.

A useful framework for understanding this relationship was provided by Popper (1980), who identified *three* worlds, each interpenetrating and influencing the others, thereby shaping this mapping. World 1 (W1) is the subjective "inner" terrain of qualia (e.g., mental states). World 2 (W2) is the objective "outer" realm of material entities (including the physical bodies of humans). The nature and relationship of these worlds have been debated for millennia (Chalmers, 1995). In addition, though, Popper adds a third world (W3): the conceptual world of abstract thought and its products. Most relevantly here, this includes language, being the "world of the products of the human mind, such as languages; tales and stories and religious myths; scientific conjectures or theories, and mathematical constructions; songs and symphonies; paintings and sculptures" (p. 144). Thus, a large part of W3 consists of mapping W1 and W2, as well as W3 itself: language can delineate territory in W1 (e.g., differentiating emotions), W2 (e.g., identifying objects), and W3 (e.g., conceptualising ideas).

As with conventional (geographical) cartography, language maps our worlds (1, 2, 3) by imposing boundaries, parsing them into cognitively digestible elements, including through grammatical structure and lexical content. Grammatical structures bring order to the complexity of the worlds (e.g., organising them according to considerations like temporal dynamics and relationships between entities). Influenced by these structures, the worlds can also be segmented into lexemes of various sorts, including delineating objects (via nouns and pronouns), processes (verbs), qualities (adjectives and adverbs), relationships (prepositions and conjunctions), and communicative acts (interjections).

Considering this process of boundary construction, four points are central to the significance of untranslatable words, namely, boundaries are somewhat fuzzy, fluid, socially constructed, and culturally dependent. First, when we delineate regions of a world using a boundary, and label it linguistically, these boundaries are not usually clean-cut. Regarding affective states, for instance, we agree to demarcate a particular region of valence, intensity, etc. as "ecstasy," and a related area as "contentment." Words can be deployed in varying ways by different people though (and even by the same person at different times), so these regions are not usually precisely defined, with unambiguous demarcation. Rather, they constitute a "fuzzy set," where the "transition between membership and nonmembership is gradual rather than abrupt" (Dubois & Prade, 1980, p. 1).

Related to the fuzziness of categories/labels is their fluidity. This was a key insight of poststructuralism, which recognised the dynamic nature of language (whereas early structuralism regarded its structures as more fixed). Consider again the notion of ecstasy, whose meaning has shifted considerably over the centuries. It originates in classical Greek, where *ékstasis* combined *ek* (outside or beyond), and *stasis* (stature or standing), connoting someone "standing outside" themselves in some manner. This notion was deployed in various ways, from the benign (e.g., astonished) to the more troubling (e.g., insanity) (Michaelsen, 1989). It was then "borrowed" by English in the 14th century, becoming a loanword, at first mainly in religious contexts, depicting forms of rapture arising from contemplating the divine (McGinn, 1987). Over time, with the secularisation of the West, these spiritual connotations were mostly eroded, with the term now generally just denoting intense pleasure. The key point, using Peirce's (1955) semiotic terminology, is there is a relatively loose link between a given signifier (e.g., "ecstasy") and the "object" it signifies (in this instance, a W1 region of affective experience). At a cultural level, the region denoted by the label can thus evolve, producing changes in what the lexeme signifies.

The fuzzy and changing nature of linguistic terms/categories leads to the third point. Linguistic boundaries are socially constructed: their drawing is somewhat arbitrary, and subject to convention, especially when boundaries are especially fuzzy, or not self-evident, as with affective states, where it is not obvious how the emotional space signified by ecstasy differs from that denoted by near-synonyms like euphoria. W3 concepts are not abstract symbols that exist in perfect and fixed correspondence with phenomena in W1 and W2.

Rather, W3 is a communal creation: developed through negotiation in cultural groups, then maintained through practice and living together in the world.

This brings us to the fourth point about boundary construction: language is a product of culture. Given there are multiple cultures, there are many linguistic "maps" globally, producing variations in how people conceptualise the world. This recognition has been called the linguistic relativity hypothesis (LRH), which dates back as least as far as Herder (1772), who argued that differences in the mentalities of countries derived partly from their language. Entering the modern era, the notion found its most prominent articulation with the anthropologists Sapir (1929) and Whorf (1940), such that the LHR is sometimes referred to as the "Sapir-Whorf Hypothesis." Per the general tenets of the LHR, they argued language shapes how people experience and understand life. As Whorf (1956) said, "We dissect nature along lines laid out by our native languages ... The world is presented as a kaleidoscopic flux of impressions which has to be organized ... largely by the linguistic systems in our minds" (pp. 213–214). One particularly interesting aspect of this theory is untranslatable words.

Untranslatable Words

So-called "untranslatable" words essentially lack an exact equivalent in one's own language. Such words have attracted much attention in recent years, both within academia (Cassin et al., 2014) and popular culture (De Boinod, 2007). The term itself can be problematic and is disliked by some linguists who prefer "unlexicalized." On one hand, arguably *no* word is truly translatable. Ever since de Saussure (1916), it's been generally accepted by post-structuralists that words are embedded within complex webs of meanings. Even if languages have rough equivalents (e.g., *Liebe* as the German counterpart to love), something is always lost in translation (McClaren, 1998). Conversely though, some scholars contend nothing is ever genuinely *un*translatable. Even if a word lacks an exact equivalent, something of its meaning can often be conveyed in a few words or sentences (Pullum, 1989). However, it's lacking an "exact match" that renders a word untranslatable in common parlance, and moreover makes it so intriguing.

Such words highlight "semantic gaps" in our language: "the lack of a convenient word to express what [one] wants to speak about" (Lehrer, 1974, p. 105). In such instances, language often simply "borrow" the word as a loanword. Not *all* cases of borrowing are due to untranslatability. Haspelmath (2009) differentiates between "core" versus "cultural" borrowings. The former is when a loanword replicates a word already in the recipient language, such as for sociolinguistic reasons, perhaps cultural capital associated with using foreign words (Blank, 1999). Such cases are not of concern here. But the second category of "cultural" borrowings is central; these are "loanwords by necessity," whereby the recipient language lacks its own word for the referent in question.

This might occur, for instance, when a new invention, practice, or idea is introduced to a culture. Absent an appropriate native word, or a new coinage, the loanword is adopted because it is cognitively and socially useful, allowing speakers to articulate concepts they previously struggled to, thereby *filling* a semantic gap. Analysing loanword adoption across languages, Tadmor (2009) found such gaps are less likely to arise in relation to phenomena which are common across cultures and less susceptible to innovation, with low levels of borrowing for phenomena like the body (of which just 14% of English words are loanwords), spatial relations (14%) and sense perception (11%). By contrast, phenomena more subject to creativity and innovation – such as religion and belief (41%), and clothing and grooming (39%) – are more likely to have culturally specific elements, meaning other cultures may have semantic gaps in relation to them, necessitating borrowing loanwords.

In our cartographic metaphor, a semantic gap denotes a region of experience not circumscribed by a word in a given language (in our case, English). This may happen for various reasons. The term might denote an experience with which English speakers overall are unfamiliar, e.g., because they lacked opportunities to experience or notice the phenomenon in question. For instance, various Eastern philosophies, and related branches of practice (from medicine to martial arts), have developed lexica pertaining to subtle forms of "energy" in/around the body, from the Chinese *qi* (Jonas & Crawford, 2003) to the Sanskrit *chakras* (Albanese, 1999). Whatever these energies actual nature, they may not necessarily be universally experienced or perceived. Potentially, for most English-speakers – except those who have consciously appraised themselves of such phenomena – these experiences might not even effectively exist. This suggests language does not only map worlds (1, 2, 3), but even *creates* dimensions of these worlds, populating them with new phenomena, such as engendering experiences of subtle energies in W1.

Another reason for untranslatability could be English-speakers are familiar with the region of experience in question, but English has carved this up differently to other languages. An example is colour perception, with cultural differences in how the colour spectrum is segmented (Lucy, 1997). A related semantic gap is when another language has mapped a phenomenon with greater specificity than English. Linguists have highlighted the vast range of experiences and relationships encompassed by "love" for example (Berscheid, 2010). By contrast, other languages have developed more nuanced lexica to depict types of love – with Greek particularly prolific in this regard (Lee, 1977; Lomas, 2018a) – thereby generating words which are untranslatable (since "love" does not capture their nuanced differences).

Whatever the reason for untranslatability, such words are significant for many reasons. First, they offer windows onto other cultures' experiences and understanding of life, as Wierzbicka's (1999) analysis of cultural "key words" has shown. These thus offer portals through which people from other cultures might gain a glimpse, however partial or obscured, into ways of being and thinking in that culture. This doesn't mean people outside the culture could actually "step into" it, fully acquiring the "experiential familiarity" that people native to those languages may have, hence understanding how such words functions in the local "stream of life" (Wierzbicka, 1999, p. 8). Nevertheless, such terms still provide some indication, however fragmented, of modes of experiences in those cultures. Moreover, beyond being informative vis-à-vis the culture that created the word, they enrich *other* lexica, with "borrowing" loanwords being central to language and cultural development, discussed above, allowing people to articulate phenomena in ways they hitherto struggled to.

For this reason, I have been creating a lexicography of untranslatable words pertaining to wellbeing, aiming to enrich the conceptual lexicon in psychology (Lomas, 2016, 2018a, 2020). Wellbeing scholarship has been critiqued as Western-centric, as has psychology generally, biased towards scholars and participants belonging to societies described by Henrich et al. (2010) as WEIRD (Western, Educated, Industrialised, Rich and Democratic). Thus, a central premise of my project is untranslatable words can enrich the nomological network in psychology (and English more broadly). Indeed, such words already *have* enhanced the discipline, including loanwords from languages like Greek (e.g., psyche), Latin (e.g., id), and German (e.g., Gestalt). These examples reinforce the contention that untranslatable words have great relevance to psychology. By providing insights into how other cultures understand and experience life, they can counter the Western-centricity of psychology, creating space for greater consideration of cultural diversity. Moreover, by helping refine our cartographic map, we can develop a better understanding of the mind itself. Furthermore, engaging with such words has the potential to enhance wellbeing literacy, as the final section considers.

Promoting Wellbeing Literacy through Untranslatable Words

At its best, education helps people develop and flourish in all aspects of life, not only intellectually, but psychologically, socially, and even spiritually. In that respect, a key area of development is around emotions, reflected in paradigms such as Social and Emotional Learning (Weissberg et al., 2015). Such learning takes many forms, but among the most prominent is cultivating emotional granularity (EG) – sometimes also called emotional differentiation – namely the "ability to make fine-grained, nuanced distinctions between similar emotions" (Smidt & Suvak, 2015, p. 48). Crucially, this capacity is not merely a fixed trait but a skill amenable to training (Kashdan et al., 2015). Indeed, school interventions have been developed to help children cultivate EG, expanding their knowledge and use of emotion words (Brackett et al., 2012). By helping people better identity, understand, and regulate their emotions, such learning is associated with myriad beneficial outcomes, such as improved wellbeing, behaviour, and academic performance (Lennarz et al., 2018).

An intriguing possibility for further enhancing EG is therefore engaging with untranslatable words. Although this possibility has not actually been explored empirically in any comprehensive way, it is supported by relevant research and theorising, such as that of Lisa Feldman Barrett (2006). Her conceptual-act model skilfully interweaves the two main perspectives on emotions in the literature: naturalistic and constructivist. The former regards emotions in an essentialist way as "natural kinds" (i.e., universal affective responses): Russell's (1980) circumplex model, for instance, positions affective states as the product of two independent neurophysiological systems, valence (pleasant vs. unpleasant), and arousal (active vs. passive); relatedly, the basic emotions paradigm associated with Ekman (2016) holds that all people experience six basic emotions (anger, disgust, fear, sadness, enjoyment, and surprise). By contrast, constructivist theories suggest emotions are not universally available inner states but are products of social interaction and the broader cultural context in which interaction occurs (Harré, 1986).

Barrett's thought incorporates insights from both perspectives. Per naturalistic theories, she proposes humans experience momentary states of "core affect" that may be relatively universal. However, the interpretation and conceptualisation of such states depend on people's linguistic-conceptual schemas, thereby incorporating the insights found in constructivist theorising. A similar dynamic is found in Matsumoto and Hwang's (2012) notion of culturally driven emotion regulation: this proposes humans inherit "a set of biologically innate emotions that are produced by a core emotion system," but how these emotions are felt, interpreted, and reacted to is culturally "calibrated" (p. 92). Thus, in these models, people's culture and language play significant roles in their experience and understanding of emotions.

This insight is central to the LRH, which holds that people's experience and conceptualisation of emotions – indeed, all aspects of life – are strongly shaped by their cultural context, especially their language. Potentially some emotional states may even only be experienced by people from particular cultures, as reflected in research into "culture-bound" psychiatric illnesses (Simons & Hughes, 2012). Conversely, other anthropological research indicates that some seemingly common emotions may not be widely experienced in certain cultures or might be felt and interpreted in ways that diverge from those in Western contexts (Beatty, 2013).

This brings us back to the significance of untranslatable words, which reveal cross-cultural differences in all aspects of wellbeing. As such, they have significant potential for enriching social and emotional learning, including enhancing EG. Beyond that, they have the potential to expand students' horizons in other ways, such as fostering awareness, appreciation, and understanding of other cultures. This latter potential is particularly valuable in terms of encouraging diversity and inclusion in the classroom, particularly in the context of multicultural societies (Bartz & Bartz, 2018), and related discussions around "decolonizing" the curriculum to make learning less Western-centric and more inclusive of other cultural perspectives (Meighan, 2019).

In that spirit, I recently made some suggestions for engaging with untranslatable words in educational settings (Lomas, 2022), grouped into two main types of activities: identifying words and engaging with words. The first involves students identifying or encountering relevant words. One option could just involve looking through my lexicography (www.drtimlomas.com/lexicography), with people encouraged to select words they either (a) just find interesting for some reason, (b) have actually experienced, or (c) have not experienced but would like to. If possible though, since many educational settings are multicultural, with students speaking diverse languages, people could be invited to introduce words from their own culture/language to the class, which would likely be more enriching. Some students may only speak English, of course, in which case they could share instances of dialect or terminology that might not be widely used in English but are meaningful to the student. Such exercises would then create lists of relevant words which can be used in the second activity.

This second type features activities to encourage students to engage productively with words that resonate with them. One could harness various creative approaches to this end, with students picking a favourite word and exploring its appeal in myriad ways, with the details depending on their age and competencies. In terms of artistic modalities, students could paint a picture to capture the meaning and significance of the word, for example, or write some music or a simple melody that likewise expresses the word's meaning and appeal, or just simply choose a song they already know that captures its sense.

Moving into a discursive space, students could write a short fiction story centred around the word; alternatively, the story could be non-fiction and focus on actual experiences in their lives. Similarly, they could write a poem that expresses the word's qualities and brings it poetically to life. Some activities could be even more involved, and harness forms of experiential learning, such as spending some time (e.g., a week) reflecting on the word, being open to how it manifests in their lives, and recording their reflections in a journal. The possibilities are almost endless. In this way, we may discover how helpful engagement with untranslatable words could be in encouraging emotional literacy.

References

Albanese, C. L. (1999). The subtle energies of spirit: Explorations in metaphysical and new age spirituality. *Journal of the American Academy of Religion*, *67*(2), 305–325.

Ardi, H. (2012). Is theory of translation needed to build students' translation competence? *International Conference on Languages and Arts*, 320–328.

Barrett, L. F. (2006). Are emotions natural kinds? *Perspectives on Psychological Science*, *1*(1), 28–58.

Bartz, J., & Bartz, T. (2018). Recognizing and acknowledging worldview diversity in the inclusive classroom. *Education Sciences*, 8(4), 196.

Beatty, A. (2013). Current emotion research in anthropology: Reporting the field. *Emotion Review*, *5*(4), 414–422.

Berscheid, E. (2010). Love in the fourth dimension. *Annual Review of Psychology*, 61, 1–25.

Blank, A. (1999). Why do new meanings occur? A cognitive typology of the motivations for lexical semantic change. In A. Blank & P. Koch (Eds.), *Historical semantics and cognition* (pp. 61–89). Mouton de Gruyter.

Brackett, M. A., Rivers, S. E., Reyes, M. R., & Salovey, P. (2012). Enhancing academic performance and social and emotional competence with the RULER feeling words curriculum. *Learning and Individual Differences*, *22*(2), 218–224.

Cassin, B., Apter, E., Lezra, J., & Wood, M. (2014). *Dictionary of Untranslatables: A Philosophical Lexicon*. Princeton University Press.

Chalmers, D. (1995). Facing up to the problem of consciousness. *Journal of Consciousness Studies*, *2*(3):200–219.

Dubois, D., & Prade, H. (1980). *Fuzzy sets and systems: Theory and applications*. Academic Press.

Ekman, P. (2016). What scientists who study emotion agree about. *Perspectives on Psychological Science*, *11*(1), 31–34.

Fogarty, F. A., Lu, L. M., Sollers, J J., Krivoschekov, S. G., Booth, R. J., & Consedine, N. S. (2015). Why it pays to be mindful: Trait mindfulness predicts physiological recovery from emotional stress and greater differentiation among negative emotions. *Mindfulness*, *6*(2), 175–185.

Harré, R. (1986). *The social construction of emotions*. Blackwell.

Haspelmath, M. (2009). Lexical borrowing: Concepts and issues. In M. Haspelmath & U. Tadmor (Eds.), *Loanwords in the world's languages: A comparative handbook* (pp. 35–55). De Gruyter Martin.

Henrich, J., Heine, S. J., & Norenzayan, A. (2010). Most people are not WEIRD. *Nature*, *466*(7302), 29.

Herder, J. G. (1966). *Essay on the Origin of Language*. University of Chicago Press.

Jonas, W. B., & Crawford, C. C. (2003). Science and spiritual healing: A critical review of spiritual healing, "energy" medicine, and intentionality. *Alternative Therapies in Health and Medicine*, *9*(2), 56–64.

Kashdan, T. B., Barrett, L. F., & McKnight, P. E. (2015). Unpacking emotion differentiation: Transforming unpleasant experience by perceiving distinctions in negativity. *Current Directions in Psychological Science*, *24*(1), 10–16.

Korzybski, A. (1933). Science and sanity: An introduction to non-Aristotelian systems and general semantics. *International Non-Aristotelian Library*.

Lee, J. A. (1977). A typology of styles of loving. *Personality and Social Psychology Bulletin*, *3*(2), 173–182. https://doi.org/10.1177/014616727700300204

Lehrer, A. (1974). *Semantic fields and lexical structures*. North-Holland Publishing Co.

Lennarz, H. K., Lichtwarck-Aschoff, A., Timmerman, M. E., & Granic, I. (2018). Emotion differentiation and its relation with emotional well-being in adolescents. *Cognition and Emotion*, *32*(3), 651–657.

Loinaz, E. S. (2019). Teachers' perceptions and practice of social and emotional education in Greece, Spain, Sweden and the United Kingdom. *International Journal of Emotional Education*, *11*(1), 31–48.

Lomas, T. (2016). Towards a positive cross-cultural lexicography: Enriching our emotional landscape through 216 'untranslatable' words pertaining to well-being. *Journal of Positive Psychology*, *11*(5), 546–558.

Lomas, T. (2018a). Experiential cartography and the significance of "untranslatable" words. *Theory and Psychology, 28*(4), 476–495.
Lomas, T. (2018b). *Translating happiness: Enriching our experience and understanding of wellbeing through untranslatable words.* MIT Press.
Lomas, T. (2021). Towards a cross-cultural lexical map of wellbeing. *The Journal of Positive Psychology, 16*(5), 622–639. https://doi.org/10.1080/17439760.2020.1791944
Lomas, T. (2022). Well-being lexicon in schools. In A. Giraldez-Hayes & J. Burke (Eds.), *Applied positive school psychology* (pp. 150–156). Routledge.
Lomas, T., Waters, L., Williams, P., Oades, L. G., & Kern, M. L. (2020). Third wave positive psychology: Broadening towards complexity. *The Journal of Positive Psychology, 16*(5), 660–674. https://doi.org/10.1080/17439760.2020.1805501
Lovtsevich, G. N. (2005). Language teachers through the looking glass: Expanding circle teachers' discourse. *World Englishes, 24*(4), 461–469.
Lucy, J. (1997). The linguistics of'color'. In L. Hardin & L. Maffi (Eds.), *Color categories in thought and language* (pp. 320–346). Cambridge University Press.
Matsumoto, D., & Hwang, H. S. (2012). Culture and emotion: The integration of biological and cultural contributions. *Journal of Cross-Cultural Psychology, 43*(1), 91–118.
McClaren, M. (1998). *Interpreting Cultural Differences: The Challenge of International Communication.* Peter Francis Publishers.
McGinn, B. (1987). Love, knowledge, and mystical union in Western Christianity: Twelfth to sixteenth centuries. *Church History, 56*(1), 7–24. https://doi.org/10.2307/3165301
Meighan, P. J. (2019). An "educator's" perspective: How heritage language pedagogy and technology can decolonize the English classroom. *TESOL Journal, 11*(2), 1–5.
Michaelsen, P. (1989). Ecstasy and possession in ancient Israel: A review of some recent contributions. *Scandinavian Journal of the Old Testament, 3*(2), 28–54.
Peirce, C. S. (1955). *Philosophical writings of Peirce* (J. Buchler Ed.). Dover Publications.
Popper, K. (1980). *Objective knowledge: An evolutionary approach.* Oxford University Press.
Pullum, G. K. (1989). The great Eskimo vocabulary hoax. *Natural Language & Linguistic Theory*, 275–281.
Russell, J. A. (1980). A circumplex model of affect. *Journal of Personality and Social Psychology, 39*(6), 1161–1178.
Sapir, E. (1929). The status of linguistics as a science. *Language, 5*(4), 207.
Saussure, F. (1916). *Course in general linguistics.* Duckworth.
Simons, R. C., & Hughes, C. C. (2012). *The culture-bound syndromes: Folk illnesses of psychiatric and anthropological interest* (Vol. 7). Springer Science & Business Media.
Smidt, K. E., & Suvak, M. K. (2015). A brief, but nuanced, review of emotional granularity and emotion differentiation research. *Current Opinion in Psychology, l*(3), 48–51.
Tadmor, U. (2009). Loanwords in the world's languages: Findings and results. In M. Haspelmath & U. Tadmor (Eds.), *Loanwords in the world's languages: A comparative handbook* (pp. 55–75). De Gruyter Martin.
Weissberg, R. P., Durlak, J. A., Domitrovich, C. E., & Gullotta, T. P. (Eds.). (2015). Social and emotional learning: Past, present, and future. In *Handbook of social and emotional learning: Research and practice.* (pp. 3–19). The Guilford Press.
Whorf, B. L. (1940). *Science and linguistics.* Bobbs-Merrill.
Whorf, B. L. (1956). *Language, Thought, and Reality: Selected writings of Benjamin Lee Whorf* (J. B. Carroll Ed.). MIT Press
Wierzbicka, A. (1999). *Emotions across languages and cultures: Diversity and universals.* Cambridge University Press.

7

WELLBEING IN VOCATIONAL COMPETENCY TAXONOMIES*

Daniel Loton, Matthew Iasiello, and Arnaldo Barone

Introduction

This chapter considers the current and potential place of wellbeing in vocational taxonomies, with an emphasis on wellbeing as a potential skillset, and the potential role of wellbeing literacy (WBL) as a mechanism and explanation of wellbeing skill acquisition. Vocational taxonomies contain hierarchies of knowledge, skills, abilities, work styles, values, and tasks, mapped to vocations – and form the backbone of many vocational education and training (VET) systems. We begin with a brief definition of WBL, including its' components and mechanisms of action for enabling wellbeing. Next we define Competence Based Training (CBT), an educational model used in VET in Australia and internationally, and consider its' relevance to wellbeing education. We then outline key vocational taxonomies and attempts to unify these into a complete set of human skills. We follow with a cursory overview of modifiable or trainable wellbeing qualities in four lines of wellbeing science inquiry, that suggest skills may be a useful way to frame these qualities -positive psychology interventions (PPIs), non-cognitive competencies in education, resilience and coping with adversity, and mental skills and techniques in peak performance. Throughout these sections, we make connections back to WBL theory and mechanisms, and argue it is a promising pathway through which skills taxonomies may enable wellbeing. Throughout the chapter, we present two hypothetical case studies of a VET graduate facing a challenging work situation: one exposed to wellbeing skills in their education; and another to mainly technical skills. Finally, we consider the limits of skills as a conceptualisation of wellbeing, especially the implication that fostering wellbeing is the sole or primary responsibility

*Author Note: *We have no known conflicts of interest to disclose.*

DOI: 10.4324/9781003644293-7

of the individual. The chapter concludes with a call to action for a research programme that leads to the holistic embedding of modifiable, wellbeing-supporting factors identified in wellbeing science within vocational taxonomies and VET.

WBL and Wellbeing within Skills Taxonomies

WBL is a capability-based model explaining how language can support wellbeing (Hou et al., 2021; Oades, 2017, Oades et al., 2020). The 'mechanics' of WBL include acquiring knowledge, comprehension, and expression, and 'dynamics' include adapting language use based on context and intentionality. Australia's forthcoming national skills taxonomy aims to establish 'a common language for employers, education institutions, government, and individuals regarding skills and certifications' (Australian Government, 2024, p. 2). Similarly, WBL stresses a similar common wellbeing-related language foundation (Oades et al., 2020).

This chapter makes two central arguments: (1) Vocational taxonomies require a comprehensive mapping to contemporary scientific wellbeing-enabling factors, to ensure wellbeing capacities are captured and enabled in vocational education. (2) The primary pathways for wellbeing in vocational taxonomies are defined and elaborated, at least in part, in WBL. A brief consideration of whether wellbeing-enabling factors can be considered skills supplements these arguments, with examples from four lines of evidence. In order to consider how vocational taxonomies may support wellbeing, we must first consider the educational model in VET.

VET: Competency Based Training

Competency Based Training (CBT) has been in place in Australia since the 1990s, and its' roots can be traced to the scientific management ideas of American engineer Frederick Winslow Taylor and behaviourist compatriot Edward Thorndike (McCowan, 1998; Neumann, 1979). Taylorist origins highlight the method's workplace focus, where competencies generally relevant to performance of work-related tasks. Behaviourist influences mean the attainment of skills (or competencies) are expressed in terms of visible, tangible, and measurable changes in physical behaviour or performance.

The method is sometimes referred to as 'Mastery Learning' or 'Learning for Mastery', since in CBT student progression occurs *only* once full mastery of a required competency is demonstrated, measured against pre-specified industry standards and assessment thresholds (Mulder & Winterton, 2017). In practice, some students will require (and gain) extensive formal training to master a skill, while others may attain this level more quickly. In some cases, students who can demonstrate mastery through a 'recognition of prior learning' process can avoid all formal training. In each case, however, progression occurs *only* after objectively verified demonstration of competency.

In Australia, competencies are defined as 'the consistent application of knowledge and skill to the standard of performance required in the workplace' (Vocational Education and Training Qualification Reform Design Group, 2024, p. 32). The pre-specified standard referenced in this quote reveals what is arguably CBT's most important aspect: its outcome or output focus, as demonstrated to standards stipulated in training documents developed by industry, who not only select the skills to be taught but also dictate the methods by which to pursue assessment.

The training documents used in Australia are referred to as Training Packages (Hodge, 2016; Smith, 2019). In all, there are currently 54 Training Packages and within each is a suite of 'units of competency', which are the skills (competencies) required for the successful performance of a given job. Australian VET has about 15,000 competencies in all that detail the tasks performed and competencies required to successfully function in every job (National Training Register, see Training.gov.au). The types of units vary, from workplace health and safety to generic skills like teamwork or wellbeing (an example of the latter being 'Assess and promote social, emotion and physical wellbeing'), to more job specific units that outline discrete work tasks. Similar principles apply in the application of vocational taxonomies to VET globally.

The conferral of wellbeing skills in CBT can be achieved in at least two ways. New units of competency can be developed in response to evolving workplace realities. Thus, it would be possible to introduce new units focused on wellbeing skills. This is by no means a simple or straightforward process, requiring meeting many regulatory hurdles. Further, it is uncertain how amenable wellbeing skills would be to the 'one size fits all' template and the demonstrable level of mastery based on observation and performance. Williams (2019) notes that pedagogy can be an instrument to develop so-called twenty-first century skills like communication, collaboration, and problem solving. This represents the second avenue, making it possible to develop wellbeing skills through pedagogies that could be achieved through appropriate teacher training and professional development. We return to CBT-specific considerations, in particular the notion of behavioural demonstration of wellbeing skills, after introducing vocational taxonomies and some of the modifiable wellbeing factors identified in the wellbeing science literature.

Vocational Taxonomies

Australia, the home of the authors, has a skills classification system known as the Australian Skills Classification (https://www.jobsandskills.gov.au/australian-skills-classification). The ASC seeks to forge links between skills and occupations by providing a common set of terms (or 'language') that operate across occupations, sectors and contexts. The ASC is soon to be replaced with a National Skills Taxonomy which, like its predecessor, seeks to create cohesion in skills nomenclature to support workforce development and mobility and align the supply and demand of skills (see https://www.jobsandskills.gov.au/data/national-skills-taxonomy). In the Unites States, O*NET (https://www.onetonline.org/), and in the European Union, ESCO (https://esco.ec.europa.eu/), have similar functions.

Crosswalks, a process of mapping and consolidating concepts across different skills taxonomies using a mix of machine earning and human coding, aim in part to create a unified set of human work-related skills (European Commission, 2022). Others unifying skills initiatives (e.g., Djumalieva & Sleeman, 2018; Foundation for Young Australians, 2020) have used 'big data' and machine learning to scrape and compile requirements of applicants from job advertisements. Attempts at grand unification of human skills has similarities to the importance WBL places on the need for an intentional and common language for achieving wellbeing (Oades et al., 2021).

Wellbeing Skills in Vocational Taxonomies

Current vocational taxonomies appear to have limitations in fostering wellbeing skills. Firstly, vocational taxonomies exhibit a more utilitarian and economic-rationalist purpose of wellbeing solely for workplace performance, for the wellbeing of service-recipients but not workers, or in limited cases for worker retention and reduction of burnout (e.g. resilience). Secondly, vocational taxonomies share a philosophical foundation with CBTs' Taylorist and behaviourist roots and emphasise demonstrable, observable, and easily measured tasks/skills (e.g., using a nail gun versus demonstrating compassion for a client). Finally, our most important critique is that a comprehensive reflection of wellbeing-enabling factors from wellbeing science is currently absent from vocational taxonomies.

Based on a cursory review, we were able to identify some coverage of wellbeing in vocational taxonomies, but they tend to be somewhat rare, generic as they fall into high-level domains, and either lack specificity and detail in their definition; or ramp together very many individual wellbeing-enabling factors. For example, in ESCO, transversal (or soft) skills have high relevance to wellbeing skills, including the higher-order categories of *thinking skills* (e.g. 'dealing with problems' and 'thinking creatively and innovatively'), and *life skills and competences*, which contains health-related, civic participation, and cultural skills and knowledge. But consider, for example, how 'applying health-related skills and competences' is defined: 'Care for own and others' mental and physical well-being and apply basic health standards, including hygiene', which conceptually does not span wellbeing skills we identify in subsequent sections. In O*NET, the category 'work styles' is relevant, including for example, jobs that require *adjustment*, defined as the job requiring 'maturity, poise, flexibility, and restraint to cope with pressure, stress, criticism, setbacks, personal and work-related problems, etc.', mapping clearly to aspects of resilience, coping from the SEARCH meta-framework (Waters & Loton, 2019), and sub-facets of the big five personality trait conscientiousness, such as persistence[1]. The work style ***achievement orientation*** is defined as the job requiring 'personal goal setting, trying to succeed at those goals, and striving to be competent in own work'; again mapping clearly to conscientiousness but also to the habits and goals domain of SEARCH. We conclude this chapter with a call for a research agenda to harmonise wellbeing science and vocational taxonomies.

Wellbeing-supporting Factors: A Skillset?

There are vocal and frequent calls by industry and employers for wellbeing in their workforce. Poor wellbeing incurs costs, such as losses in productivity (de Oliveira et al., 2023), sick leave (Santini et al., 2022), and turn over (Hassard et al., 2021). Workplaces are struggling with the new generation of workforces and shifting workplace design, and worker preferences (Wong & Greenwood, 2023). In response, there are many post-VET training, industry-led initiatives for wellbeing in the workplace, such as the National Workplace Initiative (see https://www.mentalhealthcommission.gov.au/projects/mentally-healthy-work/national-workplace-initiative) and the Mates in Construction program (see https://mates.org.au/construction/research). Australia recently introduced legislation mandating that workplaces protect employees from psychosocial hazards (Safe Work Australia, n.d.), such as meaningless work, or unreasonable workloads, for which certain worker wellbeing skills may help in minimising, managing or removing these hazards. Yet, incorporating wellbeing skills into vocational taxonomies has not yet been considered an avenue to achieve this.

Building on humanistic psychology and other progenitors, Positive Psychology was incepted to investigate maximalist wellbeing and has experienced rapid growth (Rusk & Waters, 2013), including 'positive education', where wellbeing is included in formal education – primarily primary and secondary schooling (Waters & Loton, 2021). There is no single, all-encompassing set of wellbeing factors from the field, but a thematic meta-framework named SEARCH (Waters & Loton, 2019) identified six domains in positive education: strengths, emotional management, attention and awareness, relationships, coping and habits and goals. Other, similarly broad-ranging reviews have resulted in holistic measures comprising 15 non-domain specific factors (Marsh et al., 2020). Our central point is that wellbeing science offers a wide array of wellbeing-enabling and modifiable factors that warrant consideration for inclusion in vocational taxonomies or attempts at a complete set of human skills.

Here we touch on four separate but overlapping lines of inquiry in wellbeing science that could be considered wellbeing skills or competencies. Acquisition of these is underpinned by WBL, as almost all such interventions rely on the intentional use of language to foster wellbeing (Oades et al., 2021). These four inquiry lines are:

- positive psychology interventions;
- non-cognitive skills in the domain of education;
- coping with adversity in the domain of disaster, adversity, and survival; and
- peak performance, generally in the domain of elite sport.

PPIs are generally designed for use with general populations. They are mostly short, accessible, sometimes self-led, interventions that aim to equip people with one or more wellbeing-enhancing factors. There is a plethora of interventions established and emerging, with a growing base of effectiveness research. Meta-analyses considering effectiveness suggest multi-component and longer duration or involvement PPIs net the largest and most sustained benefit (Carr et al., 2021). Theoretically, researchers have proposed unifying frameworks for PPIs, in that they can be thought of also as processes (Ciarrochi et al., 2022). Many involve elements of homework and intentional practice, which suggest both learning and skill acquisition.

Non-cognitive skills. First coined by sociologists Bowles and Gintis (1976), referring to useful traits outside those measured in intelligence quotient, generally meaning information retention and processing. They include achievement emotions, motivations, goal and aspiration setting, empathy and emotional literacy, to name a few. They are often referred to as soft, transversal, or 21st century skills, with Rammstedt et al. (2024), in a current OECD working paper describe them as 'personality traits, motivation, interests, self-concepts, and beliefs' (p. 5). Socio-emotional learning (SEL) and emotional intelligence are probably the largest areas of research and application of non-cognitive skills. SEL generally has been implemented in mainstream schooling and younger years, with meta analyses finding small effects on learning but moderate effects on wellbeing-related factors and personal growth (Cipriano et al., 2023). Studied more in adults, an emotional intelligence meta-analysis found moderate effects on a wide range of career variables, including progression but also satisfaction (Pirsoul et al., 2023)

Coping with Adversity is another somewhat separate line of scholarship that considers the qualities people need to survive, cope, recover, and thrive in the face of disasters, adversity, and trauma. Topics falling under this banner are resilience, post-traumatic growth, meaning in life, and coping. Psychiatrist Victor Frankl's Logotherapy theory outlines people's innate drive to find a sense of meaning in life, borne of his survival of the Nazi murder factories (Frankl, 1966). Recent work has sought to develop measures of a trait-like factor of meaning in life, including in relation to work (Dik et al., 2012, 2024). Resilience is often measured as a set of factors comprising persistence, community connections and willingness to identify and access support systems (Hall et al., 2024). Post-traumatic growth has been studied specifically in the difficult period of unemployment (Waters & Strauss, 2016)

Peak Performance contexts, such as elite sport, researchers have investigated the role of what are termed mental or psychological skills (Mesagno et al., 2020), and techniques (Birrer et al., 2012). Skills are generally framed as competences per CBT, such as goal setting, identity formation, motivation, confidence, recovery, arousal regulation, pain management, and aspects of attention regulation. Techniques are the practices used to attain these skills, such as imagery, self-talk, mindfulness, and cognitive restructuring (Behnke et al., 2019; Birrer et al., 2012; Noetel et al., 2019). This body of literature contains several mental or psychological skills that warrant consideration.

Next Steps

The VET sector is large. It is not hyperbole to state that society would struggle to function effectively without the skills and knowledge provided by VET. Perhaps this recognition at least partly explains moves in some countries to grow VET's role, such as India, which has set a target for 50% of students to have a VET experience (Chen & Pastore, 2024; Government of India, 2020). But VET also often (and traditionally) caters to some of the most vulnerable and disadvantaged students (Firth, 2020). While it should be recognised for the life-changing pathways it provides to many at-risk and disadvantaged cohorts, there is room for improvement. A more holistic educational offering, including by taking account of and providing the skills to facilitate wellbeing and develop the student as a whole person, was a point recently recognised in an Australian review of education (Education Council, 2020).

Given the widespread benefits of increasing wellbeing, which is an often-stated goal of employer groups, governments, and many others, we present three 'calls to action' to help achieve improved wellbeing via vocational taxonomies:

1 A comprehensive mapping of contemporary wellbeing models and modifiable enablers of wellbeing, to vocational taxonomies (or grand unified versions of them), must be undertaken, to ensure their thorough and detailed integration. Such an initiative would require substantial resources and may use similar methods to crosswalks that mapped and consolidated different vocational taxonomies. This necessary step could provide skills or expert councils, who generally decide what skills comprise qualifications, with a comprehensive 'menu' from which to select and include wellbeing-enabling skills; and also ensure holistic skills taxonomies.
2 WBL theory should be considered as a potential vehicle to explain the pathways and dynamics for more language-oriented wellbeing-enabling factors

or skills, with a mapping and outline of the mechanics and dynamics within WBL to wellbeing skills education.

3 Given the CBT-based education model that is unlikely to change in near future, and that, like vocational taxonomies, tends to favour tangible, observable, and workplace performance-oriented skills, guidelines for how CBT-based education models can effectively measure intangible, wellbeing-related factors are needed to assist skills stakeholders and educators alike.

We temper the wellbeing potential of this call to action by noting that, per the competency-based element of WBL, even a holistic incorporation of intra-individual wellbeing skills, would be a necessary but not sufficient effort to fully promote wellbeing, which involves consideration of an individual's environment (Lomas et al., 2021; Oades et al., 2021; Steger, 2025). This can also include a person's genetics and epigenetic environment, which explains a certain amount of variation in many wellbeing factors (van de Weijer et al., 2022). Notwithstanding these limitations, we contend that including contemporary wellbeing science into vocational or unified human skills taxonomies offers a powerful step forward in embedding and enhancing wellbeing, with likely flow-on effects for economies, workforces and employers.

Note

1 Note that with limited resources, the lead author attempted to use ChatGTP (GTP4) to concept map wellbeing domains to vocational taxonomies. Despite extensive attempts at concept mapping 14 domains (excluding competence) within the Wellbeing Profiler tool and all vocational elements within O*NET and the ASCF, results were impossible to reproduce, and the concept mapping often had inexplicable matches that made little sense. This analysis was abandoned.

References

Australian Government. (2023). *Measuring What Matters*. https://treasury.gov.au/sites/default/files/2023-07/measuring-what-matters-statement020230721_0.pdf

Australian Government, Jobs and Skills Australia. (2024). *National skills taxonomy discussion paper: To inform the design of a national skills taxonomy*. https://www.jobsandskills.gov.au/sites/default/files/2024-06/national_skills_taxonomy_discussion_paper.pdf

Behnke, M., Tomczak, M., Kaczmarek, L. D., Komar, M., & Gracz, J. (2019). The sport mental training questionnaire: Development and validation. *Current Psychology*, *38*, 504–516.

Birrer, D., Röthlin, P., & Morgan, G. (2012). Mindfulness to enhance athletic performance: Theoretical considerations and possible impact mechanisms. *Mindfulness*, *3*(3), 235–246. https://doi.org/10.1007/s12671-012-0109-2

Bowles, S., & Gintis, H. (1976). *Schooling in capitalist America: Educational reform and the contradictions of economic life*. Basic Books.

Carr, A., Cullen, K., Keeney, C., Canning, C., Mooney, O., Chinseallaigh, E., & O'Dowd, A. (2021). Effectiveness of positive psychology interventions: A systematic review and meta-analysis. *The Journal of Positive Psychology, 16*(6), 749–769. https://doi.org/10.1080/17439760.2020.1818807

Chen, J., & Pastore, F. (2024). Dynamics of returns to vocational education in China: 2010–2017. *Humanities and Social Sciences Communications, 11*(1), 1–15. https://doi.org/10.1057/s41599-024-02616-2

Ciarrochi, J., Hayes, S. C., Oades, L. G., & Hofmann, S. G. (2022). Toward a unified framework for positive psychology interventions: Evidence-based processes of change in coaching, prevention, and training. *Frontiers in Psychology, 12*, 809362. https://doi.org/10.3389/fpsyg.2021.809362

Cipriano, C., Strambler, M. J., Naples, L. H., Ha, C., Kirk, M., Wood, M., & Durlak, J. (2023). The state of evidence for social and emotional learning: A contemporary meta-analysis of universal school-based SEL interventions. *Child Development, 94*(5), 1181–1204. https://doi.org/10.1111/cdev.13968

de Oliveira, C., Saka, M., Bone, L., & Jacobs, R. (2023). The role of mental health on workplace productivity: A critical review of the literature. *Applied Health Economics and Health Policy, 21*(2), 167–193. https://doi.org/10.1007/s40258-022-00761-w

Dik, B. J., Eldridge, B. M., Steger, M. F., & Duffy, R. D. (2012). Development and Validation of the Calling and Vocation Questionnaire (CVQ) and Brief Calling Scale (BCS). *Journal of Career Assessment, 20*(3), 242–263. https://doi.org/10.1177/1069072711434410

Dik, B. J., Steger, M. F., & Mercurio, Z. A. (2024). Meaningful work, calling, and occupational health. In L. E. Tetrick, G. G. Fisher, M. T. Ford, & J. C. Quick (Eds.), *Handbook of occupational health psychology.* (3rd ed., pp. 423–443). https://doi.org/10.1037/0000331-021

Djumalieva, J., & Sleeman, C. (2018). An open and data-driven taxonomy of skills extracted from online job adverts. In C. Larsen, S. Rand, A. Schmid, & A. Dean (Eds.), *Developing skills in a changing world of work* (pp. 425–454). Rainer Hampp Verlag. https://doi.org/10.978.395710/3154

Education Council (2020). *Looking to the Future – Report of the review of senior secondary pathways into work, further education and training.* https://www.education.gov.au/quality-schools-package/resources/looking-future-report-review-senior-secondary-pathways-work-further-education-and-training

European Commission. (2022). *The crosswalk between ESCO and O*NET: Technical Report – September 2022.* https://esco.ec.europa.eu/system/files/2022-12/ONET%20ESCO%20Technical%20Report.pdf

Firth, J. (2020). *Review into vocational and applied learning pathways in senior secondary schooling.* Department of Education and Training (DET). https://www.vic.gov.au/review-vocational-and-applied-learning-pathways-senior-secondary-schooling

Foundation for Young Australians. (2020). *The New Work Order.* https://www.fya.org.au/app/uploads/2021/09/FYA-New-Work-Standard-2020.pdf

Frankl, V. E. (1966). Self-transcendence as a human phenomenon. *Journal of Humanistic Psychology, 6*(2), 97–106.

Government of India, Ministry of Human Resource Development. (2020). *National Education Policy 2020.* https://www.education.gov.in/sites/upload_files/mhrd/files/NEP_Final_English_0.pdf

Hall, J. R., Deery, B., Sciberras, E., Kern, M. L., & Quach, J. (2024). How are we measuring resilience in children? A systematic review. *Mental Health & Prevention, 35*, 200351. https://doi.org/10.1016/j.mhp.2024.200351

Hassard, J., Teoh, K., Thomson, L., & Blake, H. (2021). Understanding the cost of mental health at work: An integrative framework. *The SAGE handbook of organizational wellbeing* (1st edn., pp. 9–25). SAGE.

Hodge, S. (2016). Editorial– after competency-based training: Deepening critique, imagining alternatives. *International Journal of Training Research, 14*(3), 171–179.

Hou, H., Chin, T. C., Slemp, G. R., & Oades, L. G. (2021). Wellbeing Literacy: Conceptualization, measurement, and preliminary empirical findings from students, parents and school staff. *International Journal of Environmental Research and Public Health, 18*(4). https://doi.org/10.3390/ijerph18041485

Jobs and Skills Australia (2024). *National skills taxonomy discussion paper: To inform the design of a National Skills Taxonomy.* https://www.jobsandskills.gov.au/consultations/national-skills-taxonomy-discussion-paper

Lomas, T., Waters, L., Williams, P., Oades, L. G., & Kern, M. L. (2021). Third wave positive psychology: Broadening towards complexity. *The Journal of Positive Psychology, 16*(5), 660–674. https://doi.org/10.1080/17439760.2015.1137627

Marsh, H. W., Huppert, F. A., Donald, J. N., Horwood, M. S., & Sahdra, B. K. (2020). The well-being profile (WB-pro): Creating a theoretically based multidimensional measure of well-being to advance theory, research, policy, and practice. *Psychological Assessment, 32*(3), 294. https://psycnet.apa.org/doi/10.1037/pas0000787

Mates in Construction (2024). About us. https://mates.org.au/about-us

McCowan, R. J. (1998). *Origins of competency-based training.* Center for Development of Human Services, State University of New York. Accessed from https://files.eric.ed.gov/fulltext/ED501710.pdf on 29 August 2023.

Mesagno, C., Hill, D., Steptoe, K., & Brown, D. J. (2020). Sport performance interventions: Evaluating past strategies and providing future recommendations. *International Journal of Sport Psychology, 51*(6), 646. https://doi.org/10.7352/IJSP.2020.51.646

Mulder, M., & Winterton, J. (2017). 'Introduction'. In Mulder, M (Ed.), *Competence-based vocational and professional education: Bridging the worlds of work and education. Technical and vocational education and training: issues, concerns and prospects* (vol. 23; pp.361–380). Springer International Publishing AG.

National Wellbeing Initiative (2021). Creating a collaborative: How to build an industry-led initiative. Australian Government. National Mental Health Commission.

NCVER (n.d.-a). 'Competency'. *Glossary.* Accessed from https://www.asqa.gov.au/resources/glossary/c

Neumann, W. (1979). 'Educational responses to the concern for proficiency', in G. Grant, P. Elbow, T. Ewens, Z. Gamson, W. Koh li, W. Neumann, V. Olesen & D. Riesman, On Competence: A Critical Analysis of Competence-Based Reforms in Higher Education, Jossey-Bass, San Francisco, 1979, pp. 66–94. In Deakin University Course Development Centre (1994). *A Collection of Readings Related to Competency-Based Training.* Deakin University, Geelong. Accessed from https://eric.ed.gov/?id=ED384695 on 4 September 2023.

Noetel, M., Ciarrochi, J., Van Zanden, B., & Lonsdale, C. (2019). Mindfulness and acceptance approaches to sporting performance enhancement: A systematic review. *International Review of Sport and Exercise Psychology, 12*(1), 139–175.

Oades, L. G. (2017). WBL: The missing link in positive education. In M. A. White, G. R. Slemp, & A. S. Murray (Eds.), *Future directions in well-being: Education, organizations and policy* (pp. 169–173). Springer International Publishing/Springer Nature. https://doi.org/10.1007/978-3-319-56889-8_29

Oades, L. G., Jarden, A., Hou, H., Ozturk, C., Williams, P., R. Slemp, G., & Huang, L. (2021). Wellbeing literacy: A capability model for wellbeing science and practice. *International Journal of Environmental Research and Public Health, 18*(2), 719. https://doi.org/10.3390/ijerph18020719

Oades, L. G., Ozturk, C., Hou, H., & Slemp, G. R. (2020). WBL: A language-use capability relevant to wellbeing outcomes of positive psychology intervention. *The*

Journal of Positive Psychology, *15*(5), 696–700. https://doi.org/10.1080/17439760.2020.1789711

Pirsoul, T., Parmentier, M., Sovet, L., & Nils, F. (2023). Emotional intelligence and career-related outcomes: A meta-analysis. *Human Resource Management Review*, *33*(3), 100967. https://doi.org/10.1016/j.hrmr.2023.100967

Rammstedt, B., Lechner, C., & Danner, D. (2024. Beyond literacy: The incremental value of non-cognitive skill. In *OECD education working papers*, No. 311, OECD Publishing. https://doi.org/10.1787/7d4fe121-en.

Rusk, R. D., & Waters, L. E. (2013). Tracing the size, reach, impact, and breadth of positive psychology. *The Journal of Positive Psychology*, *8*(3), 207–221.

Safe Work Australia. (n.d.) https://www.safeworkaustralia.gov.au/safety-topic/managing-health-and-safety/mental-health/psychosocial-hazards

Santini, Z. I., Thygesen, L. C., Koyanagi, A., Stewart-Brown, S., Meilstrup, C., Nielsen, L., & Ekholm, O. (2022). Economics of mental wellbeing: A prospective study estimating associated productivity costs due to sickness absence from the workplace in Denmark. *Mental Health & Prevention*, *28*, 200247.

Smith, E. (2019). Apprenticeships and 'future work': Are we ready? *International Journal of Training and Development*, *23*(1), 69–88.

Steger, M. F. (2025). Regenerative positive psychology: A call to reorient wellbeing science to meet the realities of our world. *The Journal of Positive Psychology*, *20*(3), 373–396.

van de Weijer, M. P., de Vries, L. P., & Bartels, M. (2022). Happiness and well-being: The value and findings from genetic studies. In A. Tarkoni, D. Tarkoni, J. Harris, & N. Segal (Eds). *Twin research for everyone* (pp. 295–322). Academic Press. https://doi.org/10.1016/B978-0-12-821514-2.00016-7

Vocational Education and Training Qualification Reform Design Group. (2024). *Unlocking the potential of VET: Improving the relevance and transferability of Vocational Education and Training qualifications.* https://www.dewr.gov.au/skills-reform/resources/qualification-reform-design-group-initial-advice-skills-ministers

Waters, L., & Loton, D. (2019). SEARCH: A meta-framework and review of the field of positive education. *International Journal of Applied Positive Psychology*, *4*, 1–46.

Waters, L., & Loton, D. (2021). Tracing the growth, gaps, and characteristics in positive education science: A long-term, large-scale review of the field. *Frontiers in Psychology*, *12*, 774967.

Waters, L., & Strauss, G. (2016). Posttraumatic growth during unemployment: A qualitative examination of distress and positive transformation. *International Journal of Wellbeing*, *6*(1), 117–141. https://doi.org/10.5502/ijw.v6i1.441

Williams, M. (2019). *Developing twenty first century skills in VET.* International Specialised Skills Institute.

Wong, B., & Greenwood, K. (2023). The future of mental health at work is safety, community, and a healthy organizational culture. *Harvard Business Review*. https://hbr.org/2021/10/its-a-new-era-for-mental-health-at-work

8

EXPLORING AN INDIGENOUS APPROACH TO WELLBEING LITERACY THROUGH THE WORK OF ABORIGINAL COMMUNITY CONTROLLED HEALTH SERVICES

Emma Carlin, Shannon Cowdrey-Fong, Zaccariah Cox, Kristen Orazi, and Pat Dudgeon

Introduction

Wellbeing literacy refers to the vocabulary, knowledge, and language skills that can be deliberately employed to enhance or maintain one's or others' wellbeing (Oades et al., 2020). Wellbeing literacy is an emerging scholarly activity in positive psychology and positive education pedagogy. Researchers are excited by its potential for enhancing wellbeing, largely because wellbeing literacy is not considered an external 'intervention' but an internal 'language-based capability' (Hou et al., 2021). This capability consists of a set of skills and knowledges that individuals can draw on and use to empower their wellbeing. It is argued that developing such capabilities aligns with and strengthens health and wellbeing at the individual and community level (Hou et al., 2021). This chapter discusses the critical importance of wellbeing literacy initiatives for Aboriginal and Torres Strait Islander peoples in the colonial context of contemporary Australia. This chapter explains that for wellbeing literacy efforts to be acceptable and effective for Aboriginal and Torres Strait Islander people they must be culturally centred and responsive to community need.

Using a theoretical framework of social and emotional wellbeing (SEWB) (Gee et al., 2014), Aboriginal and Torres Strait Islander leaders, organisations, and communities have sought to optimise wellbeing literacy within their communities (Aboriginal Health Council of Western Australia, 2021). These efforts are strengths-based and responsive to the social, cultural, and political determinants of health that collectively shape Aboriginal and Torres Strait Islander people's experiences (Farnbach et al., 2017). This chapter explores the role of Aboriginal Community Controlled Health

DOI: 10.4324/9781003644293-8

Services (ACCHS) in designing and delivering wellbeing literacy initiatives by providing an example from the Kimberley Aboriginal Medical Services (KAMS).

This chapter illustrates how community-led strategies for improving Aboriginal and Torres Strait Islander people's SEWB broaden current conceptualisations of 'wellbeing literacy'. In an Aboriginal and Torres Strait Islander context, wellbeing literacy emphasises truth-telling, psycho-social education, raising self-awareness, improving self-care, and developing healthy coping strategies. Importantly, these efforts prioritise lived experience and shared cultural identity between facilitators and participants. In doing so, the relevancy and acceptability of these initiatives are strengthened, enhancing the health and wellbeing of Aboriginal and Torres Strait Islander peoples.

The Social and Emotional Wellbeing Framework

The Aboriginal-developed SEWB framework (Gee et al., 2014) positions an Aboriginal and Torres Strait Islander person's experience of health within historical, social, cultural, and political determinants, their individual life experiences, and the interconnectedness of their 'self' across the domains of Body, Mind, Family, Community, Culture, Country, and Spirit. The SEWB framework is often visualised and referred to as the SEWB wheel (Figure 8.1; Gee et al., 2014).

The SEWB framework identifies that SEWB is related to but broader than 'mental health' (Department of the Prime Minister and Cabinet, 2017) and the social determinants of health (Yearby, 2020). The SEWB framework provides conceptual guidance on risks and protective factors relating to Aboriginal and Torres Strait Islander SEWB (Table 8.1; Cox et al., 2022).

Aboriginal Community Controlled Health Services

ACCHS are primary health care services that are governed by a locally elected Aboriginal Board of Management and reflect Aboriginal and Torres Strait Islander peoples holistic understanding of health:

> *Health is not just the physical wellbeing of an individual but refers to the social, emotional and cultural wellbeing of the whole Community, in which each individual is able to achieve their full potential as a human being, thereby bringing about the total wellbeing of their community. It is a whole-of-life view and includes the cyclical concept of life-death-life.*
>
> (National Aboriginal Community Controlled Health Organisation, 2022)

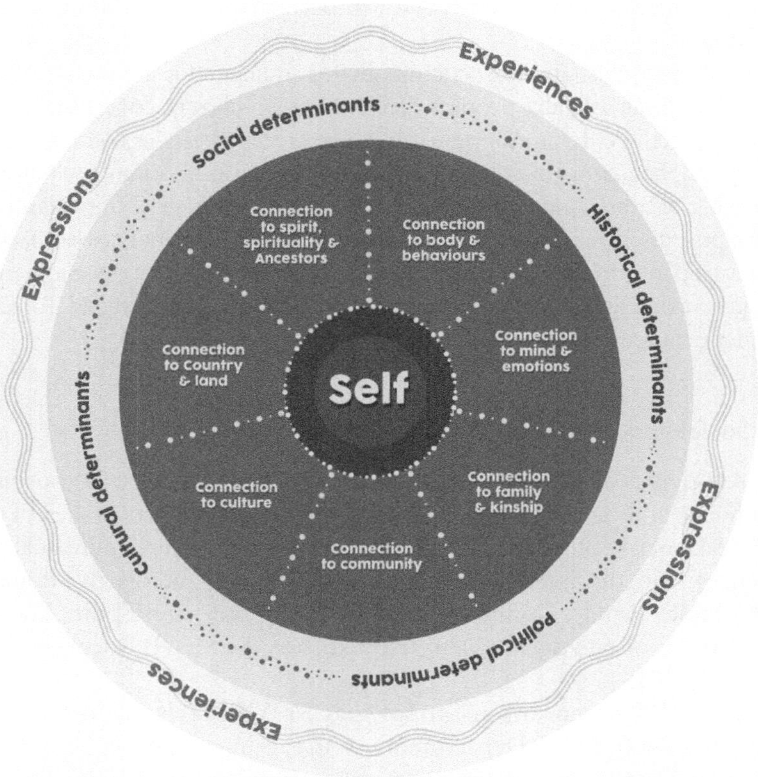

SEWB Diagram adapted from Gee et al., (2014)

FIGURE 8.1 Aboriginal and Torres Strait Islander model of social and emotional wellbeing.

Source: Working together: Aboriginal and Torres Strait Islander mental health and wellbeing principles and practice. 2nd ed. Reprinted under a CC BY license, with permission, original copyright 2013.

ACCHS are recognised as providing better health outcomes for Aboriginal and Torres Strait Islander people than mainstream health services (Panaretto et al., 2014). This demonstrates the importance of holistic and culturally secure care for Aboriginal and Torres Strait Islander people. Many ACCHS' have designated SEWB teams (Gupta et al., 2020). These teams work closely with clinical staff to support the holistic needs of Aboriginal and Torres Strait Islander people. SEWB teams provide culturally secure community development, psycho-social support, targeted interventions, and supported coordinated care (Aboriginal Health Council of Western Australia, 2021).

TABLE 8.1 An overview of risk and protective factors related to Aboriginal and Torres Strait Islander peoples social and emotional wellbeing

Domain	*Description*	*Positive/protective factors*	*Challenge/risk factors*
Connection to mind and emotions.	Includes mental health disorders and the importance of positive feelings and wellness.	Belonging. Mindfulness. Accessing services and supports. Truth-telling and treaty.	Threats to personal, family, community and cultural safety. Intergenerational trauma, experiences of racism. Misdiagnosis, and mislabelling of mental health conditions.
Connection to body and behaviours.	Considers the importance of body, health, spirit (e.g. Liyan), and mind being their best.	Sports and exercise. Hunting, gathering and other activities on Country. Traditional diets and medicines. Access to culturally safe services. Participation in cultural Lore and activities.	Smoking, alcohol, and drug misuse. Food insecurity and unhealthy foods. Chronic and communicable diseases. Exclusion from health, wellbeing, and other essential services.
Connection to family and kinship.	Includes family and kinship relations, systems of reciprocity and caring.	Learning family history. Sharing experiences with other Aboriginal peoples. Experiences of healthy relationships and family connections.	Removal of children from families. Incarceration. Family violence. Grief and loss. Lack of cultural education.
Connection to community.	Includes cultural structures of responsibility and obligation.	Self-determination and community control. Aboriginal mentors, role-models, advisors, and Elders. Cultural revitalisation and education. Participating in community activities and celebrations.	Social exclusion. Systemic racism. Lateral violence. Family feuding. Feelings of disconnection and isolation.

(Continued)

TABLE 8.1 (Continued)

Domain	*Description*	*Positive/protective factors*	*Challenge/risk factors*
Connection to culture.	Includes cultural expressions, activities, knowledges, and cultural identity.	Participating in cultural activities and knowledges to build cultural identity including ceremony, art, dance, song, storytelling, language learning.	Cultural genocide. Disconnection from language, Country and family. Stolen generation and assimilation policies.
Connection to land and Country.	Includes the experience of belonging to Country, a traditional spiritual connection to kin and culture through Country.	Returning to Country as a way of healing the body, mind, and spirit. Reconnecting with community and family on Country. Traditional medicine and diet. Land rights, Voice, Treaty.	Removal from Country. Dispossession of land. Destruction of sacred sites. Environmental degradation.
Connection to ancestors and spirituality	Includes traditional knowledges and belief systems.	Accepting traditional and evolving expressions of Indigeneity and spirituality that promote connection, and balance.	The impact of mission life and religion. Assimilation policies such as Stolen Generations. Symptoms of trauma such as misuse of drugs.

Source: *Social and emotional wellbeing: A welcome guide for the Aboriginal workforce.* Reprinted under a CC BY license, with permission, original copyright 2022.

Kimberley Aboriginal Medical Services

Established in 1986, KAMS is based in the far north of Western Australia on Rubibi (Broome), Yawuru Country, some 2000 km away from the state's capital city, Perth. KAMS is a peak body for the independent ACCHS across the Kimberley region. KAMS provides various services and support across the vast and remote region, including population health, SEWB, health promotion, information communication technology (including health informatics support), corporate services, accredited health worker training and education, research, and renal services. KAMS also operate holistic primary health care clinics in the very remote Aboriginal communities of Balgo, Billiluna, Mulan, Beagle Bay, and Bidyadanga.

KAMS recognises that Aboriginal residents of the Kimberley experience a range of health and SEWB outcome disparities that stem from colonisation, historical and contemporary trauma, structural racism, and other social determinants of health. Many Aboriginal people across the Kimberley face a high burden of disease (Western Australian Country Health Service, 2018). They are overrepresented in mental health, self harm and suicide data and are move likely to experience high rates of overrepresentation of mental health disorders (Carlin et al., 2022) and suicide and self-harming statistics (McPhee et al., 2021), and experience high rates of violence, incarceration, and child removals (Australian Institute of Health and Welfare, 2023; Dudgeon et al., 2021). There is limited availability of health and wellbeing services across the Kimberley, particularly psycho-social or therapeutic services (Carlin et al., 2022; Cox et al., 2023).

Kimberley, Empowerment, Healing, and Leadership Program

Kimberley Empowerment, Healing, and Leadership Program (KEHLP) was informed by the 'Hear Our Voices' report that was published in 2011. 'Hear Our Voices' highlighted the high rates and devastating impact of suicide for Aboriginal people across the Kimberley. Community consultations in Broome, Halls Creek, and the remote community of Beagle Bay revealed widespread distress and the need for a culturally appropriate and holistic approach to suicide prevention (Dudgeon et al., 2012). The report recommended an Aboriginal-led Empowerment, Healing, and Leadership Program to enhance local capabilities and address the determinants impacting on individual and community wellbeing (Dudgeon et al., 2012). This led to the development of the KEHLP, which focuses on personal empowerment, positive family relations, and community strengthening through culturally tailored psycho-social education and behaviour change initiatives. The KEHLP is delivered by Aboriginal and Torres Strait Islander facilitators for Aboriginal and Torres Strait Islander participants and typically involves 8–10 days of active participation. The KEHLP has been delivered by the KAMS SEWB team since 2012. KAMS has full ownership and copyright of the program and delivers across Kimberley towns, remote communities and in the West Kimberley Regional Correctional Facility (Table 8.2).

TABLE 8.2 Overview of Kimberley empowerment and healing program modules

Self module	*Family module*	*Community module*

• Creating safety
• Truth-telling
• Exploring a sense of self
• Self-care and the protective value of Culture
• Setting boundaries
• Empowerment: responsibility, forgiveness, action/ reaction, acceptance, self-worth
	• Family and Kinship
	  • Trauma
	  • Breakdown
	  • Recovery and revitalisation
	• Building Communication skills
	• Managing conflict respectfully
	• Parenting – healing the past to build the future
		• Community development history
		• Community leadership examples and qualities
		• Goal setting and, self-determination and community empowerment

Participant Profile

An evaluation of the KEHLP in 2020 (Carlin et al., 2020) found three relatively distinct groups of Aboriginal people participated in the KEHLP.

1 Self-referred: Aboriginal people who heard about the KEHLP and identified it as a learning opportunity:
2 Professionally motivated: Aboriginal professionals who attended the KEHLP as part of a workplace opportunity:
3 Service referred: Aboriginal people who were encouraged to enrol by a service provider:

All groups of participants identified wanting to learn new knowledge and skills through the KEHLP. These were focussed on improving interpersonal relationships, particularly parenting relationships, better-regulating emotions, and increasing their capacity to assist their community to be proud and self-determined.

Participant and Facilitator Reflections: Key Themes

The evaluation of the KEHLP (Carlin et al., 2020) analysed existing participant feedback mechanisms and interviewed previous participants and facilitators to understand key approaches and outcomes associated with the KEHLP.

Truth-telling

The evaluation found that participants often expressed limited formal knowledge of major policies impacting Aboriginal and Torres Strait Islander peoples. Facilitators noted how starting the KEHLP with this history provided a platform for participants to understand and reflect on their current context, experiences, and behaviours.

> *KEHLP helps our people understand and be able to explore ways that they can change their behaviour, but, in that process, we help them understand where they are. It could be historical events that have taken place, colonisation and the transgenerational trauma, learned behaviours. So, we look at lots of aspects to help a person understand who and where they are. Especially with our Aboriginal people who have never ever give thought to who they are and what their strengths are.*
> (Facilitator 06, female)

> [Participants have said] *"I didn't know that." And that's when you know it's working. This is starting to kick in, it's starting to make sense. "Yeah, I do that." "I really didn't know why I did it." "I'm angry. I don't know why I'm angry." They just know that something's happened. They just don't know what, and to the extent that it's happened. And that's when we talk about*

our transgenerational stuff. Which plays a huge part. We know something happened. But to the actual details – how it happened, when it happened. When you ask these young people about the 67 Referendum. That's only 52 years ago. Nobody hardly knows about it. Such a significant date. My mob want to know this stuff. If you don't know it, you're not going to know how to heal.

(Facilitator 02, male)

Participants emphasised the KEHLP's focus on teaching Aboriginal political history and truth-telling as important. They described it as 'surprising', 'eye-opening', and 'challenging'. These participants reported feeling that the 'true' history of Australia had not been taught in schools, and many Aboriginal people did not have ready access to this information growing up. Access to this information was seen as fundamental to identity, empowerment, and healing concepts.

It's about understanding what happened to be able to deal with it better and to know how you can understand yourself better and, move forward in your life, and understand the system.

(Facilitator 05, male)

Lived Experience

The evaluation described the content, delivery, and outcomes of KEHLP as deeply situated in the Aboriginal lived experience. Having an Aboriginal KEHLP facilitator was seen as fundamental in the knowledge exchange and learning.

Yes definitely [KEHLP has to be delivered] by an Aboriginal person, because they understand too. They go through traumas, and we understand each other. So, yes, it has to be delivered by Aboriginal people.

(Participant 04, female)

Some participant feedback emphasised the 'triggering' or 'hard' nature of the program. Several participants reflected on the course raising their own or their family's stolen generation history and the other participants talked more broadly about the course bring back 'troubling' memories or thoughts. For most participants the 'confronting' or 'hard' nature of the course was balanced by the 'healing' and 'empowerment' that came with the discussions:

It was just a group of us boys and us boys, we turned to men after that course. It was hard stuff to talk about but we ended up talking about everything and we empowered each other and we were behind each other.

(Participant 03, male)

It was the best thing, to be listened to and encouraged.

(Self-survey post course).

Exploration of Self and Self-capabilities

Several participants offered examples of how the KEHLP not only increased their knowledge of SEWB but provided them with skills and tools to facilitate them making positive changes to their own lives:

> *It's weird now after doing that course and the relationship that I have with dad. Even though we're still a bit iffy here and there, but we're comfortable. He wasn't there for the majority of my life and I just don't understand why. Why wasn't he there? But that's me as a kid. I didn't understand. Adults, I guess they go through things. There's probably answers I'll never get but it was like, well, I can't keep running back to the past. I can either build something out of this or just keep having a hatred*
>
> (Participant 03, male)

> *I have achieved courage, knowledge and confidence. And only I can make change to move forward*
>
> (Self-survey post course)

> *I got pregnant at 15, had my first child at 16. So, we had three by the time I was 21. Because we were quite young, he would still be going out drinking, coming back to the house, making noise, cooking things and everything, and we've got three kids. So, then I put in a boundary to say that, "If you are going to go drinking, and you're drunk, you need to be able to stay somewhere else and not come home". So, obviously, it didn't work straight away, but over time, that's what he started to do, and then he didn't want to drink anymore because he didn't want to sleep at someone else's house...That was one of the things that I learned* [from KEHLP] *about boundaries, if I set them and stick to it, then eventually it works*
>
> (Participant 11, female)

Social and Emotional Wellbeing Literacy

Traditional definitions of wellbeing literacy emphasise using language to describe, understand, and enhance wellbeing. Language is defined as 'multimodal symbolic systems, which may be alphabetic, pictorial, visual, aural or combinations of these' (Hou et al., 2021). To this effect literacy is understood to be more than reading and writing, and includes listening, viewing, speaking, and creating. The SEWB framework prioritises the interconnectedness of a person with their Culture, Country, identity, history, and community. SEWB knowledge is often shared and acquired through language as defined above, direct experience (e.g. being on Country, hunting, collecting bush foods) and observation (e.g. watching Elders prepare bush medicines). The KEHLP can largely be defined as having: 1. cognitive aspects focusing on wellbeing understanding and awareness, 2. experiential and existential aspects and 3. practical applications of wellbeing in everyday life. This approach to defining 'social and emotional wellbeing literacy' is aligned to but expands on the definitions of wellbeing literacy.

Using this broadened definition of literacy, we have explored the five components of wellbeing literacy outlined by Hou et al. (2021) (Table 8.3). Each of these elements plays a crucial role in fostering wellbeing by enabling individuals to understand, express, and manage their wellbeing in various contexts. However, in recognising the diverse and multifaceted nature of wellbeing, we have added an additional SEWB descriptor to each component. This SEWB descriptor is specifically designed to centre Aboriginal and Torres Strait Islander histories, cultures, and identities and reflect on the key messages of the KEHLP program that was discussed in detail. Including the SEWB descriptor emphasises the importance of

TABLE 8.3 Five-component model of wellbeing literacy

Component	*Wellbeing literacy*	*Social and emotional wellbeing literacy*
Vocabulary and knowledge about wellbeing.	Words and basic facts about wellbeing.	Understanding that colonisation and subsequent policies and practices of marginalisation have impacted the wellbeing of Aboriginal peoples and communities. Generating personal, community, and national narratives of resilience and pride.
Comprehension of multimodal text related to wellbeing.	Reading, listening and viewing about, and for, wellbeing.	Learning or strengthening cultural narratives and practices, traditional knowledges, and personal behaviours.
Composition of multimodal text related to wellbeing.	Writing, speaking, and creating about, and for, wellbeing.	Attending community programs, being on-Country, participating in Ceremony, sitting with Elders.
Context awareness and adaptability.	Awareness of and adapting language according to the specific context.	Ability to engage in and share expressions and experiences of wellbeing with family and community.
Intentionality for wellbeing.	Habit of intentionally using language to maintain or improve wellbeing of self or others.	Practice of promoting individual and collective healing through knowing, being and doing of wellbeing.

positionality – the recognition of one's social, cultural, and historical context – in building, enhancing, or sustaining wellbeing capabilities.

By incorporating the SEWB descriptors into the five components of wellbeing literacy, we acknowledge the critical importance of Aboriginal and Torres Strait Islander perspectives in understanding and fostering wellbeing. This approach not only enriches the concept of wellbeing literacy but also highlights the need for a more inclusive and culturally sensitive approach to wellbeing literacy that recognises the significance of positionality in shaping wellbeing outcomes.

Conclusion

We argue that wellbeing literacy has great potential relevance for Aboriginal and Torres Strait Islander peoples. However, its current definition and descriptors are not inclusive of their unique needs, experiences, and expressions of wellbeing literacy. We consider SEWB literacy a more appropriate framing for Aboriginal and Torres Strait Islander peoples. We have explored how this approach is already occurring across Australia in countless Aboriginal community-controlled health services and other self-determined spaces and provided a deep dive into the Kimberley Healing and Empowerment Program. Fostering culturally secure and community-controlled approaches to building wellbeing capabilities for Aboriginal and Torres Strait Islander peoples remains a national priority.

References

Aboriginal Health Council of Western Australia. (2021). *Social and emotional wellbeing service model.* AHCWA. https://timhwb.org.au/wp-content/uploads/2021/05/AHCWA_SEWBReport_JAN21.pdf

Australian Institute of Health and Welfare. (2023). *Aboriginal and Torres Strait Islander health performance framework: Report July 2023.* AIHW. https://indigenoushpf.gov.au/report-overview/overview/summary-report

Carlin, E., Cox, Z., Orazi, K., Derry, K. L., & Dudgeon, P. (2022). Exploring mental health presentations in remote aboriginal community controlled health services in the Kimberley region of Western Australia using an audit and file reviews. *International Journal of Environmental Research and Public Health, 19*(3), 1743. https://doi.org/10.3390/ijerph19031743

Carlin, E., Seear, K., Spry, E., & Ferrari, K. (2020). *Evaluation of the Kimberley empowerment healing and leadership program.* Rural Clinical School, University of Western Australia. https://research-repository.uwa.edu.au/en/publications/kimberley-empowerment-healing-and-leadership-program-evaluation

Cox, Z., Carlin, E., Derry, K., Cox, A.-R., Ansey, L., Cox, D., & Dudgeon, P. (2022). *Social and emotional wellbeing: A welcome guide for the Aboriginal workforce.* https://timhwb.org.au/wp-content/uploads/2022/09/KAMS-SEWB-MANUAL-7.pdf

Cox, Z., Carlin, E., Derry, K., & Dudgeon, P. (2023). 'It's us, or maybe no one': Yarning with aboriginal social and emotional wellbeing workers from the Kimberley region of Western Australia. *Journal of the Australian Indigenous HealthInfoNet, 4*(2), 2.

Department of the Prime Minister and Cabinet. (2017). *The national strategic framework for Aboriginal and Torres Strait Islander mental health and SEWB*. Commonwealth of Australia. https://www.niaa.gov.au/sites/default/files/publications/mhsewb-framework_0.pdf

Dudgeon, P., Blustein, S., Bray, A., Calma, T., McPhee, R., & Ring, I. (2021). Connection between family, kinship and social and emotional wellbeing. In P. Dudgeon, H. Milroy, & R. Walker (Eds.), *Produced for the indigenous mental and suicide prevention clearinghouse*. AIHW.

Dudgeon, P., Cox, K., D'Anna, D., Dunkley, C., Hams, K., Kelly, K., Scrine, C., & Walker, R. (2012). *Hear our voices: Community consultations for the development of an empowerment, healing and leadership program for Aboriginal people living in the Kimberley, Western Australia*. Centre for Research Excellence, Aboriginal Health & Wellbeing.

Farnbach, S., Eades, A.-M., Fernando, J., Gwynn, J., Glozier, N., & Hackett, M. (2017). The quality of Australian indigenous primary health care research focusing on social and emotional wellbeing: A systematic review. *Public Health Research & Practice*, *27*(4), 1–9.

Gee, G., Dudgeon, P., Schultz, C., Hart, A., & Kelly, K. (2014). Aboriginal and Torres Strait Islander social and emotional wellbeing. In P. Dudgeon, H. Milroy, & R. Walker (Eds.), *Working together: Aboriginal and Torres Strait Islander mental health and wellbeing principles and practice* (pp. 55–68). Department of Prime Minister and Cabinet.

Gupta, H., Tari-Keresztes, N., Stephens, D., Smith, J. A., Sultan, E., & Lloyd, S. (2020). A scoping review about social and emotional wellbeing programs and services targeting Aboriginal and Torres Strait Islander young people in Australia: Understanding the principles guiding promising practice. *BMC Public Health*, *20*(1), 1625. https://doi.org/10.1186/s12889-020-09730-1

Hou, H., Chin, T.-C., Slemp, G. R., & Oades, L. G. (2021). Wellbeing literacy: Conceptualisation, measurement, and preliminary empirical findings from students, parents and school staff. *International Journal of Environmental Research and Public Health*, *18*(4), 1485. https://doi.org/10.3390/ijerph18041485

McPhee, R., Carlin, E., Seear, K., Carrington-Jones, P., Sheil, B., Lawrence, D., & Dudgeon, P. (2021). Unacceptably high: An audit of Kimberley self-harm data 2014–2018. *Australasian Psychiatry*. https://doi.org/10.1177/10398562211010790

National Aboriginal Community Controlled Health Organisation. (2022). *Aboriginal definitions of health*. NACCHO. https://www.naccho.org.au/acchos/#:~:text="%E2%80%9DAboriginal%20health%E2%80%9D%20means%20not,well%2Dbeing%20of%20their%20Community

Oades, L. G., Ozturk, C., Hou, H., & Slemp, G. R. (2020). Wellbeing literacy: A language-use capability relevant to wellbeing outcomes of positive psychology intervention. *The Journal of Positive Psychology*, *15*(5), 696–700.

Panaretto, K. S., Wenitong, M., Button, S., & Ring, I. T. (2014). Aboriginal community controlled health services: Leading the way in primary care. *Medical Journal of Australia*, *200*(11), 649–652.

Western Australian Country Health Service. (2018). *Kimberley Health profile*. WACHS. https://www.wacountry.health.wa.gov.au/~/media/WACHS/Documents/About-us/Publications/Health-profiles-and-service-plans/Kimberley_Health_Profile_2018.pdf

Yearby, R. (2020). Structural racism and health disparities: Reconfiguring the social determinants of health framework to include the root cause. *Journal of Law, Medicine and Ethics*, *48*(3), 518–526.

9

MEASURING AND STUDYING WELLBEING LITERACY

Research and Methodological Horizons

Tyler Pacheco, Joël Gagnon, and Simon Coulombe

Measurement and empirical research are key ingredients to knowledge development. With wellbeing literacy theory's recent conceptualisation in 2017, identifying ways of measuring the concept has become increasingly important. However, like any other theory in infancy, wellbeing literacy is encountering measurement challenges, as well as several opportunities to empirically examine it. Part one of this chapter provides a narrative review of how wellbeing literacy has been empirically explored. Mainly, we discuss the Wellbeing Literacy 6-item (Well-Lit 6) scale's validation, correlates, and antecedents, as well as two other emerging measurement approaches. Building on this review, part two highlights prospective research ideas to stimulate future empirical research.

Wellbeing Literacy Measures and Correlates

The Well-Lit 6 Scale

As the first quantitative method of measuring wellbeing literacy, the Well-Lit 6 scale was developed by Hou et al. (2021) in English and then translated by other researchers into Brazilian Portuguese (Romano et al., submitted), Chinese (Jia et al., 2024), and Canadian French (Gagnon et al., in preparation). It is a self-report scale containing six items (Table 9.1). Each item corresponds to wellbeing literacy's working definition and measures respondents' perception of their skills on each of the concept's five core aspects: (1) vocabulary, (2) knowledge, (3) skills, (4) comprehension skills, (5) the ability to compose language, and (6) the ability to adjust language depending on

DOI: 10.4324/9781003644293-9

TABLE 9.1 The Well-Lit 6 scale (Hou et al., 2021)

Item #	*Item*
1	"I have many words I can think of to communicate about wellbeing"
2	"I know a lot about wellbeing"
3	"I know how to improve my wellbeing"
4	"I have the skills to understand information about wellbeing"
5	"I have the skills to express myself about wellbeing"
6	"I can communicate about wellbeing in multiple ways (e.g., writing, listening, drawing) to suit the needs of my audience"

context or audience (Hou et al., 2021). There have been six (un)published articles reporting tests of the Well-Lit 6's psychometric properties in diverse countries (Australia, Brazil, Canada, China) and populations (students, parents, employees, physical exercise practitioners, adults with mental health and/or addiction concerns, military academy cadets) (Table 9.2).

Reliability, Structural Validity, and Invariance

Every study provided the Well-Lit 6's psychometric properties using reliability tests (e.g., internal, homogenous, split-half) and structural validity (e.g., exploratory and confirmatory factor analysis). These articles supported Hou et al.'s (2021) conclusion of the scale's unidimensionality. Only one study tested for the invariance of the scale's structure across countries (Brazil, Canada) and genders (Romano et al., in press). Based on recommendations that Cronbach's alphas above .90 indicate item redundancy (e.g., Tavakol & Dennick, 2011), findings from several studies suggest varying degrees of concern. Four studies (Gagnon et al., in preparation; Hou et al., 2021; Romano et al., in press; Tse et al., in preparation) reported alphas of .91–.93, while Romano et al. (submitted) reported .95, and Jia et al. (2024) reported alphas of .98–.99, raising significant concerns. Two articles reported test-retest reliability, which was moderate over eight months (intraclass correlation coefficient [ICC] = .70) (Gagnon et al., in preparation) and high over three months (ICC = .91) (Tse et al., in preparation).

Convergent and Discriminant Validity

Six studies tested the Well-Lit 6's convergent and discriminant validity (Hou et al., 2021; Jia et al., 2024; Romano et al., submitted; Tse et al., in preparation). Across all the correlated external constructs (e.g., resilience, mindfulness, distress), wellbeing literacy had an absolute r-value of .17–.70. With recommendations that $r \geq .30$ and $<.80$ indicate adequate convergent and

TABLE 9.2 Well-Lit 6 reliability and validity results

Reference	*Reliability tests*		*Validity tests*					
	Reliability[a]	*Test-retest reliability*	*Structural validity*[b]	*Invariance*	*Convergent/ discriminant validity*	*Predictive validity*	*Incremental validity*	*Item response theory*[c]
Published Articles								
Jia et al. (2024)	✓		✓		✓		✓	✓
Hou et al. (2021)	✓		✓		✓		✓	
Unpublished Articles								
Romano et al. (submitted)	✓		✓		✓			✓
Gagnon et al. (in preparation)	✓	✓	✓					
Romano et al. (in press)	✓		✓	✓				
Tse et al. (in preparation)	✓	✓	✓		✓	✓		✓

Note. All Well-Lit 6 reliability and validity test results were interpreted by the authors to be satisfactory.

[a] Includes internal, homogenous, and split-half reliability and consistency.

[b] Includes internal structure.

[c] Includes item endorsement, infit/outfit, item difficulty invariance, theta level recovery, and discrimination (also distinguishing those with low trait levels).

discriminant (e.g., Brown, 2015) validity, respectively, it is observed that while some correlations for wellbeing literacy fell below the recommended threshold for ***convergent*** validity, most demonstrated adequate ***discriminant*** validity. Through an exploratory factor analysis that included the Well-Lit 6 alongside other related but distinct constructs (e.g., life satisfaction, distress, resilience), Hou et al. (2021) also concluded that the scale demonstrated adequate discriminant validity.

Predictive and Incremental Validity

One article has explored the scale's predictive validity, and two articles have explored its incremental validity. Tse et al. (in preparation) report that wellbeing literacy significantly predicted distress, flourishing, and mental health recovery at two later timepoints, while controlling for baseline levels of the predicted variable, thus indicating good predictive validity. Both articles testing the Well-Lit 6's incremental validity show that the addition of the scale predicted a significant, although small amount, of variance in wellbeing ($\Delta R2$ ranging from .003 to .03). This was after accounting for sociodemographic-related variables (e.g., gender, marital status, family parenting style) and other predictors such as emotion regulation and resilience (Hou et al., 2021; Jia et al., 2024). To better determine the scale's incremental validity and its uniqueness, future research should account for additional constructs such as mental health literacy (MHL) (i.e., knowledge regarding the recognition, management and prevention of mental health concerns; Furnham & Swami, 2018).

Item Response Theory

Three articles used Item Response Theory to validate the Well-Lit 6. The analysis revealed moderate variation in item difficulty across the answer scale range, indicating that the items are generally easy for participants to endorse (Romano et al., submitted). In Romano et al.'s (submitted) study, the scale demonstrated particular sensitivity for individuals with low to moderate wellbeing literacy, whereas Tse et al.'s (in preparation) study found that the scale tended to favour respondents with lower wellbeing literacy. These findings suggest potential limitations in the Well-Lit 6's ability to accurately assess individuals with high wellbeing literacy. No significant differences in item difficulty were found between genders (men, women), suggesting measurement invariance (Romano et al., submitted).

Correlates and Antecedents

Wellbeing literacy (via the Well-Lit 6) was found to be related to several wellbeing indicators. These relationships with wellbeing indicators have been found across the same as well as different wellbeing scales, and across diverse samples (students, parents, employees, college and military undergraduate academics, physical exercise practitioners, the public) and countries (China, Canada, Brazil, Australia). Wellbeing literacy has been negatively related to distress, depression, anxiety, stress, loneliness, and expression inhibition, and positively related to emotional, social, psychological, and subjective wellbeing, life satisfaction, emotional regulation, resilience, flourishing, recovery, mindfulness, as well autonomy, relationship and competence needs' satisfaction (Guo et al., 2024; Hou et al., 2021; Jia et al., 2024; Romano et al., submitted; Tse et al., in preparation).

Other Measurement Options

Chng et al. (2022) developed an identification task to assess participants' ability to differentiate mental health from wellbeing indicators. Unlike the Well-Lit 6, which relies on self-assessment, this task directly tests wellbeing literacy by asking participants to classify 20 expressions (e.g., "Fatigue," "Feeling happy") as mental health or wellbeing (Task 1) or both (Task 2). Results indicated that participants could distinguish between mental health and wellbeing in Task 1 but often categorised expressions as both in Task 2, raising questions about whether the public views the distinction between the two concepts as meaningful.

While valuable, this method has notable limitations. The task primarily focuses on participants' knowledge of wellbeing indicators, omitting other critical elements of wellbeing literacy, such as the ability to compose wellbeing-related language. This narrower focus means that the identification task does not fully capture the multidimensional nature of wellbeing literacy. Nevertheless, Chng et al. (2022) observed that older age, male gender, and part-time education were associated with lower wellbeing literacy, while being partnered or having a mental health diagnosis was linked to higher levels, though these effects were relatively small. Burns et al.'s (2024) international study with the same measurement approach, however, suggests that there were no sociodemographic or between-nation (Australia, the UK, Singapore, South Africa, Malaysia) differences in wellbeing literacy levels. These findings should be interpreted cautiously given the above-mentioned limitations.

Waters et al. (2022) adapted the "Draw and Write" technique to be child-centric, in which children draw pictures in response to questions (e.g., "Draw a picture showing your idea of wellbeing," p. 99) and provide a verbal description. The drawing is the main data source, with the description supporting the interpretation. Using visual narrative analysis, Waters et al. (2022) analysed three dimensions within pictures: main subject (e.g., person, pet), elements used (e.g., colour, location), and context/background (e.g., nature, park). This approach highlights arts-based research's adaptability and potential to engage participants in exploring wellbeing while generating personally relevant data.

Core Insights

Whereas the Well-Lit 6 is considered reliable and valid, several areas for improvement should be addressed. The scale narrowly measures wellbeing literacy, with one item for each core aspect. This limited scope may contribute to the high Cronbach's alphas reported in studies (e.g., Jia et al., 2024; Romano et al., submitted). When items are too homogeneous, a scale may fail to fully capture the construct, potentially affecting construct validity. Future research should validate the scale in non-western contexts and further explore its test-retest reliability, invariance, predictive, and incremental validity. Existing methods either (a) do not measure wellbeing literacy accurately, or (b) were used in a single context. Our review also suggests that a few qualitative methods investigating wellbeing literacy are emerging, although they are underdeveloped. When deciding on which method to use to measure wellbeing literacy, researchers should consider the (1) purpose of their study (e.g., strictly measuring wellbeing literacy levels versus evaluating interventions aiming to bolster such literacy) and (2) study elements (e.g., context, participants) that could affect the method's efficacy. Insights from Part One have led to positing several research challenges that should be addressed in the future.

Research Challenges

Measurement Improvement and Diversification

The Well-Lit 6's limitation in capturing the full scope of wellbeing literacy is compounded by its focus on static knowledge, overlooking the dynamic interplay between environmental conditions and individual agency central to the concept of human capability (Oades et al., 2021). This reflects the capability approach (Nussbaum, 2011; Sen, 1993), which emphasises that wellbeing is not simply about resources or predefined outcomes but about what individuals can achieve in their lives (Oades et al., 2021). Current measures, like the Well-Lit 6, fail to reflect these dynamic, personal yet interactional and collectively situated processes. Future research should incorporate participatory methods to better align wellbeing literacy assessment with the capability approach's emphasis on individual agency (Oades et al., 2021).

An innovative method for developing scales involves using natural language processing (NLP) techniques (e.g., latent semantic analysis; LSA). This approach allows for open-ended questions instead of traditional closed-ended ones (Kjell et al., 2019) providing a richer, subjective understanding of wellbeing. For example, an LSA-based method might ask respondents to list the words they use for wellbeing. These open-ended responses are then analysed using NLP, allowing to quantify complex mental states, which may be oversimplified by traditional numerical scales (e.g., Likert scale) (Kjell et al., 2019).

Although few studies have used NLP techniques like LSA for measurement, early results quantifying mental health and wellbeing (although not explicitly focused on wellbeing literacy) show promising results (Kjell et al., 2019).

LSA can also be applied to tackle issues like scale redundancy and construct proliferation by analysing semantic overlap between items. LSA can help identify when items are too similar in meaning, allowing researchers to refine scales, reduce duplication, and better differentiate between constructs (e.g., Rosenbusch et al., 2020). Future studies could build on this approach to help establish the boundaries of scales measuring closely related constructs, such as wellbeing literacy and positive MHL (see Cresswell-Smith et al. [2023]'s review).

Correlations with Key Constructs from Other Theories across Contexts and Life Stages

Discussed earlier in this chapter, wellbeing literacy (via the Well-Lit 6) has been correlated with several negative and positive wellbeing constructs. Still underexplored, however, is how wellbeing literacy is related to (a) wellbeing constructs cross-culturally and in different age groups and (b) other significant constructs important to foundational wellbeing theories. Addressing both literature gaps, we propose adding a wellbeing literacy measure to large-scale surveys conducted by governmental bodies and organisations (e.g., Gallup, World Health Organisation). Including the measure will aid researchers in better understanding how wellbeing literacy relates to several concepts (e.g., GPA, health care utilisation, employee engagement) important to other disciplines (e.g., education, public health, management). Practically, between- and within-nation differences can be used to tailor culturally, age- and setting-relevant wellbeing (literacy) interventions that better support those with lower literacy scores.

Uncovering Moderating and Mediating Roles

Given its origins in positive psychology, where many interventions are mediated by language use, wellbeing literacy has been proposed as a pathway through which environmental wellbeing opportunities or barriers, such as environmental factors and programs/interventions, translate into tangible wellbeing outcomes (Oades et al., 2021). As the first time we have seen wellbeing literacy tested as a moderator or mediator, we summarise here preliminary cross-sectional findings from a Canadian survey with over 1,500 adult workers. This survey investigated whether wellbeing literacy (via the Well-Lit 6) serves as a mediator or a moderator in workplace factors' (e.g., psychological demands, recognition, autonomy, managerial/coworker supports) associations with wellbeing indicators (burnout, thriving at work). Our findings (yet to be published) indicate that while wellbeing literacy does not moderate these associations, it does mediate them. Although these results are valuable, further research employing experimental designs as well as diverse real-life program evaluation approaches (e.g., adapted study design, Biron et al., 2018) is essential to fully understand wellbeing literacy's complexities and effects.

Intercultural Relevance

When conducting cross-cultural research on wellbeing literacy, researchers should be mindful of how wellbeing is conceptualised when (1) assessing whether the Well-Lit 6 can measure wellbeing literacy consistently across cultures, (2) comparing wellbeing literacy scores across cultural groups, and (3) adapting the Well-Lit 6 to capture cultural nuances. Regarding the first consideration, only one article (Romano et al., in press) has demonstrated the Well-Lit 6's invariance in diverse communities (Brazilian, French Canadian). Researchers should investigate invariance between other cultural groups. Regarding the second consideration, it may be of interest to detect wellbeing literacy differences across countries. Although such work has been attempted by Burns et al. (2024), the limitations we listed above affect their work's conclusions. Regarding the third consideration, it may be of interest to modify the Well-Lit 6 to explore culturally specific ways of comprehending, composing, and communicating wellbeing concepts. This may include adapting the concepts within the items (beyond linguistic translation) to represent regions' wellbeing conceptualisations or providing some examples in items to represent culturally relevant mediums used to communicate wellbeing concepts (e.g., Javanese shadow puppets; Williams et al., 2018).

Big Data and Population Wellbeing Literacy Indicators

With social media and advancements in artificial intelligence, posts on platforms like X (formerly Twitter) offer rich big data for exploring wellbeing literacy in large populations. For example, Lien et al. (2024) used machine learning to analyse X content, categorising posts into MHL facets and tracking users' MHL scores over time. This approach revealed how recognising mental illness (one aspect of MHL) influenced attitudes toward seeking mental health services. Researchers could adopt a similar method to explore variations in wellbeing literacy levels across populations based on posts aggregated by geographical locations (e.g., country, region, state), as well as its association with relevant community-level indicators (e.g., disease rates). Leximancer (Leximancer, n.d.; Ward et al., 2014), a text mining software using nonlinear dynamics and machine learning, can extract concepts from various sources related to wellbeing (e.g., government policies, social media posts). It generates a concept map showing key themes, as well as their prevalence and relationships. Researchers can interpret this map to identify recurring themes and connections within wellbeing vocabulary. Additionally, large language models in artificial intelligence (e.g., ChatGPT, Claude) can analyse similar documents to assess similarities and differences in how wellbeing and wellbeing literacy are discussed across contexts.

Broadening Methodological Designs

When developing new methods to understand better and improve wellbeing literacy, researchers are encouraged to consider the construct's context-specific and multimodal nature. Like Waters et al.'s (2022) drawing method, others may adapt art-based research designs to examine and bolster wellbeing literacy. For teenagers in school, writing monologues or creating theatre performances to showcase their understanding of wellbeing can be beneficial, as these methods not only strengthen their wellbeing literacy but also serve as creative avenues for exploring this concept; similarly, other approaches can be adapted to better investigate wellbeing literacy in older populations in specific contexts (e.g., workplaces, retirement homes). Photovoice (i.e., an adaptable method where people use cameras to identify, represent, and enhance their community; Wang & Burris, 1997), in particular, has been used across several disciplines (e.g., community psychology, education, social work) to study wellbeing. Photovoice's efficacy has particularly been useful in understanding and promoting diverse adults' wellbeing (e.g., see Cabassa et al., 2013). Such an approach seems particularly beneficial for those unable to communicate about wellbeing verbally but can do so through other modalities. Adopting a participatory action research approach (i.e., involving those experiencing issues in participation and leadership) may enhance the success of using arts-based approaches to assess wellbeing literacy, contrasting with traditional post-positivist methods (Nelson & Evans, 2014).

Concluding Remark

Given these complex methodological challenges, researchers should combine the expertise and tools of diverse disciplines (e.g., education, social work, psychology, management, public health, computer science) to support wellbeing literacy research's flourishing. Cross-disciplinary fertilisation is believed to strengthen what we know about wellbeing literacy and increase its measurement and practical applications.

Glossary

Reliability The degree to which a measure produces identical results under equal conditions, whether over time (test-retest), across raters (inter-rater), or in different contexts.

Validity The degree to which a measure accurately captures the intended construct and supports its intended interpretations and uses.

Test-retest reliability Test results' consistency over time, determined by administering the same measure to the same participants at two timepoints and assessing their scores' similarity.

Structural validity The extent to which a measure's structure aligns with the construct's theoretical dimensions it aims to measure.

Invariance A measure's ability to retain the same underlying structure, meaning, and relationships across diverse groups or conditions, ensuring comparability of results.
Convergent validity A form of construct validity that evaluates whether a measure correlates strongly with other instruments/methods measuring the same construct.
Discriminant validity A form of construct validity that examines whether a measure is sufficiently distinct from measures of theoretically unrelated constructs.
Predictive validity The extent to which a measure predicts outcomes it is expected to predict.
Incremental validity The extent to which a measure contributes unique and meaningful explanatory power beyond what is accounted for by existing measures or variables.
Item response theory (IRT) A statistical framework used to understand how people respond to a measure's items based on their underlying abilities/traits. It helps determine which items are easier or harder, and how well they measure what the test is trying to assess.

References

Biron, C., Parent-Lamarche, A., Ivers, H., & Baril-Gingras, G. (2018). Do as you say: The effects of psychosocial safety climate on managerial quality in an organizational health intervention. *International Journal of Workplace Health Management*, *11*(4), 228–244. https://doi.org/10.1108/IJWHM-01-2018-0009

Brown, T. A. (2015). *Confirmatory factor analysis for applied research*. Guilford Publications.

Burns, R. A., Sargent, K., & Crisp, D. A. (2024). Mental health and wellbeing literacy: A cross-national comparison. *Applied Research in Quality of Life*, 1–26. https://doi.org/10.1007/s11482-024-10330-z

Cabassa, L. J., Nicasio, A., & Whitley, R. (2013). Picturing recovery: A photovoice exploration of recovery dimensions among people with serious mental illness. *Psychiatric Services*, *64*(9), 837–842.

Chng, J., Burns, R., Murray, K., & Crisp, D. (2022). A community mental health and wellbeing literacy study among Australian adults. *Journal of Happiness and Health*, *2*(1), 12–30. https://doi.org/10.47602/johah.v2i1.13

Cresswell-Smith, J., Solin, P., Wahlbeck, K., & Tamminen, N. (2023). Conceptualising and measuring positive mental health literacy: A systematic literature review. *Journal of Public Mental Health*, *22*(2), 47–59. https://doi.org/10.1108/JPMH-12-2022-0128

Furnham, A., & Swami, V. (2018). Mental health literacy: A review of what it is and why it matters. *International Perspectives in Psychology*, *7*(4), 240–257. https://doi.org/10.1037/ipp0000094

Gagnon, J., Coulombe, S., Pacheco, T., Hou, H., Slemp, G., & Oades, L. (in preparation). Construct validity of the French well-being literacy scale among the general population.

Guo, J., Xie, Y., & Wang, F. (2024). The relationship between anxiety, depression, and well-being literacy in college students: Based on a Dual-Factor Model of Mental Health. In *2024 5th International Conference on Mental Health, Education and Human Development (MHEHD 2024)* (pp. 65–70). Atlantis Press.

Hou, H., Chin, T. C., Slemp, G. R., & Oades, L. G. (2021). Wellbeing literacy: Conceptualization, measurement, and preliminary empirical findings from students, parents and school staff. *International Journal of Environmental Research and Public Health*, *18*(4), 1–13. https://doi.org/10.3390/ijerph18041485

Jia, Z., Zheng, F., Wang, F., & Yang, G. (2024). Psychometric properties of the Wellbeing Literacy 6-item scale in Chinese military academy cadets. *Frontiers in Psychology*, *15*, 1–10. https://doi.org/10.3389/fpsyg.2024.1293845

Kjell, O. N. E., Kjell, K., Garcia, D., & Sikström, S. (2019). Semantic measures: Using natural language processing to measure, differentiate, and describe psychological constructs. *Psychological Methods*, *24*(1), 92–115. https://doi.org/10.1037/met0000191

Leximancer. (n.d.). *Publish or perish? … Thrive with us.* https://www.leximancer.com/
Lien, Y.-J., Feng, H.-P., Chen, C.-H., Tseng, Y.-H., & Tseng, W.-H. (2024). Exploring causal relationships in mental health literacy through Twitter content: A machine learning approach. *European Psychiatry, 67*(S1), S112–S113. https://doi.org/10.1192/j.eurpsy.2024.268
Nelson, G., & Evans, S. D. (2014). Critical community psychology and qualitative research: A conversation. *Qualitative Inquiry, 20*(2), 158–166. https://doi.org/10.1177/1077800413510873
Nussbaum, M. C. (2011). *Creating capabilities: the human development approach.* Belknap Press of Harvard.
Oades, L. G., Baker, L. M., Francis, J. J., & Taylor, J. A. (2021). Wellbeing literacy and positive education. In: M. L. Kern & M. L. Wehmeyer (Eds.), *The Palgrave handbook of positive education.* Palgrave Macmillan. https://doi.org/10.1007/978-3-030-64537-3_13
Romano, A. R., Peixoto, E. M., Gagnon, J., Coulombe, S., & Oades, L. G. (in press). Exploring the invariance of the Wellbeing Literacy 6-item (Well-Lit 6) Scale between Brazilian and French-Canadian populations. *Revista Latinoamericana de Psicología.*
Romano, A. R., Peixoto, E. M., Gagnon, J., Coulombe, S., & Oades, L. G. (submitted). Cross-cultural adaptation and psychometric properties of the Wellbeing Literacy 6-item (Well-Lit 6) in Brazil.
Rosenbusch, H., Wanders, F., & Pit, I. L. (2020). The semantic scale network: An online tool to detect semantic overlap of psychological scales and prevent scale redundancies. *Psychological Methods, 25*(3), 380–392. https://doi.org/10.1037/met0000244
Sen, A. (1993). Capability and well-being. In M. C. Nussbaum & A. Sen (Eds.), *The quality of life* (pp. 30–53). Oxford University Press.
Tavakol, M., & Dennick, R. (2011). Making sense of Cronbach's alpha. *International Journal of Medical Education, 2*, 53–55. https://doi.org/10.5116/ijme.4dfb.8dfd
Tse, S., Gagnon, J., & Coulombe, S. (in preparation). Psychometric validation of the Wellbeing Literacy Scale with a sample of Canadians experiencing mental health and addiction issues.
United Nations. (2023). *Widening digital gap between developed, developing states threatening to exclude world's poorest from next industrial revolution, speakers tell second committee.* https://press.un.org/en/2023/gaef3587.doc.htm#:~:text=He%20estimated%20that%20only%2036,2.7%20billion%20people%20still%20offline%E2%80%9D.
Wang, C., & Burris, M. A. (1997). Photovoice: Concept, methodology, and use for participatory needs assessment. *Health Education & Behavior, 24*(3), 369–387. https://doi.org/10.1177/109019819702400309
Ward, V., West, R., Smith, S., McDermott, S., Keen, J., Pawson, R., & House, A. (2014). The role of informal networks in creating knowledge among health-care managers: A prospective case study. *Health Services and Delivery Research, 2*(12), 1–132.
Waters, L., Dussert, D., & Loton, D. (2022). How do young children understand and action their own well-being? Positive psychology, student voice, and well-being literacy in early childhood. *International Journal of Applied Positive Psychology, 7*(1), 91–117. https://doi.org/10.1007/s41042-021-00056-w
Williams, C., Stewart, D. E., Bendrups, D., Laksono, B., Susilo, J., Amaral, S., Kurscheid, J., & Gray, D. J. (2018). Shadow puppets and neglected diseases (2): A qualitative evaluation of a health promotion performance in rural Indonesia. *International Journal of Environmental Research and Public Health, 15*(12), 1–12. https://doi.org/10.3390/ijerph15122829

10

WELLBEING LITERACY

A Social Discourse Approach to Lay Concepts

Annalise Roache, Elizabeth du Preez, and Lindsay G. Oades

Introduction

Wellbeing literacy is defined as "the intentional use of wellbeing relevant vocabulary, knowledge and language skills to maintain or improve the wellbeing of oneself, others and the world" (Hou et al., 2021, p. 1). Lay concepts are understood to represent subjective and informal understandings of the world, which permeate all aspects of life, including health, education, and wellbeing (Furnham, 1988). These lay beliefs, which may resonate with or diverge from scientific knowledge, are shaped by personal experiences, culture, and social influences, significantly impacting attitudes and behaviours (Furnham, 1988). As the subjective nature of lay beliefs dictates, they vary among individuals, yet commonalities exist that can offer insights. As such, the study of lay concepts provides an opportunity to explore individuals' wellbeing literacy and language choices, which in turn construct wellbeing opportunities across all aspects of life.

Studies have explored how laypeople conceptualise health and wellbeing across different contexts (e.g., vocation and educational settings) and demographics (e.g., age and ethnicity), revealing diverse perspectives on belief composition (Zedelius et al., 2017). For instance, lay concepts encompass beliefs regarding illness causation and treatment choices within health and education settings (Huang et al., 2020; Jarden et al., 2021). Over time, lay beliefs evolve through encounters with new experiences and cultural shifts, shaping individuals' perceptions and interpretations of shared information (Kilby & Sherman, 2018; Zedelius et al., 2017).

Lay beliefs offer two paths of inquiry: firstly, they provide insight into the concepts and language individuals use to define, describe, and enact wellbeing,

DOI: 10.4324/9781003644293-10

and secondly, they offer avenues for intervention by introducing evidence-based viewpoints and knowledge that can potentially expand wellbeing literacy and shape new lay beliefs that positively influence wellbeing outcomes.

A Social Constructionism Lens to Wellbeing

Within the parent movement of postmodern thought, the field of psychology acknowledges a body of ideas which is loosely called social constructionism (Burr, 1995; Harre, 1989; Shotter & Gergen, 1989). Social constructionism is not a unitary paradigm, as both epistemic and ontological forms of social constructionism are described in literature on the application of social constructionism. This chapter will focus on epistemic social constructionism, poststructuralist and postmodern perspectives in social psychology (Gergen, 1985, 1994) as it affords the authors to consider how wellbeing, as a social construct, is shaped through language choices and to explore more specifically further, how wellbeing literacy shape and create possibilities of wellbeing actions for lay people (Oades et al., 2021). For example, when cultural value is placed on "being well" through community support and connectedness, these actions will be embedded in lay beliefs and language choices. In contrast, other cultural understandings might prioritise and action the individual pursuit of wellbeing through a linguistic focus on personal agency and independence.

Potter and Wetherell (1987) state that language is used to construct the self and the world we live in to arrive at a meaningful and coherent understanding of identity and context. In using stories/narratives as a coherent container of meaning (Parker, 1992; Potter & Wetherell, 1987), it shapes our choices about which self-narratives are storied and which ones remain silenced (Doan, 1997; Freedman & Combs, 1996; Weingarten, 1998). Narratives that are storied by the individual are usually those narratives that are viewed as significant and meaningful in a person's life (Du Preez, 2006). These are sometimes called dominant narratives because of their ability to shape peoples' experiences within their specific meaning framework. Anderson and Goolishian (1988) also state that "meaning and understanding do not exist prior to the utterances of language" (p. 378), emphasising the fact that language not only creates experience but that meaning and understanding are constructed in conversation. Meaning and language then become inseparable as narratives that are unstoried are usually believed to be insignificant enough that they do not have constitutive or shaping power (Du Preez, 2006). If wellbeing is storied and understood as "essential," people are more likely to take up action possibilities in ways that support their wellbeing, and if it is storied as "indulgent," then it is less likely to increase behaviours that support wellbeing.

From the perspective of social constructionism then, people's interpretations of the world, their experiences and personal stories are always guided by shared social discourses (McNamee & Gergen, 1992). Language is generated, sustained, and/or rejected through social interactions and creates "reality" for those involved in meaning-making through language. Kerka (1997) supports this by stating that people are continually constructing experiences in interaction and through the languaging of experiences.

Researchers working within the social constructionist philosophy accept the notion of specific and local knowledge as a valid construction of meaningful events through developing an anti-theoretical version of knowledge. This aligns well with the first author's research privileging lay perspectives on wellbeing (Roache, 2025). By focusing on local narratives and acknowledging the possibility of consensus on the meaning of language, this recognition of lay or local knowledge recognises that the power to create relevant theory exists within communities. Social constructionist discourses have, therefore, made possible new ways of looking at the process of intellectual knowledge production (Kelly et al., 2000). A non-relativist stance within social constructionist inquiry is, therefore, possible and requires not only that the subjective experiences of participants should be heard but also that conditions or contextual discourses that made these subjective experiences possible be acknowledged and explored (Willig, 1999).

Lay Concepts as Part of Wellbeing Literacy

Furnham and Cheng (2000) categorise theories into three main types: scientific, folk, and lay. Scientific theories are systematically developed and empirically tested to predict phenomena, grounded in rigorous research. In contrast, folk theories are communal and rooted in cultural traditions shared among specific groups. Lay theories, however, are more individualised, emerging from personal experiences and beliefs. These informal yet structured explanations help people navigate both straightforward and complex situations (Dweck et al., 1995; Plaks et al., 2009). They provide a framework that informs daily decisions and actions, allowing individuals to make sense of their world.

Lay theories can be seen as the everyday, non-expert explanations that people construct to interpret their environment. Furnham (1988) suggests that individuals naturally seek stability, predictability, and comprehensibility in their surroundings. Through this process, they develop explanations for phenomena that matter to them, creating an internal model of the world that is functional and meaningful. These lay theories are not merely casual thoughts; they are deeply embedded cognitive frameworks that shape perceptions, attitudes, and behaviours (Molden & Dweck, 2006).

The term "lay" signifies ideas that are not based on formal academic expertise. This does not imply a lack of education or intelligence; instead, it emphasises that these beliefs are formed through everyday experiences rather than systematic research or scholarly evidence (Furnham, 2017). These lay understandings significantly influence beliefs about an event or activity's nature, value, antecedents, and outcomes. "Nature" refers to the core components of the concept; "value" relates to the perceived benefits and significance; "antecedents" involve the prerequisites necessary for the event to occur; and "outcomes" denote the consequences or results of the experience (Joshanloo, 2019).

Similar to how scientists use theories to interpret data, laypeople rely on their lay theories to make sense of their experiences, leading to consistent patterns of behaviour (McMahan et al., 2013). By constructing informal theories, individuals can create a sense of certainty, predictability, and control over their lives (Furnham, 1988; Levy et al., 2006). However, lay theories are not always accurate or aligned with scientific understanding. Research has shown that individuals often distort or disregard information that contradicts their pre-existing beliefs to maintain their worldview (Plaks & Stecher, 2007; Plaks et al., 2005, 2009). Nonetheless, growing evidence suggests overlaps between lay beliefs and scientific theories, even as some differences remain (Delle Fave et al., 2011; Joshanloo, 2019; Karnaze & Levine, 2020; Roache, 2025).

A Social discourse lens provides a valuable perspective for exploring lay theories, particularly within the context of wellbeing literacy. This approach explores how language reflects broader societal norms and cultural values, highlighting the ways in which individuals articulate their understanding of wellbeing. By scrutinising the language choices embedded in these "lay beliefs," researchers can uncover how people conceptualise wellbeing, what they prioritise, and how these perceptions shape their actions and behaviours (Roache, 2025).

The Capability Model of Wellbeing Literacy is a framework to understand, analyse and promote effective wellbeing-related language use. It can be used to integrate insights from lay concept studies to provide content to populate the five core dimensions. The first dimension involves proficiency in vocabulary, knowledge, and language skills specific to wellbeing (Gee, 1991). Understanding the vocabulary of wellbeing includes articulating personal values and grasping evidence-based principles related to those values. The second dimension emphasises the ability to comprehend multimodal texts, such as reading, listening, and viewing. In the digital age, this extends to engaging with diverse media forms, including books, podcasts, reels, and online articles that discuss wellbeing (Oades et al., 2020). The third dimension focuses on the production of multimodal texts, encompassing writing, speaking, and other creative forms of expression. Individuals express their wellbeing experiences through various mediums, from social media posts to in-person conversations, art, and storytelling. The fourth dimension highlights the importance of context in communication, acknowledging that effective discussions about wellbeing must adapt to the audience and setting. For instance, language use may differ between formal and informal settings, such as in the home, workplace, school, or online platform. Those with high wellbeing literacy demonstrate an ability to tailor their language to suit different contexts and audiences. The final dimension of wellbeing literacy emphasises intentionality – an ongoing, mindful intention to enhance or maintain the wellbeing of oneself, others, or the broader community. Individuals who are highly literate in wellbeing use language deliberately to promote positive outcomes. This intentional use of language can be likened to a form of mindfulness, where communication is carefully adapted to meet the specific needs of each context. Thus, literacy is not merely a technical skill but a purposeful practice where individuals make conscious choices about how to engage based on their desired outcomes (Perry, 2012).

A systematic review by Sollis et al. (2022) examines the complexities of defining wellbeing across diverse populations. Analysing 121 studies using participatory methodologies, the authors developed a participatory wellbeing framework that captures community-based dimensions of wellbeing, a good life, and quality of life. This framework prioritises participant engagement, grounding definitions of wellbeing in real-world perceptions rather than academic constructs. Open-ended questions and thematic analysis were used to explore participants' understandings, offering insights into everyday language around wellbeing.

Excluding studies on ill-being, poverty, and context-specific aspects (e.g., educational settings), the review identified 30 wellbeing dimensions, including relationships, health, financial security, community, education, work, spirituality, personal growth, and civic engagement. These dimensions extend beyond traditional academic models, which often focus on subjective mental experiences (Keyes, 2002; Keyes & Martin, 2017; Oades & Mossman, 2017; Roache, 2025; Seligman, 2011). The participatory framework also highlights connections between wellbeing, physical health, and economic security, areas often overlooked in conventional models (VanderWeele, 2017).

These findings underscore that wellbeing is a multidimensional construct, with varying conceptualisations both within and across different communities and regions. Although common themes emerge, significant variations suggest that a nuanced, context-sensitive approach is essential for defining, measuring, and intervening in wellbeing (Jarden & Roache, 2023; Roache, 2025). This resonates closely with the principles of wellbeing literacy and social discourse analysis, which emphasise the need to understand the language and cultural nuances that inform people's lay theories of wellbeing.

Integrating insights from participatory research (Delle Fave et al., 2011; Roache, 2025; Sollis et al., 2022) into discussions on wellbeing literacy is crucial, as it underscores the importance of contextual language and the diversity of conceptual understandings. Social discourse analysis helps to unpack how distinct groups articulate wellbeing, revealing the varied lay theories that influence individual perceptions and behaviours. Through this lens, improving wellbeing literacy is not solely about building vocabulary and knowledge;

it also involves appreciating and adapting to diverse cultural expressions of wellbeing (Gee, 2020). By acknowledging and valuing these differences, researchers and practitioners can promote more inclusive, empathetic, and effective communication and intervention strategies that foster intentional and mindful engagement with wellbeing concepts across various contexts.

The interplay between lay theories and wellbeing literacy reveals the importance of context, intentionality, and the practical application of knowledge. Understanding people's lay beliefs about wellbeing offers valuable insights into how they perceive, manage, and enhance their mental health and wellbeing. Social discourse analysis enables researchers to identify patterns in how people discuss wellbeing, providing a deeper understanding of the implicit narratives that shape their intentional wellbeing enhancing practices. Developing wellbeing literacy skills empowers individuals to navigate the complex interplay of values, contexts, and behaviours, fostering a more holistic sense of wellbeing that is attuned to their personal and cultural realities and context.

Conclusion

In conclusion, the dynamic interplay between language and wellbeing highlighted in this chapter affirms that how people talk about their experiences is integral to how they perceive and respond to the world around them. The construction of lay concepts through everyday language reflects deeper social, cultural, and individual values, making it a critical study area for those interested in promoting holistic and flourishing lives. By adopting a nuanced, context-sensitive approach, practitioners and researchers can leverage the power of language to foster intentional practices that benefit wellbeing. Future work in this area should continue to explore the diverse ways lay beliefs are articulated while also seeking to align these understandings with evidence-based practices to create effective policies and interventions that are both effective and respectful of individual and cultural differences.

References

Anderson, H., & Goolishian, H. (1988). Human systems as linguistic systems: Preliminary and evolving ideas about the implications for clinical theory. *Family Process, 27(4)*, 371–393.

Burr, V. (1995). *Introduction to social constructionism.* Routledge.

Delle Fave, A., Brdar, I., Freire, T., Vella-Brodrick, D., & Wissing, M. P. (2011). The Eudaimonic and Hedonic components of happiness: Qualitative and quantitative findings. *Social Indicators Research, 100*(2), 185–207.

Doan, R. E. (1997). Narrative therapy, postmodernism, social constructionism, and constructivism: Discussion and distinctions. *Transactional Analysis Journal, 27*(2), 128–133. https://doi.org/10.1177/036215379702700208

Du Preez, E. (2006). *The social construction of counsellor identity in a South African context* [Doctoral dissertation, University of Pretoria]. http://hdl.handle.net/2263/27350

Dweck, C. S., Chiu, C. Y., & Hong, Y. Y. (1995). Implicit theories and their role in judgments and reactions: A word from two perspectives. *Psychological Inquiry, 6*(4), 267–285.

Freedman, J., & Combs, G. (1996). *Narrative therapy: The social construction of preferred realities.* Norton.

Furnham, A. (1988). *Lay theories: Everyday understanding of problems in the social sciences.* Pergamon Press.

Furnham, A. (2017). How lay theories influence our mental health. In B. C. M. C. M. Zedelius & J. W. Schooler (Eds.), *The science of lay theories: How beliefs shape our cognition, behavior, and health* (pp. 354–374). Springer International Publishing.

Furnham, A., & Cheng, H. (2000). Lay theories of happiness. *Journal of Happiness Studies, 1*(2), 227–246. https://doi.org/10.1023/A:1010027611587

Gee, J. (1991). Socio-cultural approaches to literacy (Literacies). *Annual Review of Applied Linguistics, 12*, 31–48. https://doi.org/10.1017/S0267190500002130

Gee, J. P. (2020). *What is a human?: Language, mind, and culture/James Paul Gee.* Palgrave Macmillan.

Gergen, K. J. (1985). The social constructionist movement in modern psychology. *American Psychologist, 40*, 266–275.

Gergen, K. J. (1994). *Realities and relationships: Soundings in social constructionism.* Harvard University Press.

Harre, R. (1989). Language games and the texts of identity. In J. Shotter & K. J. Gergen (Eds.), *Texts of identity.* Sage.

Hou, H., Chin, T. C., Slemp, G. R., & Oades, L. G. (2021). Wellbeing literacy: Conceptualization, measurement, and preliminary empirical findings from students, parents and school staff. *International Journal of Environmental Research and Public Health, 18*(4), 1485.

Huang, L., Kern, M. L., & Oades, L. G. (2020). Strengthening university student wellbeing: Language and perceptions of Chinese international students. *International Journal of Environmental Research and Public Health, 17*(15), 5538.

Jarden, A., & Roache, A. (2023). What is wellbeing? *International Journal of Environmental Research and Public Health, 20*(6), 5006. https://www.mdpi.com/1660-4601/20/6/5006

Jarden, R. J., Jarden, A. J., Weiland, T. J., Taylor, G., Brockenshire, N., Rutherford, M., Carbery, C., Moroney, K., & Gerdtz, M. (2021). Nurse wellbeing during the coronavirus (2019) pandemic: A qualitative descriptive study. *Collegian, 28*, 709–719.

Joshanloo, M. (2019). Lay conceptions of happiness: Associations with reported well-being, personality traits, and materialism. *Frontiers in Psychology, 10*, 2377.

Karnaze, M. M., & Levine, L. J. (2020). Lay theories about whether emotion helps or hinders: Assessment and effects on emotional acceptance and recovery from distress. *Frontiers in Psychology, 11*, 183.

Kelly, P., Hickey, C., & Tinning, R. (2000). Educational truth telling in a more reflexive modernity. *British Journal of Sociology of Education, 21*(1), 111–123.

Kerka, S. (1997). Postmodernism and Adult Education. Retrieved August 7, 2001, from http://www.cete.org/acve/textonly/docgen.asp?tbl=tia&ID-105

Keyes, C., & Martin, C. (2017). The complete state model of mental health. In M. Slade, L. Oades, & A. Jarden (Eds.), *Wellbeing, recovery and mental health* (pp. 86–97). Cambridge University Press.

Keyes, C. L. (2002). The mental health continuum: From languishing to flourishing in life. *Journal of Health and Social Behavior, 43*(2), 207–222.

Kilby, C. J., & Sherman, K. A. (2018). Lay beliefs. In M. Gellman (Ed.), *Encyclopedia of behavioral medicine* (pp. 1–3). Springer. https://doi.org/10.1007/978-1-4614-6439-6_101997-1

Levy, S. R., Chiu, C.-Y, & Hong, Y. (2006). Lay theories and intergroup relations. *Group Processes & Intergroup Relations, 9*(1), 5–24.

McMahan, E. A., Dixon, K. J., & King, L. M. (2013). Evidence of associations between lay conceptions of well-being, conception-congruent behavior, and experienced well-being. *Journal of Happiness Studies*, *14*, 655–671.
McNamee, S., & Gergen, K. J. (1992). *Therapy as social construction*. Sage.
Molden, D. C., & Dweck, C. S. (2006). Finding" meaning" in psychology: A lay theories approach to self-regulation, social perception, and social development. *American Psychologist*, *61*(3), 192.
Nightingale, D. J., & Cromby, J. (Eds.). (1999). *Social constructionist psychology*. Open University Press.
Oades, L., & Mossman, L. (2017). The science of wellbeing and positive psychology. In M. Slade, L. Oades, & A. Jarden (Eds.), *Wellbeing, recovery and mental health* (pp. 7–23). Cambridge University Press.
Oades, L. G., Jarden, A., Hou, H., Ozturk, C., Williams, P., R Slemp, G., & Huang, L. (2021). Wellbeing literacy: A capability model for wellbeing science and practice. *International Journal of Environmental Research and Public Health*, *18*(2), 719.
Oades, L. G., Ozturk, C., Hou, H., & Slemp, G. R. (2020). wellbeing literacy: A language-use capability relevant to wellbeing outcomes of positive psychology intervention. *The Journal of Positive Psychology*, *15*(5), 696–700. https://doi.org/10.1080/17439760.2020.1789711
Parker, I. (1992). *Discourse dynamics: Critical analysis for social and individual psychology*. Routledge.
Perry, K. H. (2012). What is literacy? A critical overview of sociocultural perspectives. *Journal of Language and Literacy Education*, *8*(1), 50–71.
Plaks, J. E., Grant, H., & Dweck, C. S. (2005). Violations of implicit theories and the sense of prediction and control: Implications for motivated person perception. *Journal of Personality and Social Psychology*, *88*(2), 245.
Plaks, J. E., Levy, S. R., & Dweck, C. S. (2009). Lay theories of personality: Cornerstones of meaning in social cognition. *Social and Personality Psychology Compass*, *3*(6), 1069–1081.
Plaks, J. E., & Stecher, K. (2007). Unexpected improvement, decline, and stasis: A prediction confidence perspective on achievement success and failure. *Journal of Personality and Social Psychology*, *93*(4), 667.
Potter, J., & Wetherell, M. (1987). *Discourse and social psychology: Beyond attitudes and behaviour*. Sage.
Roache, A., (2025). *Mapping Wellbeing: Exploring Lay Concepts of Wellbeing and How They Compare with Positive Psychology Approaches - A Mixed Methods Study of New Zealand Adults*. [Doctoral thesis, Auckland University of Technology].
Seligman, M. E. (2011). *Flourish: A visionary new understanding of happiness and well-being*. Simon and Schuster.
Shotter, J., & Gergen, K. J. (1989). *Texts of identity*. Sage.
Sollis, K., Yap, M., Campbell, P., & Biddle, N. (2022). Conceptualisations of wellbeing and quality of life: A systematic review of participatory studies. *World Development*, *160*, 106073. https://www.sciencedirect.com/science/article/pii/S0305750X22002637
VanderWeele, T. J. (2017). On the promotion of human flourishing. *Proceedings of the National Academy of Sciences*, *114*(31), 8148–8156.
Weingarten, K. (1998). The small and the ordinary: The daily practice of a postmodern narrative therapy. *Family Process*, *37*, 3–15.
Willig, C. (1999). Beyond appearances: A critical realist approach to social constructionist work. In D.J. Nightingale & J. Cromby (Eds.), *Social constructionist psychology: A critical analysis of theory and practice* (pp. 37–51). Open University Press.
Zedelius, C. M., Müller, B. C., & Schooler, J. W. (2017). *The science of lay theories*. Springer.

11

EXPLORING THE INTERSECTION OF WELLBEING LITERACY AND STORYING METHODS

Rachel Colla, Paige Williams, and Lindsay G. Oades

A Background to Storying and Participatory Methods in Wellbeing

Wellbeing is a complex concept that can incorporate both objective and subjective experience. As such, defining wellbeing involves both describing what it is and evaluating what it should be – a philosophical concept known as a 'thick concept' (Alexandrova & Fabian, 2022). When such a concept is defined and measured by a limited group, such as academics, it can fail to capture the nuances of how people experience wellbeing in their daily lives. To address this issue, scholars have argued for a more inclusive approach to understanding wellbeing in context, where knowledge is co-produced with the people being studied (Alexandrova & Fabian, 2022; Hayes et al., 2012; Henriques et al., 2014). Participatory research methods offer a way to achieve this and can contribute to a more holistic understanding of wellbeing.

Story-based methods are a powerful example of participatory approaches that provide a democratic means of illustrating and informing theories about the nuanced experiences of wellbeing. Stories, defined simply as "discourse designed to connect a series of happenings" (Webster, 1969), are a fundamental way that humans make sense of the world and communicate experiences (Clandinin & Rosiek, 2007; Phillips & Bunda, 2018). As human beings, we are 'storying' beings (Chawla, 2011, p. 16). Stories are a natural mode of expression used by people of all backgrounds, and using storying methods can democratise the research process by allowing diverse voices and perspectives to be represented (Gottschall, 2012; Hutchens, 2015).

Holman Jones (2016) eloquently describes the benefits of sharing stories to create deeper understanding as a "dance of collaborative engagement"

DOI: 10.4324/9781003644293-11

between the story-sharer and listener (p. 229). Indeed, narrative methods have long been used in psychology and other disciplines to foster a more nuanced understanding of complex experiences like wellbeing. However, in many narrative methods, the researcher (listener) takes the lead in interpretation (Riley & Hawe, 2005). Phillips and Bunda (2018), however, argue for a more participatory term: 'story/ing', defined as the "act of making and remaking meaning through stories" (p. 8), more reflective of the collaborative dance described by Holman Jones. The verbification of 'story/ing' is intentional, as they position the process of storying throughout the entire research cycle: from conceptualising the investigation, collecting stories, analysing and theorising, and finally, in the presentation of the research. It is relevant at this juncture to distinguish storying from the term storytelling. While Mair (1988) posits that we live in and through stories, it is the co-creation of sharing stories that Phillips and Bunda reference as a core principle in their approach. This relational understanding differs from the more unidirectional nature of story*telling* with the intention to 'tell' or communicate key messages rather than create shared understanding.

Phillips and Bunda (2018) locate five principles of researching through, with, and as storying methodologies. These include (a) storying nourishes thought, body, and soul; (b) storying is embodied relational meaning-making; (c) storying intersects past and present as living oral archives; (d) storying claims voice in the silenced margins; and (e) storying enacts collective ownership and authorship. These principles of storying facilitate a more democratic and embodied process to understand the unique experience of wellbeing in different contexts. They additionally point to the possibility of enabling wellbeing through the exploration of sharing stories.

Storying is not limited to those that can share through oral methods. Images, like stories, also tap into methods used in everyday life as we create, interpret and use images, often without conscious attention (Knowles & Cole, 2008). Images can be used to express complex human experiences, highlighting both concrete and abstract concepts in an economical manner, making them an excellent source of knowledge production (Barbrook-Johnson & Penn, 2022; Knowles & Cole, 2008). Arts-informed methods, such as image-based modes of representation, draw on aesthetic ways of knowing, best understood as emotional, perceptual and sense-based forms of knowledge (Archibald & Gerber, 2018; Douglas & Carless, 2018). Incorporating these methods into research and practice enables awareness and new ways of understanding that can tap into preverbal sensory and emotional knowledge that may not be facilitated through language-based methods of inquiry (Archibald & Gerber, 2018; Barbrook-Johnson & Penn, 2022; Knowles & Cole, 2008). Through the use of metaphor and symbolism, visual images can communicate underlying theories effectively and eloquently (Knowles & Cole, 2008). They allow the capacity to simultaneously view the whole and interrelationships between the parts, which makes their use an ideal method for understanding the complex dynamic experience of wellbeing.

Pictorial mapping diagrams, like rich picture maps, are a good example of a storying tool to create a shared understanding of an experience like wellbeing (Barbrook-Johnson & Penn, 2022). The value of rich picture maps lies not in their objective representation of reality but rather as a technique that can prompt systems thinking, surfacing mental models and identification of interconnected relationships that can generate new insights (Bell & Morse, 2013; Conte & Davidson, 2020). Drawing a rich picture map invokes a process of iterative thinking, understanding and refining understanding through the creation of the map (Fathulla, 2008; Monk & Howard, 1998). Additionally, rich picture maps can be used throughout an inquiry process to engage participants in sense-making and/or as an output to engage key stakeholders in a reflexive process on the insights from the research (Bell & Morse, 2013; Conte & Davidson, 2020). These multimodal methods provide a rich toolkit to uncover and develop a deeper understanding of how different cohorts experience and understanding thick concepts like wellbeing.

Wellbeing Literacy: From the Mechanics to the Dynamics of Language Use

Oades et al. (2021) proposed the capability model of wellbeing literacy – conceptualising how we intentionally communicate about and for wellbeing and adapt to the context of the communication. This was developed as a formal model (Table 11.1) so that it could be used to conceptualise language-use in multiple language contexts, with the overarching value commitment to wellbeing (i.e. thick concept) of the communicators. The capability model can be a useful way to make sense of some of the mechanisms that underpin a participatory storying method.

Within this model, wellbeing literacy is multimodal (using different modes of communicating, e.g., speaking, writing, visual imagery), reflecting a real-world, societal view of literacy (Perry, 2012). The multimodality is recognised formally within the model in terms of how *comprehension* of wellbeing information occurs through reading, listening, and viewing. In parallel, *composition* of wellbeing occurs through writing, speaking, and creating (ACARA; *Literacy*, https://www.australiancurriculum.edu.au/f-10-curriculum/general-capabilities). (Table 11.1). Literacy is understood here as pivotal for relationships and wellbeing, as a sociocultural phenomenon, and as occurring between people (Gee, 1991, 2005). Hence, wellbeing literacy, like contemporary versions of literacy, is more than reading and writing, that occurs in a fluid and

TABLE 11.1 Capability model of wellbeing literacy

Component	*Mechanics and dynamics*	*Description and relevance to storying*
1. Vocabulary and knowledge *about* wellbeing	The 'what' and denotive use of language. *Mechanics*	Words and information about wellbeing – possessing words (vocabulary) and knowledge about wellbeing
2. Comprehension related to wellbeing	The 'how' of receptive communication. *Mechanics*	Comprehension in multiple modes including viewing, listening, and reading about and for wellbeing. We can view, listen or read stories.
3. Composition related to wellbeing	The 'how' of expressive communication. *Mechanics*	Student's expression in multiple modes, including writing, creating and speaking about and for wellbeing. We can write, create and tell stories.
4. Context awareness and adaptability	The 'who' and 'where' of language use. May be considered a higher order skill. A form of adaptation to external conditions. *Dynamics*	Awareness of differences across contexts and adapting use of language to fit the relevant context. We can modify comprehension or composition of stories depending on context (see Jayda example below).
5. Intentionality *for* wellbeing	The 'why' of language use and adapting for context. A form of internal/external regulation. *Dynamics*	Habit of intentionally using language to maintain or improve wellbeing of self or others. We may deliberately comprehend or compose, new, old or evolved stories about and/or for wellbeing.

ongoing way across society, in real-life contexts, not only in educational contexts. Literacy is a sociocultural phenomenon, humans use language together in dynamic contexts – language use is relational by definition – that is, there is no such thing as a private language.

To further examine the interactive and relational aspects of the wellbeing literacy model, and assist with its understanding as a capability, the terms 'mechanics' and 'dynamics' are useful. Using the analogy and language from physics, of mechanics and dynamics to understand important differences between the first three components of the capability model of wellbeing literacy and the latter two components, as illustrated in Table 11.1. The first three components (vocabulary and knowledge about wellbeing, comprehension of wellbeing language and composition of wellbeing language) may be considered the mechanics of wellbeing language use. If mechanics deals with the behaviour of bodies when subjected to forces, these components examine how people best read, listen and view information about wellbeing, or how they write, speak or create about wellbeing – what helps put them in motion. Dynamics is more about what happens when they are in motion using language, that is they are using wellbeing vocabulary and knowledge, using the skills of reading, listening and viewing, and the skills of writing, speaking and creating. It also speaks to the dynamics within and around them: how does their language use change because of context (e.g. interpersonal interactions) or development of intentionality? This is an underdeveloped area of the capability model of wellbeing literacy, and the concept and practice of storying provide an excellent opportunity to elaborate the notion of wellbeing literacy as a capability, particularly in terms of the potential enabling and limiting influences of dynamics.

Storying as a Capability

Storying supports both the composition of wellbeing literacy through sharing of stories and the comprehension of it through listening. It requires the utility of the mechanics of Wellbeing Literacy (Table 11.1) and is influenced by the dynamics of the individual and context. Stories – the content of storying – are inherently situated within context (Creswell, 2013) including the subjective, rich complexities and meaning that an individual layers into them. Locally situated truths take primacy over objective truth (Phillips & Bunda, 2018) as stories narrate a time-based journey of experience (McAdams, 2001), create a coherent thread of meaning and insight, and provide insights to causal factors for specific experiences (McAdams & McLean, 2013).

How might storying be a capability that supports wellbeing?

In the Capability Approach (CA), economist Amyrta Sen suggests that for a conceptualisation of wellbeing to be effective, there must be a genuine opportunity to experience it in a way that makes sense for the individual (Sen, 1980, 1985, 1993). This shifts the emphasis away from wellbeing measures that focus on economic resources or pre-defined outcomes, to what Sen refers to as capabilities: 'what people can be or do'. Capabilities comprise the things that are of value and that people seek to 'be and do'. These are referred to as 'functionings' and may be as simple as eating breakfast and going to the market, or more complex, such as the desire to love and be loved or to be culturally aware. It is likely that an individual will hold multiple functionings in their lives and at multiple levels.

A unique aspect of the CA in contrast to other economic models is its recognition that resources or achievements (functionings) are only valid as measures of a society's wellbeing if they can be 'realised' into meaningful wellbeing achievements as defined by the individual. Capabilities are the opportunities (or 'freedoms' as Sen conceptualises them) that allow that conversion to take place. The Capability Model of Wellbeing Literacy presents wellbeing literacy as a mediator (or moderator) in the wellbeing experience; a capability that influences the experience of wellbeing. Could storying similarly be a capability that mediates the experience of wellbeing?

Although stories are used in everyday language and are a natural way in which we make sense of our experiences, there are conditions that influence how – or if – we share them. The Inside-out Outside-in (IO-OI) model (Williams et al., 2016) suggests that the experience of wellbeing is influenced by factors 'outside' of the individual and factors 'inside' the individual. *Outside factors* are those that are in the external context that influence an individual's experience such as the social environment (e.g., family, friends, culture), economic and educational environments (e.g., employment, national economy, availability of schooling, resources and infrastructure) and physical environments (e.g., safety, clean drinking water, pollution). *Inside factors* are the personal attributes that influence an individual's experience and include physical considerations such as health and psychological ones including identity, values, beliefs, and attitudes. The IO-OI model further suggests that it is the dynamic interplay between inside-out and outside-in factors that will influence an individual's experience of wellbeing.

IO-OI is a useful framework to analyse storying practices as an example of wellbeing literacy as it speaks to the 'contextually embedded' nature of storying developing as a capability. Stories shape and are shaped by 'outside factors' such as social and cultural structures and power dynamics; in turn, these broader stories can also shape the 'inside factors' of people's experiences, thoughts, and behaviours, which inform the stories they hold about themselves and share into the world. This highlights a potential emancipatory function in storying, through the ability of vulnerable or disenfranchised groups to envisage an alternate story of their future. However, it also highlights some of the limits to the democratic function, noting that capability is influenced by the contextual environment. We suggest the relationship between inside-out and outside-in factors may create and enable storying 'freedom' (capability) or limit/prevent it at three levels – Me (intrapersonal), We (interpersonal), and Us (sociocultural) (Jarden, 2015), and that these *dynamics* operate independently from the *mechanics* of storying (Table 11.1).

For example, Jayda is the eldest child in her family and has four younger brothers. Every day, she and her mother look after the family home and two youngest boys while her father and the two eldest sons work in a local factory. Jayda is intelligent, and whilst formal schooling is not available to her, she is keen to learn and has taken every opportunity she can to learn to read, draw and write. She has hopes beyond life with her family and, using her vibrant imagination shares stories of future adventures with her younger brothers as they walk to and from the market each day.

The mechanics and dynamics for wellbeing literacy (Table 11.1) are all present in Jayda – she has the right intentionality, knowledge, and vocabulary and can comprehend and compose language to a high level. However, she also has context sensitivity, and this tells Jayda that when her father and brothers are home, her sharing of stories must stop. She has an internal belief that she must be 'seen and not heard' (inside-out, Me level), an external environment experience with her Father shouting at her to be quiet that reinforces this (outside-in, We level), and a broader cultural context that normalises this attitude towards females (outside-in, Us level). Despite the storying ***mechanics*** available to Jayda, the ***dynamics*** at each of the three levels limit her storying freedom (capability) and as such also her experience of wellbeing.

Bringing This to Life through the 'Stories of Hope' Project

Let us now illustrate the power of storying and participatory-based methods to build wellbeing literacy through the story of a research project designed to understand how hope emerges in university students. The investigation was a multi-phased qualitative study that sought to incorporate youth voices into our research inquiries using Participatory Narrative Inquiry (PNI). PNI is a storying approach that senses patterns in the social system through the shared exploration of stories, prioritising participants as experts in their own experience (Kurtz, 2014). PNI can be used as a research or community change methodology, moving through three core phases to foster collective understanding and reveal insights that can shape practice (Figure 11.1). These phases include participants sharing stories of their experience (*story collection*), working together to make sense of these experiences (*sense-making*) and then

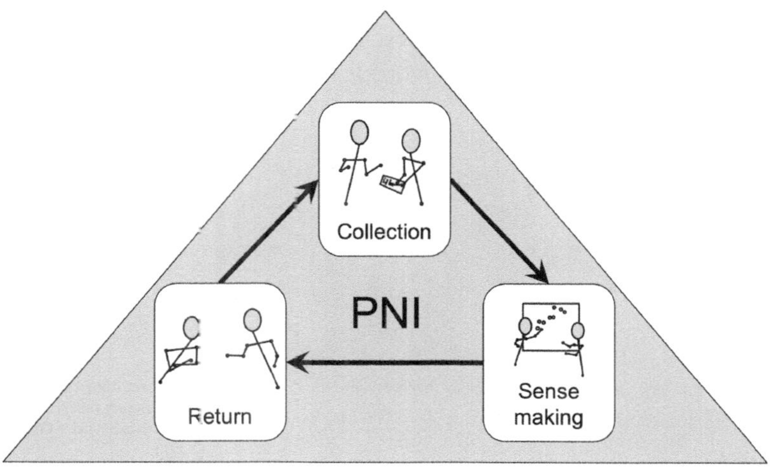

FIGURE 11.1 Three core phases of PNI methodology.

Source: Image used with permission from Kurtz (2014).

considering how to story the collective experiences back to the community to create a call to action (*return*).

The project drew on multimodalities of expression to uncover how participants used language to understand and make sense of their experiences of hope. Participants were invited to share a story of an experience of hope in text form, including identifying some of the factors that enabled hope in their story. A subset of participants were engaged as co-researchers in a series of sense-making workshops, using a variety of storying methods, such as rich picture mapping, visual depictions, and storyboards to depict the common themes they identified in the shared stories of hope. An example of some of the images they created to communicate how hope is experienced is depicted in Figure 11.2. A crucial part of enabling the efficacy of these methods resulted from the environment that was designed to create a sense of safety and trust for participants to share their stories and work together to foster shared understanding. Intentional practices were built in to create the *outside*-in conditions for these storying capabilities to emerge.

Participants' sense-making of the stories moved beyond examining some of the factors that students considered central to the experience of hope to a shared understanding of how they see the dynamic interplay *between* these factors leading to the experience itself. For example, students determined that social enablers inspire hope in the individual and activate their own internal resources that elicit the ideation of potential pathways and motivational energy. The use of different modalities facilitated a richness to this sense-making that could not be enabled solely through verbal or written modes. That is, such capabilities were enabled through broadening the mechanics that participants could draw upon to story their experience of hope.

As we have explored in this chapter, language is a powerful mechanism for communicating ideas and creating shared understanding across different audiences. Perhaps this is best illustrated by Wittgenstein's (1953) famous quote: "the meaning of a word is in its use in the language" (p. 43).

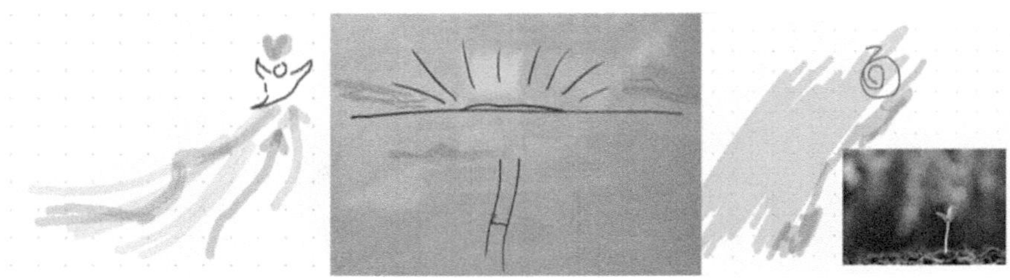

(a) Soaring, flight, uplift

(b) Hope draws you into the future

(c) Breakthrough – sparks of hope and strength that spirals one into a blossoming, like a flower in spring

FIGURE 11.2 Visual images created by students to depict the experience of hope.

Social constructionist scholars pose that language is not only used to describe concepts but as a communication system that is used to process ideas both intrapersonally and interpersonally (Burr, 2015). In fact, the role of language in shaping the psychosocial realm is well evidenced across cultures and contexts (Brooks et al., 2017; Sivak et al., 2019; Sun et al., 2020). Not only does language help communicate our understanding of a particular concept, but language also influences or constructs our experience, that is we understand experiences through language (Brothers, 2005). Therefore, it is imperative to discern the language that populations use around hope, and this language may also be used as a lever for making shifts in the experience of hope. This was certainly evident in the data from the student co-researchers experience in the project.

The co-researchers identified a range of generative benefits through participating in the research, building their knowledge of hope through their explorations while also deepening their critical analysis skills. They reported that the methods expanded their understanding and pathways to hope through their exploration of other student stories, including experiencing a sense of hope in the process. Wellbeing literacy poses that if you have more words, you have more concepts to construct your experience (Oades et al., 2021). In essence, literacy builds agency, which is a core component of hope (Snyder, 2002). The co-researchers also reported experiencing a sense of wellbeing and growth through this process, which could be explained by some of the processes used to integrate need-supportive practices and facilitate the *outside*-in environmental conditions for wellbeing to emerge. These examples may help illuminate how storying methods like those used in PNI approach can help in building wellbeing literacy capabilities.

Finally, it is worth noting that methods that enable the coproduction of knowledge, such as PNI, can also enhance research translation to practice as we learn more about how language can be tailored to better communicate to our target audience (Conte & Davidson, 2020; Oades et al., 2021). For example, students spoke about possibilities, not pathways, and willpower, rather than agency. Intentionally drawing on the language that resonates with students is one of the pathways through which we can develop wellbeing literacy, which has been suggested as an important mediator or moderator between interventions and outcomes (Hou et al., 2021; Oades et al., 2020).

Conclusion

In this chapter, we have explored the powerful synergy between storying practices and developing wellbeing literacy. Stories are a fundamental way that humans make sense of their experiences and share understanding across cultures. From ancient oral traditions to modern digital narratives, storying taps into our natural capacity for contextualising complex concepts and awakening empathy (Smith et al., 2017). As such, they can be useful methods through which we can develop wellbeing literacy capabilities. Creating the freedom to share stories of wellbeing experiences in a safe and trusting environment not only enables the story sharer to construct and make sense of their experience but also fosters the necessary empathy that can give voice to diverse perspectives.

This chapter has shone a new light on the capability model of wellbeing literacy by elucidating the dynamics that influence language use for wellbeing, beyond just the mechanics. Rather than reducing people's experiences to decontextualised data points, stories and arts-based methods can holistically illuminate some of the dynamics that interact to enable or inhibit wellbeing (Colla & Kurtz, 2024). The Stories of Hope project illustrated some of the processes through which participatory storying approaches can build wellbeing literacy capabilities in generative ways. By sharing personal stories through multiple modalities like writing, visuals, and mapping, participants expanded their vocabulary and concepts around the experience of hope, while the sense-making process facilitated greater contextual awareness as they explored patterns across stories.

Looking ahead, participatory storying methods offer a valuable process through which we can further explore the capability model of wellbeing literacy. Identifying the necessary conditions for such capabilities to emerge could provide useful insights into how we foster wellbeing literacy in different contexts. By democratising whose experiences of wellbeing are included and uplifting diverse ways of knowing, we can construct more emancipatory and action-oriented models to facilitate wellbeing. We believe that storying is a profound capability through which people can, not just describe, but reshape the outside-in and inside-out dynamics influencing their own and others' wellbeing journeys.

References

Alexandrova, A., & Fabian, M. (2022). Democratising measurement: Or why thick concepts call for coproduction. *European Journal for Philosophy of Science*, *12*(1). https://doi.org/10.1007/s13194-021-00437-7

Archibald, M. M., & Gerber, N. (2018). Arts and mixed methods research: An innovative methodological merger. *American Behavioral Science*, *62*(7), 956–977. https://doi.org/10.1177/0002764218772672

Barbrook-Johnson, P., & Penn, A. S. (2022). *Systems mapping*. Palgrave Macmillan.

Bell, S., & Morse, S. (2013). How people use rich pictures to help them think and act. *Systemic Practice and Action Research*, *26*(4), 331–348. https://doi.org/10.1007/s11213-012-9236-x

Brooks, J. A., Shablack, H., Gendron, M., Satpute, A. B., Parrish, M. H., & Lindquist, K. A. (2017). The role of language in the experience and perception of emotion: A neuroimaging meta-analysis. *Social Cognitive and Affective Neuroscience*, *12*(2), 169–183. https://doi.org/10.1093/scan/nsw121

Brothers, C. (2005). *Language and the pursuit of happiness: A new foundation for designing your life, your relationships and your results*. New Possibilities Press.

Burr, V. (2015). *Social constructionism* (3rd ed.). Routledge. https://doi.org/10.4324/9781315715421

Chawla, D. (2011). Between stories and theories: Embodiments, disembodiments and other struggles. In D. Chawla & A. Rodriguez (Eds.), *Liminal traces: Storying, performing, and embodying postcoloniality* (pp. 13–24). Sense Publishers.

Clandinin, D. J., & Rosiek, J. (2007). Mapping a landscape of narrative inquiry: Borderland spaces and tensions. In D. J. Clandinin (Ed.), *Handbook of narrative inquiry: Mapping a methodology* (pp. 35–76). Sage.

Colla, R. H., & Kurtz, C. F. (2024). Storying research: Exploring the benefits of participatory narrative inquiry as a methodology for wellbeing research. *International Journal of Applied Positive Psychology*. https://doi.org/10.1007/s41042-024-00147-4

Conte, K. P., & Davidson, S. (2020). Using a 'rich picture' to facilitate systems thinking in research coproduction. *Health Research Policy & Systems*, *18*(1), 14. https://doi.org/10.1186/s12961-019-0514-2

Creswell, J. W. (2013). *Qualitative inquiry and research design: Choosing among five approaches* (3rd ed.). Sage.

Douglas, K., & Carless, D. (2018). Engaging with arts-based research: A story in three parts. *Qualitative Research in Psychology*, *15*(2-3), 156–172. https://doi.org/10.1080/14780887.2018.1429843

Fathulla, K. (2008). Understanding diagrams: A pointer to the development of diagramming software. *Visible Language*, *42*(3), 265–284.

Gee, J. (1991). Socio-cultural approaches to literacy (literacies). *Annual Review of Applied Linguistics*, *12*, 31–48. https://doi.org/10.1017/S0267190500002130

Gee, J. (2005). The new literacy studies: From 'socially situated' to the work. In D. Barton, M. Hamilton, & R. Ivanic (Eds.), *Situated literacies: Theorising Reading and writing in context* (pp. 177–193). Taylor and Francis. https://doi.org/10.4324/9780203984963

Gottschall, J. (2012). *The storytelling animal: How stories make us human*. Houghton Mifflin Harcourt.

Hayes, S. C., Barnes-Holmes, D., & Wilson, K. G. (2012). Contextual behavioral science: Creating a science more adequate to the challenge of the human condition. *Journal of Contextual Behavioral Science*, *1*(1-2), 1–16. https://doi.org/10.1016/j.jcbs.2012.09.004

Henriques, G., Kleinman, K., & Asselin, C. (2014). The nested model of well-being: A unified approach. *Review of General Psychology*, *18*(1), 7–18. https://doi.org/10.1037/a0036288

Holman Jones, S. (2016). Living bodies of thought. *Qualitative Inquiry*, *22*(4), 228–237. https://doi.org/10.1177/1077800415622509

Hou, H., Chin, T. C., Slemp, G. R., & Oades, L. G. (2021). Wellbeing literacy: Conceptualization, measurement, and preliminary empirical findings from students, parents and school staff. *International Journal of Environmental Research and Public Health*, *18*(4). https://doi.org/10.3390/ijerph18041485

Hutchens, D. (2015). *Circle of the nine muses*. John Wiley & Sons.

Jarden, A. (2015). Introducing workplace wellbeing to organisations: The "Me, We, Us" model. https://www.aaronjarden.com/uploads/3/8/0/4/3804146/the_me_we_us_model_final.pdf

Knowles, J., & Cole, A. (2008). *Handbook of the arts in qualitative research: Perspectives, methodologies, examples, and issues*. Sage. https://doi.org/10.4135/9781452226545

Kurtz, C. (2014). *Working with stories in your community or organization: Participatory narrative inquiry* (3rd ed.). Kurtz-Fernhout Publishing.

Mair, M. (1988). Psychology as storytelling. *International Journal of Personal Construct Psychology*, *1*(2), 125–137. https://doi.org/10.1080/10720538808412771

McAdams, D. P. (2001). The psychology of life stories. *Review of General Psychology*, *5*(2), 100–122. https://doi.org/10.1037/1089-2680.5.2.100

McAdams, D. P., & McLean, K. C. (2013). Narrative identity. *Current Directions in Psychological Science*, *22*(3), 233–238. https://doi.org/10.1177/0963721413475622

Monk, A., & Howard, S. (1998). The rich picture: A tool for reasoning about work context. *Interactions*, *5*, 21–30. https://doi.org/10.1145/274430.274434

Oades, L. G., Jarden, A., Hou, H., Ozturk, C., Williams, P., Slemp, G. R., & Huang, L. (2021). Wellbeing literacy: A capability model for wellbeing science and practice. *International Journal of Environmental Research and Public Health*, *18*(2). https://doi.org/10.3390/ijerph18020719

Oades, L. G., Ozturk, C., Hou, H., & Slemp, G. R. (2020). Wellbeing literacy: A language-use capability relevant to wellbeing outcomes of positive psychology intervention. *The Journal of Positive Psychology*, *15*(5), 696–700. https://doi.org/10.1080/17439760.2020.1789711

Perry, K. H. (2012). What is literacy? A critical overview of sociocultural perspectives. *Journal of Language and Literacy Education*, *8*, 50–71.

Phillips, L. G., & Bunda, T. (2018). *Research through, with and as storying*. Routledge. https://doi.org/10.4324/9781315109190-5

Riley, T., & Hawe, P. (2005). Researching practice: The methodological case for narrative inquiry. *Health Education Research*, *20*(2), 226–236. https://doi.org/10.1093/her/cyg122

Sen, A. (1980). Equality of what? In S. M. McMurrin (Ed.), *Tanner lectures on human values* (Vol. 1). Cambridge University Press.

Sen, A. (1985). *Commodities and capabilities*. Oxford University Press.

Sen, A. (1993). Capability and well-being. In M. Nussbaum & A. Sen (Eds.), *The quality of life* (pp. 30–53). Oxford University Press. https://doi.org/10.1093/0198287976.003.0003

Sivak, L., Westhead, S., Richards, E., Atkinson, S., Richards, J., Dare, H., Zuckermann, G., Gee, G., Wright, M., Rosen, A., Walsh, M., Brown, N., & Brown, A. (2019). "Language breathes life"- Barngarla community perspectives on the wellbeing impacts of reclaiming a dormant Australian aboriginal language. *International Journal of Environmental Research and Public Health*, *16*(20). https://doi.org/10.3390/ijerph16203918

Smith, D., Schlaepfer, P., Major, K., Dyble, M., Page, A. E., Thompson, J., Chaudhary, N., Salali, G. D., Mace, R., Astete, L., Ngales, M., Vinicius, L., & Migliano, A. B. (2017). Cooperation and the evolution of hunter-gatherer storytelling. *Nature Communications*, *8*(1), 1853. https://doi.org/10.1038/s41467-017-02036-8

Snyder, C. R. (2002). Hope Theory: Rainbows in the mind. *Psychological Inquiry*, *13*(4), 249–275. https://doi.org/10.1207/S15327965PLI1304_01

Sun, J., Schwartz, H. A., Son, Y., Kern, M. L., & Vazire, S. (2020). The language of well-being: Tracking fluctuations in emotion experience through everyday speech. *Journal of Personality and Social Psychology*, *118*(2), 364–387. https://doi.org/10.1037/pspp0000244

Webster, N. (1969). *webster's third new international dictionary of the English language, unabridged: A Merriam-Webster*. Riverside.

Williams, P., Kern, M., & Waters, L. (2016). inside-out-outside-in: A dual approach process model to developing work happiness. *International Journal of Wellbeing*, *6*(2), 30–56. https://doi.org/10.5502/ijw.v6i2.489

Wittgenstein, L. (1953). *Philosophical investigations* (G. E. M. Anscombe, Trans.). Oxford.

12

LANGUAGE, LITERACY AND WELLBEING IN THE EARLY YEARS

What Happens Early Matters

Lisa M. Baker

Wellbeing and Childhood

> Children are like little trees. In the early years, they are growing roots – learning the ways of their people, their land, their stories. This is when they are most open to the knowledge of the ancestors, and we must nurture that growth carefully.

These words, from Ngangiwumirr elder, artist and educator, Dr. Miriam-Rose Ungunmerr-Baumann (About Miriam Rose Foundation – Miriam Rose Foundation), reflects a long-held belief in the importance of the early childhood years. Likening children's development to the foundation of tree roots, this serves to focus us on the vitality of the early years of childhood for deep and lasting growth and wellbeing. Decades of research, particularly that from neuroscience, supports views such as that of the Ngangiwumirr people, and the knowledge that early childhood is an undeniably critical life stage where children's capacity to construct knowledge is fundamentally shaped (MCEECDYA, 2010; NSCDC, 2004). For development, health, learning and wellbeing, the years between birth and eight are profoundly influential – not just for this immediate early childhood period, but for establishing a positive life trajectory across multiple, interrelated domains. Rapid and cumulative development occurs in early childhood, encompassing physical, socio-emotional, psychological, cognitive, language and self-regulatory skills and capacities, laying roots for lifelong learning, health and positive outcomes (Berger, 2020; Shonkoff & Phillips, 2000). While 'early childhood' is not a developmental window with hard borders and is instead a distinctly individual, intersectional, and contextual continuum encompassing the time before birth and age eight,

DOI: 10.4324/9781003644293-12

the profound effects for shaping long-term trajectories are undisputed (Kelly & Allen, 2015, UNICEF, 2023).

Wellbeing can be an amorphous concept – complex, intangible, multifaceted, contested – and has been debated for millennia (Jarden & Roache, 2023). The idea of 'wellbeing' goes beyond merely the absence of 'illbeing' or dysfunction, with research confirming a strong sense of wellbeing is linked to a wide range of life outcomes, including enhanced functioning, greater happiness, success, improved relationships, better health, and increased longevity (Huppert, 2009; Lyubomirsky et al., 2005). Wellbeing is also impacted by interconnected and contextual factors including those related to the economy, human rights, the environment, an individual's psychological characteristics, social circumstances, and cultural forces (McNulty & Fincham, 2012; Myers & Diener, 2018). These ecological, internal, and external factors are particularly relevant when discussing children's wellbeing.

Childhood is a unique time of interdependence and vulnerability in the world. The influence of cultural and contextual limitations, expectations, and opportunities upon children impacts their learning, development, and wellbeing (Pollard & Lee, 2003; White, 2008). Additionally, childhood is a distinctive and time-sensitive phase marked by rapid neurological, psychological, and physical growth; both dynamic and evolving (OECD, 2023). The concept of child wellbeing therefore pertains not only to children's immediate lives and experiences but also the long-term effects on their future development and opportunities (Ben-Arieh et al., 2014). Furthermore, child wellbeing can be examined and understood from diverse perspectives – including cultural and contextual views about its impacts on economic sustainability and government policy; moral obligations and ecological considerations related to children having strong wellbeing; how learning, development and education are connected; and wellbeing in regard to child rights and child voice (Baker et al., 2021; Jarden & Roache, 2023). With that complexity in mind, a broad definition of wellbeing, relevant to childhood, is offered here to guide the following discussion. The combined views of Dodge et al. (2012) and Huppert and So (2013) suggest that wellbeing is a balanced state of being able to feel good, do good, and function well within one's context. How children's wellbeing relates to language, literacy, and the early years is of particular interest to this chapter.

Young Children's Language and Literacy Development

Humans have an innate ability to use language. Whether spoken, signed, or through the body, language skills begin in infancy – babies are predisposed to babbling and speaking begins without being taught (Al-Harbi, 2020). From birth (and prior) the use of language is everywhere, impacting children's experiences, interactions, knowledge, and meaning-making. Along with language acquisition, literacy development also occurs organically in the early years as children are immersed in their social and cultural worlds. Children grow, encounter and are informed by others more knowledgeable than them, rapidly developing language, literacy, and the capacity to use them in all their forms – written, visual, oral, and auditory (Raban, 2012).

Conceptions of literacy have evolved in recent decades, but the traditional western idea of literacy, and how the layperson may still frame literacy skills, is predominantly the ability to read and write. Traditional literacy has long been viewed as a linear, individual, and developmental outcome of formal education, where we learn to extract information through reading and communicate through writing (Razfar & Gutiérrez, 2003). New parents eagerly await their child being able to read or write their names, with these skills prized as milestones in the modern world. However, literacy scholars have expanded the view of literacy from an individual, cognitive process (where reading and writing is an internal, mental practice), to a sociocultural one, occurring between people and within a context (Gee, 2015). We have moved from the page to the screen as our dominant text structure and expanded our views of what it is to be literate. We recognise that reading and writing are not the only literacy valuable in a volatile, virtual, technological and hyper-connected world. There is an understanding of the need to be literate in many ways across multiple domains, and the concept of multiple literacies has emerged (Gee, 2015) with terms like 'financial literacy', 'digital literacy', 'emotional literacy', and 'health literacy' increasingly used in western vernacular. In understanding literacy as a communication and meaning-making tool, requisite for developing knowledge, feeling good, and functioning in the world, we also appreciate the many language modes it employs. Beyond written or oral modes, language and 'text' can be generated and received in multi-modal ways, including visually (via still or moving images; watching or viewing); aurally (music, sounds; hearing and listening); sensorily (tactile representations of touch, smell, taste); gesture (face and body movements; dance, ceremony and rituals) and/or spatially (architecturally, through proximity and interpersonal distance) (Cope & Kalantzis, 2009).

Here, in these contemporary views of literacy as sociocultural, multiple, and multi-modal, the concept of 'wellbeing literacy' finds a nexus. Moreover, in the dynamic and cumulative impactful early childhood years, a wellbeing literacy crucible exists.

Wellbeing Literacy

Simply defined as 'the mindful use of language for and about wellbeing' (Hou et al., 2021, p. 1), the concept of wellbeing literacy has much to offer contemporary literacy, wellbeing, and child development discourse. Wellbeing literacy is the ability to communicate intentionally about and for wellbeing and involves language skills that are used in context and for the direct purpose

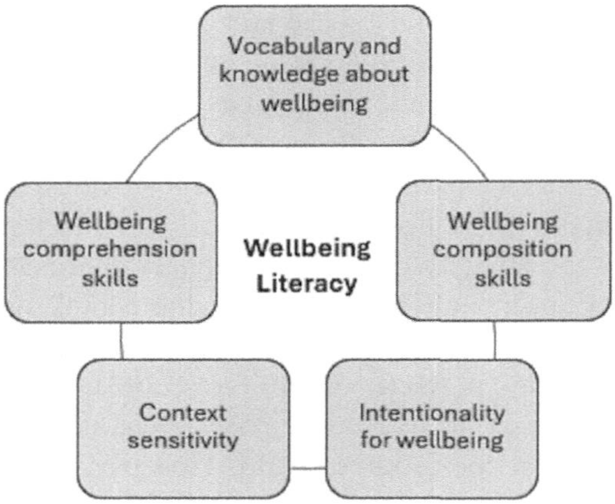

FIGURE 12.1 The wellbeing literacy capability model.

Source: Adapted from Oades et al. (2021).

of wellbeing creation. These include developing words and knowledge about wellbeing, being able to understand and express wellbeing languages, being aware of and adapting to our context and having an intention for wellbeing (Oades et al., 2021). These five necessary components combine as the capability of wellbeing literacy (see Figure 12.1).

In line with multiple literacies and sociocultural views of literacy as constructing and making meaning within and between people, wellbeing literacy draws attention to the language people have and use around their wellbeing (Oades et al., 2021). Language is central to human experience, and an innate and powerful lever for impacting human development and wellbeing (Hou et al., 2021). Wellbeing literacy can be taught, nurtured and learned, beginning at any age, and in all situations, for oneself, others, or the world (Hou et al., 2021). Wellbeing literacy has been studied in primary school children (aged 5–10 years) through visual narrative analysis of children's drawings (Waters & Higgins, 2022; Waters et al., 2022) and via a brief online positive psychological intervention (Francis et al., 2020) providing children with the opportunity to identify what assists their wellbeing. However, many more opportunities for exploration exist. This chapter proffers that despite its recent arrival in wellbeing scholarship, wellbeing literacy can be argued as the most vital literacy of all to begin in early childhood as children are rapidly establishing their communication and wellbeing roots (Baker et al., 2021).

Wellbeing Literacy in the Worlds of Children

Where do wellbeing literacy and early childhood meet? Important influences on learning, development, and wellbeing in childhood are family (parents, caregivers, siblings, and kin) and the early education and care services and schools they attend (National Research Council, 2015). These family and education settings hold the first audiences for children's communication and are drivers of their wellbeing. As primary channels they are therefore key contexts in which wellbeing literacy can and should be taught and supported.

To function in these key environments, children need strong expressive and receptive language skills, yet their ability to understand the world around them and participate in it socially, physically, and cognitively differing vastly with age and experience. What a toddler can say, comprehend, and do for their own wellbeing will naturally be very different to that of a seven-year-old. However, language, in its many modes, is core to young children's desire to engage, and they are constantly adapting and learning to feel good and function well. Even babies will find ways to communicate and be heard for the purposes of their own thriving!

Initial suggestions for how wellbeing literacy may look for children in these early years is offered in Table 12.1, informed by the author's early childhood education pedagogy and experience, data collected from early childhood educators, and discussions with other wellbeing literacy and education practitioners. Specific (but not universal) ideas that families and educators may adopt or adapt to support the development of young children's wellbeing literacy are offered within the table, but caveats to these suggestions exist. The nascent position of wellbeing literacy means empirical data, scholarly perspectives, and real-world examples of its application to families, children, and early education settings are lacking. While this author and other wellbeing literacy and early education scholars have proffered the applicability and relevance of wellbeing literacy to the crucial life stage of the early years, more information is needed. Moreover, it is acknowledged that parenting and educating young children is bound by contextual, developmental and sociocultural constraints, opportunities, expectations, and experiences. Not all strategies or affordances may be comprehensively relevant, appropriate, or desired by individual families or educational settings.

I suggest those working with or parenting young children could also think of many examples of wellbeing literacy in 'action', other than the above, when using the five components of the wellbeing literacy capability model as a framework to view children's wellbeing communication and behaviours. Consider the 18-month-old who has mastered the ability to tell the family 'Alexa' to play 'The Wiggles' so she can dance at will. Or the 4-year-old offering his stuffed toy and suggesting singing their favourite song when he notices his mother feeling upset at school drop-off time. Or the caregiver who is teaching a 1-year-old key-sign language for basic concepts such as 'more', 'help', 'milk', and 'all done' to increase communication options and reduce frustration. The teacher who introduces their class of 7-year-olds to the idea of being 'the boss of your body' along with strategies for calming and personal boundary setting

TABLE 12.1 How wellbeing literacy might appear and be taught in the early childhood years (adapted from Baker et al., 2021; Oades et al., 2021)

Wellbeing literacy component and description		*How this might look in the early childhood years*	*How might this skill be taught to or used by a young child (at home or in education settings)*
The WHAT? of Wellbeing Literacy - *about* wellbeing	**Knowledge and Vocabulary about wellbeing** – Having words, information about wellbeing that are consistent with our values and social context.	*Children are learning words they can use, and that other people understand, to help themselves and/or others feel good and function well.*	Children are introduced to vocabulary and knowledge of their possible strengths of character for making sense of interacting with self and others, e.g., kindness, teamwork, gratitude, self-control (see also www.viacharacter.org). Children learn about breathing techniques as ways to regulate their mind and bodies.
The HOW?	**Wellbeing Comprehension** – Being able to understand texts* relevant to wellbeing in many ways, including listening, reading, viewing about, and for wellbeing.	*Children are using their receptive language skills about and for wellbeing – they have to opportunity to hear, see, watch, read, and/or understand ways to feel good and contribute to others wellbeing.*	Children read books, sing songs, and perform dances that are focused on emotions to understand a spectrum of feelings and that they are all important and valid. Children can create and/or view resources (such as photographs or drawings of people, places, animals, or things) so they can look them and think about the people who love them and supports they have, particularly at times when they are feeling sad or lonely. Children are supported to learn breathing exercises they can do when they want to calm their body or get ready for daily rest time. This may be informally or through free guided mindfulness apps, such as 'Smiling Mind' or 'Headspace'.
	Wellbeing composition – Being able to produce texts* relevant to wellbeing in many ways, including speaking, writing, and creating about and for wellbeing.	*Children are using their expressive language skills about and for wellbeing – they have to opportunity to write, draw, make, create, dance, sign, and/or talk about things to help themselves feel good and function well.*	Children are taught ways move their bodies and encouraged to dance with sibling or friends when they are feeling restless or want to have fun. This may be with adult support or accessing appropriate resources online (such as their favourite performers or musician). Provisions are available to children to create pictures of themselves (for example painting/drawing supplies; craft, found or natural materials) to share with friends, family or others in their lives. And/or to access anytime for creative pleasure.

(*Continued*)

TABLE 12.1 (Continued)

Wellbeing literacy component and description		*How this might look in the early childhood years*	*How might this skill be taught to or used by a young child (at home or in education settings)*
The WHO? WHEN? WHERE?	**Context sensitivity** – Having an awareness of context and being able to adapt wellbeing to language suit.	*Children begin to understand that receiving and expressing wellbeing language can be different in different places, with different people, and different circumstances.*	Parents and carers share information with teachers about language and strategies they each use with children – about labelling feelings or favourite songs and dances – in languages relevant to the lives of the children, so they can use and adapt these across both home and educational contexts. Children begin to understand that words and strategies they use for feeling good and functioning with family and with peers are different and may be changed depending on where they are – for example, excitement and high energy may be able to be expressed at home through loud music and dancing, while this may adapted at school to be channelled through creating with playdough or drawing.
The WHY? of Wellbeing Literacy - *for* wellbeing	**Intentionality for wellbeing** – the habit of intentionally communicating for the purposes of wellbeing.	*Children are mindfully or skilfully using language modes (such as listening, viewing, speaking, writing, drawing, and/or creating) to purposefully maintain or improve their own or other's wellbeing.*	Children have a selection of music they play each night to calm themselves before going to bed, and/or they are taught a range of songs, breathing techniques, and movements that assist in emotional regulation and soothing. Sensory and creative provisions, such as sand, water, and art materials, are always available to children for them to experience, regulate, and express their emotions and ideas.

Note: 'Text' means a piece of spoken, written, visual, gestural, or audio material that you can see, interpret, or assign meaning to. This may be an oral conversation, written words (from a traffic sign to a letter or book), a digital message (a text, gif, emojis, or video clip), music, or something physically and spatially created or performed (such as a drawing, sculpture, or dance) (Cope & Kalantzis, 2009).

they can use when they feel dysregulated or in need of space. Or the family who tell stories of 'what went well today' over dinner each night, sharing how this makes them feel and why acknowledging the positive helps them feel and function well. These small but mindful uses of multi-modal communication with a desire for the wellbeing of self and/or others, can and do occur in the early childhood years, developing children's wellbeing literacy. Perhaps we have not viewed them as such before, or we have lacked the express intention or knowledge of them as practices about or for wellbeing. Either way, their power and potential to help young children feel good, do good and function well, is important and can be recognised as such through the lens of wellbeing literacy.

Wellbeing Literacy in Early Childhood

Science is iterative and the world is complex; new ideas rise and fall. It is iteration and complexity that support the application of wellbeing literacy and its capability model to the lives of young children. Conceptions and definitions of wellbeing have been fascinating to humans across time, from richly rooted indigenous stories and the musings of philosophers to modern science, global policy, and measures. Child wellbeing specifically is a topic of global concern and discourse with the facilitation of flourishing viewed as a contemporary educational outcome as important as academic proficiency (De Ruyter et al., 2020; OECD, 2017). Wellbeing also remains the primal interest of parents as they hold their newborn or send a young child off to school.

Just as shifts have occurred in literacy understanding and notions of wellbeing, so to have perceptions of young children and what they need and deserve. Contemporary perspectives advocate for children as holders of rights, with capabilities and to be respected and heard (United Nations, 1989). Our focus for children has moved beyond mere survival and protection from life's negative aspects, to focusing on their strengths, immediate experiences and their self-perceptions and viewpoints, away from solely what they contribute to the future – from 'well-becoming' to 'well-being' (Ben-Arieh et al., 2014, p. 570).

In this context a literacy of wellbeing is pertinent and timely. Wellbeing literacy is a contemporary literacy more relevant in the early years than the narrow and traditional perspective, which can no longer be viewed as wholly addressing modern-day demands. There is a need in the early years to prioritise children's wellbeing and language development for functioning and flourishing. Wellbeing literacy addresses this need through a comprehensive capability model that can be used across contexts, highlighting what children can be and do with language strengths and capabilities. It is a positive, language-based resource and framework that can support families to raise wellbeing literate children, and for early childhood services and government programs to share a strength-based common language around and for children's wellbeing.

Wellbeing literacy is a capability that can be taught, learned and used within families and in early childhood programs, schools and services. The five-component model (Table 12.1) recognises context and illuminates the words, vocabulary and knowledge that children and families can have for and about their wellbeing. Moreover, wellbeing literacy is a lifelong, ongoing capability that can be built with intention and carried across contexts, rather than a single wellbeing intervention that is 'done' to children by adults. In recognising literacy as a sociocultural phenomenon and that children are socialised into the dominant discourses where they are culturally and socially situated, wellbeing literacy is also relevant to first nations and indigenous settings. The protective factors for children's wellbeing of cultural identity, kinship structures and connection are applicable within the five components of the wellbeing literacy model, respecting place-based approaches to wellbeing, ways of being, and ancestral knowledge systems of indigenous cultures.

Contemporary discourse about early childhood respects the fact that young children are contributing citizens of the world, with rights and capabilities, whose wellbeing should be prioritised. This along with ancient wisdoms such as that of the Ngangiwumirr people of valuing children 'growing roots – learning the ways of their people, their land, their stories', support wellbeing literacy as a place to shine our collective light, policy, and scholarship. Parents, professionals, and policymakers can and must put aside a pushed-down agenda of hurrying children into traditional literacy that no longer fully serves us. We must marvel instead at the 18-month-old facilitating her own flourishing through the modes of music, dance, and technology. Aspire to the intentionality of the 4-year-old adapting to the context of his family and seeking feeling-good for his mother. Respect the 7-year-old who has the words and information to be the boss of their mind and body. It is time to understand, prioritise and promote wellbeing literacy as we know what happens early matters.

REFERENCES

Al-Harbi, S. S. (2020). Language development and acquisition in early childhood. *Journal of Education and Learning (Edulearn)*, *14*(1), 69–73.

Baker, L. M., Oades, L. G., & Raban, B. (2021). Wellbeing literacy and early childhood education. *New Zealand International Research in Early Childhood Education*, *23*(2), 4–19.

Ben-Arieh, A., Casas, F., Frønes, I., & Korbin, J. E. (2014). Multifaceted concept of child well-being. In A. Ben-Arieh, F. Casas, I. Frønes, & J. E. Korbin (Eds.), *Handbook of child well-being: Theories, methods and policies in global perspective*. Springer. https://doi.org/10.1007/978-90-481-9063-8_134

Berger, K. S. (2020). *The developing person through childhood and adolescence* (12th ed.). Worth Publishers.

Cope, B., & Kalantzis, M. (2009). "Multiliteracies": New Literacies, New Learning. *Pedagogies: An International Journal*, *4*(3), 164–195. https://doi.org/10.1080/15544800903076044

De Ruyter, D., Oades, L., & Waghid, Y. (2020). Meaning (s) of human flourishing and education. *Research brief by the International Science and Evidence based Education Assessment. An Initiative by UNESCO MGIEP.*

Dodge, R., Daly, A., Huyton, J., & Sanders, L. (2012). The challenge of defining wellbeing. *International Journal of Wellbeing*, *2*(3), 222–235

Francis, J., Chin, T. C., & Vella-Brodrick, D. (2020). Examining emotional literacy development using a brief on-line positive psychology intervention with primary school children. *International Journal of Environmental Research and Public Health*, *17*(20), 7612.

Gee, J. P. (2015). The new literacy studies 1. In J. Rowsell & K. Pahl (Eds.), *The Routledge handbook of literacy studies* (pp. 35–48). Routledge.

Hou, H., Chin, T. C., Slemp, G. R., & Oades, L. G. (2021). Wellbeing literacy: Conceptualization, measurement, and preliminary empirical findings from students, parents and school staff. *International Journal of Environmental Research and Public Health*, *18*(4), 1485.

Huppert, F. (2009). Psychological well-being: Evidence regarding its causes and consequences. *Applied Psychology: Health and Well-Being*, *1*(2), 137–164.

Huppert, F. A., & So, T. T. C. (2013). Flourishing across Europe: Application of a new conceptual framework for defining well-being. *Social Indicators Resource*, *110*(3), 837–861.

Jarden, A., & Roache, A. (2023). What is wellbeing? *International Journal of Environmental Research and Public Health*, *20*(6), 5006.

Kelly, B. B., & Allen, L. (Eds.). (2015). *Transforming the workforce for children birth through age 8: A unifying foundation*. National Academies Press.

Lyubomirsky, S., King, L., & Diener, E. (2005). The benefits of frequent positive affect: Does happiness lead to success? *Psychological Bulletin*, *131*(6), 803–855.

MCEECDYA (Ministerial Council for Education, Early Childhood Development and Youth Affairs) (2010). Engaging families in the early childhood development story. Neuroscience and early childhood development: Summary of selected literature and key messages for parenting. Ministerial Council for Education, Early Childhood Development and Youth Affairs. Neuroscience and early childhood development: Summary of selected https://www.yumpu.com/en/document/view/10997282/neuroscience-and-early-childhood-development-summary-of-selected

McNulty, J., & Fincham, F. (2012). Beyond positive psychology? Toward a contextual view of psychological processes and well-being. *American Psychologist*, *67*, 101–110. https://doi.org/10.1037/a0024572

Myers, D. G., & Diener, E. (2018). The scientific pursuit of happiness. *Perspectives on Psychological Science*, *13*(2), 218–225.

National Research Council. 2015. *Transforming the workforce for children birth through age 8: A unifying foundation*. The National Academies Press. https://doi.org/10.17226/19401

NSCDC (National Scientific Council on the Developing Child). (2004). Children's emotional development is built into the architecture of their brains: Working Paper No. 2. http://www.developingchild.net

Oades, L. G., Baker, L. M., Francis, J. J., & Taylor, J. A. (2021). Wellbeing literacy and positive education. In M. L. Kern & M. L. Wehmeyer (Eds.), *The Palgrave handbook of positive education* (pp. 325–343). Springer International Publishing.

Oades, L. G., Jarden, A., Hou, H., Ozturk, C., Williams, P., R. Slemp, G., & Huang, L. (2021). Wellbeing literacy: A capability model for wellbeing science and practice. *International Journal of Environmental Research and Public Health*, *18*(2), 719.

OECD. (2017). *How's life? 2017: Measuring well-being*. OECD Publishing. https://doi.org/10.1787/how_life-2017-en

OECD (2023). *Integrated policy making for child well-being: Common approaches and challenges ahead*. OECD Papers on Well-being and Inequalities, No. 16, OECD Publishing. https://doi.org/10.1787/1a5202af-en

Pollard, E. L., & Lee, P. D. (2003). Child well-being: A systematic review of the literature. *Social Indicators Research*, *61*, 59–78.

Raban, B. (2012). Early literacy-audience, context and purpose. *Practically Primary*, *17*(2), 4–5.

Razfar, A., & Gutiérrez, K. (2003). Reconceptualizing early childhood literacy: The sociocultural influence. In N. Hall, J. Larson, & J. Marsh (Eds.), *Handbook of early childhood literacy*. SAGE. (pp. 34–47).

Shonkoff, J. P., & Phillips, D. A. (Eds). (2000). *From neurons to neighborhoods: The science of early childhood development*. National Academy Press.

United Nations (1989, November 20). Convention on the Rights of the Child (UNCRC). https://www.ohchr.org/en/professionalinterest/pages/crc.aspx

United Nations Children's Fund (UNICEF). Division of Data, Analytics, Planning and Monitoring (2023). *The early childhood development index 2030: A new measure of early childhood development*. UNICEF.

United Nations Educational Scientific and Cultural Organization (UNESCO) (1990) Convention on the Rights of the Child. (1990). Available from https://www.unicef.org/child-rights-convention

Waters, L., Dussert, D., & Loton, D. (2022). How do young children understand and action their own well-being? Positive psychology, student voice, and well-being literacy in early childhood. *International Journal of Applied Positive Psychology*, *7*(1), 91–117.

Waters, L., & Higgins, M. C. (2022). The impact of a teacher-based positive education intervention on student wellbeing literacy. *Journal of School and Educational Psychology*, *2*(1), 22–43. https://doi.org/10.47602/josep.v2i1.12

White, S. C. (2008). But What is Wellbeing? A Framework for Analysis in Social and Development Policy and Practice. WeD Working Paper No. 43. Wellbeing in Developing Countries. ESRC Research Group, University of Bath, 18 pp.

13

WELLBEING LITERACY IN COMMUNITY

Translating Wellbeing Literacy Research into Practice

Jacqui Francis and Alex Couley

Introduction

Translating wellbeing research into effective practice remains a well-recognised challenge (Durlak & DuPre, 2008; Holtrop et al., 2021), including within community contexts (Kwan et al., 2019). Yet better understanding translation, delivery, and sustained application of research for health promotion and ill-health prevention is key (Meyers et al., 2012). Paradoxically, wellbeing itself is not necessarily foregrounded in the processes and practices of wellbeing research translation and implementation, where cooperative and sensitive interpersonal relationship (collaboration) (APA, 2024) are fundamental. Since relationships are core to collaboration (Hattori & Lapidus, 2004), and wellbeing (Baumeister & Leary, 1995; Dudgeon et al., 2022; Ryan & Deci, 2017), it is likely that communicating about and for wellbeing is important for effective researcher/practitioner collaborative relationships. We are therefore curious to explore how a research community and practitioner community can collaborate to translate wellbeing literacy research into successful practice, in ways that also support researcher and practitioner wellbeing.

As researcher and practitioner, we came together with different personal experiences in wellbeing literacy research translation. Contextually dependent and sensitive wellbeing literacy involves intentional, and consistent communication about and for wellbeing (Oades et al., 2021). We are curious to explore our different perspectives of the collaborative practices and processes necessary for successful research translation.

This chapter engages duoethnography (Norris & Sawyer, 2012). Our process is modelled on ethnographic research exploring the emotional experiences and diverse perspectives stemming from a shared phenomenon

DOI: 10.4324/9781003644293-13

(Lemon et al., 2024). We reflect on, interpret and transform our perspectives through our critical examination of shared vignettes (Alexakos, 2015). We highlight our emergent learnings as we respond to key questions, articulate our experiences and thoughts, iteratively and reflexively respond, and share our evolving and transforming perspectives. We delve deep into the heart of collaborative partnerships in research translation, and examine the role of values, goals, and communication, in sustaining quality relationships and collaboration, within the complex process of research translation. The conclusion proposes recommendations for peers and colleagues to review and consider, and potentially adopt when translating wellbeing literacy research into practice.

Wellbeing Literacy and Community

Wellbeing literacy involves intentional wellbeing communication (comprehending and composing) in contextually suitable and sensitive ways, for the benefit of self or others (Oades et al., 2021). Since wellbeing literacy is associated with greater wellbeing (Hou et al., 2021), promoting wellbeing literacy beyond individual and towards community capability holds potential to positively influence societal wellbeing.

Community can be defined as a group of people with shared characteristics or interests, which may or may not be a geographically based group (UNESCO, 2024). Community wellbeing is a complex, multi-layered, multi-level concept (Choi et al., 2020), involving 'the combination of social, economic, environmental, cultural, and political conditions identified by individuals and their communities as essential for them to flourish and fulfill their potential' (Wiseman & Brasher, 2008, p. 358). While historically rooted in assumptions of the autonomous self, the nuance and experience of community wellbeing is also related to collective living, community cohesion, values, and belonging (Atkinson et al., 2020). Here we represent two individuals from both separate and overlapping researcher and practitioner communities. We are interested in exploring the relational space between these two communities, as we seek to tease apart what facilitates and hinders successful wellbeing literacy translation.

Translation of Wellbeing Literacy Research

Implementation science has long sought to identify and articulate the pragmatics of implementation success (Wandersman et al., 2008). Frameworks inform research synthesis, delivery, and implementation and encourage consideration of practitioner needs and resources (Meyers et al., 2012). Human and environmental resources include competency, administrative, and leadership implementation drivers (Fixsen et al., 2015), and planning and assessment tools can help guide research translation and application (Glasgow et al.,

2019), from contemplation and preparation through to action (Prochaska & Velicer, 1997). However, for the people involved, what is the experience of research translation? How does it look and feel? What are the personal stories? Are there key elements that thread through the pragmatic aspects of implementation? If so, do these elements also support wellbeing?

Methodology

Here wellbeing literacy research translation within community is explored through duo ethnography. Following, methodological decisions are discussed before presenting an analysis of our adjacent narratives.

Duoethnography

Duoethnography is qualitative research that involves the co-construction of new knowledge through the sharing of personal narratives and self-reflection (Norris & Sawyer, 2012). This postpositivist, constructionist storying approach situates individual narratives within the wider social context and associated narratives (Benwell & Stokoe, 2006) and assumes storied productions of self and society (Chase, 2018). Life stories are juxtaposed, analysed, and synthesised to share multiple world perspectives (Lawrence & Lowe, 2020; Norris & Sawyer, 2012),

Participants

As duoethnographers we come from different geographic locations, organisational communities and cultures, life experience, and perspectives. As researcher and practitioner engaged in research translation, we join to examine the same phenomenon. Jacqui is an early-career wellbeing scholar, lecturer, and researcher. Jacqui seeks to facilitate equitable access to wellbeing knowledge and skills through engagement and dissemination projects with community. Alex has been a mental health practitioner for more than forty years. He currently holds a senior leadership position in a psychosocial support organisation. We met when Alex's organisation engaged Jacqui's organisation to help translate and embed wellbeing literacy knowledge and skills into community.

Our Process

We present our stories based on our separate experiences, creating a tapestry of perspectives. This is not a collective account of shared experience, nor do we refer to specific projects when creating our stories. Sequential process stages involve individual reflection, individual reflection of each other's perspectives, and collaborative synthesis. We began by writing an autoethnographic account of our research translation experiences, responding to the question: *How can the research community and practitioner community collaborate to translate wellbeing literacy research into successful practice?* We then responded through free writing to each other's reflections. As we reflected and responded, we considered: What similarities and synergies exist? What differences or challenges have shown up? Once completed we shared.

We present in vignettes the themes emerging from our reflections, responses, and collaborative synthesis. The final transformation stage represents our evolved thinking and consideration of the concluding question: *How does wellbeing literacy play a role in the research-translation process, for us in community?*

In the following discussion, we use our first names, Jacqui and Alex, reflecting our status as co-participants to this duo ethnographic research (Sawyer & Norris, 2012).

Analysis of Juxtaposed Texts and Emerging Themes

Following we introduce the two key themes which emerged from the synthesis of our reflections; these are supported and illustrated by our personal vignettes.

Values and Goals

The importance of shared values and shared goals stood out as a major theme of our reflections. Values are an umbrella term that relate to what matters to people (Witteman et al., 2021), and have been identified as important in community-based research translation (McKenney, 2016). Since internal values and goal pursuit are associated with quality motivation and wellbeing (Ryan et al., 2008), clarifying underpinning values may enable effective goal pursuit and wellbeing.

Jacqui's Reflection

I see effective collaboration as rooted in effective communication, trust-based relationships, and shared values and goals. These notions of communication, relationships, and goal achievement are fundamental to human existence. Valuing the opportunity to truly learn from each other allows different perspectives to be heard – through shared stories, experiences, and ideas. A climate of respect, trust, and reciprocity supports a safe psychological climate that enables robust and courageous dialogue, to explore what works for who and why. In my experience when there is an expectation of honesty, openness, and authenticity, more sustainable relationships are enabled.

Alex's Reflection

I have been blessed to ask the question of hundreds of individuals in training sessions 'What is a value?'. Most people struggle to answer. I am often drawn to the words of an ex-colleague. 'Values act to guide individuals, teams or organisations. Crucially they are not a destination point but are like the horizon'. You move towards your value, but you never tick it off and it's done. Another way to describe this is as follows. When people used to sail around the world, prior to compasses and the GPS they would use the stars as their guide. The stars were not the destination but a guide to keep them heading in broadly the right direction … Goals, however, are destinations. They are much more concrete. Many collaborative projects are based upon shared goals and indeed this is commonly the starting point … a key point for me is that it is okay for the respective parties to have differing goals … I think that whilst it is important that the overarching goals are the same it is natural that there would be individual goals at play too.

Jacqui's Transformation

Researcher practitioner collaborations are relational. Understanding each other's values and goals may not always be straightforward or comfortable, but (understanding) is necessary for a collaborative process that is meaningful, engaging and motivating, and optimally successful. Surfacing values and goals, in a contextually sensitive manner, by sharing stories to intentionally support wellbeing among collaborators, illustrates how wellbeing literacy can be used as a valuable part of the collaboration process. I see enhanced communication, through modes such as storying as an opportunity to understand others and their values better. Stories help break down barriers.

Alex's Transformation

Shared values emerge in the 'doing', the stories we tell, the way we respond to challenges and our willingness to step into each other's worldview. The stories are driven by our emotive and embodied reactions to the inevitable highs and lows of a joint research venture. At its heart I would suggest that we used an ethnographic reflective process throughout our shared journey … (Importantly) if you don't have a shared value base, then the goals become meaningless. If you haven't explored separate and shared goals, then what are you communicating about? Indeed values, goals, and stories seem to interact together to enhance science communication through various practices to help understand each other's values such as leveraging the power of stories, to uncover values (Merkle et al., 2021) and inform goals. Similarly, a strong researcher, practitioner community can be formed through the power of stories which facilitate understanding and articulating our shared values and goals.

Communication

Communication was a key theme identified as crucial for successful wellbeing literacy research translation. Defined as the '... transmission or exchange of information, knowledge, or ideas, by means of speech, writing, mechanical or electronic media etc.' (OECD, 2021), etymology stems from French (interpersonal contact), and Latin (consultation/discussion) origins. Combined communication is the interpersonal exchange of information through multimodal pathways. From a public health perspective effective communication is considered accessible and inclusive (OECD, 2021), and within interdisciplinary teamwork, communication is recognised as a key competency for success (Nancarrow et al. 2013). Communication has been identified as key in successful researcher-practitioner community collaboration (Lane et al., 2004). Effective communication is a vital capability for successful research translation, which is impacted by contextual factors and the people within those contexts drawing our attention beyond simple messages of composition and interpretation (Ratna, 2019). Factors identified as relevant for effective organisational communication, may also be relevant for community-based research. Communication style, the state of peace or conflict, transparency and trust, and the opportunity to speak and be heard (Musheke & Phiri, 2021), likely impact communication effectiveness and wellbeing.

Jacqui's Reflection

Communication is a deeply social process, a process of being seen, heard, acknowledged, and understood. Where communication is authentic, reciprocal, and respectful, opportunity for *effective* communication exists. Communication is the glue that holds everything together. Communication and a genuine intention to understand each other and the needs of each other. I have found serendipitously wellbeing literacy can also function as a tool for effective research translation ... in the ways that people communicate to support quality relationships and wellbeing within and between the researcher-practice communities.

Alex's Reflection

As communities come together it is often unintentional miscommunication that becomes an issue. All communities have their own artefacts, rituals, and symbols. These become part of how they interact with one another and are a form of communication. Jacqui refers to a 'genuine intent to understand one another'. I think that includes exploring sometimes-overlooked communication pathways. What are the artefacts, rituals, and symbols of your community and why do they matter? What messages do they convey? I would suggest that the deepest level of communication between two communities occurs when they begin to evolve their own mutual artefacts, rituals, and symbols.

Jacqui's Transformation

Individuals and their communities can strive to communicate accurately, with care and sensitivity, and with wellbeing intention, endeavouring to support effective communication and collaboration between two separate communities. However, it is possible a shared researcher/practitioner community space may emerge, a space where both reside, where place and people communicate in shared ways (language and/or artefacts) that supports effective collaboration. I wonder if in this instance shared artefacts and rituals that support effective collaboration and research translation may be evidenced?

Alex's Transformation

Why does all of this matter? Alongside our values and goals, we have talked about the critical importance of respectful communication. As I reflect more deeply, I find myself merging the idea of communication and storytelling. We are a narrative species and storytelling as a communication methodology is ingrained in who we are.

Wellbeing Literacy as a Tool in Research Translation

We began our duoethnographic inquiry with the question: *How can the research community and practitioner community collaborate to translate wellbeing literacy research into successful practice?* Through our reflections, vignettes, and collaborative synthesis, we identified the key themes of values, goals, and communication. The aim of our final transformation stage was to consider the concluding question: *How does wellbeing literacy play a role in the research – translation process, for us in community?* We feel wellbeing literacy can play an important role in the *translation* of wellbeing literacy research to practice – particularly through the power of stories. A key takeaway from our work is that wellbeing literacy may facilitate successful research translation in diverse contexts, and particularly within other contexts similar to our own – wellbeing literacy research being translated into the not-for-profit psychosocial support sector. Table 13.1 illustrates examples of wellbeing literacy used for research translation purposes

TABLE 13.1 The use of wellbeing literacy in research translation and implementation (adapted from Oades et al., 2022)

Wellbeing Literacy component and description		*How might this look when translating research into practice*
The WHAT (about wellbeing)	**Knowledge and Vocabulary about wellbeing** – values aligned and socially suitable words and information	The 'language' of research and the 'language' of practice, may in part diverge, however building a space of shared understanding (including asking questions as needed), supports the building of a shared researcher/practitioner language, and clarity in relation to values, goals and translation processes. **Practical tip:** During project planning explicitly identify and name underpinning practitioner and researcher values and goals.
The HOW	**Wellbeing Comprehension** – understanding information related to wellbeing by reading, listening or viewing about and for wellbeing.	Reading the espoused values of communities involved (researcher and practitioner communities). Listening to each other's articulated values and goals. Observing values illustrated in community artefacts (artefacts from the researcher or practitioner communities, and artefacts from the shared researcher/practitioner community), e.g., annual reports, commissioned artwork, visible displays, workspace design. **Practical tip:** Foster psychological safety and curiosity, enabling question-asking, clarification, and exploration of ways forward when values or goals misalign.
	Wellbeing Composition – producing information related to wellbeing in different modes.	Incorporate ethnographic approaches to share personal and community stories that illustrate what is meaningful within the community/ies, enabling deep communication, relationship building, and collaboration. **Practical tip:** Intentionally create time and space to tell and hear stories. This might be informally captured at the beginning of a meeting, or more formally captured in planned self-storying at the commencement of a collaboration or partnership.
The WHO? WHEN? WHERE?	**Context sensitivity** – awareness of context and adjusting language to suit the context.	Foster open, honest, reflective communication that is actively and dynamically adjusted as needed. **Practical tip:** Connect regularly throughout the project, clearly but compassionately reflect on goals, progress, group needs, and achievable action (Brown & Grant, 2010).
The WHY? (*for* wellbeing)	**Intentionality for wellbeing** – habitually communicating for wellbeing.	Consider co-designing contextually suited rituals, intentionally designed to support and enable wellbeing. **Practical tip:** Where possible seek to foster trusting, generative, values aligned and sustained researcher/practitioner relationships, support and celebrate these.

Conclusion

Here the subjective and relational aspects inherent in the complexities of community wellbeing (Atkinson et al., 2020) are highlighted, and recognised as opportunities for effective research translation, where communicating with deep listening and reciprocity, enables researchers, leaders, employees, and community members to understand each other better. Using a duoethnographic approach, we shared our own stories of translating wellbeing literacy research into organisational community practice. Researcher/practitioner understanding, and communication were identified as key to successful collaboration, particularly in relation to values held and intended goals. Shared narratives of personal and community stories were identified as one modality to achieve communication and understanding. Serendipitously we recognised wellbeing literacy itself as valuable in the research-translation process. Wellbeing literacy may enable wellbeing-supportive environments, that in turn support more effective collaboration and research translation, for those within both the researcher and practitioner communities, and in the sustenance and maintenance of the shared researcher/practitioner community.

References

Alexakos, K. (2015). *Being a teacher | Researcher. a primer on doing authentic inquiry research on teaching and learning*. Sense Publishers. https://doi.org/10.1007/978-94-6300-295-0

American Psychological Association (APA) (2024). APA Dictionary of Psychology. Collaboration. https://dictionary.apa.org/collaboration

Atkinson, S., Bagnall, A. M., Corcoran, R., South, J., & Curtis, S. (2020). Being well together: Individual subjective and community wellbeing. *Journal of Happiness Studies*, *21*(5), 1903–1921. https://doi.org/10.1007/s10902-019-00146-2

Baumeister, R. F., & Leary, M. R. (1995). The need to belong: Desire for interpersonal attachments as a fundamental human motivation. *Psychological Bulletin*, *117*(3), 497.

Benwell, B., & Stokoe, E. (2006). *Discourse and identity*. Edinburgh University Press.

Brown, S. W., & Grant, A. M. (2010). From GROW to GROUP: Theoretical issues and a practical model for group coaching in organisations. *Coaching: an International Journal of Theory, Research and Practice*, *3*(1), 30–45. https://doi.org/10.1080/17521880903559697

Chase, S. (2018). Narrative inquiry toward theoretical and methodological maturity. In N. Denzin & Y. Lincoln (Eds.), *The sage handbook of qualitative research* (5th ed., pp. 546–560). Sage.

Choi, N., Kim, J., & Lee, S. J. (2020). The usefulness of intersubjective community wellbeing as a community development indicator: Evidence from comparing three approaches to measuring community wellbeing. *International Journal of Community Well-Being*, *3*, 173–192. https://doi.org/10.1007/s42413-020-00059-6

Dudgeon, P., Derry, K. L., Mascall, C., & Ryder, A. (2022). Understanding aboriginal models of selfhood: The national empowerment Project's cultural, social, and emotional wellbeing program in Western Australia. *International Journal of Environmental Research and Public Health*, *19*(7), 4078. https://doi.org/10.3390/ijerph19074078

Durlak, J. A., & DuPre, E. P. (2008). Implementation matters: A review of research on the influence of implementation on program outcomes and the factors affecting implementation. *American Journal of Community Psychology*, *41*(3–4), 327–350. https://doi.org/10.1007/s10464-008-9165-0

Fixsen, D. L., Blase, K., Naoom, S. F., & Duda, M. (2015). *Implementation drivers: Assessing best practices. national implementation research network (NIRN). 2013.* Frank Porter Graham Child Development Institute, University of North Carolina Chapel Hill. https://doi.org/10.13140/RG.2.2.20415.30885

Glasgow, R. E., Harden, S. M., Gaglio, B., Rabin, B., Smith, M. L., Porter, G. C., & Estabrooks, P. A. (2019). RE-AIM planning and evaluation framework: Adapting to new science and practice with a 20-year review. *Frontiers in Public Health*, *7*, 64. https://doi:10.3389/fpubh.2019.00064

Hattori, R. A., & Lapidus, T. (2004). Collaboration, trust and innovative change. *Journal of Change Management*, *4*(2), 97–104. https://doi.org/10.1080/14697010320001549197

Holtrop, J. S., Estabrooks, P. A., Gaglio, B., Harden, S. M., Kessler, R. S., King, D. K., & Glasgow, R. E. (2021). Understanding and applying the RE-AIM framework: Clarifications and resources. *Journal of Clinical and Translational Science*, *5*(1), e126. https://doi.org/10.1017/cts.2021.789

Hou, H., Chin, T.-C., Slemp, G. R., & Oades, L. G. (2021). Wellbeing literacy: Conceptualization, measurement, and preliminary empirical findings from students, parents and school staff. *International Journal of Environmental Research and Public Health*, *18*(4), 1485. https://doi.org/10.3390/ijerph18041485

Kwan, B. M., McGinnes, H. L., Ory, M. G., Estabrooks, P. A., Waxmonsky, J. A., & Glasgow, R. E. (2019). RE-AIM in the real world: Use of the RE-AIM framework for program planning and evaluation in clinical and community settings. *Frontiers in Public Health*, *7*, 492438. https://doi.org/10.3389/fpubh.2019.00345

Lane, J., Turner, S., & Flores, C. (2004). Researcher-practitioner collaboration in community corrections: Overcoming hurdles for successful partnerships. *Criminal Justice Review*, *29*(1), 97–114. https://doi.org/10.1177/073401680402900107

Lawrence, L., & Lowe, R. J. (2020). An introduction to duoethnography. *Duoethnography in English language teaching: Research, reflection and classroom application*, 1–26.

Lemon, N., Francis, J., & Baker, L. M. (2024). Well-being literacy in the academic landscape: Trioethnographic inquiry into scholarly writing. *Brock Education Journal*, *33*(1), 27–48. https://doi.org/10.26522/brocked.v33i1.1120

McKenney, S. (2016). Researcher-practitioner collaboration in educational design research: Processes, roles, values, and expectations. In M. A. Evans, M. J. Packer, & R. K. Sawyer (Eds.), *Reflections on the learning sciences* (pp. 155–188). Cambridge University Press.

Merkle, B. G., Valdez-Ward, E., Shukla, P., & Bayer, S. R. (2021). Sharing science through shared values, goals, And stories: An evidence-based approach to making science matter. *Human–Wildlife Interactions*, *15*(3), 27. https://doi.org/10.26077/9wss-av78

Meyers, D. C., Durlak, J. A., & Wandersman, A. (2012). The quality implementation framework: A synthesis of critical steps in the implementation process. *American Journal of Community Psychology*, *50*(3-4), 462–480. https://doi:10.1007/s10464-012-9522-x

Musheke, M. M., & Phiri, J. (2021). The effects of effective communication on organizational performance based on the systems theory. *Open Journal of Business and Management*, *09*(02), 659–671. https://doi.org/10.4236/ojbm.2021.92034

Nancarrow, S. A., Booth, A., Ariss, S., Smith, T., Enderby, P., & Roots, A. (2013). Ten principles of good interdisciplinary team work. *Human Resources for Health*, *11*(1). https://doi.org/10.1186/1478-4491-11-19

Norris, J., & Sawyer, R. D. (2012). Toward a dialogic methodology. In J. Norris, R. D. Sawyer, & D. Lund (Eds.), *Duoethnography: Dialogic methods for social, health, and educational research* (pp. 9–40). Left Coast Press.

Oades, L., Hanchao, H., Francis, J., Baker, L., & Huang, L. (2022). Language use as a way to contextualise the process of positive education. In K.-A. Allen, M. J. Furlong, D. Vella-Brodrick, & S. Suldo (Eds.), *Handbook of positive psychology in schools* (pp. 91–103). Routledge.

Oades, L. G., Jarden, A., Hou, H., Ozturk, C., Williams, P., R Slemp, G., & Huang, L. (2021). wellbeing literacy: A capability model for wellbeing science and practice. *International Journal of Environmental Research and Public Health*, *18*(2), 719. https://www.mdpi.com/1660-4601/18/2/719

OECD (2021), *OECD report on public communication: The global context and the way forward*. OECD Publishing. https://doi.org/10.1787/22f8031c-en

Oxford English Dictionary (OED), 2024. Communication. https://www.oed.com/dictionary/communication_n?tl=true

Prochaska, J. O., & Velicer, W. F. (1997). The transtheoretical model of health behavior change. *American Journal of Health Promotion*, *12*(1), 38–48. https://doi.org/10.4278/0890-1171-12.1.38

Ratna, H. (2019). The importance of effective communication in healthcare practice. *Public Health Review*, *23*, 1–6. https://www.jstor.org/stable/48546767

Ryan, R., Huta, V., & Deci, E. L. (2008). Living well: A self-determination theory perspective on eudaimonia. *J Happiness Stud*, *9*, 139–170. https://doi.org/10.1007/s10902-006-9023-4

Ryan, R. M., & Deci, E. L. (2017). *Self-determination theory: Basic psychological needs in motivation, development, and wellness*. The Guilford Press.

Sawyer, R. D., & Norris, J. (2012). *Duoethnography*. Oxford University Press.

UNESCO (2024). Community. https://uis.unesco.org/en/glossary-term/community

Wandersman, A., Duffy, J., Flaspohler, P., Noonan, R., Lubell, K., Stillman, L., & Saul, J. (2008). Bridging The gap between prevention research and practice: The interactive systems framework for dissemination and implementation. *American Journal of Community Psychology*, *41*(3-4), 171–181. https://doi:10.1007/s10464-008-9174-z

Wiseman, J., & Brasher, K. (2008). Community wellbeing in an unwell world: Trends, challenges, and possibilities. *Journal of Public Health Policy*, *29*(3), 353–366. https://doi:10.1057/jphp.2008.16

Witteman, H. O., Ndjaboue, R., & Vaisson, G., et al. (2021). Clarifying values: An updated and expanded systematic review and meta-analysis. *Medical Decision Making*, *41*(7), 801–820. https://doi.org/10.1177/0272989X211037946

14

"YOU ARE ENOUGH. YOU ARE WHOLE": CENTRING COMMUNAL WELLBEING IN TEACHER EDUCATION

Linda Noble, Malgorzata Powietrzynska, Sharon Holmes, Katherine Knutsen, Riana Kolari, D.J. Nemat-Nasser, and Kaitlin Rice

Framing Our Journey

This chapter is an invitation to share in an ongoing exploration of wellbeing literacy, broadly defined as the ability to understand the concept and language of wellbeing (Waters & Charles Higgins, 2021). The journey began with two teacher educators (Malgorzata and Linda) planting seeds for teaching | learning about mindfulness and self-care in a School of Education program based in New York City, USA (Noble & Powietrzynska, 2023). The threads that comprise this tapestry of narratives were woven together by the two instructors and a group of 5 students in a graduate-level course. In our pursuit to elevate educators' wellness, we (Malgorzata and Linda) align with Oades et al.'s (2021a) framing of wellbeing literacy as the capability to comprehend and compose wellbeing language across contexts with the intention to maintain or improve the wellbeing of oneself and others. Furthermore, we believe that the promotion of wellbeing literacy must necessarily involve considerations that are epistemological, ontological, and axiological in nature. Thus, we understand wellbeing literacy as having the knowledge of as well as demonstrating and valuing competence in skills essential for personal health and collective happiness.

In the design of the Mindfulness in Teaching and Learning course, we intentionally applied a methodological bricolage (Tobin, 2018) in both content and pedagogy. Our conceptual framework includes what the Greater Good Science Center (2024) refers to as building blocks of individual and community wellbeing. In addition, our work is informed by Seligman's (2011) principles of PERMA as well as the path-breaking work within the field of science of wellbeing and human flourishing (cf. Frederikson & Losada, 2005)

DOI: 10.4324/9781003644293-14

including literature focused on educator self-care (Lemon, 2024). To that end, our course features a series of mindfulness topics paired up with corresponding character strengths including: Mindfulness and Wellbeing/Happiness; Mindfulness and Self-Care/Compassion; Mindfulness for Teachers/Empathy; Mindfulness and Mental Health/Forgiveness; Mindfulness in Sociocultural Contexts/Diversity; and Ecological Mindfulness/Gratitude.

In cultivating our understanding of wellbeing literacy, we collectively embrace a pedagogical approach to course implementation that reflects our philosophical commitment to contemplative pedagogy (cf. Zajonc, 2013) with an equity lens informed by Peter Kaufman's (2017) synthesis of contemplative and critical (Freire, 2000) educational practices. Since wellbeing is often viewed as a skill that can be developed through purposeful practice (Davidson & Schuyler, 2015), our pedagogy deliberately aims to centre the course participants' experience through mindfulness-based openings and transitions, "playlists" of choiceful and multimodal course materials, guided personal journaling (Lemon, 2024), collaborative reflections, as well as cooperative activities.

Importantly our course has matured under the compassionate and creative stewardship of its ardent participants, whose voices comprise the ensemble for this chapter. In developing wellbeing literacy, our community of learners seamlessly transitioned from a knowledge base of cognitive awareness to a somatic sense of embodied practice curating activities that reflected the five components of wellbeing literacy including writing, creating, and speaking *about* and *for* wellbeing (Oades et al., 2021b). Our respective and collective vignettes speak of laughter, shared camaraderie, empathic teachable moments, and surprising turns.

In the following sections we use the 5-components capability model of wellbeing literacy proposed by Oades et al. (2021a) that include: vocabulary and knowledge; multimodal comprehension and composition; as well as context sensitivity and intentionality. We illustrate how each component was woven into our course. In our approach, we align with Waters and Charles Higgins (2021) in arguing that since wellbeing literacy is about the words people use, "student voice" is the most appropriate way to assess wellbeing literacy. To that end, we adopted the methodology of "short written narratives" (Czarniawska, 2004) of the course participants; students and instructors alike.

Vocabulary and Knowledge

While wellbeing vocabulary reflects language associated with the wellbeing of oneself and of others (e.g., words such as mindfulness, perspective, and belonging); wellbeing knowledge includes declarative knowledge about wellbeing (Oades et al., 2021a). In the following vignette, Riana articulates words such as "anxiety" and expresses how it made her feel. The arc of Riana's wellbeing literacy appears to be a movement from anxiety to empathy, by using vocabulary, knowledge, and language skills to affect her own wellbeing. Riana notes,

> This course not only allowed me to experience a new way of learning, but it allowed me to understand myself better by pushing me *out of my comfort zone*. I was able to practise *mindfulness*, as well as teach it to my peers in the classroom. In doing so, I utilised my *empathic abilities* and refined my teaching skills by sharing these experiences alongside my classmates.
>
> I (Riana) reflect on growing up in a strict household and always being a timid student. I never wanted to raise my hand. I was scared that what I had to say wasn't valuable so I kept to myself for most of my school life. I have also struggled with anxiety since the age of fifteen, which only added to my fears. However, I now realise that my wellbeing is related to social connection as I always wanted to share my thoughts. This course challenged me because it was different from other classes in the way that I had to immerse myself into the content and conquer my presentation anxiety. The course focused on different aspects of mindfulness, such as empathy, compassion, happiness, forgiveness, and so forth. In our presentation on forgiveness (Luskin, 2010), my group and I introduced the topic by stressing the importance of being able to forgive oneself before forgiving others. We asked our classmates to write on index cards and share a time in which they struggled to forgive themselves or another. Afterwards, the cards were shuffled and distributed to the class, for others to read and decide if they would choose to forgive and/or how they would have handled the situation if they were the ones experiencing it. I was initially worried that students might not participate because the topic of forgiveness requires an immense amount of vulnerability (Brown, 2013), but I was delighted to see that my classmates were brave and open. In having students give their perspective on a situation that wasn't their own, they were practising and applying empathy (Marsh, 2005). In the closing activity students were asked to write something that they would like to let go of, whether that be hatred, trauma, anger, grudges, or so forth. When prompted, students would shred the piece of paper and let go of whatever it was that they wrote about.

For Riana, becoming a wellbeing literate individual involved a growth mindset (Dweck, 2017). In the framework of the five-component capability model, the language we use is a reflection of our current perceptions, attitudes, beliefs, choices, and freedoms (Oades et al., 2020). Riana's narrative demonstrates her capability to transform how she engaged with language for the betterment of her own and others' wellbeing.

Multimodal Comprehension

Communicating *about* and *for* wellbeing involves understanding and generating aspects of literacy in multiple modalities. For example, our students listen to and create a class playlist to embrace a sense of belonging in a culturally sustaining environment. We kinaesthetically experience gallery walks to mirror back feeling vulnerable and/or courageous while embodying these emotions. We read from and write on Padlets to articulate thoughts, feelings, and sensations associated with self-care. Sharon's narrative below references her experience with different course modalities.

> Hard to believe that out of seven siblings, I (Sharon) was my dad's favourite. Although I lost him at the tender age of fifteen, he and his strong belief that education is the one thing no one can take away from you lives inside of me. When I lost him, I assumed the role of the glue that kept my family together. I became everything for everyone while becoming very little for myself. While working as a New York City Police Officer during COVID-19, I remember saying how hard it was being essential both at home and at work.
>
> This class found me right when I needed it. My therapist recommended mindfulness practices one week before the start of class. I felt as though the universe was listening, and I am grateful that I received what it was saying. After re-assessing my strengths and challenges (VIA Institute on Character, 2024), I realise I've come a long way in such a short period. I've learned to let go of perfection and fear, and my commitment to going all in and trusting the process has taken over me. My "love letter to myself," my bad habit audit, and writing about my sphere of control, I loved it all. Sitting with myself and my thoughts is something that I never take for granted. It's nice to know that in this chaotic world there is peace within all of us. These days I prioritise MY wellbeing. I write in my journal regularly to clear my mind. I go on solo dates, and spend time with my nineteen and three-year-old. I unfollow people, places, and things from my social media that no longer serve me. I am also very big on my self-care, just to name a few of my mindfulness practices. When I lost my favourite niece to an overdose, I gave myself the permission to live the life that I've always dreamed of. Hence the reason I've been putting myself first, sold my house and retired from the Police Department early to do what I've always dreamt of, become a high school English teacher.

Sharon's narrative provides a unique and invaluable lesson about the power of multimodal comprehension in fostering wellbeing literacy. The way in which students understand and talk about their own wellbeing is an important predictor of mental health, yet only limited research has investigated how this capability can be promoted (Waters & Charles Higgins, 2021). Sharon's vignette illustrates the way in which the multimodal instructional scaffolds that included journal entries, group work, presentations, and in-class activities can create openings for vulnerability and personal "Growth" with the potential to enhance wellbeing.

Multimodal Composition

Writing, speaking, and creating are examples of multimodality of wellbeing communication composition. As noted by Gee (1998), literacy may be understood as crucial for relationships and wellbeing, a sociocultural phenomenon occurring between people. Wellbeing experiences are likely composed in congruence with values and the sociocultural context (Oades et al., 2022). Our course examples of intentionally composing for wellbeing include writing and trading post-its as simulations for the exchange of "rumours" about awareness, belonging, and courage among classmates to strengthen our sense of shared values. One example of speaking for wellbeing involves deliberately reciting quotes to uplift and boost morale throughout our course. In addition, as described by D.J. below, freewrites and collaging are opportunities to enact composition for wellbeing (Figure 14.1).

> I (D.J.) navigated early adulthood in XYZ City as a freshly "out" queer person, often finding myself drawing on lessons around mindfulness, self-care, empathy, and community building that I learned in my youth to find and cultivate safe spaces. When my project partner, Katherine, and I began brainstorming for our lesson on empathy, we knew our end goal was to build and strengthen a sense of community. Since the course required each of us to access and share the sensitive aspects of our minds and bodies, Katherine and I hoped to help peers let down their defences and begin to build bonds. We started with freewriting as an invaluable tool for centring oneself, venting out stressors, and self-reflection - a crucial first step into vulnerability, which in turn could facilitate empathy (Brown, 2013). For the main activity, we wanted students to create a small group collage with different strategies for cultivating empathy. Those strategies were active listening, identifying shared identity, "putting a face to feelings," and eliciting altruism (The Greater Good Science Center, 2024). In addition to engaging with the content and building community, we hoped the collaging would remind our cohort what it's like to be a high school student. It can feel awkward when you are placed into a group of strangers and are tasked with making art together. The act of pushing through that awkwardness would be a triumph of empathy. Afterwards, an invitational prompt for a free write was "what is something you're struggling with right now." Indeed, the moving show of community took Katherine and I by surprise.

FIGURE 14.1 Creating *for* and *about* wellbeing.

As D.J. illustrates in their narrative above, creating *for* and *about* wellbeing involved a group composition of a collage, representing the power in community. In this multimodal composition collaging activity students moved beyond curators of content to collaborative creators in a micro workshop setting. In the closing activity, one student after another demonstrated their trust by telling the class about their struggles with family conflict, recent deaths of loved ones, financial difficulties, a desire to break bad habits, and more.

Context Sensitivity

Since the meaning of language varies with context, wellbeing literacy requires context identification and appropriately adaptive language use. An individual demonstrates sensitivity to context, when they are able to select language and communication modes that meet different situations. The final project in our course involved designing and delivering a mindfulness workshop. Student groups were asked to choose different target audiences with whom to conduct the workshop. In each workshop there was evidence of context sensitivity in that the wellbeing language and related wellbeing practices were customised for a specific target audience such as mindful hiking in a park with teens. Kaitlin highlights the importance of context sensitivity as she reflects on her own identity, relationships, and her group's workshop that explores the topic of diversity.

> I (Kaitlin) always felt left out in my family dynamic. As the youngest, I never felt like I had a comfortable place to build relationships. I've also struggled with my identity. I come from a large indigenous family, but due to living so far from the reservation where so many of my cousins live, I feel such a great disconnect. They live lives that are so completely foreign to me, growing up in such a large city. When I visit, during the tourist season, I feel like one of those tourists as well.
>
> The mindfulness workshop that I co-created with my peers centred around diversity and how we navigate our identities in a richly diverse city. My favourite activity was when we created our own "I Am" poems (Momaday, 1992). I really found a connection with mindfulness and the way I view myself, and my relationship with who I want to be, especially as a teacher. One motto that I've found myself adopting is living in a constant state of content. I've always found myself pushing to experience the highest highs and getting stuck when I hit my lows. I've found that I am happiest when I float in the middle and push a lot of those extreme emotions away. I choose to focus on what I can handle, instead of being overwhelmed, or even underwhelmed My victories throughout my days consist of the small things, like making my coffee just right or actually putting all my laundry away once it's done instead of letting it sit. Acknowledging the little things makes my day so much more relaxed and helps me to concentrate on letting myself decompress.

As an indigenous woman with the lived experiences of feeling marginalised, isolated, and alone, Kaitlin leveraged the context sensitivity of wellbeing literacy she developed in becoming "ok to be with myself at my own pace." Kaitlin's narrative shares her experience conducting a context-sensitive workshop focused on identity. At the same time, she reminds us that when we follow the middle way we can remain balanced despite the dynamic nature of circumstances.

Intentionality

Intentionality relates to the component of wellbeing literacy; that is not just what language is about or signifies, but why it is being used. Language does not use itself; it has the user's intentions and awareness of contexts in which they use the language. A single act of intervention for the wellbeing of self or others is simply a wellbeing activity and does not assume or create literacy. Rather, wellbeing literacy denotes awareness, values, and goals, which motivate a habit of intention. In Katherine's words, "Every session in our course was a call to adventure, and I drew such delight from leaping in without hesitation, my eyes and heart wide open to the raw beauty of this precious experience." Katherine's narrative below is an example of intentionality that emerged from our course.

> Linda, Malgorzata and my beautiful, brilliant colleagues caught me (Katherine) and held me during one of the most difficult years of my life. We were so alive. Together, our devotion to the practice of mindfulness and the cultivation of a truly safe space allowed us to transcend from class to community. We braved icebreaker activities which made us cringe and giggle, watched lectures from leaders in the field who inspired us and assured us that we were on the right path, and mused about the healing power of our profession in the life of a child. Every session was a call to adventure, and I drew such delight from leaping in without hesitation, my eyes and heart wide open to the raw beauty of this precious experience.
>
> Still, I struggled mightily that winter, as I often do when the frigid months roll around and the sun goes into hibernation. One particularly cold evening, I felt the heinous icy breath of the monster upon my soul. I knew from experience I had to dig deep and fight back against the chilling despair, or risk succumbing to darkness. On a whim, I opened my laptop, thinking I'd use my old magic trick of distraction to delay the inevitable. Checking my school email through half-lidded eyes, I saw a reminder to meditate from Monique Rhodes' daily practice (Rhodes, 2018) introduced to me by Linda and Malgorzata. Immediately, my mind flashed to the last time I tried meditating consistently – against my will in an inpatient psychiatric unit while nine months pregnant with my son. I remembered the terror I felt closing my eyes in that bleak atmosphere, so vulnerable, surrounded by strangers, whilst my unborn baby kicked me, urging me not to give up. The hot shame poured over me all over again as I remembered being so hopeless during what should have been the happiest time of my life. Desperate to stop the torrent of memories, I clicked on the link and laid back on my bed, suppressing a sob. I remember thinking, I'll try anything.
>
> ...And I kept trying. Day after day, I returned to my bed, surprised by how soothed I felt listening to Monique's gentle voice. There were days when my mind wandered and ran marathons as she spoke. There were days when I cried hard and fast at her gentle words caressing my tortured spirit. There were days when I floated away and felt held by her message. Slowly, I realised that I was doing it – I was meditating, and that every single day mattered and was meaningful. Even outside of the classroom, the power of mindfulness was transforming me, one day at a time.

Katherine's narrative is testimony of a transformative shift due to the development of the skill of intentionality manifested in an ongoing mental state,

You are enough. You are whole
by Katherine Knutsen

This too shall pass –
Or so they say
Dust to dust, ash to ash
Will it, someday?
In every breath, a gentle dance,
A soft rhythmic tune guiding a mindful trance.
Awareness blooms in this silent winter air
the present hums, tender and rare –
How can we live without care?
Will mindfulness teach us at last?
Should I breathe with my fingers or perhaps a mere gentle grasp?

Happiness is only real when shared
Don't let your emotions leave you ensnared
Breathe in, breathe out
Confront the sea, scream and shout –

A distant whisper from someone dear,
Reminding you to live without fear –
From your fingers to your toes,
You are enough, you are whole.

FIGURE 14.2 This too shall pass.

rather than a solitary instance or action. For Katherine cultivating intentionality in wellbeing literacy was emancipatory and transformative (Figure 14.2).

"This Too Shall Pass" – Parting Words

According to Lemon et al. (2024), well-being literacy embraces the building, maintaining, and protecting of wellbeing in order for individuals, collectives, and systems to flourish. Rather than being a "quick fix" or focusing on what is broken, wellbeing literacy is about a sustained shift in wellbeing, focusing on what is possible. The 5-component model of wellbeing literacy offers an approach that has the potential to teach people the vocabulary, knowledge, and skills to positively affect their own wellbeing, as well as the wellbeing of others. Based on our experience, we propose wellbeing literacy as a capability that should be recognised and utilised towards positive wellbeing outcomes in education. As noted by Oades et al. (2021b), wellbeing literacy can support the future of education in building, individual, collective, societal, and ecological wellbeing.

References

Brown, B. (2013). *Embracing vulnerability* [Video]. YouTube. https://www.youtube.com/watch?v=AO6n9HmG0qM

Czarniawska, B. (2004). *Narratives in social science research*. SAGE Publications, Ltd. https://doi.org/10.4135/9781849209502

Davidson, R. J., & Schuyler, B. S. (2015). Neuroscience of happiness. In J. Helliwell, R. Layard, & J. Sachs (Eds.), *World happiness report 2015* (pp. 88–105). Sustainable Development Solutions Network.

Dweck, C. (2017). *Mindset - updated edition: Changing the way you think to fulfil your potential*. Little, Brown Book Group.

Frederikson, B. L., & Losada, M. F. (2005). Positive affect and the complex dynamics of human flourishing. *American Psychologist*, *60*(7a), 678–686.

Freire, P. (2000). *Pedagogy of the oppressed*. Continuum.

Gee, J. P. (1998). What is literacy? In V. Zamel & R. Spack (Eds.), *Negotiating academic literacies: Teaching and learning across languages and cultures* (pp. 51–59). Lawrence Erlbaum.

Kaufman, P. (2017). Critical contemplative pedagogy. *Radical Pedagogy*, *14*(1), 1–20.

Lemon, N. (2024). *The 'How' of self-care for teachers*. Routledge.

Lemon, N., Francis, J., & Baker, L. M. (2024). Well-being literacy in the academic landscape: Trioethnographic inquiry into scholarly writing. *Brock Education Journal*, *33*(1), 27–48. https://doi.org/10.26522/brocked.v33i1.1120

Luskin, F. (2010, August 19). *What is forgiveness?* Greater Good Magazine. https://greatergood.berkeley.edu/article/item/what_is_forgiveness

Marsh, J. (2005, September 1). *Acting on empathy*. Greater Good Magazine. https://greatergood.berkeley.edu/article/item/acting_on_empathy

Momaday, N. S. (1992). *The delight song of Tsoai-talee*. https://www.poetryfoundation.org/poems/46558/the-delight-song-of-tsoai-talee

Noble, L., & Powietrzynska, M. (2023). "It be's that way sometime": Mindfully recalling our time during COVID-19. In N. Lemon, H. Harju-Luukkainen, & S. Garvis (Eds.), *Practising compassion in higher education: Caring for self and others through challenging times* (pp. 15–30). Routledge.

Oades, L. G., Baker, L. M., Francis, J. J., & Taylor, J. A. (2021a). Wellbeing literacy and positive education. In M. L. Kern & M. L. Wehmeyer (Eds.), *The Palgrave handbook of positive education* (pp. 325–343). Palgrave Macmillan. https://doi.org/10.1007/978-3-030-64537-3_13

Oades, L. G., Hou, H., Francis, J., Baker, L. M., & Huang, L. (2022). Well-being literacy: Language use as a way to contextualise the process of positive education. In K.-A. Allen, M. J. Furlong, D. Vella-Brodrick, & S. Suldo (Eds.), *Handbook of positive psychology in schools: Supporting process and practice* (3rd ed., pp. 91–103). Routledge.

Oades, L. G., Ozturk, C., Hou, H., & Slemp, G. R. (2020). Wellbeing literacy: A language-use capability relevant to wellbeing outcomes of positive psychology intervention. *The Journal of Positive Psychology*, *15*(5), 696–700. https://doi.org/10.1080/17439760.2020.1789711
Oades, L. G., Taylor, J. A., Francis, J., & Baker, L. M. (2021b). Wellbeing literacy as an emancipatory and transformative capability. In M. A. White & F. McCallum (Eds.), *Wellbeing and resilience education: COVID-19 and its impact on education* (pp. 209–231). Routledge.
Rhodes, M. (2018). *The 10 minute mind*. https://the10minutemind.com
Seligman, M. E. P. (2011). *Flourish: A visionary new understanding of happiness and well-being*. Free Press.
The Greater Good Science Center. (2024). *Keys to well-being*. https://greatergood.berkeley.edu/key
Tobin, K. (2018). Methodological bricolage. In S. M. Ritchie, & K. Tobin (Eds.), *Eventful learning* (pp. 31–55). Brill. https://doi.org/10.1163/9789004377912_003
VIA Institute on Character (2024). *Discover your strengths*. https://www.viacharacter.org/
Waters, L., & Charles Higgins, M. (2021). The impact of a teacher-based positive education intervention on student wellbeing literacy. *Journal of School and Educational Psychology*, *2*(1), 22–43. https://doi.org/10.47602/josep.v2i1.12
Zajonc, A. (2013). Contemplative pedagogy: A quiet revolution in higher education. *New Directions for Teaching and Learning*, *134*, 83–94. https://doi.org/10.1002/tl.20057

15

CULTIVATING WELLBEING LITERACY IN UNIVERSITY CONTEXTS

A Dialogue for Systemic Change

Narelle Lemon and Lanxi Huang

Introduction

In the context of higher education, and explicitly universities, there is growing attention of wellbeing and self-care and the challenges regarding the wellbeing of their diverse community members including undergraduate, postgraduate and international students, research candidates, postdoctoral researchers, and professional and academic staff (Edwards et al., 2021; Evans et al., 2018; Huang et al., 2020).

Academic staff in universities face intensifying pressures that significantly affect their wellbeing, stemming from multifaceted role demands and systemic challenges within higher education. Research demonstrates that academics consistently report high levels of stress and burnout due to increasing workload intensity across teaching, research, and administrative responsibilities (Urbina-Garcia, 2020). The digitalisation of academic work, coupled with performative expectations, has eroded traditional work-life boundaries, creating an environment where work becomes perpetual and increasingly difficult to manage (Fetherston et al., 2020). While social connections and institutional support mechanisms can enhance wellbeing through fostering workplace belonging and community engagement (Thissen et al., 2023), many academics struggle with limited resources and systemic barriers to accessing support. Evidence suggests that effective interventions require both structural and cultural changes, moving beyond individual-focused solutions to address institutional practices that impact academic wellbeing (Brewster et al., 2021).

University students encounter multiple challenges that significantly affect their wellbeing, including financial tensions, academic pressures, social adjustments, and personal development demands. Contemporary research demonstrates

DOI: 10.4324/9781003644293-15

that students' experiences of wellbeing are intrinsically linked to both academic and social dimensions of university life (Brooker & Vu, 2020). While institutions implement various support mechanisms, students consistently identify the need for more integrated approaches that encompass enhanced teaching practices, accessible support services, and inclusive campus environments (Baik et al., 2019). Participatory research indicates that students benefit most from holistic support systems that actively involve them in decision-making processes and programme design (Lister et al., 2022).

The interconnected nature of academic staff and student wellbeing in universities creates a dynamic environment where the experiences of one group significantly influence the other. Brewster et al. (2021) captured this relationship succinctly in their research finding that institutions must look after the staff as they would look after the students, highlighting the cascading effect of wellbeing support. These challenges create a complex ecosystem where staff and student wellbeing are intrinsically linked. Research indicates that academic wellbeing significantly influences teaching quality and student experiences (Brewster et al., 2021), while institutional support structures affect both populations' capacity to thrive. Universities increasingly recognise that isolated interventions are insufficient; instead, comprehensive approaches that address both structural and cultural aspects of university life are essential (Baik et al., 2019). Academic staff experiencing high levels of stress and burnout often find their capacity to provide quality teaching and support diminished, directly affecting student experiences and outcomes (Urbina-Garcia, 2020). When academics struggle with excessive workloads and blurred work-life boundaries (Fetherston et al., 2020), their reduced availability and emotional resources can impact student engagement and academic support quality. Conversely, positive academic wellbeing fosters environments where staff can fully engage in their teaching and mentoring roles, creating more supportive learning experiences for students. Students, particularly those in research degrees for example, often model their academic practices and work-life balance approaches on their supervisors and mentors. Research indicates that academic staff wellbeing influences departmental culture and, consequently, shapes student perceptions of academic career sustainability (Morgan et al., 2023). This relationship becomes particularly significant in research supervision, where the supervisor's wellbeing can affect the quality of guidance and support provided to research candidates.

Institutional responses to wellbeing must therefore adopt an integrated approach. Universities implementing successful wellbeing initiatives recognise that supporting staff wellbeing creates a ripple effect throughout the institution. When academic staff feel supported and valued, they are better positioned to contribute to positive student experiences and outcomes. This symbiotic relationship suggests that universities should consider staff and student wellbeing not as separate challenges but as interconnected aspects of a healthy academic environment.

While some existing interventions show promise in addressing some of these challenges, there is a pressing need for more comprehensive, context-sensitive approaches that consider the diverse needs of the higher education population. Integrating wellbeing literacy within the higher education framework has the potential to promote sustained, relational, and person-centred approaches to wellbeing. In this complex landscape of interconnected wellbeing challenges, wellbeing literacy emerges as a critical framework that enables both staff and students to better understand, communicate about, and actively manage their wellbeing needs. By developing shared language and understanding around wellbeing, this approach has the potential to bridge the gaps between different stakeholder experiences while facilitating more effective institutional responses. Wellbeing literacy thus serves as both a protective factor against the challenges outlined above and a catalyst for creating more sustainable, relationship-centred approaches to wellbeing within higher education communities.

We present our chapter as an ethnographic conversation, sharing our voices as a way to explore our meaning-making as well as that around us, in this case, the university context as two researchers from two very different career stages, one a professor with a focus on academic and student wellbeing and the other an emerging scholar with a focus on international student wellbeing from two different settings and with one united interest, being the change we want to see. We draw from journaling, conversations in situ and the method of writing as conversation (Watkins & Swidler, 2009) as we reveal our reflexivity as a distributed process to strengthen the ethnographer's interpretative authority and to constantly push the conceptual boundaries of the participating disciplines and professions (Bieler et al., 2021; Breault, 2016; Docherty-Skippen & Beattie, 2018). As such this chapter is conversational, inspirational, and delves into the topic of wellbeing in higher education in a unique way that invites the conversation to continue beyond this chapter itself.

Understanding the Landscape of Wellbeing in Universities

Narelle: From my observations, wellbeing in universities is often misunderstood, neglected, and misrepresented. But wellbeing literacy in this context offers a unique chance to reimagine how we understand and communicate about and for wellbeing, both individually and collectively. It's an opportunity to intentionally reframe our perspective and approach within the university setting.

Lanxi: Absolutely, I couldn't agree more. What I find particularly compelling about wellbeing literacy in this context is how it prompts us (as authors, the sector, those working and studying in universities) to step back and reconsider how we approach and communicate about wellbeing. It's not just about a surface-level understanding; it's about diving into the intricacies of how wellbeing affects everyone involved. Students navigate academic pressures while teaching staff, researchers, and professional personnel coordinate their diverse responsibilities. The policies and procedures that form our institutional framework unite these elements into a cohesive academic ecosystem. Moreover, there's the public face of higher education institutions, which needs to reflect their commitment to wellbeing, alongside the candid corridor conversations where the real challenges and solutions often emerge. Leadership, too, plays a vital role in setting the tone and ensuring wellbeing is prioritised across all levels. It's about creating a culture where we intentionally support each other's wellbeing through diverse modes of communication and collaboration across all stakeholders (students, leaders, teachers, professional staff, etc), ultimately fostering a more inclusive and supportive higher education environment for all.

Narelle: The concept of wellbeing literacy provides a novel perspective on the role of language in shaping wellbeing experiences and outcomes. As Oades, Jarden, et al (2021); Oades et al. (2021) state, "If people can develop language capability related to wellbeing, they have more choices about their construction of wellbeing through language" (p. 2). I'm thinking about a project I am working on at the moment where we as an academic team are introducing university students to character strengths (Buckingham, 2008; Clifton & Harter, 2003; Park et al., 2004) as intentional language for and as wellbeing. We are scaffolding across year levels within degrees, thinking through the connection to curriculum and assessment in engaging ways, and establishing links to learning with one another across university and work integrated learning contexts as an act for and as wellbeing. In this example, we are providing a sustained scaffolded experience of wellbeing literacy to empower individuals and the student body as a group to actively influence their own and others' wellbeing. This is what I hope is the future; providing opportunities to scaffold in sustained ways choice and freedom plus multi-modal ways to explore our wellbeing as a way to interrupt the current issues that exacerbate experiences of being unwell or languishing.

Lanxi: In the realm of wellbeing literacy, leadership assumes a pivotal role in shaping organizational cultures that prioritise holistic wellbeing. Effective leaders are able to transcend traditional hierarchical paradigms by fostering environments where wellbeing serves as a foundational principle guiding organizational practices and policies (Barr & Nathenson, 2022). They adeptly integrate wellbeing considerations into strategic decision-making processes, recognizing the profound impact of wellbeing on individual and collective productivity, satisfaction, and organizational resilience. Leaders' adept in wellbeing literacy exhibit a commitment to fostering supportive climates that acknowledge and address the diverse challenges encountered by individuals across hierarchical strata within the organization. This commitment manifests in behaviours, actions, attitudes, practices and advocacy for policies that mitigate prevalent stressors such as overwork and resource scarcity while simultaneously promoting initiatives designed to cultivate work-life balance and robust mental health support mechanisms (Bryan & Wilson, 2014; Hammoudi Halat et al., 2023). Furthermore, with support and permission of institutions, leaders can champion inclusive practices that prioritise the strengths and resilience of their teams, fostering a culture where wellbeing is intrinsic to professional development and organizational sustainability (Dooris et al., 2021). By leveraging their influence and credibility, these leaders create environments where individuals are empowered to prioritise their wellbeing without fear of stigma or professional repercussions, thereby cultivating healthier, more engaged, and more sustainable organizational cultures (Jayman et al., 2022). This proactive approach not only enhances individual resilience and satisfaction but also fosters a robust organizational climate conducive to innovation, collaboration, and sustained excellence in higher education and beyond.

Narelle: Leadership in wellbeing extends beyond formal titles – it's inherent in every member of the university community. This collective responsibility (Oades, jarden et al., 2021) demands attention within universities (Lemon, 2024) as we foster cultures of inclusion and support. As Noddings (2012) emphasises, authentic caring relationships in education require genuine listening and responsive action rather than assumptions about needs.

Through wellbeing literacy, staff and students can develop the capacity to listen deeply, communicate effectively, and create inclusive learning environments that prioritise mutual care. This distributed approach to leadership enables transformative change across the institution.

Messaging and Language

Lanxi: The discourse surrounding wellbeing is complex, often hindered by inconsistent terminology and definitions that create misunderstandings. Cultural differences significantly shape how wellbeing concepts are understood and expressed across different contexts (Lomas, 2021). This implies potential discrepancies between the wellbeing expected by our institutions and that which students and staff possess while navigating these systems. Chinese international students, for instance, may interpret wellbeing in ways shaped by their cultural perspectives, encompassing both positive and negative aspects, potentially influenced by overlapping definitions of "mental health," "mental illness," and "wellbeing" found in the literature (Huang et al., 2022). However, institutional resources and services may focus narrowly, such as at the University of Melbourne, the "health and wellbeing" section primarily addresses mental health issues, with a predominant focus on stress management strategies (University of Melbourne, 2024). This selective emphasis may not fully align with the comprehensive view of wellbeing that encompasses broader facets beyond mental health alone. Thus, there exists a pertinent gap between institutional frameworks and the nuanced understandings of wellbeing held by international students, underscoring the need for a more universally understood language when discussing wellbeing concepts, especially considering the perspectives of lay individuals who may not have specialised knowledge in this area (Huang et al., 2022). Without a shared language, individuals may struggle to articulate their wellbeing needs or access appropriate support systems, further complicating efforts to promote holistic wellbeing within educational and societal settings. Addressing these barriers requires fostering a shared understanding of wellbeing that transcends linguistic and cultural boundaries, thereby enabling more inclusive and effective approaches to supporting wellbeing across diverse populations.

Narelle: The language of wellbeing literacy demands precise consideration within university contexts. Terms like "mental health," "wellbeing," and "self-care" carry distinct cultural meanings and interpretations that significantly impact their effectiveness in policy and practice. For instance, the concept of self-care varies markedly across cultures – some communities prioritise collective care over individual wellbeing, while others emphasise personal care as foundational.

Consider initiatives like "R U OK Day" (R U OK, 2025) which, while well-intentioned as a suicide prevention strategy, highlights the complexities of language choice in wellbeing literacy. The casual phrasing may create barriers for some cultural groups, while others seek deeper engagement beyond the initial question. This exemplifies how wellbeing initiatives, even when aiming for accessibility, can inadvertently exclude through their choice of language.

Universities must carefully examine their wellbeing terminology within policy frameworks, ensuring alignment with diverse cultural perspectives and existing health literacy strategies. This thoughtful approach to language selection strengthens the holistic implementation of wellbeing initiatives across the institution.

Lanxi: Wellbeing literacy, therefore, assumes critical importance, encompassing the ability to comprehend, articulate, and apply wellbeing-related knowledge effectively across different cultural and contextual settings (Oades, Jarden et al., 2021). This literacy not only involves understanding the diverse manifestations of wellbeing but also navigating these within culturally sensitive frameworks that respect and incorporate local norms and values. By fostering wellbeing literacy, educators and leaders can bridge these communication gaps, ensuring that messages about wellbeing are clear, accessible, and inclusive. This approach not only enhances the collective understanding of wellbeing but also empowers individuals to make informed decisions that positively impact their own and others' wellbeing outcomes in diverse societal contexts. Thus, a comprehensive approach to wellbeing literacy serves as a foundation for promoting holistic wellbeing practices and fostering resilience in communities and organizations alike.

Narelle: This is what excites me with wellbeing literacy – foundation, holistic, and a bridge for cultural and contextual accessible, clear, and scaffolded multimodal initial language for and as wellbeing. This the university context so needs, the opportunities for change agent moves are rich in the sector especially as we consider the ripple effects – wellbeing literate academic and professional staff working together, wellbeing literate academic staff modelling to students, wellbeing literate students experiencing a university context that supports their wellbeing that they then transfer to their various workplaces upon graduation across diverse discipline areas, these workplaces becoming wellbeing literate, wellbeing literate families, and so on. The ripples are massive!

The Top-Down and Bottom-Up Approaches

Narelle: I'm thinking about opportunities here as well to build on the intentionality to compose and comprehend for and about wellbeing in higher education. I've built from Oades, Baker et al. (2021) and Oades, Jarden, et al. (2021) conceptualization to consider the context of higher education as well as some opportunities and future directions across the Five Component Model of Wellbeing Literacy (see Table 15.1) as a way to invite us to consider what might be possible.

Can this be the beginning of systems level and systematic ways of considering the I [original notes as 'me'), we, and us (Jarden, 2016) of wellbeing in high education? Is it bottom-up and top-down meeting each other?

TABLE 15.1 The five component model of wellbeing literacy for university

Component	*Description*	*University context*	*Opportunities and future directions*
1. Vocabulary and knowledge	Words and basic facts about wellbeing (i.e., content that is signified).	• Incorporating wellbeing concepts into course curricula • Providing workshops and seminars on wellbeing for students and staff • Encouraging research and discourse on wellbeing	• Developing a common language and understanding of wellbeing across disciplines • Integrating wellbeing literacy into professional development for educators with a focus on a series that builds wellbeing literacy across time and contexts rather than one-off sessions • Exploring the impact of wellbeing literacy on student success and retention • Codesign bottom-up initiatives
2. Comprehension of multimodal text	Reading, listening, viewing about and for wellbeing	• Offering resources that explore wellbeing through various media (e.g., literature, videos, podcasts) • Encouraging critical analysis of wellbeing information from diverse sources • Promoting understanding of evidence-based approaches to wellbeing	• Developing students'/staff skills in evaluating the quality and personal/professional relevance of wellbeing information • Investigating the effectiveness of different modes of delivering wellbeing content • Exploring the role of technology in enhancing wellbeing literacy comprehension
3. Composition of multimodal text	Writing, speaking, creating about and for wellbeing	• Providing opportunities for students/staff to share their wellbeing experiences and insights • Encouraging creative expression related to wellbeing	• Examining the impact of creating wellbeing content on students'/staff own wellbeing • Exploring the potential for student/staff-generated wellbeing content to influence the broader community • Investigating the effectiveness of different modalities for expressing wellbeing knowledge

(*Continued*)

TABLE 15.1 (Continued)

Component	*Description*	*University context*	*Opportunities and future directions*
4. Context awareness and adaptability	Awareness of differences across contexts and adapt use of language to fit the relevant context.	• Discussing how wellbeing concepts and strategies may apply differently across personal, academic, and professional contexts • Encouraging reflection on how cultural, socioeconomic, and other factors influence wellbeing • Providing opportunities to practice applying wellbeing literacy in diverse settings	• Investigating how context influences the expression and understanding of wellbeing • Developing strategies for tailoring wellbeing literacy to specific populations and settings • Exploring the role of higher education in promoting context sensitive wellbeing literacy
5. Intentionality for wellbeing	Habit of intentionally using language to maintain or improve wellbeing of self or others.	• Modelling intentional use of language to support wellbeing in educational settings • Providing opportunities for students to practice intentional communication for wellbeing • Encouraging the development of habits that prioritise wellbeing	• Investigating the impact of intentional wellbeing language on individual and community wellbeing • Exploring strategies for sustaining intentional wellbeing practices beyond the educational setting • Examining the potential for intentional wellbeing language to influence institutional culture, policy, practices, decision-making, systems and processes • Redesign of "everyday practices" (e.g., staff approach to meetings can integrate wellbeing strategies in design or enactment, or in the classroom wellbeing can underpin decisions that support engagement, communication and relationship development)

Lanxi: Yes, I believe so. This could indeed mark the start of systematic approaches to considering the personal (I), communal (we), and collective (us) aspects of wellbeing in higher education. It signifies a convergence of grassroots initiatives and institutional strategies, fostering a holistic approach to wellbeing that integrates perspectives from both individual experiences and broader institutional frameworks.

In higher education, integrating wellbeing literacy is increasingly recognised as pivotal for fostering a supportive and thriving campus environment. Policies and strategic plans that prioritise mental health and wellbeing, coupled with specialized health and wellbeing teams, play a crucial role in promoting wellbeing awareness and understanding among students. By establishing clear guidelines and initiatives, institutions empower individuals to navigate challenges effectively and seek necessary support (Eloff et al., 2023). For example, one student shared that their introduction to the term 'wellbeing' occurred during the University Open Day, where they learned about numerous supportive services and resources, including meditation sessions, counselling services, gym facilities, and various student associations dedicated to enhancing student wellbeing.

Narelle: I spoke with a doctoral student from Vietnam just yesterday. She joined a Shut Up and Write session I host every Tuesday. It is an invitation for anyone to join us. She said at the end of our two hours of writing in a shared space that this was her first feeling of wellbeing, that she has been welcomed for the first time and felt that she belonged. This after being in Australia for 9 months. This is a reminder of the assumptions we make, institutionally and individually within the institutions of how wellbeing is being scaffolded, developed, and supported.

Lanxi: At the heart of student life is a vibrant community where students actively build connections and foster a sense of belonging. Through initiatives like recording and sharing tips and creating visual narratives, students engage meaningfully with one another and the broader university community. The University of Melbourne's Twitter account plays an important role in this interaction, serving as a platform where students showcase their experiences and insights. Whether it's offering study tips, sharing campus adventures, or celebrating academic achievements, these posts not only connect students but also inspire and support their journey towards personal and academic growth. This collaborative spirit enriches the university experience, promoting a culture of learning, creativity, and mutual support among students.

Narelle: The Instagram account for Edith Cowan University (ECU) also engages in such practices. Students host student voice in videos, peer-to-peer interviews, and there is an account called ECU Well Being. It is the multimodality of building and in some cases codesigning wellbeing literacy in these spaces away from university systems that are enriching, offering much potential.

Lanxi: Also, courses and subjects covering personal, organizational, and community wellbeing, such as Wellbeing, Motivation and Performance (WMP), and Positive Psychology and Organisation (PPO), are available for students to explore wellbeing conceptualizations, theories, and interventions across different contexts. These efforts not only enhance personal academic success but also contribute to holistic development, encompassing physical, mental, and emotional wellbeing and sustainability as a collective whole.

Narelle: The possibility for intentional integration and mapping across curriculum with subjects, year levels and degrees is calling.

Lanxi: Through collaborative efforts and accessible resources, higher education institutions aim to cultivate a culture where wellbeing is not only understood but actively practiced and prioritised across campus communities.

Concluding Thoughts: Cultivating Wellbeing Literacy Within the Academic Community

Universities are increasingly recognising that wellbeing literacy extends beyond awareness to encompass practical knowledge and actionable steps. This initiative empowers students and staff to navigate challenges and enhance their mental, emotional, and physical health through integrated support systems and resources. The emphasis has shifted from isolated programs to a fundamental reimagining of how institutions approach education and professional development.

The cultivation of wellbeing literacy demands a systems-level transformation, where these principles are woven into institutional policies, strategic planning, and curriculum development. For students, this means embedding wellbeing concepts within their academic journey. For staff, it necessitates incorporating wellbeing literacy into professional development frameworks, positioning it alongside pedagogical expertise.

This integrated approach operates across three key dimensions:

- Individual: Development of personal wellbeing literacy practices
- Communal: Creation of supportive relationships and communities of practice
- Institutional: Implementation of systems and structures that embed wellbeing literacy into organisational DNA

By fostering a culture where wellbeing literacy is actively cultivated, universities create an environment where the entire academic community can flourish personally and professionally. This transformation requires ongoing reflection, advocacy for systemic change, and the embodiment of wellbeing principles in daily practices.

References

Baik, C., Larcombe, W., & Brooker, A. (2019). How universities can enhance student mental wellbeing: The student perspective. *Higher Education Research & Development*, *38*(4), 674–687. https://doi.org/10.1080/07294360.2019.1576596

Barr, T. L., & Nathenson, S. L. (2022). A holistic transcendental leadership model for enhancing innovation, creativity and well-being in health care. *Journal of Holistic Nursing*, *40*(2), 157–168. https://doi.org/10.1177/08980101211024799

Bieler, P., Bister, M. D., Hagner, M., Kraftner, L., Lipphardt, V., & Schlünder, M. (2021). Distributing reflexivity through collaborative ethnography. *Journal of Contemporary Ethnography*, *50*(1), 77–98. https://doi.org/10.1177/0891241620968271

Breault, R. A. (2016). Emerging issues in duoethnography. *International Journal of Qualitative Studies in Education*, *29*(6), 777–794. https://doi.org/10.1080/09518398.2016.1162866

Brewster, L., Jones, E., Priestley, M., Wilbraham, S. J., Spanner, L., & Hughes, G. (2021). 'Look after the staff and they would look after the students' cultures of wellbeing and mental health in the university setting. *Journal of Further and Higher Education*, *46*(4), 548–560. https://doi.org/10.1080/0309877X.2021.1986473

Brooker, A., & Vu, C. (2020). How do university experiences contribute to students' psychological wellbeing? *Student Success*, *11*(2), 99–108. https://doi.org/10.5204/ssj.1676

Bryan, L. K., & Wilson, C. A. (2014). *Shaping work-life culture in higher education: A guide for academic leaders*. Routledge. https://doi.org/10.4324/9780203118887

Buckingham, M. (2008). *Go put your strengths to work: Six powerful steps to achieve outstanding performance*. Simon & Schuster UK.

Clifton, D. O., & Harter, J. K. (2003). Investing in strengths. In K. Cameron & J. E. Dutton (Eds.), *Positive organizational scholarship* (pp. 111–121). Berrett-Koehler.

Docherty-Skippen, S., & Beattie, K. (2018). Duoethnography as a dialogic and collaborative form of curriculum inquiry for resident professionalism and self-care education. *Canadian Medical Education Journal*, *9*(3), e76–82. https://doi.org/10.36834/cmej.42981

Dooris, M., Powell, S., Parkin, D., & Farrier, A. (2021). Health promoting universities: Effective leadership for health, well-being and sustainability. *Health Education*, *121*(3), 295–310. https://doi.org/10.1108/HE-12-2020-0121

Edwards, M. S., Martin, A. J., & Ashkanasy, N. M. (2021). Mental health and psychological well-being among management students and educators. *Journal of Management Education*, *45*(1), 3–18. https://doi.org/10.1177/1052562920978252

Eloff, I., O'Neil, S., & Kanengoni, H. (2023). Students' well-being in tertiary environments: Insights into the (unrecognised) role of lecturers. *Teaching in Higher Education*, *28*(7), 1777–1797. https://doi.org/10.1080/13562517.2021.1931836

Evans, T. M., Bira, L., Gastelum, J. B., Weiss, L. T., & Vanderford, N. L. (2018). Evidence for a mental health crisis in graduate education. *Nature Biotechnology* *36*(3), 282–284. https://doi.org/10.1038/nbt.4089

Fetherston, C., Fetherston, A., Batt, S., Sully, M., & Wei, R. (2020). Wellbeing and work-life merge in Australian and UK academics. *Studies in Higher Education*, *46*(12), 2774–2788. https://doi.org/10.1080/03075079.2020.1828326

Hammoudi Halat, D., Soltani, A., Dalli, R., Alsarraj, L., & Malki, A. (2023). Understanding and fostering mental health and well-being among university

faculty: A narrative review. *Journal of Clinical Medicine*, *12*(13), 4425. https://doi.org/10.3390/jcm12134425
Huang, L., Kern, M., & Oades, L. (2022). Chinese International students' conceptualizations of wellbeing: A prototype analysis. *Frontiers in Psychology*, *13*, 939576. https://doi.org/10.3389/fpsyg.2022.939576
Huang, L., Kern, M. L., & Oades, L. G. (2020). Strengthening university student wellbeing: Language and perceptions of Chinese international students. *International Journal of Environmental Research and Public Health*, *17*(15), 5538. https://doi.org/10.3390/ijerph17155538
Jarden, A. (2016). Introducing workplace wellbeing to organizations: The "Me, we, us" model. *Positive Work and Organizations: Research and Practice*, *1*, 1–4.
Jayman, M., Glazzard, J., & Rose, A. (2022). Tipping point: The staff wellbeing crisis in higher education. *Frontiers in Education*, *7*, 929335. https://doi.org/10.3389/feduc.2022.929335
Lemon, N. (2024). *The 'How' of self-care for teachers: Building your wellbeing toolbox*. Routledge.
Lister, K., Riva, E., Kukulska-Hulme, A., & Fox, C. (2022). Participatory digital approaches to embedding student wellbeing in higher education. *Frontiers in Education*, *7*, 924868.
Lomas, T. (2021). Towards a cross-cultural lexical map of wellbeing. *The Journal of Positive Psychology*, *16*(5), 622–639. https://doi.org/10.1080/17439760.2020.1791944
Morgan B, Simmons L and Ayles N (2023) Flourish-HE: An online positive education programme to promote university student wellbeing. *Frontiers in Education*, *8*, 1124983. https://doi.org/10.3389/feduc.2023.1124983
Noddings, N. (2012). The caring relation in teaching. *Oxford Review of Education*, *38*(6), 771–781. https://doi.org/10.1080/03054985.2012.745047
Oades, L. G., Baker, L. M., Francis, J. J., & Taylor, J. A. (2021). Wellbeing literacy and positive education. In M. L. Kern & M. L. Wehmeyer (Eds.), *The Palgrave handbook of positive education* (pp. 325–343). Springer International Publishing. https://doi.org/10.1007/978-3-030-64537-3
Oades, L. G., Jarden, A., Hou, H., Ozturk, C., Williams, P., R. Slemp, G., & Huang, L. (2021). Wellbeing literacy: A capability model for wellbeing science and practice. *International Journal of Environmental Research and Public Health*, *18*(2), Article 2. https://doi.org/10.3390/ijerph18020719
Park, N., Peterson, C., & Seligman, M. E. P. (2004). Strengths of character and wellbeing. *Journal of Social and Clinical Psychology*, *23*(5), 603–619. https://doi.org/10.1521/jscp.23.5.603.50748
R U OK. (2025). *R U OK? For University and TAFE*. Retrieved January 14, 2025, from https://www.ruok.org.au/university
R U OK. (2025). *R U OK? For University and TAFE*. Retrieved January 14, 2025, from https://www.ruok.org.au/university
Thissen, L., Biermann-Teuscher, D., Horstman, K., & Meershoek, A. (2023). (Un)belonging at work: an overlooked ingredient of workplace health. *Health Promotion International*, *38*(3), daad061. https://doi.org/10.1093/heapro/daad061
University of Melbourne. (2024). *Student health and wellbeing digital hub*. Students. https://students.unimelb.edu.au/student-support/health-and-wellbeing
Urbina-Garcia, A. What do we know about university academics' mental health? A systematic literature review. *Stress Health* 2020, 36, 563–585
Watkins, S. C., & Swidler, A. (2009). Hearsay ethnography: Conversational journals as a method for studying culture in action. *Poetics*, *37*(2), 162–184. https://doi.org/10.1016/j.poetic.2009.03.002

16

IMPROVING HOW WE USE SOCIAL MEDIA

The Role of Wellbeing Literacy

Lu Li, Jacqui Francis, and Lindsay G. Oades

Introduction

Social media provides a device, digital application, or tool for communication (Nesi et al., 2018), as well as a novel *context* within which communication occurs (McFarland & Ployhart, 2015). The notion of context is diverse, however narrowing our focus to social media allows consideration of it as a context for wellbeing, and as such also wellbeing literacy. While acknowledging the issues associated with social media communication and illbeing, we see opportunity to refocus and redirect this online communication for good. Wellbeing literacy within the social media context, holds potential to educate and inform, and to shape communication that is intended to protect and promote wellbeing.

Wellbeing Literacy

Wellbeing literacy is defined as the capability to comprehend and compose wellbeing language, across contexts, with the intention of using such language to maintain or improve the wellbeing of oneself, others or the world (Oades et al., 2021). It consists of five components, including vocabulary and knowledge about wellbeing, comprehension and composition of multimodal text related to wellbeing, context awareness and adaptability, and intentionality for wellbeing (Oades et al., 2021). Social media, as a technology, enables the composition and comprehension of wellbeing knowledge and vocabulary across a wide population at a faster speed. In addition, as a context with unique attributes, it provides a stage where wellbeing literacy can play its role in improving individual and communal wellbeing.

DOI: 10.4324/9781003644293-16

Social Media and Context

For over a decade, researchers from various disciplines, such as computer science, marketing, communications, organisational studies, and psychology, have attempted to define what social media is. One of the most common approaches is to conceptualise it from a techno-centrical perspective (Carr & Hayes, 2015; McFarland & Ployhart, 2015), either inclusively or with a discipline-specific focus. For example, a maximally inclusive definition of social media presents it as 'media used for social interaction, or any digital applications or tools that allow users to share content and communicate with others' (Nesi et al., 2018, p. 270). Other definitions have focused on specific devices, such as mobile phones, and tool affordances, such as editability which affords users to craft and recraft content (Treem & Leonardi, 2013). Some definitions also involve viewing social media as information infrastructure or a collection of platforms and applications, like Facebook and YouTube, that enable users to generate, distribute, and consume digital content (Howard & Parks, 2012).

These definitions may be broad enough to encompass a wide range of technologies. And it might be straightforward to agree on which apps, platforms, or tools qualify as social media. Yet, reaching a consensus on why they should be categorised as such is more challenging and underexplored (Carr & Hayes, 2015). Key to understanding social media is its contextual attributes that denote the environments in which these technologies afford communicative activities. It is these features that distinguish social media from other forms of communication such as face-to-face interactions, emails, or text messages (McFarland & Ployhart, 2015; Nesi et al., 2018).

Eight core and distinguishing characteristics of the social media context include physicality, accessibility, latency, interdependence, synchronicity, permanence, verifiability, and anonymity (McFarland & Ployhart, 2015), as summarised in Table 16.1. These contextual features indicate that temporal aspects are among the most significant differences between social media and non-digital contexts, as three of them – latency, synchronicity, and permanence – are directly related to time.

Social Media and Wellbeing

Social media as a technology has been consistently linked to individuals' wellbeing, with studies revealing conflicting influences. On one hand, researchers have highlighted the positive impacts of social media, acknowledging benefits such as increased social capital and connectedness (Ellison et al., 2007) as well as enhanced self-esteem (Gonzales, 2014). These improvements in wellbeing have been observed across various populations, including for adolescents (Quinn & Oldmeadow, 2013), university students (Pang, 2020), and individuals with different personality traits, particularly those who are introverted and self-concealing (Magsamen-Conrad & Greene, 2014) or experiencing emotional issues (Naslund et al., 2020). For example, in a cross-sectional study involving 1004 students from

TABLE 16.1 Eight characteristics of the social media context

Components	*Interpretation*	*Features in social media*
Physicality	Tangible constraints imposed by a context	Less relevant
Accessibility	The opportunity to join a network	Relatively open
Latency	Time required to share content on a network	Typically shorter
Interdependence	How interactions between members are interconnected	Generally greater
Synchronicity	Whether interactions occur simultaneously (synchronous) or not (asynchronous)	Both types of engagement are supported
Permanence	The duration that posted content remains available	More enduring
Verifiability	The ease with which information can be checked or reviewed	Often easier to verify
Anonymity	The degree to which individuals can be identified	Tend to be more anonymous

Source: Adapted from McFarland and Ployhart (2015)

135 Chinese universities, social media usage was found positively correlated with students' psychological and subjective wellbeing, mediated by self-esteem and online social support (Zhang et al., 2023).

However, the negative effects of social media have been demonstrated in various longitudinal, experimental, and meta-analysis studies (Verduyn et al., 2020), such as reduced subjective wellbeing (Kross et al., 2013), reduced life satisfaction (Shakya & Christakis, 2017), and greater depression (Boers et al., 2019). Frequent use of social media platforms can increase the exposure to disinformation and harmful or unhealthy content (Kim, 2017), which can lead to distress (Sampasa-Kanyinga & Lewis, 2015), anxiety (Twenge & Campbell, 2018), social isolation (Primack et al., 2017), and sadly suicidal ideation (Sampasa-Kanyinga & Lewis, 2015; Twenge et al., 2018). For instance, increased time spent on social media is a pivotal risk factor for anxiety, according to regression analyses of data collected from 563 emerging adults in the United States (Vannucci et al., 2017).

The discrepant findings in the growing body of literature have been further amplified during the COVID-19 pandemic, since the use of social media surged during times of lockdowns, quarantine and physical distancing (Volkmer, 2021). These channels for connection and information sharing mobilised social and emotional support during the crisis, benefiting people's wellbeing (Tkáčová et al., 2021; Volkmer, 2021). Yet, for some, spending excessive time on social media brought harm to physical health and/or mental health, with stress, anxiety, and fear triggered from overwhelming and at times false or misleading digital information (infodemics) (Burns et al., 2020).

Social media is omnipresent. And while the negative impact of social media cannot be ignored, there remains the potential for good. We, therefore, see ourselves presented with not only an opportunity but perhaps even an obligation to leverage the unique aspects of the social media context, through the lens of wellbeing literacy, to communicate in ways that protect and promote wellbeing.

Communicating for Wellbeing Within the Social Media Context

The ease of access and lack of physical constraints on social media allow anyone with an internet connection and a device to compose and comprehend, creating content and contributing to ongoing dialogues. From a positive perspective, this means that wellbeing literate individuals can communicate online and share their emotions and personal experiences through a wide variety of language forms, such as written words, videos, audios, and visual symbols like emoticons and emojis, fostering conversations about and for wellbeing across different cultures and communities. The enormous user-generated content in turn feeds information to consumers and enables them to accumulate knowledge and vocabulary surrounding wellbeing. Two examples of this are The Happy Words Project (Lomas, n.d.-a) on Facebook and the Positive Lexicography Project (Lomas, n.d.-b). People were invited to share words related to wellbeing from their own language and culture via Facebook, X (formerly Twitter), and Instagram. Thanks to the physicality, interdependence, and permanence of social media, users from different backgrounds collectively contribute to the ongoing building of positive lexicology, facilitating the spread of wellbeing vocabulary and knowledge.

Yet, some key features of social media, especially anonymity, along with the evolving digital technology, have made the context ever-changing and challenging. Although the anonymous nature of social media increases self-disclosure (Schlosser, 2020) and thus improves wellbeing (Kim et al., 2014), it provides a hotbed for inappropriate online behaviour such as hostile language and negative comments (Lapidot-Lefler & Barak, 2012). Technological advancements, while enhancing social media functionality, also introduce predicaments. For instance, developments like AI and big data might be employed to produce and spread unauthentic content such as fake news and dis- or mis-information (Aïmeur et al., 2023; Kaplan, 2020), which can ultimately harm wellbeing. In face of these complexities, users equipped with wellbeing literacy can react proactively, while keeping in mind the contextual attributes of social media and the intentionality to care about the wellbeing of themselves and others.

Figure 16.1 illustrates this interaction between the components of the social media context and the wellbeing literacy model, followed by an illustrative vignette.

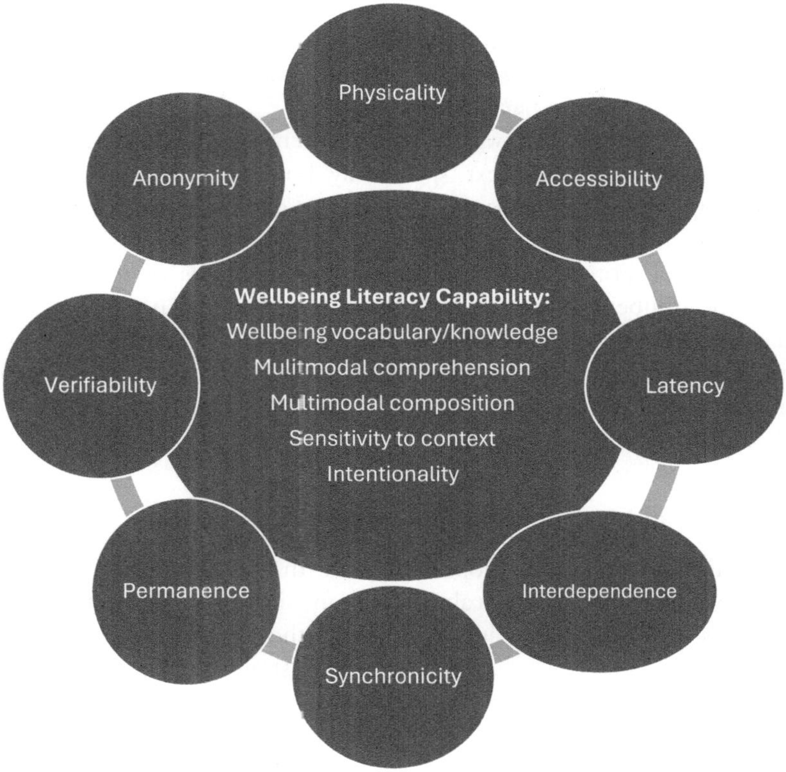

FIGURE 16.1 Wellbeing literacy capability within a social media context.

Social Media and Wellbeing Literacy – A Vignette

Huan recently began studying at a university in Australia. Before coming to Australia, Huan ate with their family each evening, and on the weekend would spend time with their grandmother (Nainai), making dumplings. Now based in a big city on the other side of the world, eating is often a solitary experience, and at times Huan feels lonely and misses home, especially Nainai and Nainai's dumplings. To boost their sense of connection to family, to connect with their passion for Chinese food, including cooking and eating Nainai's dumplings, and to connect with other people, Huan creates an Instagram profile 'Food with Nainai'. Huan posts a short video of making Nainai's dumplings, sharing about happy childhood memories of being with and cooking with Nainai, remembering her loving and gentle teaching. Huan encourages others to post their favourite 'Nainai' foods. Huan's first post reaches 120 people. Over time Huan generates worldwide interest: Grandchildren and grandparents alike post favourite dishes. People from across the globe share their favourite 'Nainai' dishes, and their stories of cooking and eating with family. Sometimes Huan eats while viewing these videos. They feel glad to have connected with so many people. Stories shared make Huan feel less alone. Huan's Nainai is also happy to know her dumplings are famous! Although occasionally unfriendly comments are received, Huan can evaluate the intention behind the comments and respond accordingly.

Table 16.2 illustrates how the vignette demonstrates wellbeing literacy within the social media context, specifically, how communication was intentionally adapted in response to those contextual components, to communicate for the wellbeing of the self and others.

It should be noted that the contextual components of social media sit around the wellbeing literacy capability model. They do not align explicitly with particular components of the model. Moreover, Table 16.2 only provides some illustrative examples of how wellbeing literacy is related to the social media context and influences users' communication choices to cater to the wellbeing of the self and others.

Implications and Recommendations for Social Media Use

With rapid technological development, and with the advancement of AI, criticism, scepticism, and pessimism about social media mounts. Recent news about universities, secondary schools and primary schools suffering from deepfake pornography (Oaten & Lee, 2024), and the Australian Federal Government's plan to set an age limit for social media users (Long, 2024), reflect the need to support better use of social media. Various stakeholders such as platforms and governments have taken actions to improve the social media environment. For example, companies like Facebook have introduced content removal and labelling interventions to manage the creation and spread of malicious and harmful content (Yadav, 2021). The Chinese government has mandated that social media platforms establish monitoring and reporting systems, enabling users to report issues about network information security (Niu & Yuan, 2020).

Yet, these actions are far from sufficient, and their effectiveness remains questionable. Social media communication is complicated. The responsibility for improvement sits with all stakeholders alike, including not only platforms and governments but also individual users. Wellbeing literacy provides a model to guide contextually suitable communication that supports wellbeing. The following recommendations are therefore proposed for further consideration:

- Individuals – Acquire and accumulate wellbeing-related knowledge and skills in daily life and apply them to online communication. Consciously consider ways to communicate with awareness and responsiveness to the contextual components of social media to support the wellbeing of the self and others. For example, when engaging online, take into consideration that physical cues such as facial expressions are absent in online communication (Nesi et al., 2018) to minimise potential misunderstanding.

TABLE 16.2 Wellbeing literacy capability and social media contextual components matched to aspects of the illustrative vignette

Vignette – sample section	*Wellbeing literacy capability model components*	*Components of social media context influencing communication choices*
Huan's creation of an Instagram profile to boost a sense of connection to family and others	**Wellbeing vocabulary, knowledge and skills** Huan's known connection with family supports their wellbeing, and cooking boosts their sense of satisfaction and competence by creating something personally meaningful. **Intentionality** Utilising skills and passions to meet an identified need to connect and support one's own wellbeing.	**Accessibility** The communication topic (cooking and family stories) is adaptable and can suit many people in different locations, with different family structures and experiences. Diverse tools (phones, iPads or computers) provide diverse and inclusive creation and usage options. **Permanence** The profile and its content can exist as long as the creator keeps them and can even be restored after being deleted. Audience can review past and present posts, repeatedly, and share their feelings through comments or re-sharing of the posts. **Anonymity** Users can freely decide the extent of anonymity on social media. Huan may decide to use their real names when creating the Instagram profile. In addition, when posting photos or videos online, Huan can also decide to disclose their faces or not. With the capability to intentionally look after their own wellbeing, Huan can make decisions accordingly. **Verifiability** There is a possibility that Huan's story and the story of many others with their grandmothers might be fake, but users with wellbeing literacy have the ability to evaluate the authenticity of sources, relying on their past experiences or conducting their own research. They can also respond thoughtfully to the content, avoiding upward social comparison or hostile communication that could harm their own wellbeing or that of others.

(*Continued*)

TABLE 16.2 (Continued)

Vignette – sample section	*Wellbeing literacy capability model components*	*Components of social media context influencing communication choices*
Huan's short video post of making Nainai's dumplings and sharing of happy memories	**Composing in multimodal ways** Creating video to share about cooking, family, love and connection. Talking and captioning in the video.	**Accessibility** Composers can choose their preferred modality by which to communicate - video, audio, text, emojis. **Physicality** Although Huan is physically away from family, the action of making videos and sharing on social media helps break the physical constraints, connecting Huan with their homeland and people. Audiences from around the world can echo feelings of connection regardless of their geographical location.
Others' comments and sharing of similar experience and dishes	**Comprehending in multimodal ways** Viewing videos and chat comments of others. Listening to the stories of others as they share about their Nainai food experiences.	**Interdependence** There is mutual benefit for contributors in composing and comprehending shared posts. **Latency** The videos posted by Huan and people worldwide can be spread very quickly across diverse platforms through the sharing and re-sharing in different communities, influencing a wider audience and achieving collective wellbeing. **Synchronicity** Communication on social media can be synchronous or asynchronous. Viewers can converse asynchronously by commenting on the videos of Huan and other people or sharing the videos to other platforms to reach a wider audience and thus improve their emotional wellness.
The convention to eat with family and spend weekend making dumplings with Nainai versus the experience of studying in Australia and connecting with home using social media	**Sensitivity to context** Huan demonstrates communication that is responsive to different contexts: The context of being an international student away from home and the context of using social media to stay connected with home.	**Physicality** The sensitivity to the change of contexts (from physical context to online) enables Huan to adjust the mode of communication. Social media can connect them with their family and reduce to certain extent, the loneliness of being away from home.

- Social media companies – Take the responsibility to provide technological assistance for wellbeing literate use of social media. Consider: In what ways can damaging communication be eliminated, and in what ways can wellbeing literate communication be promoted? AI coaches to assist the application of wellbeing literacy may be embedded into platforms to support users in posting, responding and interpreting communication, in ways that protect and promote wellbeing. These AI coaches could use the five components of the wellbeing literacy model to cue both those composing (writing, speaking, creating) social media, and those comprehending (reading, listening, viewing) social media. Whilst this is not the same as autocorrect, it could be a tool for more wellbeing enhancing social media use, but still providing autonomy for users.

In this chapter, we asserted that although social media as a technology is often deemed as related to illbeing, wellbeing literacy as a capability model can play a positive role in improving and protecting wellbeing in the virtual realm by aligning to the contextual characteristics of social media. When communicating online, users with wellbeing literacy are aware of those contextual features and can adjust their use of language – either texts, videos, audios, emojis, or other forms – for the wellbeing of the broader public. Social media as a modality and context is complex. Similarly, the relationship between social media, wellbeing literacy, and wellbeing is sophisticated and multi-directional. Social media holds opportunity to enable wellbeing-supportive communication, while wellbeing literacy may enable wellbeing-supportive social media use.

References

Aïmeur, E., Amri, S., & Brassard, G. (2023). Fake news, disinformation and misinformation in social media: A review. *Social Network Analysis and Mining*, *13*(1). https://doi.org/10.1007/s13278-023-01028-5

Boers, E., Afzali, M. H., Newton, N., & Conrod, P. (2019). Association of screen time and depression in adolescence. *JAMA Pediatrics*, *173*(9), 853–859. http://doi.org/10.1001/jamapediatrics.2019.1759

Burns, D., Dagnall, N., & Holt, M. (2020). Assessing the impact of the COVID-19 pandemic on student wellbeing at universities in the United Kingdom: A conceptual analysis. *Frontiers in Education*, *5*, 582882. https://doi.org/10.3389/feduc.2020.582882

Carr, C. T., & Hayes, R. A. (2015). Social media: Defining, developing, and divining. *Atlantic Journal of Communication*, *23*(1), 46–65. https://doi.org/10.1080/15456870.2015.972282

Ellison, N. B., Steinfield, C., & Lampe, C. (2007). The benefits of Facebook "friends:" Social capital and college students' use of online social network sites. *Journal of Computer-Mediated Communication*, *12*(4), 1143–1168. https://doi.org/10.1111/j.1083-6101.2007.00367.x

Gonzales, A. L. (2014). Text-based communication influences self-esteem more than face-to-face or cellphone communication. *Computers in Human Behaviour*, *39*, 197–203. https://doi.org/10.1016/j.chb.2014.07.026

Howard, P. N., & Parks, M. R. (2012). Social media and political change: Capacity, constraint, and consequence. *Journal of Communication*, *62*(2), 359–362. https://doi.org/10.1111/j.1460-2466.2012.01626.x

Kaplan, A. (2020). Artificial intelligence, social media, and fake news: Is this the end of democracy. In A. A. Gul, Y. D. Erturk, & P. Elmer (Eds.), *Digital transformation in media & society* (pp. 149–161). Istanbul University Press.

Kim, H. H. S. (2017). The impact of online social networking on adolescent psychological well-being (WB): A population-level analysis of Korean school-aged children. *International Journal of Adolescence and Youth*, *22*(3), 364–376. https://doi.org/10.1080/02673843.2016.1197135

Kim, J. Y., Chung, N., & Ahn, K. M. (2014). Why people use social networking services in Korea: The mediating role of self-disclosure on subjective well-being. *Information Development*, *30*(3), 276–287. https://doi.org/10.1177/0266666913489894

Kross, E., Verduyn, P., Demiralp, E., Park, J., Lee, D. S., Lin, N., Shablack, H., Jonides, J., & Ybarra, O. (2013). Facebook use predicts declines in subjective well-being in young adults. *PloS One*, *8*(8), e69841. https://doi.org/10.1371/journal.pone.0069841

Lapidot-Lefler, N., & Barak, A. (2012). Effects of anonymity, invisibility, and lack of eye-contact on toxic online disinhibition. *Computers in Human Behavior Reports*, *28*(2), 434–443. https://doi.org/10.1016/j.chb.2011.10.014

Lomas, T. (n.d.-a). *The Happy Words Project* [Facebook page]. Facebook. Retrieved September 10, 2024, from https://www.facebook.com/drtimlomas/

Lomas, T. (n.d.-b). *The Positive Lexicography Project*. Tim Lomas, PhD. Retrieved September 10, 2024, from https://www.drtimlomas.com/lexicography/cm4mi

Long, C. (2024). Social media ban for children to be introduced this year, but age limit undetermined. *ABC News*. https://www.abc.net.au/news/2024-09-09/government-plans-social-media-porn-site-age-limit/104329920

Magsamen-Conrad, K., & Greene, K. (2014). Technology addiction's contribution to mental wellbeing: The positive effect of online social capital. *Computers in Human Behaviour*, *40*, 23–30. https://doi.org/10.1016/j.chb.2014.07.014

McFarland, L. A., & Ployhart, R. E. (2015). Social media: A contextual framework to guide research and practice. *Journal of Applied Psychology*, *100*(6), 1653. http://dx.doi.org/10.1037/a0039244

Naslund, J. A., Bondre, A., Torous, J., & Aschbrenner, K. A. (2020). Social media and mental health: Benefits, risks, and opportunities for research and practice. *Journal of Technology in Behavioural Science*, *5*, 245–257. https://doi.org/10.1007/s41347-020-00134-x

Nesi, J., Choukas-Bradley, S., & Prinstein, M. J. (2018). Transformation of adolescent peer relations in the social media context: Part 1—A theoretical framework and application to dyadic peer relationships. *Clinical Child and Family Psychology Review*, *21*, 267–294. https://doi.org/10.1007/s10567-018-0261-x

Niu, J., & Yuan, X. (2020). The Chinese government regulations on social media and its implications. In J. Hong (Ed.), *China In the era of social media: an unprecedented force for an unprecedented social change* (pp. 333–352). Lexington Books, the Rowman & Littlefield Publishing Group.

Oades, L. G., Jarden, A., Hou, H., Ozturk, C., Williams, P., Slemp, G. R., & Huang, L. (2021). Wellbeing literacy: A capability model for wellbeing science and practice. *International Journal of Environmental Research and Public Health*, *18*(2), 719. https://doi.org/10.3390/ijerph18020719

Oaten, J., & Lee, S. (2024). Deepfake pornography ring linked to South Korean university uncovered after years-long sting. *ABC News*. https://www.abc.net.au/news/2024-09-08/south-korea-deepfake-pornography-telegram-app-sex-crimes/104314174

Pang, H. (2020). Examining associations between university students' mobile social media use, online self-presentation, social support and sense of belonging. *Aslib Journal of Information Management*, *72*(3), 321–338. https://doi.org/10.1108/AJIM-08-2019-0202

Primack, B. A., Shensa, A., Sidani, J. E., Whaite, E. O., yi Lin, L., Rosen, D., & Miller, E. (2017). Social media use and perceived social isolation among young adults in the US. *American Journal of Preventive Medicine*, *53*(1), 1–8. https://doi.org/10.1016/j.amepre.2017.01.010

Quinn, S., & Oldmeadow, J. A. (2013). Is the *i*generation a 'we' generation? Social networking use among 9-to 13-year-olds and belonging. *British Journal of Developmental Psychology*, *31*(1), 136–142. https://doi.org/10.1111/bjdp.12007

Sampasa-Kanyinga, H., & Lewis, R. F. (2015). Frequent use of social networking sites is associated with poor psychological functioning among children and adolescents. *Cyberpsychology, Behavior, and Social Networking*, *18*(7), 380–385. https://doi.org/10.1089/cyber.2015.0055

Schlosser, A. E. (2020). Self-disclosure versus self-presentation on social media. *Current Opinion in Psychology*, *31*, 1–6. https://doi.org/10.1016/j.copsyc.2019.06.025

Shakya, H. B., & Christakis, N. A. (2017). Association of Facebook use with compromised well-being: A longitudinal study. *American Journal of Epidemiology*, *185*(3), 203–211. https://doi.org/10.1093/aje/kww189

Tkáčová, H., Pavlíková, M., Jenisová, Z., Maturkanič, P., & Králik, R. (2021). Social media and students' wellbeing: An empirical analysis during the covid-19 pandemic. *Sustainability*, *13*(18), 10442. https://doi.org/10.3390/su131810442

Treem, J. W., & Leonardi, P. M. (2013). Social media use in organizations: Exploring the affordances of visibility, editability, persistence, and association. *Annals of the International Communication Association*, *36*(1), 143–189. https://doi.org/10.1080/23808985.2013.11679130

Twenge, J. M., & Campbell, W. K. (2018). Associations between screen time and lower psychological well-being among children and adolescents: Evidence from a population-based study. *Preventive Medicine Reports*, *12*, 271–283. https://doi.org/10.1016/j.pmedr.2018.10.003

Twenge, J. M., Joiner, T. E., Rogers, M. L., & Martin, G. N. (2018). Increases in depressive symptoms, suicide-related outcomes, and suicide rates among US adolescents after 2010 and links to increased new media screen time. *Clinical Psychological Science*, *6*(1), 3–17. https://doi.org/10.1177/2167702617723376

Vannucci, A., Flannery, K. M., & Ohannessian, C. M. (2017). Social media use and anxiety in emerging adults. *Journal of Affective Disorders*, *207*, 163–166. https://doi.org/10.1016/j.jad.2016.08.040

Verduyn, P., Gugushvili, N., Massar, K., Täht, K., & Kross, E. (2020). Social comparison on social networking sites. *Current Opinion in Psychology*, *36*, 32–37. https://doi.org/10.1016/j.copsyc.2020.04.002

Volkmer, I. (2021). *Social media and COVID-19: A global study of digital crisis interaction among gen z and millennials*. University of Melbourne.

Yadav, K. (2021). *Platform interventions: How social media counters influence operations*. The Carnegie Endowment for International Peace. Retrieved January 10, 2025 from https://carnegieendowment.org/posts/2021/01/platform-interventions-how-social-media-counters-influence-operations?lang=en#platform-interventions/?lang=en

Zhang, C. A., Tang, L., & Liu, Z. (2023). How social media usage affects psychological and subjective well-being: Testing a moderated mediation model. *BMC Psychology*, *11*(1). https://doi.org/10.1186/s40359-023-01311-2

17

USING THE ARTS TO EXPLORE THE MULTI-MODALITY OF WELLBEING TO GROW WELLBEING LITERACY

Narelle Lemon, Jason Goopy, and Megan McPherson

Introduction

Wellbeing literacy encompasses the mindful and intentional use of language to enhance wellbeing, incorporating vocabulary, comprehension, composition, and contextual adaptation (Oades et al., 2020, 2021). High wellbeing literacy enables expanded language choices for personal and collective wellbeing, recognising that wellbeing itself is both individual and experiential (Oades et al., 2020).

As artists and educators, we explore wellbeing literacy through multimodality – engaging multiple forms of communication beyond traditional reading and writing to include visual, auditory, and kinaesthetic elements (Albers & Harste, 2007; Moffatt et al., 2016). This approach enables expression through diverse channels such as visual arts, music, and digital media, allowing complex emotions and cultural meanings to be conveyed when words alone prove insufficient.

Multimodal composition in wellbeing literacy encourages both individual and collective expression through various creative forms. For instance, intergenerational digital storytelling projects combine interviews, photography, and narrative to articulate perspectives on wellbeing across ages and experiences. This integration of multiple modes enables richer expression and deeper connection to wellbeing concepts.

Communication for wellbeing requires intentional language use to foster psychological safety and emotional wellbeing (Oades et al., 2021). Multimodal approaches enhance this through varied strategies – from visual aids in mental health discussions to intimate audio storytelling in podcasts – allowing individuals to explore wellbeing literacy through personally meaningful channels.

DOI: 10.4324/9781003644293-17

Our Dialogical Conversation

In this chapter, we present a dialogical conversation consisting of dynamic texts and visuals to invite the reader to observe us engaging in narrative exposure and reconceptualisation, as we critically examine and redefine our previously held beliefs. Dialogue, as a method of inquiry (Norris & Sawyer, 2012; Placier et al., 2005), highlights the emergent aspects of research and writing. Helin (2016) suggests that dialogical writing shifts the focus from finalised to emergent writing, recognising how writing can be used for inquiring, feeling, listening, and connecting. This approach contrasts with traditional academic writing, which often aims for stable and solid texts.

Dialogue allows for tentative, developmental, and emergent conversations and writing, enabling individuals and groups to collaboratively construct new meaning (Smith, 2015). We move away from a traditional academic structure; instead of a separate literature review, we integrate literature discussion within our dialogue. In writing about ways that we might create spaces for wellbeing, we see the process of dialogic writing as a way of starting to open a space, and of inviting others into the conversation and the endeavour.

Who Are We?

Narelle: I'm an interdisciplinary scholar drawing on arts, education and positive psychology. I'm a retired classical musician and my true love is photography. In my research at the moment I am adapting photo voice methodology working with still and moving image and audio to foster a deeper understanding of everyday self-care practices. By empowering participants to become "citizen wellbeing scientists," this initiative encourages individuals to document and share their personal self-care routines using various multimedia tools. Through this process, participants not only enhance their own wellbeing literacy but also contribute to a growing community of knowledge. As these diverse experiences are shared in an anonymous online space, a dialogue emerges that transcends individual practices. This collaborative approach to exploring wellbeing creates a supportive environment where participants can reflect on their own habits, draw inspiration from others, and collectively build a richer understanding of what it means to prioritise self-care in our daily lives in multimodal ways. By bringing together people from all walks of life, the project aims to democratise wellbeing knowledge and empower individuals and groups to take an active role in nurturing their own health and happiness. This is where we are all citizens of everyday acts of self-care; sharing, growing, contributing, enhancing, and collectively supporting one another build a wellbeing literacy.

Jason: I am a passionate music educator and scholar deeply interested in how learning music can positively transform lives. My research operates at the interface of music, education, and psychology, and I am particularly invested in the stories of youth and their uses of music. My featured project examines the role of trauma-informed music education in supporting the wellbeing of young people facing challenging life circumstances. In this project, I worked with music education programs that had a focus on developing life skills through and with music for youth experiencing disengagement, mental illness, trauma, substance abuse, unemployment, and homelessness. Wellbeing literacy was both a method and topic of investigation, with data generated using narrative share and tell interviews. While musical products were consumed by youth as a resource for wellbeing, the process of listening, making, and learning was also an act of wellbeing. Music for and as wellbeing processes were multilayered and multimodal, and interconnected and complex.

Megan: I am a non-Indigenous artist, educator and researcher based in Naarm (Melbourne). My research is focused on how artists learn how to be artists. In this space, I am working with First Peoples artists and becoming artists to build skills and capacities to build artistic careers, and with all this, encompassing cultural and creative multimodal practices. How these actions build and maintain and share literacies in all areas of wellbeing and healing, entrepreneurial competencies and artistic careers inform how this research is co-designed and co-facilitated through printmaking and art making workshops in remote and regional Communities. By bringing in opportunities to build skills in printmaking, there are discussions and wellbeing literacy building through ideas of self-determination and its links to wellbeing supported through cultural and creative practice.

Conversational Considerations...

Narelle: The integration of diverse communication modes is essential for a comprehensive approach to understanding and promoting wellbeing. By engaging these multiple channels of communication, individuals can enhance their comprehension and composition of wellbeing-related content. Moreover, this layered approach to expression enriches the actions of "communicating for and about wellbeing" (Oades et al., 2021), making these interactions more effective, engaging, and inclusive. As such, the deliberate use of varied expressive forms stands as a pivotal element in the advancement of wellbeing literacy, contributing to the holistic development of individuals and groups. If we build on the five components of wellbeing literacy (Oades et al., 2020) in Table 17.1 and look for

TABLE 17.1 Multimodal opportunities and future directions in composing and comprehending about and for wellbeing

Component	*Description*	*Multimodal opportunities and future directions*
1. Vocabulary and knowledge about wellbeing	Words and basic facts about wellbeing (i.e., content that is signified).	• Developing interactive digital resources (e.g., apps, websites, podcasts) to facilitate learning and engagement with wellbeing vocabulary and concepts • Creating visually compelling infographics and videos to convey key wellbeing information • Exploring the use of virtual and augmented reality to immerse learners in wellbeing-related content
2. Comprehension of multimodal text related to wellbeing	Reading, listening, viewing about and for wellbeing	• Designing multimedia case studies and scenarios that challenge learners to analyse and interpret wellbeing related content across various formats • Incorporating interactive elements (e.g., simulations, mobile documentary making, visual narratives, etc.) to assess and reinforce comprehension of multimodal wellbeing texts • Investigating the effectiveness of different multimodal formats in facilitating wellbeing literacy comprehension across diverse audiences
3. Composition of multimodal text related to wellbeing	Writing, speaking, creating about and for wellbeing	• Encouraging others to create and share their own wellbeing-related content using various media (e.g., blogs, podcasts, videos) • Providing opportunities for learners to collaborate on multimodal wellbeing projects, fostering creativity and shared understanding • Exploring the potential for learner-generated multimodal content to contribute to the broader discourse on wellbeing literacy
4. Context awareness and adaptability	Awareness of differences across contexts and adapt use of language to fit the relevant context.	• Developing case studies and role-playing activities that challenge learners to adapt their wellbeing communication to different contexts and audiences • Encouraging learners to critically analyse how wellbeing is represented and discussed across various media and cultural contexts • Investigating the impact of context-specific multimodal communication on wellbeing literacy and outcomes
5. Intentionality for wellbeing	Habit of intentionally using language to maintain or improve wellbeing of self or others.	• Providing opportunities for learners to practise intentional communication for wellbeing using various multimodal formats • Encouraging learners to reflect on their own multimodal communication habits and their impact on personal and collective wellbeing • Exploring the potential for intentional multimodal communication to foster a culture of wellbeing and inspire positive change

multimodal future directions, what does our future look like? From your perspective Jason and Megan, what is it that we can offer from our respective arts that allows us to understand wellbeing further?

Knowledge and language are embedded in social, cultural, historical, and communal contexts. The creation of theories, ideas, truths, beliefs, realities, and practical knowledge is an interactive interpretive process that unfolds through social discourse within knowledge communities. These communities collaboratively develop and sustain these concepts through language, thus blurring the distinction between "knower" and "non-knower" (Anderson, 2012). Language, the medium of knowledge, encompasses any mode or means used for communication, articulation, or expression, whether through words, gestures, facial expressions, or hand movements. This is what I am really curious as to how we can embrace the arts and the multi-modality that comes with the flow of process and product and the intersection as, of and for wellbeing. What do you think Jason and Megan?

Jason: Our views of wellbeing literacy can be expanded by considering the substantive body of research on arts and literacies, that is, the multiple ways people can make meaning of their lives and the world using various media, movement, and sound (Barton, 2019). In the case of music, it is established that most people listen to and consume music to support their wellbeing (Rickard, 2012). My research with young people suggests that wellbeing outcomes could be amplified by youth directly participating in music processes (e.g., making and learning music) and generating their own musical products (e.g., original songs). These processes and products are multimodal and multisensory. For example, young people writing original songs fuse a range of arts literacies, including crafting and singing lyrics; experimentation with and playing musical ideas on instruments; digital audio and video recording and production skills; conversations and sharing of music ideas with peers and mentors; reflection and refinement; and, publishing and promoting on digital platforms. Music processes and products without lyrics can be equally or even more powerful. Game and film music strongly resonate with youth and are examples of music that can generate deep meaning, typically without language involved. It is also important to recognise the ways that people use and respond to music processes and products for and as wellbeing is personalised, dynamic, and contextualised, including for identity formation, self-expression, self-regulation, connection, and reflection.

Megan: I consider how the artist-researchers and communities I work with inform my understanding of what multimodal ways for understanding how creating artwork and the intentions are informed through Place and contexts (Martin & Mirraboopa, 2003). The artists I work with are involved in cultural and creative practices as an important part of their lives. Many of the artists I work with will have multiple practices encompassing song, dance, storytelling and art making. Many have cultural responsibility to stories, Place and how these stories and practices are passed on intergenerationally. The creation of artworks that reflect Place, story, cultural knowledges and practice makes statements and actions of what ways of knowing, being and doing (Martin & Mirraboopa, 2003) can do in relational ways with ongoing responsibilities for cultural continuance and thrivance (Jolivétte et al., 2021). In writing about Indigenist research, Martin and Mirraboopa argue on the importance of ontology, "It is through ontology that we develop an awareness and sense of self, of belonging and for coming to know our responsibilities and ways to relate to self and others" (Martin & Mirraboopa, 2003, p. 206). The term thrivance is an acknowledgement of continuing Indigenous cultures, not just surviving, but thriving and with joy. This joy, as seen in art making, dance, and song, for example, is an Indigenous response to colonial violence. It is a decolonisation force with Indigenous Knowledge systems, creative and cultural practices, and relational embodiment between place, community, ceremony, culture and cultural responsibilities at the centre (Jolivétte et al., 2021). This stance informs the ways I understand how the relational becomes all important to notions of multimodal literacies for wellbeing. Wellbeing is relational, through individual and community's context, Culture and Place, the intention in the creative making, and how wellbeing literacies are multimodal.

Narelle: I've taken a risk recently and shared an idea that is underpinned with the multi-modality of comprehending and composing for and as wellbeing called Citizen Wellbeing Scientist (CWS). Megan your connection to community and co-design resonates with me, with CWS, I'm involving all of us, (citizens of the world) to document our everyday self-care acts as a way to build our capacity, understanding, capacity to relocate the self of self-care as relational - we learn with and from one another as we care for self in order to care for one another (Lemon, 2024). Everyday documentation through photography, video or audio recording serves as both a representation of wellbeing and a wellbeing practice in itself (see Figures 17.1 and 17.2). There is an acknowledging of one's own practice, a composing and communicating what this is in text paired with a creative expression form, then a sharing this, and inviting others to comment. This way meaning making isn't happening in isolation – there is interaction with others allowing for perspectives to be engaged

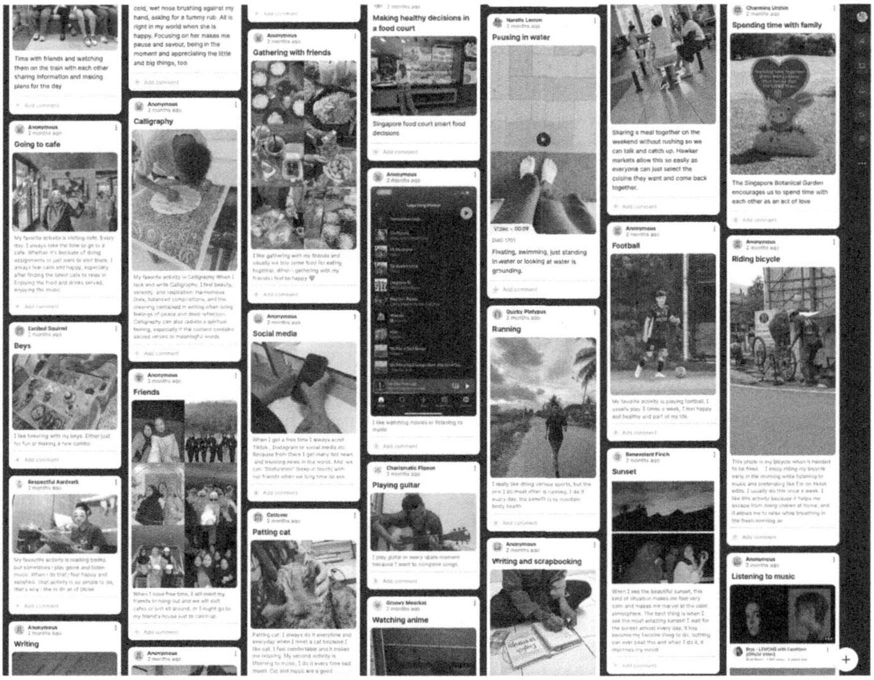

FIGURE 17.1 A curated collection of images from Narelle's citizen wellbeing scientist project, showcasing diverse representations of everyday self-care generated by community members across the world.

with and through knowledge affirmation, making, questioning, processing, reflecting, etc grow occurs for self and others as an act of sharing. Similar to music-making, as you shared Jason, these activities involve capturing moments, honing skills, and creating original content. They provide avenues for emotional expression and regulation while engaging individuals and groups in a process that enhances wellbeing through creation and reflection.

Jason: Building on my previous work using narrative inquiry and draw and tell tasks (Goopy, 2024), I designed narrative share and tell interviews that facilitate multi-modal wellbeing literacy. Interviews consisted of a two-phase share and tell task, which involved participants drawing and then sharing music with reflections. Young people were first presented with a draw and tell task, which involved responding to a single open question such as "What do you enjoy about music?" (Figure 17.3) and "How does music help you?" (Figure 17.4). The product of the drawing was not the focus of investigation but rather the stories generated through the process of drawing and comprehension. In the second phase,

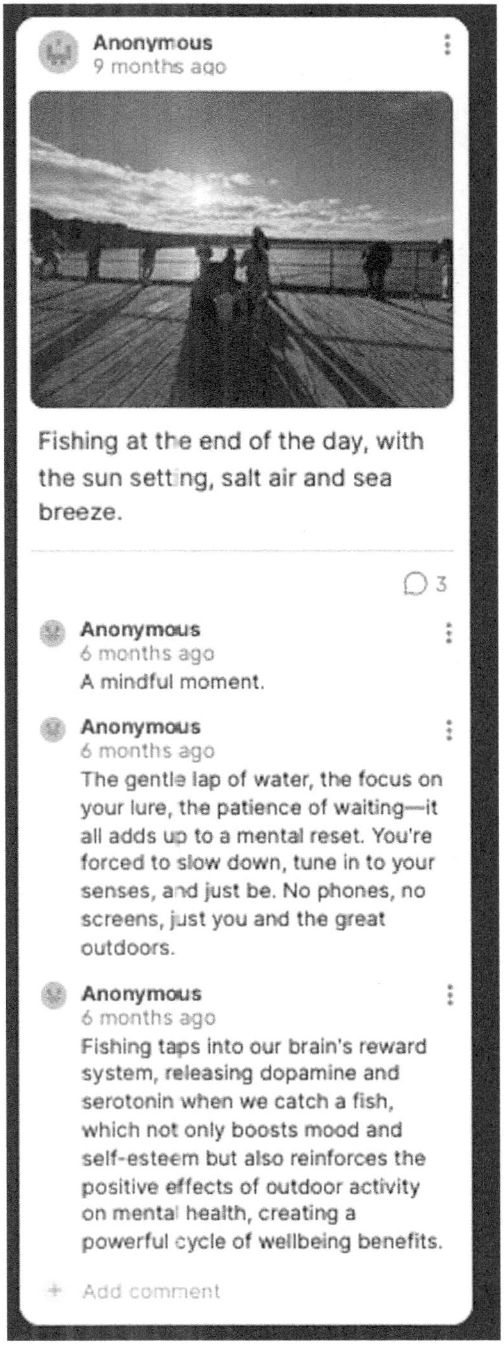

FIGURE 17.2 Building shared wellbeing literacy: From individual post to community response.

FIGURE 17.3 Narrative share and tell interviews facilitated multi-modal wellbeing literacy for young people. Rowan's drawing represents artists and audience coming together as a community.

FIGURE 17.4 Drawing in share-and-tell interviews provided space for young people to compose and comprehend their thoughts about their wellbeing. Mia's drawing represents how music can connect different people.

participants shared music as a salient example of what they previously described. Often, these examples were from participants' Spotify playlists, including their own original songs. We then listened to music together in the interview with follow-up questions. This process of making and sharing art provided multiple angles for deepening participant reflection, evident in the richness of their transcripts. Participants often commented on how these interviews provided them with a rare opportunity to pause and consciously consider the influential role of music in supporting their wellbeing.

Narelle: Jason, could you describe a specific instance of how song writing supported a young person's wellbeing, highlighting the multimodal aspects of the process?

Jason: I visited a non-selective music-focused senior secondary school for students with a passion for music and the arts who were previously disengaged from school. In this setting, most students were creating and performing their own original songs. I was struck by the powerful role that music played in supporting these students' wellbeing. For example, Ellie (Year 11) was already a prolific singer-songwriter. Ellie took on multiple roles in songwriting, including generating lyrics and musical ideas, singing and playing instruments, and being part of the production and promotion process. For Ellie, music was her way of processing her emotions and communicating with the world, especially those most close to her. She shared with me a song from her personal Spotify channel, which describes a painful relationship with a family member where the person is both a "heartbreaker" and "heartmender" (https://open.spotify.com/track/0GJLMRoxenLKplEdaUojqP?si=98f6205265d54b5c). This song acted as a circuit breaker and a way to start a conversation about a healthier relationship with this family member. In this instance, music creation and performance provided a more personally accessible and resonating method of self-expression to communicate wellbeing meaning than words alone. Megan, how about you?

Megan: During the six hour drive to my fieldwork location in the Kimberley in the remote north of Western Australia, my eyes became attuned to a lemon yellow flower endemic in the landscape (see Figure 17.5). This large petal yellow flower of the Kapok tree contrasted against the fluffy mauve of mulla-mullas. I stopped the 4WD by the side of the road multiple times on my trip into the Kupungarri Community to look closely at both flowers. While facilitating printmaking workshops in the Community, the artists decided on what images that they wanted to create. They discussed that making images of

FIGURE 17.5 Megan's attunement to the kapok flower in the Kimberley region of Western Australia.

plants was a way of making images of cultural knowledge they felt comfortable in sharing. The Kapok flower was a feature in one of the linocuts created by the artists. The artists discussed how the fluffy seed heads after the flowers were used as fire starters, that the flowers came out in the Dry season, and that they were important culturally. The fluffy seed pod insides are used as body and costume decoration for ceremony (Kenneally et al., n.d.). While creating an image of the Kapok flower, the artists discussed the importance of Place to them. The artist felt comfortable in creating this image with cultural knowledge whereas other themes and topics for images and knowledge use may not have met with community approval. How this creation of an image of a common flower is then thought of as an indicator of wellbeing in this community speaks to how self-determination and agency are expressed. The artist felt confident that this image showed knowledge that they were responsible for and that they had the right to tell this seasonal story. It is their story to share with as they hold these responsibilities. How these ideas are shared are important to the public and within community. In this discussion of wellbeing, the emphasis on cultural expression is a part of the Community's wellbeing and demonstrates the Community's self-determination to "shape their own lives" (Australian Human Rights Commission, n.d.) Self-determination informed the artist's agency in what one can be and done in making the image and the artist's intention of sharing their knowledge about wellbeing within the community. The artist considered the wellbeing of themselves, place and community in their practices, and set the agendas of how wellbeing is intentional for them.

Narelle: The integration of cultural contexts and social settings in multimodal wellbeing literacy acknowledges the heterogeneous nature of wellbeing across diverse cultures, communities, and social environments. Your work Megan illustrates First Peoples artists and likewise Jason's experiences in varied musical education settings, emphasises several key aspects as well. Firstly, it recognises the deep-rooted cultural responsiveness of wellbeing practices, exemplified by the integration of storytelling, dance, and art-making that reflect place, cultural knowledge, and intergenerational responsibilities. The importance of contextual adaptation, noting that wellbeing practices may have varying impacts in different settings. The approach also underscores the influence of social dynamics on wellbeing practices, ranging from collaborative community music programs to shared experiences in which we also feature in the CWS project. All of our work incorporates a relational ontology that emphasises the interconnectedness of self, community, and Place. This perspective illuminates that effective wellbeing literacy necessitates adaptability to different cultural and social contexts, crucial for creating inclusive and effective wellbeing practices.

Where to next with arts and wellbeing literacy? The arts offer unique pathways for advancing wellbeing literacy through diverse expression. Whether creating, viewing, or participating, artistic engagement enables multiple channels of understanding that transcend traditional verbal communication. This natural synthesis between artistic expression and wellbeing literacy creates accessible entry points for diverse audiences, while deepening both personal and collective understanding of wellbeing concepts.

Jason: I am really interested in the ways that the arts can facilitate deeply meaningful, highly engaging, and creative ways for individuals and communities to live well. Wellbeing is a personalised act and we need to further explore the multiplicities in which people can realise their potential. Participating in and creating arts augments existing conversations surrounding wellbeing literacies, and acknowledges that people do and want to make meaning of the world differently. How can we not explore every avenue to support all people, especially those marginalised and vulnerable in society?

Megan: I am interested in how we can foster and express our understanding of wellbeing through this very multi-modality that then grows a wellbeing literacy for self and others. Narelle, you talk of a "multi-modal potential"; this idea is powerful and engaging through its conceptualisation of multiple ways of thinking about wellbeing literacies. Creative and cultural practices express through multi-modal potentials which in turn can inform wellbeing literacies, intentionality and interconnectivities. What is becoming apparent in these relationships in my work is where wellbeing literacies strengthen and broaden conceptions of what wellbeing is, and this wellbeing literacy can be through creative and cultural practices.

In a recent study of Creating Arts and Crafts (CAC) and wellbeing, researchers found that creating arts and craft may be beneficial in improving subjective wellbeing in the general population. This quantitative study reveals some interesting benefits to increases in life satisfaction (Keyes et al., 2024). What these benefits may indicate and translate for artists in this interconnected space of wellbeing and wellbeing literacies may inform how we think about wellbeing in different ways. Being fluent in how we speak, draw, paint, make music, dance and do these creative and cultural practices can inform how we think, do and make wellbeing literacies together.

Conclusion

This chapter examined how the arts enrich wellbeing literacy through diverse modalities. Our dialogical exploration revealed that artistic practices – from music to visual arts and cultural expressions – offer unique pathways for understanding and embodying wellbeing beyond traditional linguistic boundaries.

Key insights emerged through our discussion. The arts provide multiple channels for experiencing and articulating wellbeing, enabling inclusive approaches that honour diverse learning preferences and cultural contexts. This is particularly evident in First Peoples' art, where Place-based knowledge and intergenerational practices demonstrate the importance of cultural responsiveness in wellbeing literacy.

Artistic engagement facilitates personalised meaning-making while emphasising the interconnectedness of self, community, and environment. Through creative practices, individuals and communities can assert agency in defining wellbeing on their own terms, transforming abstract concepts into tangible, lived experiences.

The integration of arts as wellbeing literacy opens new possibilities for understanding and cultivating wellbeing. This approach not only deepens our conceptual understanding but provides practical methods for active participation in wellbeing journeys. As we continue exploring this intersection, we invite ongoing dialogue about the multimodality of wellbeing literacy. Will you join us?

References

Albers, P., & Harste, J. C. (2007). The arts, new literacies and multimodality. *English Education*, *40*(1), 6–20. https://doi.org/10.58680/ee20076423

Anderson, H. (2012). Collaborative relationships and dialogic conversations: Ideas for a relationally responsive practice. *Family Process*, *51*(1), 1–19.

Australian Human Rights Commission. (n.d.). *Self-determination (webpage)*. https://humanrights.gov.au/our-work/aboriginal-and-torres-strait-islander-social-justice/self-determination

Barton, G. (2019). *Developing literacy and the arts in schools*. Routledge. https://doi.org/10.4324/9780429316067

Goopy, J. (2024). *Teenage boys, musical identities, and music education: An Australian narrative inquiry*. Routledge. https://doi.org/10.4324/9781003438878

Helin, J. (2016). Dialogical writing Co-inquiring between the written and the spoken word. *Culture and Organization*, *25*(1), 1–15. https://doi.org/10.1080/14759551.2016.1197923

Jolivétte, A. (2021). American Indian Leadership: On indigenous geographies of gender and thrivance. In M. Walter, M. Walter, T. Kukutai, A. A. Gonzales, R. Henry (Eds.), *The Oxford handbook of indigenous sociology* (online edn). Oxford Academic.

Kenneally, K., Thomson, C., Done, C., & Wheeler, J. (n.d.). *Common plants of the Kimberley*. Western Australia Department of Conservation and Land Management. https://library.dbca.wa.gov.au/static/FullTextFiles/016899.pdf

Keyes, H., Gradidge, S., Forwood, S. E., Gibson, N., Harvey, A., Kis, E., Mutsatsa, K., Ownsworth, R., Roeloffs, S., & Zawisza, M. (2024). Creating arts and crafting positively predicts subjective wellbeing. *Frontiers in Public Health*, *12*, 1417997. https://doi.org/10.3389/fpubh.2024.1417997

Lemon, N. (2024). *The 'How' of self-care for teachers: Building your wellbeing toolbox*. Routledge.

Martin, K., & Mirraboopa, B. (2003). Ways of knowing, being and doing: A theoretical framework and methods for indigenous and indigenist re-search. *Journal of Australian Studies*, *27*(76), 203–214. https://doi.org/10.1080/14443050309387838

Moffatt, A., Barton, G., & Ryan, M. (2016). Multimodal reflection for creative facilitators: An approach to improving self-care. *Reflective Practice*, *17*(6), 762–778. https://doi.org/10.1080/14623943.2016.1220935

Norris, J., & Sawyer, R. D. (2012). Toward a dialogic methodology. In J. Norris, R. D. Sawyer, & D. Lund (Eds). *Duoethnography* (pp. 9–39). Routledge.

Oades, L. G., Jarden, A., Hou, H., Ozturk, C., Williams, P., R. Slemp, G., & Huang, L. (2021). wellbeing literacy: A capability model for wellbeing science and practice. *International Journal of Environmental Research and Public Health*, *18*(2), 719. https://doi.org/10.3390/ijerph18020719

Oades, L. G., Ozturk, C., Hou, H., & Slemp, G. R. (2020). Wellbeing literacy: A language-use capability relevant to wellbeing outcomes of positive psychology intervention. *Journal of Positive Psychology*, 696–700. https://doi.org/10.1080/17439760.2020.1789711

Placier, P., Pinnegar, S., Hamilton, M. L., & Guilfoyle, K. (2005). Exploring the concept of dialogue in the self-study of teaching practices. In C. Kosnik, C. Beck, A. R. Freese, & A. P. Samaras (Eds.), *Making a difference in teacher education through self-study: Studies of personal, professional and program renewal* (pp. 51–64). Springer.

Rickard, N. S. (2012). Music listening and emotional well-being. In N. S. Rickard & K. McFerran (Eds.), *Lifelong engagement with music: Benefits for mental health and well-being* (pp. 207–238). Nova Science.

Smith, D. (2015). Exploring interprofessional collaboration and ethical practice: A story of emancipatory professional learning. *Reflective Practice*, *16*(5), 652–676. https://doi.org/10.1080/14623943.2015.1071246

18

WORKPLACE WELLBEING LITERACY

A Business Imperative for Enhanced Workplace Experiences

Margo Lydon, Berni Cooper, and Sandra Surace

The rapidly evolving work environment has elevated mental health and wellbeing from a peripheral concern to a core business imperative. Despite growing recognition of its importance, organisations struggle to translate empirical knowledge into practical applications. In creating healthier, more collaborative, and supportive work environments, it is necessary to transcend mental health literacy (MHL), embracing a broader understanding and promotion of wellbeing. In this chapter, we propose a new concept, workplace wellbeing literacy (WWL), that builds on Oades et al.'s (2021) wellbeing literacy (WL) model and adapts it specifically for workplace contexts. By integrating WL into workplace systems, organisations can transform worker experiences and amplify positive, sustainable outcomes, benefitting workers, organisations, and society. We argue that WWL is essential for effectively promoting wellbeing, boosting engagement, productivity, and cultivating a flourishing workforce.

Challenges and Opportunities for Workplace Wellbeing

Workplace wellbeing is a prerequisite for sustainable productivity, innovation, engagement, and overall organisational success (Bhatt et al., 2023). Work experiences affect both individual workers and workgroup wellbeing, including their collective functioning. As organisations increasingly recognise these impacts, many seek to implement strategies to enhance wellbeing and measure outcomes. This is complex work, exacerbated by varied interpretations of wellbeing across different fields and contexts.

McKinsey Health Institute (Brassey et al., 2023) research highlights that Australian workers exhibit higher rates of burnout, exhaustion, disengagement, and cognitive impairment compared to global averages. Concurrently,

DOI: 10.4324/9781003644293-18

Australia's productivity has declined over numerous years (Parliament of Australia, n.d.). Troubling is a 36.9 per cent rise in work-related psychological injury claims between 2017 and 2022 (Safe Work Australia, 2024); a problem not limited to Australia, as global trends indicate that worker wellbeing is at a crisis point (Schulte et al., 2024).

These statistics reflect experiences in a rapidly evolving workplace where worker wellbeing faces complex challenges. The pace of change stems from diverse drivers, such as five generations in the workforce and post-COVID-19 shifts in work dynamics. Widespread disruptions to operating models, increasing global challenges, and competition place further strain on workforces. So too, do precarious market forces such as the supply chain and geopolitical fluctuations. Compounding all of this are the nuanced attributes of each industry.

Many workplaces address these challenges by implementing "wellbeing/wellness" programs. Mostly aimed at individuals, common programs include subsidised gym memberships, yoga, step challenges, counselling services, and ad hoc training. While these initiatives represent progress, interventions targeting only individual workers prove insufficient for supporting mental health or developing wellbeing (Brassey et al., 2023; Fleming, 2024). Successful interventions require balanced and holistic strategies that also encompass workgroup and organisational-level approaches (Brassey et al., 2023).

Australia's various Codes of Practice for managing psychosocial hazards[1] at work (Australian Government, 2024; Safe Work Australia, 2022) and the international ISO 45003 standard (International Organization for Standardization, 2021) represent additional responses to workforce challenges. While leaders and health and safety professionals implement psychosocial risk management frameworks to support worker safety and wellbeing, these compliance-focused approaches may inadequately address psychosocial risks (Metzler et al., 2019). By primarily focusing on preventing harm through controlling hazards and mitigating risks, they overlook positive enablers of psychosocial factors. Supporting worker wellbeing necessitates learning a new language and knowledge that influences safety AND wellbeing, as enablers of flourishing across multiple organisational levels.

Accurate usage and understanding of wellbeing terminology is foundational to transforming workplace wellbeing experiences. The current landscape is cluttered with poorly defined language across multiple disciplines. Terms like wellbeing, mental health, and mental illness are often used interchangeably and incorrectly (Iasiello et al., 2024) with mental health often serving as a proxy for wellbeing. While interconnected, these concepts require distinction. Wellbeing extends beyond mental health presence and contributes to flourishing (Keyes, 2002), characterised by positive experiences. The absence of a universally accepted wellbeing definition compounds conceptual confusion.

Wellbeing is multifaceted, commonly understood as combining feeling good and functioning well (Huppert, 2009), both crucial elements in workplace wellbeing. The language used to discuss wellbeing shapes social reality and enhances opportunities for workers, workgroups, and organisations to flourish.

Defining Workplace Wellbeing Literacy

WL is the ability to understand and intentionally use language in various contexts, such as the workplace, to enhance the wellbeing of oneself, others, or the world (Oades et al., 2021). To illustrate, imagine entering an engineering plant with no prior knowledge or understanding of engineering concepts; the lack of literacy makes it difficult to comprehend, communicate, and contribute effectively. The five components of WL (vocabulary and knowledge, comprehension, composition, context, and intentionality) provide a way to enhance wellbeing.

To augment understanding and applicability in workplace settings, we propose a definition of **WWL** as *the vocabulary, knowledge, skills, and competencies that enable people, individually or collectively, to understand, access, adapt, and use information, tools, and resources to intentionally improve worker, workgroup, and organisational wellbeing experiences.*

Applying Workplace Wellbeing Literacy to Workplace Systems

Wellbeing at work does not exist in isolation, but in a complex, interconnected system operating on multiple levels (Kern et al., 2020): intrapersonal (worker), interpersonal (workgroup), and organisational. WWL applies to all three levels, thereby increasing "the capability of language-use…about and for wellbeing" (Oades et al., 2021, p. 9).

To translate this theory and illustrate the practical application of WWL, the following workplace vignettes showcase the five components of WL across all three levels. These examples, while not exhaustive, have been compiled from the authors' combined experiences and do not refer to real people or situations.

Intrapersonal (Worker): Fostering Personal Wellbeing at Work

Developing intrapersonal WWL entails acquiring vocabulary and knowledge to deepen awareness and understanding of one's own wellbeing. This includes cultivating emotional intelligence for self-awareness and self-management, enabling effective processing of personal responses. Nurturing a self-compassionate internal narrative helps workers observe negative self-talk without judgement and leverage personal strengths to meet situational demands, which can improve work performance.

Vignette

In a busy healthcare environment, paramedics, Ren and Frankie, face stressors including emergencies and high patient loads. During a natural disaster, the system and workers were strained; ambulances lined up, patients filled corridors and understaffing created chaos. Overwhelmed, Frankie provided incorrect patient advice. When informed of the error, Frankie withdrew from the team. Internally, Frankie engaged in negative self-talk and self-criticism. In contrast, Ren remained calm, leveraging strengths of perspective and self-regulation, managing emotional responses. Ren confidently took charge, directing staff to support critical patients. After the shift, Frankie felt like a failure blaming external factors such as patient rudeness. Conversely, Ren experienced accomplishment and reflected on performance with self-compassion, objectivity, and non-judgement, considering future improvements. This illustrates the impact of high WWL (Ren) and low WWL (Frankie) at the intrapersonal level.

Interpersonal (Workgroup): Strengthening Relational Wellbeing at Work

Intrapersonal capabilities form the foundation for interpersonal WWL, fostering effective communication and wellbeing within workgroups. Communication styles significantly affect worker experiences encompassing all workplace interactions from emails to verbal exchanges. For example, a leader's approach is particularly influential, with warm, empathetic communication fostering support, even during challenges (Goleman, 2006). Empathy enhances coworker interactions through emotional understanding. In workplace communications, it builds trust and enables psychological safety (Edmondson, 2019). Conversely, directive communication can undermine worker autonomy and competence by reducing motivation and wellbeing.

Education and training become essential for developing interpersonal WWL. Active learning bridges theory and practice (Hattie, 2009), helping workers apply wellbeing concepts in real-time. Understanding concepts such as job crafting, active constructive responding, emotional intelligence, high-quality connections, and flow experiences can help workgroups establish a shared vocabulary, improving interactions and wellbeing outcomes while valuing diversity.

Vignette

In a bustling office, coworkers encountered a project challenge requiring a proposal for senior management. Despite differing opinions, they managed their workplace relationship, using emotional intelligence, rather than letting their differences escalate. They maintained open, active, and respectful communication, approaching disagreements with curiosity and genuine interest in alternative perspectives. Their nonverbal communication, relaxed posture, and calm tone created psychological safety, transcending seniority or hierarchy. No one resorted to shouting, sarcasm, or dismissive behaviours. Through this approach, the coworkers preserved their wellbeing while successfully co-creating the proposal for senior management.

Organisational: Fostering Workplace Wellbeing

Deliberately using WWL at the organisational level involves cultivating adaptable interventions, such as job crafting with autonomy support (Slemp et al., 2015) alongside strategic planning and consistent action. For scalable and sustainable impact, WWL is best embedded into all systems, policies, processes, and practices. An example is an employee handbook that incorporates WWL into the organisation's narrative, serving as a guide for all workers. This requires carefully selecting vocabulary, sharing knowledge, and creating widespread understanding, linking wellbeing with various business operations and decisions. Undeniably, the WWL of policy-writers, decision-makers, and system designers is crucial. Aligning policies, processes, and visible action prevents the possibility of wellbeing washing, a tokenistic approach to workplace wellbeing that occurs when wellbeing is not genuinely prioritised or understood.

Another way to build WWL at scale is through targeted training. Gayed et al. (2018) found that managerial training on addressing worker mental health needs significantly improved managers' knowledge, attitudes, and behaviour, benefitting workers. These findings translate to wellbeing, inferring that cultivating leadership WWL alongside MHL supports the entire workforce. While leadership significantly shapes organisational culture (Schein, 2017), collective worker behaviour contributes to overall wellbeing, emphasising a need for both strong leadership and organisation-wide learning to improve WWL. As workers develop greater WWL, their capacity to enhance and maintain it expands, mirroring findings in education where increased wellbeing knowledge led to better choices and improved wellbeing outcomes (Waters & Higgins, 2022).

Viewed through a maturity model (Hudson, 2007), WWL evolves through stages. In the early WWL maturity stages, organisations concentrate on operational efficiencies, considering wellbeing secondary. With higher WWL, organisations more readily adopt inclusive practices, like Shared Value (Porter & Kramer, 2011), a strategic methodology for solving societal problems profitably, benefitting workers, community, and partners. According to Laloux (2014), wellbeing should serve as a fundamental component of organisational operations rather than a tokenistic afterthought, reflecting a mature WWL environment.

Vignette

Fictitious Firm administered an annual survey, assessing worker experiences related to workplace wellbeing, leadership, psychosocial factors, and work practices, while inviting suggestions for improvement. Each survey included a CEO email espousing positive culture and affirming leadership's commitment to worker wellbeing. Despite this, survey results declined continuously with no visible action on workers' suggestions, such as implementing flexible work arrangements. Workers became disillusioned amid increasing workloads and rejected flexible work requests, resulting in rising turnover and workforce shortages. Many viewed the survey and CEO's address as wellbeing washing. Fictitious Firm lacked the capability to effectively address working conditions impacting worker and workplace wellbeing, demonstrating low WWL.

Down the road at Example Co., Jaime and the executive team led a major project using shared value principles, collaborating with partners to address community issues while balancing profit and wellbeing. As the deadline loomed, workloads mounted. The organisation implemented a co-developed psychosocial risk management process and policy. They invested in WWL for leaders and the workforce, understanding wellbeing drivers, alongside identifying potential hazards. The company created multimodal knowledge-sharing avenues to improve wellbeing understanding and embedded these processes. During a regular review, workers raised concerns about workloads and inadequate support. With high WWL, the executives addressed excessive job demands and poor support, by implementing wellbeing strategies including job crafting with autonomy support. This improved workers' satisfaction while maintaining project progress. Example Co.'s approach to wellbeing integration, emphasising meaning, purpose, and wellbeing citizenship, transcended mere hazard mitigation to actively enhance wellbeing.

Reframing Perspectives: From the Language of Hazards to Drivers of Wellbeing

Psychosocial work factors can be harmful or helpful. This duality provides a framework, recognising that fostering positive influences is as important as addressing deficits. Although language and tools to assess psychosocial hazards are increasingly used in workplaces, Nebbs et al. (2023) observed potential to expand psychosocial hazard scales to also evaluate the existence of positive factors, an aspect presently underexplored. Currently, organisations lack tools, language, and workforce understanding to incorporate positive elements within risk management strategies.

WWL balances the risk management approach, providing a complete picture that enables flourishing. By embracing psychosocial factors as drivers of job satisfaction, performance, and creativity, organisations transcend from compliance-driven literacy to WWL. This would amplify the integrated nature of LaMontagne et al.'s (2014) seminal approach to Workplace Mental Health.

Job demands and organisational change management are two psychosocial factors that exemplify the duality of hazards and drivers, as illustrated below and in Figure 18.1.

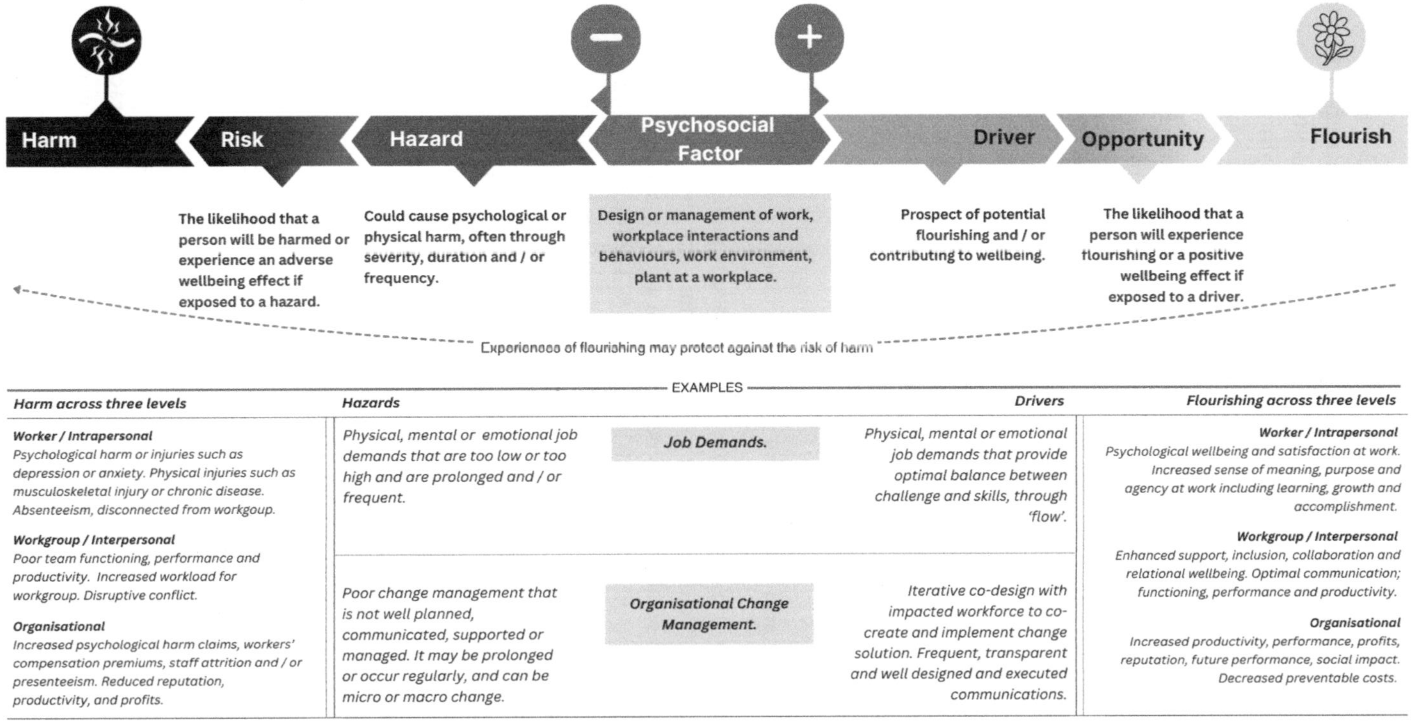

FIGURE 18.1 © using WWL to expand psychosocial risk management to enable Flourishing[a]

Note: Psychosocial hazard, risk, and harm information sourced from "*Managing Psychosocial Hazards at Work. Code of Practice*" by Safe Work Australia (2022).

[a]This model may not apply to all psychosocial hazards.

Job Demands

Job demands constitute a psychosocial risk when they require too much or too little physical, mental, or emotional effort, especially when sustained over time (Safe Work Australia, 2022). Alternatively, the Job-Demands-Resources (JD-R) model demonstrates that job demands when paired with appropriate resources, boost wellbeing, personal growth, mastery, and performance (Bakker & Demerouti, 2017). Furthermore, when job demands match a worker's skills and provide optimal challenge, they can induce a state of flow, characterised by deep focus and engagement, improving wellbeing (Csikszentmihalyi, 1997).

Organisational Change Management

Organisational change imposed without genuine consultation and feedback opportunities can detrimentally affect wellbeing and performance. Conversely, when individual workers and workgroups co-design change, using strengths-based change methodologies, they become empowered to champion the transformation. This approach creates opportunities for autonomy, mastery development, and enhanced connectedness.

Maturing Practices and Frameworks

While attention to workplace wellbeing has increased, significant advancements in workplace mental health have been at the forefront. The Integrated Approach to Workplace Mental Health has influenced research and practice in Australia and globally (LaMontagne et al., 2014, 2019; Nielsen & LaMontagne, 2024). This evidence-based, multidisciplinary model consolidates over ten scientific disciplines, each with nuanced literacies, into three threads: protecting workers from harm, addressing mental ill-health/injury, and promoting the positive elements of work.

Workplaces value simplicity. Simplifying workplace wellbeing language, knowledge, and capabilities remains a persistent request from the business community. The literacy focus within the Integrated Approach emphasises workplace MHL, defined as "the knowledge, beliefs, and skills that aid in the prevention of mental disorders in the workplace, and the recognition, treatment, rehabilitation, and return to work of working people affected by mental disorders" (LaMontagne et al., 2014, p. 11). Recognising the essential benefits of workplace wellbeing, the MHL definition evolved to explicitly include the "promotion of well[-]being in the workplace" (LaMontagne et al., 2019, p. 220). This important inclusion emphasises the wholistic nature of the three threads. However, incorporating wellbeing into a workplace MHL's definition does not fully capitalise on the benefits that workplace wellbeing **literacy** could contribute to the Integrated model. Although WL and MHL in the workplace share common goals in creating healthy work environments, they remain conceptually distinct. Articulating this distinction clearly could reduce workplace confusion regarding these terms.

To better incorporate wellbeing, we propose incorporating it into the model explicitly as: the *Integrated Approach to Workplace Mental Health **and Wellbeing*** and clearly including both MHL and WWL (see Figure 18.2). Integrating WWL may enable organisations to expand beyond mental health and mental illness/injury to encompass broader workplace wellbeing. Overtly elevating wellbeing to equal consideration with mental health brings gravitas to the Integrated Approach and reinforces the foundational need for WWL.

FIGURE 18.2 Evolution of the integrated approach to workplace mental health and wellbeing

Note: Adapted from *Integrated approach to workplace mental health,* by A. D. LaMontagne et al., 2014, BMC Psychiatry, *14*(1), (https://doi.org/10.1186/1471-244X-14-131) and *Prevention and intervention. Multi-level workplace interventions to improve employee mental health* by K. Nielsen & A. D. LaMontagne, 2024, In M. C. W. Peeters, J. de Jonge, & T. W. Taris (Eds), An Introduction to Contemporary Work Psychology, 2nd ed., pp 505–523, Wiley-Blackwell. Copyright A.D. LaMontagne. Used with permission.

The Future with Workplace Wellbeing Literacy

Looking to the future of work, the World Economic Forum (2020) identified that most skills needed will be cognitively and emotionally based encompassing critical thinking, analysis, self-management, resilience, and flexibility. This underscores the urgent need for an approach centred on improving WWL, allowing organisations to surpass surface-level initiatives and address complex factors contributing to diminishing wellbeing.

Implementing WWL through clear, adaptable, and embedded practices can help organisations overcome challenges and achieve economic and social benefits. Research by De Neve et al. (2024) demonstrates that organisations cultivating positive workplace cultures exhibit increased profitability and superior market outcomes, indicating that positive workplace wellbeing predicts both current and future success. Complementing this, Krekel et al. (2019) discovered that higher worker wellbeing led to increased profitability, analysing over 1.8 million workers across 82,000 business units. Similarly, PricewaterhouseCoopers (2014) emphasised the value of investing in mentally healthy workplaces, yielding an average return of $2.30 for every dollar invested. Brassey et al. (2023) argue that the current state of organisations may lead to worker confusion, isolation, disengagement, and reduced productivity. To address this, taking a maturity approach to implementing WWL is crucial to enhance wellbeing for all workers, workgroups, and organisations, amid the escalating pressures of a rapidly evolving world.

Conclusion

Articles about mental health and wellbeing in the workplace often start with painting a dark picture of rising injury, illness and burnout, low morale, and declining productivity. While Australia's work, health, and safety response is positive, it risks focusing solely on compliance-driven, problem-oriented language. As words create worlds, this neglects exploration of wellbeing-promoting protective factors derived from experiencing psychologically safe workgroups and positive cultures. For a complete investigation of workplace wellbeing experiences, including safety, WWL is foundational. The authors' experience across various industries led them to observe that well-intentioned organisations trying to create optimal work environments are constrained by time, resources, energy, knowledge, language, vision, and insufficient WWL.

It is unsurprising that WWL is limited, given:

1. The crowded and confusing workplace wellbeing ecosystem drawing from multiple disciplines, using inconsistent language.
2. Much of contemporary research and interventions have focused on the individual worker, with efforts only now starting to address other levels of the system.
3. There is no consistently accepted language that envisions how psychosocial hazards and psychosocial drivers interact.

Maturity is necessary for organisations to conceptualise and design work systems that ensure safety and promote flourishing. WWL demands context-sensitive adaptability to various system levels, as demonstrated through the vignettes. This literacy must accommodate different industries, workplaces, and roles, and be intentionally applied.

In this chapter, we have reimagined WL in the context of workplaces (WWL) in response to the evidence indicating an urgent need for change. This requires further research. WWL is a business imperative; essential for enhanced workplace experiences that foster environments where organisations, workgroups, and workers can flourish.

Note

1 Anything at work that harms someone's mental health (Safe Work Australia, 2022).

References

Australian Government. (2024). *Work health and safety (managing psychosocial hazards at work) Code of Practice 2024* https://www.legislation.gov.au/F2024L01380/latest/downloads

Bakker, A. B., & Demerouti, E. (2017). Job demands-resources theory: Taking stock and looking forward. *Journal of Occupational Health Psychology, 22*(3), 273–285. https://doi.org/10.1037/ocp0000056

Bhatt, J., Bordeaux, C., & Fisher, J. (2023, March 13). *The workforce well-being imperative*. Deloitte Insights. https://www2.deloitte.com/us/en/insights/topics/talent/employee-wellbeing.html

Brassey, J., Herbig, B., Jeffery, B., & Ungerman, D. (2023, November 2). *Reframing employee health: Moving beyond burnout to holistic health*. McKinsey & Company. https://www.mckinsey.com/mhi/our-insights/reframing-employee-health-moving-beyond-burnout-to-holistic-health

Csikszentmihalyi, M. (1997). *Finding flow: The psychology of engagement with everyday life*. Basic Books.

De Neve, J.-E., Kaats, M., & Ward, G. (2024). *Workplace wellbeing and firm performance*. University of Oxford Wellbeing Research Centre Working Paper 2304. https://doi.org/10.5287/ora-bpkbjayvk

Edmondson, A. C. (2019). *The fearless organization: Creating psychological safety in the workplace for learning, innovation, and growth*. John Wiley & Sons.

Fleming, W. J. (2024). Employee well-being outcomes from individual-level mental health interventions: Cross-sectional evidence from the United Kingdom. *Industrial Relations Journal. 55*, 162–182. https://doi.org/10.1111/irj.12418

Gayed, A., Milligan-Saville, J. S., Nicholas, J., Bryan, B. T., LaMontagne, A. D., Milner, A., Madan, I., Calvo, R. A., Christensen, H., Mykletun, A., Glozier, N., & Harvey, S. B. (2018). Effectiveness of training workplace managers to understand and support the mental health needs of employees: A systematic review and meta-analysis. *Occupational and Environmental Medicine, 75*(6), 462–470. https://doi.org/10.1136/oemed-2017-104789

Goleman, D. (2006). *Social intelligence: The new science of human relationships*. Bantam Books.

Hattie, J. (2009). *Visible learning: A synthesis of over 800 meta-analyses relating to achievement*. Routledge.

Hudson, P. (2007). Implementing a safety culture in a major multi-national. *Safety Science*, *45*(8), 697–722. https://doi.org/10.1016/j.ssci.2007.04.005

Huppert, F. A. (2009). Psychological well-being: Evidence regarding its causes and consequences. *Applied Psychology: Health and Well-Being*, *1*(2), 137–164. https://doi.org/10.1111/j.1758-0854.2009.01008.x

Iasiello, M., Ali, K., van Agteren, J., Kolovos, E., Kyrios, M., Kashdan, T. B., & Fassnacht, D. B. (2024). What's the difference between measures of wellbeing, quality of life, resilience, and coping? An umbrella review and concept map of 155 measures of positive mental health. *International Journal of Wellbeing*, *14*(2), 3621, 1–25. https://doi.org/10.5502/ijw.v14i2.3621

International Organization for Standardization. (2021). *Occupational health and safety management—Psychological health and safety at work—Guidelines for managing psychosocial risks* (ISO Standard No. 45003:2021). https://www.iso.org/standard/64283.html

Kern, M. L., Williams, P., Spong, C., Colla, R., Sharma, K., Downie, A., Taylor, J. A., Sharp, S., Siokou, C., & Oades, L. G. (2020). Systems informed positive psychology. *The Journal of Positive Psychology*, *15*(6), 705–715. https://doi.org/10.1080/17439760.2019.1639799

Keyes, C. L. M. (2002). The mental health continuum: From languishing to flourishing in life. *Journal of Health and Social Behavior*, *43*(2), 207–222. https://doi.org/10.2307/3090197

Krekel, C., Ward, G., & Neve, J.-E. (2019). Employee wellbeing, productivity, and firm performance. *SSRN Electronic Journal*. https://doi.org/10.2139/ssrn.3356581

Laloux, F. (2014). *Reinventing organizations: A guide to creating organizations inspired by the next stage of human consciousness*. Nelson Parker.

LaMontagne, A. D., Martin, A., Page, K. M., Reavley, N. J., Noblet, A. J., Milner, A. J., & Keegel, T. (2014). Workplace mental health: Developing an integrated intervention approach. *BMC Psychiatry*, *14*(1), 13. https://doi.org/10.1186/1471-244X-14-131

LaMontagne, A. D., Martin, A., Page, K. M., Reavley, N. J., Noblet, A. J., Milner, A. J., Keegel, T., Allisey, A., Papas, A., Witt, K., & Smith, P. M. (2019): Developing an integrated approach to workplace mental health. In H. L. Hudson, J. A. S. Nigam, S. L. Sauter, L. C. Chosewood, A. L. Schill, & J. Howard (Eds.), *Total worker health* (pp. 211–228). American Psychological Association. https://doi.org/10.1037/0000149-013

Metzler, Y. A., von Groeling-Müller, G., & Bellingrath, S. (2019). Better safe than sorry: Methods for risk assessment of psychosocial hazards. *Safety Science*, *114*, 122–139. https://doi.org/10.1016/j.ssci.2019.01.003

Nebbs, A., Martin, A., Neil, A., Dawkins, S., & Roydhouse, J. (2023). An integrated approach to workplace mental health: A scoping review of instruments that can assist organizations with implementation. *International Journal of Environmental Research and Public Health*, *20*(2), 1192. https://doi.org/10.3390/ijerph20021192

Nielsen, K., & LaMontagne, A. D. (2024). Prevention and intervention. Multi-level workplace interventions to improve employee mental health. In M. C. W. Peeters, J. de Jonge, & T. W. Taris (Eds.), *An introduction to contemporary work psychology* (2nd ed., pp. 505–523). Wiley-Blackwell.

Oades, L. G., Jarden, A., Hou, H., Ozturk, C., Williams, P., Slemp, G. R., & Huang, L. (2021). Wellbeing literacy: A capability model for wellbeing science and practice. *International Journal of Environmental Research and Public Health*, *18*(2), 1–12. https://doi.org/10.3390/ijerph18020719

Parliament of Australia. (n.d.). *Australia's productivity slowdown*. https://www.aph.gov.au/About_Parliament/Parliamentary_departments/Parliamentary_Library/pubs/BriefingBook47p/AustraliasProductivitySlowdown

Porter, M. E., & Kramer, M. R. (2011). Creating shared value: How to reinvent capitalism - and unleash a wave of innovation and growth. *Harvard Business Review*. https://hbr.org/2011/01/the-big-idea-creating-shared-value

PricewaterhouseCoopers (PwC). (2014). *Creating a mentally healthy workplace: Return on investment analysis*. PwC and Beyond Blue. https://www.pwc.com.au/publications/pdf/beyondblue-workplace-roi-may14.pdf

Safe Work Australia. (2022). *Model code of practice: Managing psychosocial hazards at work*. https://www.safeworkaustralia.gov.au/doc/model-code-practice-managing-psychosocial-hazards-work

Safe Work Australia. (2024, Feb 27). *New report on psychological health in Australian workplaces*. https://data.safeworkaustralia.gov.au/sites/default/files/2024-02/Psychological-health-in-the-workplace_Report_February2024.pdf

Schein, E. H. (2017). *Organizational culture and leadership* (5th ed.). John Wiley & Sons.

Schulte, P. A., Sauter, S. L., Pandalai, S. P., Tiesman, H. M., Chosewood, L. C., Cunningham, T. R., Wurzelbacher, S. J., Pana-Cryan, R., Swanson, N. G., Chang, C.-C., Nigam, J. A. S., Reissman, D. B., Ray, T. K., & Howard, J. (2024). An urgent call to address work-related psychosocial hazards and improve worker well-being. *American Journal of Industrial Medicine*, *67*, 499–514. https://doi.org/10.1002/ajim.23583

Slemp, G. R., Kern, M. L., & Vella-Brodrick, D. A. (2015). Workplace well-being: The role of job crafting and autonomy support. *Psychology of Well-Being*, *5*, 7. https://doi.org/10.1186/s13612-015-0034-y

Waters, L., & Higgins, M. C. (2022). The impact of a teacher-based positive education intervention on student wellbeing literacy. *Journal of School and Educational Psychology*, *2*(1), 22–43. https://doi.org/10.47602/josep.v2i1.12

World Economic Forum. (2020). *The future of jobs report*. https://www.weforum.org/publications/the-future-of-jobs-report-2020/

19

WELLBEING LITERACY AND NEED-SUPPORTIVE PARENTING

Kelly A. Ferber and Emma L. Bradshaw

Introduction

This chapter explores the concept of wellbeing literacy in the context of parenting, aiming to highlight multiple ways parents support and shape their children's wellbeing from the perspective of Self-Determination Theory (SDT). According to SDT, parents who support their children's basic psychological needs for autonomy (volition and agency), competence (capability and effectiveness), and relatedness (closeness with others), fundamentally support their wellbeing. Basic psychological need support leads to basic psychological need satisfaction, which facilitates the organismic integrative process through which children internalise values, develop a cohesive sense of self, and flourish. Indeed, in this chapter, we will review several published meta-analyses that demonstrate the connection between need-supportive parenting and a range of outcomes that benefit children, including greater wellbeing, and the capacity to set need-supportive goals that foster wellbeing. Therefore, we will propose that parents' wellbeing literacy should include an understanding of how to provide need-supportive environments. To this end, this chapter will also describe and provide examples of need-supportive parenting practices and illustrate why they undergird parents' wellbeing literacy, thus enabling parents to create environments that support child wellbeing.

We also acknowledge the nuances within the parent-child relationship and reiterate the importance of applying need-supportive practices in developmentally and contextually appropriate ways. For instance, child age, individual differences, and circumstantial factors can require considered and evolving applications of need-supportive strategies. We also emphasise the importance of considering the process by which parents can best be supported to adopt need-supportive parenting practices.

DOI: 10.4324/9781003644293-19

In summary, we emphasise that wellbeing literacy is fundamentally relational and grounded in the features of proximal environments such as parents. We invite readers to reflect on how the parenting environment itself serves as a platform for wellbeing literacy. Wellbeing literacy therefore includes knowing what constitutes a need-supportive environment and actively applying this knowledge in the relational dynamics between parent and child.

Parenting researchers and practitioners are increasingly recognising the potent role parents' wellbeing literacy plays in supporting their children's wellbeing (Hou et al., 2021; Sanders, 2019). A parent's wellbeing literacy is enriched by understanding how their own behaviours support and shape their children's wellbeing. SDT provides a valuable lens through which parents can gain deeper insight into the ways they can foster their children's wellbeing, thus providing valuable knowledge that should be within the scope of wellbeing literacy in the context of parenting (Ryan & Deci, 2017).

Parents arguably represent one of the most powerful relational and contextual aspects of a child's life, and from the perspective of SDT, there are specific relational behaviours and contextual factors that have been shown to support children's innate, active tendency towards greater integration, unity, and effectiveness in functioning (Joussemet et al., 2008). In particular, SDT suggests that the provision of an environment that supports children's basic psychological needs for autonomy, competence, and relatedness is crucial to the wellbeing of children. This chapter outlines parental need support and explores how knowledge about its application offers a fuller understanding of how parents can bolster the wellbeing of their children. Throughout this chapter, we discuss wellbeing through the lens of SDT, how and why parents could use needs-based approaches in their everyday lives, as well as the role of other parent and contextual factors in promoting child wellbeing. We propose that while there are multiple ways that parents influence their children's wellbeing, parents' knowledge about and ability to provide a need-supportive environment is fundamental to the wellbeing of their children and is therefore an important aspect of parents' holistic wellbeing literacy.

Wellbeing from the SDT Perspective

A key component of wellbeing literacy is *knowledge* – specifically, knowledge that promotes the wellbeing of self and others. To cultivate knowledge within the context of wellbeing literacy, it is crucial to first define and understand what constitutes wellbeing, that is, what is it that parents are aiming for when they wish for their child to experience wellbeing? SDT takes a eudaimonic view of wellbeing, holding that wellbeing is defined as being vital, optimally functioning, and being able to actualise one's potential (Ryan & Martela, 2016). Wellbeing defined in this way is crucially and fundamentally dependent on the extent that people experience the satisfaction of their basic psychological needs

(Ryan et al., 2013). SDT posits three basic psychological needs – autonomy, competence, and relatedness (Ryan & Deci, 2017). *Autonomy* involves a sense of personal agency and volition, where individuals feel that their actions are self-endorsed. *Relatedness* concerns the inherent need to feel a sense of belonging and connection with others, characterised by reciprocity, mutual respect, emotional support, and a sense of unconditional acceptance for who one is at their core. *Competence* refers to an individual's innate need to master their environment and attain a sense of efficacy. Competence reflects an individual's desire to learn, grow, and master new skills. Support for and satisfaction of these three needs is foundational to human wellness (Ryan & Deci, 2017). Therefore, parents' wellbeing literacy will be enriched by their awareness of how to foster their children's basic psychological needs.

Promoting the Wellbeing of Children through Basic Psychological Need Support

Parents have the potential to support or thwart their children's basic psychological needs, and therefore their wellbeing, via the conditions they create (Grolnick & Pomerantz, 2009; Grolnick et al., 1991). Decades of research have shown a positive link between basic psychological need support and child wellbeing (Bradshaw et al., 2024; Şimşek & Demir, 2013; Vasquez et al., 2016). The parental strategies that have been consistently found to support children's basic psychological needs are – autonomy support, involvement, and structure (Ryan & Deci, 2017). Autonomy support is the practice of promoting an individual's self-endorsed, congruent actions (Joussemet et al., 2008). Involvement refers to the degree to which parents are interested in, knowledgeable about, and spend time relating to their children's activities and experiences (Grolnick et al., 1991). Structure involves parents providing clear and consistent guidelines and expectations (Grolnick et al., 1997). Through the use of these need-supportive behaviours, parents create conditions in which children are more likely to develop a strong sense of self-worth, feel more volitional and in control of what they do, face optimal challenges and experience competence, feel more connected, and set goals that directly meet their psychological needs (Grolnick et al., 1997; Şimşek & Demir, 2013).

In contrast, need-thwarting parenting practices hinder the development of children's innate tendencies and authentic self-expression by prompting them to suppress their natural inclinations or depriving them of the necessary support and resources to cultivate their sense of identity and meaningful goals. These environments also disrupt their experiences of relatedness, as relationships in such contexts tend to be inconsistent or unreliable. Need-thwarting tactics include psychological control, chaos, and permissiveness (Ryan & Deci, 2017). Psychological control refers to behaviours such as guilt induction, harsh punishment, intrusiveness, and invalidation of thoughts and feelings which thwart children's curiosity, exploration, and fosters a conditional sense of worth. Chaos involves unpredictable or erratic behaviour that disrupts a child's sense of stability and competence. Permissiveness is characterised by a lack of parental guidance, or minimal emotional involvement. Unsurprisingly, need-thwarting parenting practices have been linked with numerous ill-being outcomes (Bradshaw et al., 2024). With the awareness of which parenting behaviours support or thwart children's needs, comes the capacity to make more informed choices about parenting behaviours to reduce, with the knowledge that such behaviours are likely to hinder children's wellbeing.

The How of Need Support

Below, we further outline key need-supportive parenting practices – autonomy support, involvement, and structure – and offer examples of the types of communication and language that typify these behaviours. We note that need-supportive parenting practices encompass an array of verbal and non-verbal communication behaviours, which are intended to be adapted to the individual and their context.

Autonomy Support

Parental autonomy support involves behaviours such as perspective-taking, offering meaningful choices, and providing meaningful rationales for requested behaviours (Ryan & Deci, 2017). Perspective-taking is crucial to autonomy-supportive parenting, as it enables parents to attune to their child's experiences and create a space where initiative is encouraged and supported. An atmosphere of perspective-taking entails ongoing consideration for an individual's values, interests, and needs. Language that enables parents to take the perspective of their child, might include open-ended curiosity such as "what do you think about…?" or "how do you feel about…?" or "tell me about…" or "what do you like the most.?" or "what is the hardest thing about…?". For instance, a parent who listens to their child's feelings about a challenging homework assignment and acknowledges their frustration before offering options about how to help is engaging in perspective-taking.

Perspective-taking is fundamental to two other key components of autonomy support: offering meaningful choices and rationales. A common misconception is that autonomy support is simply about providing options – for example, "You can choose from A or B". While offering age-appropriate choices can foster autonomy, the options must be relevant and meaningful to the child's experiences and interests to truly support their sense of agency. When choice is not possible or children face an uninteresting task, such as cleaning up or doing homework, providing meaningful rationales has been shown to make such activities feel more valuable and important (Joussemet et al., 2004). Thus, moving away from phrases such as "because I say so..." and replacing them with personally relevant, descriptive rationales offers greater autonomy support. Based on these components of autonomy support, it is clearly distinct from independence, with which autonomy support is sometimes confused. Independence focuses on the promotion of self-sufficiency or detachment from others, whereas autonomy support fosters self-endorsement of choices, which may involve self-sufficiency, but one can also willingly seek and accept support when needed.

A recent meta-analysis consolidated the abundant evidence supporting the link between autonomy-supportive parenting and child wellbeing, across cultures and a variety of developmental and demographic variables (Bradshaw et al., 2024). The meta-analysis included 238 studies and found a moderate positive link between parental autonomy support and child wellbeing. Meanwhile, parental psychological control (the opposite of autonomy support and a key aspect of need-thwarting), which is characterised by tactics like guilt induction and coercion, was linked with greater child illbeing. The meta-analysis confirmed that the effects of autonomy support and psychological control on child wellbeing and illbeing are distinct and independent. Even when controlling for psychological control, autonomy support continued to show a positive association with child wellbeing, and vice versa. The distinction suggests that fostering wellbeing requires more than just eliminating controlling parenting practices; it necessitates the active promotion of autonomy-supportive behaviours.

Involvement

Involvement refers to the dedication of time, engagement, and resources towards a child. Everyday acts of involvement can take the form of showing interest, paying attention, spending time together, participating in daily activities, or providing material resources (Grolnick & Slowiaczek, 1994). Involvement can be expressed in both autonomy-supportive and controlling ways, and recognising the difference is essential in becoming literate in need-supportive parenting practices. For instance, autonomy-supportive involvement prioritises offering resources in a way that is attuned to the child's needs and perspectives. For instance, showing interest might involve using descriptive statements or open-ended questions that encourage curiosity and self-expression, such as "Show me how you did that!" or "What was the most fun part of making that project?" Investing in the child could involve paying attention to and recognising their passions and supporting them through encouragement and access to experiences that align with their interests. Material resources can also be provided in autonomy-supportive ways, such as offering tools, books, or learning materials that align with the child's interests. Controlling involvement instead includes providing resources with contingencies attached – where a parent's involvement is conditional on the child meeting their expectations. Being *overly* involved can also be controlling because it can make children feel untrusted (undermining competence) and surveilled (undermining autonomy). Clearly, autonomy-supportive involvement is better able to help children feel attuned, understood, and supported in ways that respect their autonomy.

Structure

Structure involves the provision of clear and consistent guidelines and expectations and the creation of an optimally challenging environment for a child. Effective parenting strategies that offer structure include giving feedback that supports development, creating experiences in which children can experience mastery, and setting clear limits and expectations (Grolnick & Pomerantz, 2009). A central component of structure is using language and communication that scaffolds expectations and learning experiences appropriately, guiding children in a way that promotes mastery and effectiveness. For example, a person with no swimming experience should not be expected to swim in the deep end immediately. Instead, their learning should be scaffolded by breaking it down into manageable steps. Engaging with a child to provide structure requires thoughtful involvement. At times communication used within the provision of structure could involve guiding a child by saying, "let's do the first few together".

Like involvement, structure can also be provided in both autonomy-supportive and controlling ways, and discerning the two is essential to its effective use. Autonomy-supportive structure is responsive to the level of structure a child needs in a given context. At times, a high degree of structure can foster autonomy and competence by providing clear expectations and guidance, whereas in other situations, even minimal structure can feel intrusive if it undermines a child's sense of ownership over their actions. When structure is provided in an autonomy-supportive way – such as through collaboration in setting rules and expectations, offering choices on how to meet guidelines, and explaining the rationale behind limits – it promotes engagement, competence, and performance (Grolnick et al., 2015). Conversely, structure that is rigid, arbitrary, or imposed without consideration of the child's perspective and capacity can diminish autonomy and autonomous motivation.

By understanding and incorporating autonomy support, involvement, and structure into the parent-child dynamic, parents deepen their wellbeing literacy, enabling them to create environments that better understand and nurture their children's psychological needs and, therefore their ability to flourish.

The Many Ways Parents Shape Their Children's Wellbeing

We propose that understanding the many ways parents influence their children's wellbeing – both directly and indirectly – can enhance parents' wellbeing literacy. In addition to the more direct influences of parents' need support and/or need thwarting, parents also shape their children's wellbeing in less explicit ways, such as through their own need satisfaction, and life goals. The following sections explore these multiple parental influences.

Contagion Between Parents' and Children's Need Satisfaction

Given that parents are among the most influential socialisation figures in the lives of their children, it is unsurprising that one of the ways in which wellbeing-related behaviours might transfer between parent and child is through contagion – when similar behaviours (and their consequences) spread between people. Research has shown, for example, that when parents experience more basic psychological need satisfaction, so do their children (Lo Cricchio et al., 2021; Nishimura et al., 2021; Rodriguez-Meirinhos et al., 2021). Parents who report more basic psychological need satisfaction likely occupy contexts that are consistently need-supportive, leading to their own need satisfaction, and arguably bolstering their ability to support and satisfy the basic psychological needs of their children. There is a saying that parents should "fill their own cup", which this evidence suggests may be true in the case of basic psychological need support.

Contagion Between Parents' and Children's Life Goals

A meta-analysis of 49 studies found that when parents prioritise goals that promote their own wellbeing, such as having close relationships, investing in their personal growth, and community giving, their children are also more likely to do so (Ferber et al., 2024). SDT terms these types of goals as intrinsic goals because they lead directly to experiences of basic psychological need satisfaction (e.g., striving for warm, reciprocal relationships supports experiences of relatedness). Whereas extrinsic – or materialistic – goals such as for money, notoriety, or image are those that rely on extrinsic contingencies and are less likely to fulfil basic psychological needs. The meta-analysis also found that regardless of whether the goals were intrinsic or extrinsic, children tended to aspire in similar ways to their parents (Ferber et al., 2024). Thus, parents influence children's wellbeing not only by adopting goals that enhance their personal need satisfaction but also by modelling and thereby transmitting these goal orientations to their children.

In addition to the content of parents' goals, evidence suggests that the context in which goals are fostered influences the degree to which children may also come to value goals that promote wellbeing (i.e., intrinsic goals). Lekes et al. (2011) observed that mothers' and adolescents' levels of intrinsic goal striving were greater when the adolescents experienced more basic psychological needs satisfaction. Evidence also supports a process called *value origination*, in which people's intrinsic goals arise organically, as a function of prior experiences of need support (Ahn & Reeve, 2020; Grolnick et al., 1997). Meaning that need-supportive environments help adolescents focus more on intrinsic goals that better support their wellbeing. Indeed, Ferber et al. (2024) showed meta-analytically that need support was moderately, positively linked with children's intrinsic goals. Taken together, this evidence shows that the provision of need support also facilitates the degree to which children adopt intrinsic goals, which tend to also better support their wellbeing.

The Role of Context and Individual Differences in Needs-Based Wellbeing Literacy

A key aspect of wellbeing literacy is recognising that wellbeing is contextually bound and different contexts and developmental stages require the adoption of informed, targeted approaches Understanding individual differences – such as age, developmental stages, varying abilities, and neurodiversity – is crucial for the effective application of need-supportive parenting strategies. As children develop, their needs evolve, and parenting practices need to adapt to these changes. For younger children, need support is necessary to help them build foundational developmental capacities, such as executive functions, which in turn contribute to later skills like academic achievement in school (Bindman et al., 2015). As children transition into adolescence, a prominent focus becomes providing autonomy support in a way that encourages them to explore their values and make authentic decisions that shape their identity (Côté-Lecaldare et al., 2016). Need support should also be responsive to a child's cultural background and personal circumstances. What fosters a sense of connection may vary across cultural contexts, with different traditions, values, and social norms shaping how children experience and express relatedness. Creating optimally need-supportive environments requires recognising that children have varying abilities, with some benefiting from high levels of autonomy-supportive structure and tools such as social stories and communication aids. While the basic psychological needs for autonomy, relatedness, and competence are universally important to wellbeing, the ways in which they can be best supported varies depending on individual circumstances.

Facilitating the Adoption of Need-Supportive Parenting Practices

In this chapter, we have focussed on the *content* of need-supportive parenting. But, SDT also holds that, to be effective, the *process* of learning need support should itself be need-supportive. As this chapter outlines, need support bolsters wellbeing, but it also supports the development of optimal forms of motivation in a process SDT calls ***internalisation***. Internalisation refers to the process by which behaviours and values become personally meaningful and self-endorsed rather than externally imposed.

Some parents might initially strive to adopt more need-supportive practices to avoid their child's meltdowns; we would call this ***external regulation***, which is when one does something to avoid punishment or to receive a reward. Over time, when the same parents continue practising need-supportive strategies, they may begin to experience internal pressure, such as guilt or self-criticism, when they slip back into more controlling approaches. This internal pressure reflects ***introjected regulation***, which – while still involving a sense of obligation – is more relatively autonomous than external regulation and a step towards greater internalisation of need-supportive values. While external and introjected regulations can initiate behaviour change, it is often unsustainable in the long term. By teaching parenting practices in need-supportive ways, we can support parents to engender more autonomous forms of motivation such as identifying with the importance and benefits of need-supportive parenting practices (***identified regulation***) and integrating the behaviour set with other deeply held personal values (***integrated regulation***). Identified and integrated regulation are more relatively autonomous forms of motivation, and better sustain behaviours over the long term. However, the process may be gradual so parents should not be disheartened by setbacks or a lack of instant mastery. So, how do we teach parents need support in a need-supportive way? Programs such as the "*How to Talk So Kids Will Listen & Listen So Kids Will Talk*" (Faber & Mazlish, 2012) offer need support consistent with the principles we have outlined here; offering perspective taking and responsiveness to parental experiences and concerns allows parents to feel understood and better able to integrate new skills. The provision of structured opportunities for skill development – such as guided practice, role-playing, and the use of meaningful rationales – helps parents build the confidence and capability to implement and adapt these strategies effectively. The more interesting and valuable a parent comes to find the provision of need support, the more likely they are to maintain it in the future, which stands to benefit their children.

Conclusion

Our hope for this chapter is that it contributes to parents' understanding of basic psychological needs and the vital role they play in fostering children's wellbeing; as well as how to support them both directly (need support) and indirectly (parents' own wellbeing-related behaviours and goals). In building this knowledge, we strive to add to parents' wellbeing literacy and therefore the wellbeing of their children.

References

Ahn, J. S., & Reeve, J. (2020). Developmental pathways of preadolescents' intrinsic and extrinsic values: The role of basic psychological needs satisfaction. *European Journal of Personality*, *35*(2), 151–167. https://doi.org/10.1002/per.2274

Bindman, S. W., Pomerantz, E. M., & Roisman, G. I. (2015). Do children's executive functions account for associations between early autonomy-supportive parenting and achievement through high school? *Journal of Educational Psychology*, *107*(3), 756–770. https://doi.org/10.1037/edu0000017

Bradshaw, E. L., Duineveld, J. J., Conigrave, J. H., Steward, B. A., Ferber, K. A., Joussemet, M., Parker, P. D., & Ryan, R. M. (2024). Disentangling autonomy supportive and psychologically controlling parenting: A meta-analysis of self-determination Theory's dual process model across cultures. *American Psychologist*. https://doi.org/10.1037/amp0001389

Côté-Lecaldare, M., Joussemet, M., & Dufour, S. (2016). How to support toddlers' autonomy: A qualitative study with child care educators. *Early Education and Development*, *27*(6), 822–840. https://doi.org/10.1080/10409289.2016.1148482

Faber, A., & Mazlish, E. (2012). *How to talk so kids will listen & listen so kids will talk*. Scribner.

Ferber, K. A., Bradshaw, E. L., Noetel, M., Wong, T. Y., Ahn, J. S., Parker, P. D., & Ryan, R. M. (2024). Does the apple fall far from the tree: A meta-analysis linking parent factors to children's intrinsic and extrinsic goals. *Psychological Bulletin*, *150*(10), 1155–1177. https://doi.org/10.1037/bul0000448

Grolnick, W. S., Deci, E. L., & Ryan, R. M. (1997). Internalization within the family: The self-determination theory perspective. In J. E. Grusec & L. Kuczynski (Eds.), *Parenting and children's internalization of values: A handbook of contemporary theory* (pp. 78–99). Wiley.

Grolnick, W. S., & Pomerantz, E. M. (2009). Issues and challenges in studying parental control: Toward a new conceptualization. *Child Development Perspectives*, *3*(3), 165–170. https://doi.org/10.1111/j.1750-8606.2009.00099.x

Grolnick, W. S., Raftery-Helmer, J. N., Flamm, E. S., Marbell, K. N., & Cardemil, E. V. (2015). Parental provision of academic structure and the transition to middle school. *Journal of Research on Adolescence*, *25*(4), 668–684. https://doi.org/10.1111/jora.12161

Grolnick, W. S., Ryan, R. M., Deci, E. L., & Levin, J. R. (1991). Inner resources for school achievement: Motivational mediators of children's perceptions of their parents. *Journal of Educational Psychology*, *83*(4), 508–517. https://doi.org/10.1037/0022-0663.83.4.508

Grolnick, W. S., & Slowiaczek, M. L. (1994). Parents' involvement in children's schooling: A multidimensional conceptualization and motivational model. *Child Development*, *65*(1), 237–252. https://doi.org/10.1111/j.1467-8624.1994.tb00747.x

Hou, H., Chin, T. C., Slemp, G. R., & Oades, L. G. (2021). Wellbeing literacy: Conceptualization, measurement, and preliminary empirical findings from students, parents and school staff. *International Journal of Environmental Research and Public Health*, *18*(4), 1485. https://doi.org/10.3390/ijerph18041485

Joussemet, M., Koestner, R., Lekes, N., & Houlfort, N. (2004). Introducing uninteresting tasks to children: A comparison of the effects of rewards and autonomy support. *Journal of Personality*, *72*, 139–166. https://doi.org/10.1111/j.0022-3506.2004.00259.x

Joussemet, M., Landry, R., & Koestner, R. (2008). A self-determination theory perspective on parenting. *Canadian Psychology/Psychologie Canadienne*, *49*(3), 194–200. https://doi.org/10.1037/a0012754

Lekes, N., Joussemet, M., Koestner, R., Taylor, G., Hope, N. H., & Gingras, I. (2011). Transmitting intrinsic value priorities from mothers to adolescents: The moderating role of a supportive family environment. *Child Development Research*, 2011. https://doi.org/10.1155/2011/167146

Lo Cricchio, M. G., Costa, S., & Liga, F. (2021). Adolescents' well-being: The role of basic needs fulfilment in family context. *British Journal of Developmental Psychology*, *39*(1), 190–204. https://doi.org/10.1111/bjdp.12360

Nishimura, T., Bradshaw, E. L., Deci, E. L., & Ryan, R. M. (2021). Satisfaction of basic psychological needs in an interdependence model of fathers' own aspirations and those of their adolescent children. *Social Development*, *30*(1), 293–310. https://doi.org/10.1111/sode.12473

Rodriguez-Meirinhos, A., Antolın-Suarez, L., & Oliva, A. (2021). Psychological needs in parents and clinically referred adolescents: An integrative model via parenting and parental mindfulness. *Journal of Family Psychology*, *35*(7), 906–915. https://doi.org/10.1037/fam0000863

Ryan, R., Huta, V., & Deci, E. L. (2013). Living well: A self-determination theory perspective on eudaimonia. In A. Delle Fave (Ed.), *The exploration of happiness* (pp. 117–139). Springer. https://doi.org/10.1007/978-94-007-5702-8_7

Ryan, R. M., & Deci, E. L. (2017). *Self-determination theory: Basic psychological needs in motivation, development, and wellness*. Guilford Press.

Ryan, R. M., & Martela, F. (2016). Eudaimonia as a way of living: Connecting Aristotle with self-determination theory. In J. Vitterso (Ed.), *The handbook of eudaimonic wellbeing*. Springer.

Sanders, M. R. (2019). Harnessing the power of positive parenting to promote wellbeing of children, parents and communities over a lifetime. *Behaviour Change*, *36*(2), 56–74. https://doi.org/10.1017/bec.2019.3

Şimşek, Ö. F., & Demir, M. (2013). Parental support for basic psychological needs and happiness: The importance of sense of uniqueness. *Social Indicators Research*, *112*(3), 661–678. https://doi.org/10.1007/s11205-012-0075-z

Vasquez, A. C., Patall, E. A., Fong, C. J., Corrigan, A. S., & Pine, L. (2016). Parent autonomy support, academic achievement, and psychosocial functioning: A meta-analysis of research. *Educational Psychology Review*, *28*(3), 605–644. https://doi.org/10.1007/s10648-015-9329-z

20

UNLOCKING POLICY POTENTIAL

Leveraging Wellbeing Literacy for Enhanced Wellbeing Policy

Diane Bowles and Kate Sollis

Introduction

To improve how economic and political systems can deliver better outcomes for people and planet amid complex challenges of escalating climate change impacts, growing inequality, rising mental health challenges (particularly among young people), and a rapid decline in biodiversity, governments are changing the way they develop and implement policy. This involves making wellbeing a central pillar and objective of governments, sometimes referred to as 'wellbeing government', 'wellbeing policymaking', or 'wellbeing policy approaches'. This is a departure from conventional practices, that primarily focus on the country's Gross Domestic Product (GDP) and productivity growth. The current approaches to policymaking often are siloed and narrowly focused on economic rationalism, such as cost-benefit analysis. In contrast, wellbeing policy approaches seek to ensure that policymaking is goal-oriented, participatory, contextual, experimental, holistic, evidence-based, and strengths-based (Wellbeing Economy Alliance, 2021).

Wellbeing literacy can serve as a transformative tool for policymakers, enabling them to better integrate wellbeing policy approaches into decision-making. The five components of wellbeing literacy – knowledge, comprehension, composition, context, and intentionality (Oades et al., 2021) – interact dynamically at different stages of policymaking, providing the necessary framework for effective wellbeing policy. This chapter discusses how enhancing the wellbeing literacy of policymakers through these five different components can help transform the way policymakers develop and implement policy, ultimately fostering greater wellbeing for individuals, communities, and the global society.

DOI: 10.4324/9781003644293-20

We first provide an outline of wellbeing policy and the wellbeing economy movement before discussing how policymakers currently learn about and approach wellbeing. We then go on to detail how increasing wellbeing literacy of policymakers can help support them to develop more effective policies to improve the wellbeing of people and the planet. We conclude with some recommendations on how wellbeing literacy can be better incorporated into training for policymakers, as well as the educational curriculum more broadly, to ensure we develop a society that enables greater wellbeing.

Policy and Economy-Enablers for Wellbeing

The wellbeing system encompasses laws, economy, politics, and culture that shape and influence the wellbeing of individuals, communities, and the environment (Kern et al., 2020; Seligman & Csikszentmihalyi, 2000). The current polycrisis is disrupting this system, which consists of interconnected layers: the individual, the microsystem (family, friends, school, work), the exosystem (local community, policies, media, health resources, amenities), and the mesosystem (interactions between micro and exosystems), which are all shaped by the macrosystem (economy, politics, law, culture) (Bronfenbrenner, 1979). In response, governments across the world are increasingly prioritising the wellbeing of people and the sustainability of the planet when developing policy. This movement stems from an increased awareness throughout society that these systems are failing to serve both people and the planet (Raworth, 2017; Stiglitz, 2019). Humanity is facing crises on multiple fronts. This includes the escalation of climate change and its impacts on humans, a rapid decline in biodiversity, worsening mental health issues and rising inequality (Tooze, 2021).

This global movement advocates for governments to transition from the business-as-usual (BAU) approach to a wellbeing approach in developing policy. The BAU approach has traditionally included an over-reliance on GDP as a measure of societal wellbeing, with a focus on continuous productivity improvement and a 'growth-at-all-costs' mindset. In contrast, taking a wellbeing approach to developing policy helps ensure that the economy and policy deliver wellbeing outcomes through instruments such as taxes, subsidies, business models, and policy instruments (Trebeck & Smith, 2024).

Various governments worldwide have started on a wellbeing approach in different levels of governance – from local communities to regions, nations, and international organisations. At a national level, governments have embraced wellbeing approaches, budgeting, and frameworks, including Scotland, Wales, Iceland, Denmark, Bhutan, Australia, and Finland. The Wellbeing Economy movement is made up of 17 global hubs. Multilateral organisations are also embracing and promoting the adoption of wellbeing policy approaches. The OECD's wellbeing framework and Better Life Index were developed to support governments in adopting wellbeing indicators to measure progress (OECD, 2020). The European Union has endorsed the concept of a wellbeing economy (Council of the European Union, 2019). Additionally, the World Health Organisation launched the European Wellbeing Economy initiative to influence central banks and ministries of finance to invest in initiatives that improve health equity and the wellbeing of people (World Health Organization, 2023).

The movement towards incorporating wellbeing approaches into policy development is gaining momentum. However, to ensure that policy is developed in an effective and sustainable way that increases the wellbeing of individuals and communities, the wellbeing literacy of policymakers must be improved. This is particularly the case for policymakers who work across multidisciplinary fields and are responsible for delivering wellbeing outcomes. Throughout this chapter, we outline where the current limitations are and how wellbeing literacy would help to enhance the way policy is developed and implemented.

The Current State of Play

Policymakers often lack formal training in wellbeing science and wellbeing policy. There is limited professional development available for policymakers to increase their wellbeing literacy to develop policy using a wellbeing approach. To the authors' best knowledge, no government has provided the policymakers responsible for developing and implementing a wellbeing policy framework with comprehensive professional development. Relevant policymakers therefore currently learn about wellbeing in an ad-hoc, incidental manner.

Despite this gap, good-practice principles in developing wellbeing policy frameworks can inherently enhance the wellbeing literacy of policymakers. For example, a deeper consideration of key wellbeing dimensions and indicators can significantly increase policymaker's understanding of wellbeing and their approach to policymaking.

This process is particularly apparent in the context of developing wellbeing frameworks, which can provide a structured way of implementing a wellbeing policy approach. A study undertaken by Sollis (2023) with developers of wellbeing frameworks found that being involved in the process helped them to gain a deeper understanding of wellbeing. This was emphasised by one participant in the study:

> At the heart of it, just having those in-depth and challenging conversations pushed us in our awareness...You can't really develop awareness without talking and listening and challenging and being challenged.

Importantly, incorporating participatory approaches in the development of wellbeing frameworks can further enhance the wellbeing literacy of policymakers. Given that wellbeing can have different meanings for different population groups (Jarden & Roache, 2023; Sollis et al., 2022), participatory approaches ask community members how they define wellbeing through interviews and focus groups. This approach can help support policymakers to develop a deeper understanding of the contextual factors influencing how a population group defines wellbeing, which may go on to influence policy indirectly (Sollis, 2023). Additionally, it is also crucial that policymakers from a diverse range of portfolios related to the wellbeing of people and the planet are engaged in the development of wellbeing frameworks. Scott (2012, p. 166) contends that if policymakers are more heavily involved in selecting wellbeing indicators, they will develop a deeper understanding of the nature and complexity of wellbeing.

Thus, while the way policymakers learn about wellbeing literacy is currently ad-hoc and incidental, the processes used to develop wellbeing frameworks can implicitly improve wellbeing literacy. When developing wellbeing frameworks, policymakers are compelled to consider different wellbeing indicators and how they relate to the population of interest. Incorporating participatory approaches to engage with individuals directly and hear what wellbeing means to them can further increase wellbeing literacy. These are important processes, however; they can be further enhanced through more intentional professional development opportunities designed to increase policymakers' knowledge of wellbeing science.

Embedding Wellbeing Literacy in Policymaking

Policymakers have a crucial role in transitioning to a wellbeing government and economy. Embedding wellbeing approaches into decision-making will substantially transform the way policy is made. The foundations of wellbeing policymaking are preventative, participatory, contextual, holistic, evidence-based, and strengths-based. Essentially, a wellbeing policy approach facilitates greater collaboration amongst policy areas, different line agencies and government departments to address the complex, interconnected nature of societal issues.

This is in stark contrast to the linear process used in traditional policymaking of identifying a problem, setting an agenda, evaluating options, making decisions, implementing policies, and evaluation (Jann & Wegrich, 2017; Moran et al., 2008). This process often occurs in silos, with a narrow focus and a reliance on traditional economic reasoning like cost-benefit analysis.

This section outlines how enhancing wellbeing literacy through its five components of wellbeing literacy put forward by Oades et al. (2021), would help to enhance policies that seek to promote wellbeing. We firstly discuss the knowledge and comprehension components, defined as increasing language, reading, and understanding about/for wellbeing. We then outline composition, defined as creating multimodal texts about and for wellbeing, before noting the importance of context and intentionality, defined as awareness of different cultures and contexts along with intentional use of the new capabilities to improve the wellbeing of oneself or others.

Knowledge and Comprehension

The term 'wellbeing' is used to mean a number of different things (Huppert, 2017). For example, in popular culture, it is often attributed to concepts such as mindfulness and wellness. For practitioners in the clinical psychology space, it is often used synonymously with mental health. For wellbeing researchers, it can refer to concepts such as life satisfaction, quality of life, or thriving. When you ask individuals about what their own wellbeing means, it can include more personal definitions such as inner harmony, work-life balance, sense of purpose and meaning, and connection to culture (Jarden & Roache, 2023; Sollis et al., 2022). Wellbeing is generally agreed to be a multidimensional concept, comprising of multiple areas that one needs to be thriving in to be said to have a good life (Huppert & So, 2013; Ruggeri et al., 2020).

Policymakers must deepen their understanding of wellbeing science and foundational wellbeing theory to understand what fosters and sustains the wellbeing of individuals, communities, and nations in which they live. Knowledge of wellbeing – such as how to achieve and maintain it, and the benefits of doing so – provides a clear rationale and an answer to the 'why' of wellbeing. Being wellbeing literate involves not only possessing this knowledge but also having the ability to communicate effectively about and for wellbeing. As people gain more knowledge, cultural and structural norms can evolve to better support wellbeing at all levels, which is crucial for driving transformative change (Chan et al., 2020).

The potential benefits of increasing policymakers' wellbeing literacy include:

- Strengthening policymakers' ability to ground their decisions in evidence-based wellbeing theories.
- Boosting confidence in designing long-term impactful policy that reflects an understanding of the time needed to improve the wellbeing of people and communities.
- Empowering policymakers to create holistic policies by understanding interconnectedness, enabling systems change and a focus on prevention rather than primarily addressing the symptoms.
- Enhancing policymakers' communication skills about and for wellbeing, enabling them to effectively convey the 'why' behind the policy. This helps to secure better buy-in from stakeholders, colleagues, and the public, resulting in greater trust in government and participation in new initiatives.

- Increasing policymakers' understanding of the essential basic psychological needs for human wellbeing (Ryan & Deci, 2000). This can contribute to more sophisticated, goal-oriented policy, which could lead to better outcomes.
- Being more adaptable and better equipped to respond to new information or changing circumstances with improved wellbeing.

Unlocking the Potential Composition

The wellbeing literacy component of composition occurs when policymakers create policy. Many wellbeing frameworks developed and used today have similar themes, one being 'connection and relationships' (Barrington-Leigh & Escande, 2018). We will use this theme as an example of how increased comprehension of wellbeing science, its theories, and understanding of the 'why' can assist in creating more sustainable, effective policies that can help prevent issues from occurring in the first place.

While the importance of relationships and belonging is widely acknowledged, wellbeing science provides the theoretical foundation needed to fully comprehend why these connections are vital. For example, a deeper understanding of two foundational theories – the Need to Belong theory by Baumeister and Leary (1995) and the Basic Psychological Needs (BPN) theory by Ryan and Deci (2000) – is critical for understanding this theme. Learning about these two theories can increase the comprehension needed to create more effective wellbeing policies.

The Need to Belong Theory asserts that humans have an innate drive to form and maintain lasting, close, positive relationships. This fundamental need is crucial for psychological wellbeing and social functioning. When unmet, it can lead to severe adverse outcomes such as loneliness, depression, and anxiety. Notably, the theory emphasises that it is not just any relationships that matter but close, enduring bonds that are essential for overall wellbeing to function well (Baumeister & Leary, 1995).

Similarly, the BPN theory, part of the broader Self-Determination Theory developed by Ryan and Deci (2000), identifies three core psychological needs – competence, autonomy, and relatedness – essential for an individual's wellbeing. These needs must be fulfilled for a person to thrive; when thwarted, they lead to negative consequences. For example, when the need for relatedness is not met, the individual may experience social isolation, exclusion, and loneliness, leading to more severe mental health issues (Cacioppo et al., 2010). Both theories have been extensively tested with new findings continuing to emerge that are important for policymakers to understand and incorporate into decision-making processes.

Recent research underscores the critical importance of early interventions based on these foundational theories and subsequent research. Studies on brain and neural connections have shown that bullying can distort a young person's perception of belonging, particularly following social isolation that can lead to a heightened vulnerability to loneliness in adulthood (Fowler et al., 2021).

To effectively apply these insights, policymakers must ensure that the measurement captures the complexity of relationships and connections. For instance, the closeness of a relationship and how the individual perceives it affects how a person feels and the extent to which they feel lonely (Fowler et al., 2021). However, common metrics such as how many relatives or friends people can count on to help them in times of need and time spent in social interactions relationships (OECD, 2020) may overlook the depth and quality of those relationships that are needed to thrive.

For example, recent research posits that there are varied concepts and perspectives of belonging, Allen et al. (2021), propose that it is dynamic and is composed of four interrelated components: competencies, opportunities, motivation, and perceptions. Incorporating more relevant and recently developed indicators on belonging and loneliness such as the Perceived Relational Value Scale, the Sense of Belonging Scale (Mellinger et al., 2024) and the Dual Continuum Scale of Loneliness (Lim et al., 2021) would provide a more nuanced understanding of connection and relationships. This can enable earlier identification of loneliness risks, allowing for more targeted policy interventions to mitigate issues later in life. However, achieving better measurements will require a long-term investment from governments to expand existing data collection processes.

Context and Intentionality

Context and intentionality are also critical components of wellbeing literacy. The satisfaction of the Basic Psychological Needs varies across different contexts, life stages, and social interactions (Allen et al., 2022). To develop effective policy, policymakers must recognise that wellbeing is not a static concept; it evolves over time and in response to changing circumstances. As such, wellbeing measures must be regularly reviewed and updated to ensure they accurately reflect the latest understanding of these factors.

Going back to our example of relationships and connection, the rising global challenge of loneliness highlights the urgency of more effective policies. Loneliness, as US surgeon general Vivek Murthy has noted, is akin to hunger – a signal that something essential for survival is missing (The Guardian, 2024). In Australia, loneliness costs an estimated $2.7 billion annually in healthcare and lost productivity (Groundswell Foundation, 2022). The effects of loneliness include a 26% increase in mortality risk, higher incidences of cancer and cardiovascular disease, a greater likelihood of dementia, and poorer mental health outcomes. Additionally, loneliness can contribute to antisocial behaviour, bullying, and aggression and is often linked to excessive internet use and deteriorating social skills (Burns et al., 2020).

With increased wellbeing literacy, policymakers can craft more effective, prevention-focused, collaborative policies that promote the ability for individuals to develop strong relationships and connect with others. For example, understanding the connection between childhood bullying and adult loneliness highlights the need for a comprehensive national anti-bullying strategy focused on prevention. Currently, there is no national definition, leaving anti-bullying programs in Australia to be initiated by individual schools; many do not include families and communities that play a critical role in prevention resulting in varied outcomes (Australian Education Authorities, 2024).

The final component of wellbeing literacy, intentionality, occurs when policymakers choose to use their new wellbeing literacy capabilities to create new policies. Currently, policymakers use different types of assessments as part of the policy development process. Traditional Cost Benefit Analyses (CBA) are used to project economic outcomes of proposed policies. With the introduction of wellbeing frameworks and measurements, new tools are being developed to assess the likely impacts of wellbeing policy. For example, the Australian Capital Territory government incorporates wellbeing impact assessments early in their policy development (ACT Government, n.d.).

Frayman et al. (2024) have recently called for better assessments when spending public money, such as improving the Green Book and utilising Wellbeing-adjusted life years (WELLBYs) as a metric. Additionally, new policy tools could be developed to assess the impact of policies on wellbeing by using the lens of Basic Psychological Needs to evaluate how proposed policies could satisfy or thwart the basic psychological needs of competence, autonomy, and relatedness before finalising policy. With increased wellbeing literacy, policymakers can implement evidence-based programs to create environments that support strong and enduring relationships from an early age throughout the lifespan.

Conclusion

The shift towards a wellbeing approach to policymaking represents a transformative opportunity to address the root causes of many societal issues. As a result, policymakers need better education. Wellbeing literacy should be integrated into university public policy courses, additional training and eventually included in national curriculums and teacher training to build widespread knowledge. Education is widely accepted as a key factor in transforming communities, and by increasing wellbeing literacy, capabilities are increased, and more choices can be made (Oades et al., 2021).

With increased wellbeing literacy, we can create a more equitable, healthy, and sustainable society by grounding policies in a deep understanding of wellbeing science, embracing a shared language across disciplines, and actively involving the public in the policymaking process. The benefits of this approach are clear: more effective policies, improved public trust and engagement, and ultimately, a society where everyone can thrive.

References

ACT Government. (n.d.). *Wellbeing impact assessment.* Retrieved September from https://www.act.gov.au/wellbeing/wellbeing-framework/embedding-wellbeing.

Allen, K.-A., Gray, D. L., Baumeister, R. F., & Leary, M. R. (2022). The need to belong: A deep dive into the origins, implications, and future of a foundational construct. *Educational Psychology Review*, *34*(2), 1133–1156.

Allen, K.-A., Kern, M. L., Rozek, C. S., McInerney, D. M., & Slavich, G. M. (2021). Belonging: A review of conceptual issues, an integrative framework, and directions for future research. *Australian Journal of Psychology*, *73*(1), 87–102.

Australian Education Authorities. (2024). *Research snapshot from a literature review.* The State of Queensland. https://bullyingnoway.gov.au/understanding/Documents/research-snapshots-bullying-combined.pdf

Barrington-Leigh, C., & Escande, A. (2018). Measuring progress and well-being: A comparative review of indicators. *Social Indicators Research*, *135*, 893–925.

Baumeister, R., & Leary, M. (1995). The need to belong: Desire for interpersonal attachments as a fundamental human motivation. *Psychological Bulletin*, *117*, 497–529. https://doi.org/10.1037/0033-2909.117.3.497

Bronfenbrenner, U. (1979). The ecology of human development: Experiments by nature and design. *Harvard University Press Google Scholar*, *2*, 139–163.

Burns, A., Leavey, G., Ward, M., & O'Sullivan, R. (2020). The impact of loneliness on healthcare use in older people: Evidence from a nationally representative cohort. *Journal of Public Health*, *30*, 1–10.

Cacioppo, J. T., Hawkley, L. C., & Thisted, R. A. (2010). Perceived social isolation makes me sad: 5-year cross-lagged analyses of loneliness and depressive symptomatology in the Chicago health, aging, and social relations study. *Psychology and Aging*, *25*(2), 453.

Chan, K. M., Boyd, D. R., Gould, R. K., Jetzkowitz, J., Liu, J., Muraca, B., Naidoo, R., Olmsted, P., Satterfield, T., Selomane, O., Singh, G. G., Sumaila, R., Ngo, H. T., Boedhihartono, A. K., Agard, J., de Aguiar, A. P. D., Armenteras, D., Balint, L., Barrington-Leigh, C., … Brondízio, E. S. (2020). Levers and leverage points for pathways to sustainability. *People and Nature*, *2*(3), 693–717.

Council of the European Union. (2019). *Economy of wellbeing: The council adopts conclusions.* https://www.consilium.europa.eu/en/press/press-releases/2019/10/24/economy-of-wellbeing-the-council-adopts-conclusions/

Fowler, C. H., Lin, L. C., Rudolph, K. D., & Telzer, E. H. (2021). Like me back: Neural correlates of low perceived relational value in peer victimized youth. *Journal of Research on Adolescence*, *31*(2), 435–450.

Frayman, D., Krekel, C., Layard, R., MacLennan, S., & Parkes, I. (2024). Value for money: How to improve wellbeing and reduce misery. *CEP Reports* (44).

Groundswell Foundation. (2022). *Connections matter - A report on the impacts of loneliness in Australia.* https://www.groundswellfoundation.com.au/post/connectionsmatter-a-report-on-the-impacts-of-loneliness-in-australia

Huppert, F. A. (2017). Challenges in defining and measuring well-being and their implications for policy. In M. A. White, G. R. Slemp, & A. S. Murray (Eds.), *Future directions in well-being: Education, organizations and policy* (pp. 163–167). Springer International Publishing/Springer Nature. https://doi.org/10.1007/978-3-319-56889-8_28

Huppert, F. A., & So, T. T. (2013). Flourishing across Europe: Application of a new conceptual framework for defining well-being. *Social Indicators Research*, *110*, 837–861.

Jann, W., & Wegrich, K. (2017). Theories of the policy cycle. In F. Fischer, G. J. Miller, & M. S. Sidney (Eds.), *Handbook of public policy analysis* (pp. 69–88). Routledge.

Jarden, A., & Roache, A. (2023). What is wellbeing? *International journal of environmental research and public health*, *20*(6), 5006.

Kern, M. L., Williams, P., Spong, C., Colla, R., Sharma, K., Downie, A., Taylor, J. A., Sharp, S., Siokou, C., & Oades, L. G. (2020). Systems informed positive psychology. *The Journal of Positive Psychology*, *15*(6), 705–715.

Lim, M. H., Allen, K.-A., Furlong, M. J., Craig, H., & Smith, D. C. (2021). Introducing a dual continuum model of belonging and loneliness. *Australian Journal of Psychology*, *73*(1), 81–86.

Mellinger, C., Fritzson, A., Park, B., & Dimidjian, S. (2024). Developing the sense of belonging scale and understanding its relationship to loneliness, need to belong, and general well-being outcomes. *Journal of Personality Assessment*, *106*(3), 347–360.

Moran, M., Rein, M., & Goodin, R. E. (2008). *The Oxford handbook of public policy*. Oxford University Press.

Oades, L. G., Jarden, A., Hou, H., Ozturk, C., Williams, P., R. Slemp, G., & Huang, L. (2021). Wellbeing literacy: A capability model for wellbeing science and practice. *International Journal of Environmental Research and Public Health*, *18*(2), 719.

Oades, L. G., Taylor, J. A., Francis, J., & Baker, L. M. (2021). Wellbeing literacy as an emancipatory and transformative capability. In *Wellbeing and resilience education* (pp. 209–231). Routledge.

OECD. (2020). *How's life? 2020*. https://www.oecd.org/en/publications/how-s-life/volume-/issue-_9870c393-en/full-report/component-14.html#chapter-d1e14471

Raworth, K. (2017). A doughnut for the Anthropocene: humanity's compass in the 21st century. *The Lancet Planetary Health*, *1*(2), e48–e49.

Ruggeri, K., Garcia-Garzon, E., Maguire, Á., Matz, S., & Huppert, F. A. (2020). Well-being is more than happiness and life satisfaction: A multidimensional analysis of 21 countries. *Health and Quality of Life Outcomes*, *18*, 1–16.

Ryan, R. M., & Deci, E. L. (2000). Self-determination theory and the facilitation of intrinsic motivation, social development, and well-being. *American Psychologist*, *55*(1), 68.

Scott, K. (2012). *Measuring wellbeing: Towards sustainability?* Routledge. https://doi.org/10.4324/9780203113622

Seligman, M. E., & Csikszentmihalyi, M. (2000). *Positive psychology: An introduction* (Vol. 55). American Psychological Association.

Sollis, K. (2023). Participatory wellbeing frameworks and the secret to impact. *Journal of Human Development and Capabilities*, 1–31. https://doi.org/10.1080/19452829.2023.2200238

Sollis, K., Yap, M., Campbell, P., & Biddle, N. (2022). Conceptualisations of wellbeing and quality of life: A systematic review of participatory studies. *World Development*, *160*, 106073. https://doi.org/10.1016/j.worlddev.2022.106073

Stiglitz, J. E. (2019). *Measuring what counts: The global movement for well-being*. The New Press.

The Guardian. (2024). *US surgeon general Vivek Murthy: "Loneliness is like hunger, a signal we're lacking something for survival"*. Retrieved September 13, 2024, from https://www.theguardian.com/lifeandstyle/2024/jan/29/us-surgeon-general-vivek-murthy-loneliness-mental-health-epidemic-social-media

Tooze, A. (2021). *Shutdown: How Covid shook the world's economy*. Penguin.

Trebeck, K., & Smith, W. (2024). *The wellbeing economy in brief.* https://cpd.org.au/work/wellbeing-economy-in-brief/
Wellbeing Economy Alliance. (2021). *Designing public policy.* WEAll. Retrieved September from https://weall.org/designing-public-policy
World Health Organization. (2023). *WHO European well-being economy initiative.* Retrieved September 13 from https://www.who.int/europe/initiatives/who-european-well-being-economy-initiative

21

WELLBEING LITERACY AND ITS ROLE IN EVIDENCE-BASED COACHING

Suzy Green, Aylin Dulagil, and Lisa M. Baker

Introduction

Coaching has become ubiquitous as a cross-disciplinary intervention to improve performance, facilitate individual and organisational change, and enhance wellbeing (Grant, 2005). Meta-analyses of coaching research suggest numerous positive benefits including leadership improvement (Thach, 2002), enhanced application of formal learning to real workplace situations (Miller et al., 2004), and increased wellbeing, resilience, and goal-attainment (Duijts et al., 2008; Grant et al., 2010).

Despite a historical focus on performance outcomes in coaching, since COVID-19 there has been an increased focus on wellbeing in coaching, primarily driven by the increased awareness of mental ill-health and the promotion of mental health and wellbeing in the workplace (McQuaid et al., 2020). Research shows that, among other outcomes, workplace wellbeing is a key factor in enhancing employee engagement (Langford, 2010; Rasool et al., 2021), worker productivity (Harter et al., 2002), and greater discretionary effort (Hesketh & Cooper, 2023), and thus represents an important mechanism for organisations. Furthermore, there is now a recognition of the shared responsibility for mental health and wellbeing between organisations and individuals (ISO45003). In Australia, this has led to legislative changes (Work Health and Safety Act 2011 (Cth)) that require organisations to reduce psychosocial hazards. In addition, many workplaces are moving beyond compliance towards a proactive approach of implementing initiatives, such as wellbeing coaching (Green et al., 2021).

Wellbeing coaching may be seen as a proactive approach to assist individuals to review and enhance their current levels of wellbeing through the use of

DOI: 10.4324/9781003644293-21

evidence-based practices. Whilst wellbeing coaching is still in its infancy, there is also a move towards the inclusion of wellbeing goals within traditional executive and leadership development (Grant, 2017). As such, we argue there is a need for evidence-based coaches to be knowledgeable in wellbeing science and to develop their own and their coaching clients' wellbeing literacy (WBL) in order to facilitate sustained wellbeing.

WBL is a relatively new construct from the field of wellbeing science that encourages us to think beyond short-term wellbeing gains that positive psychology and other interventions are designed to achieve, moving instead towards language and communication skills that can be carried beyond the intervention (Oades & Johnston, 2017). While positive psychology interventions (PPIs) have received much attention in the psychological literature over the last 20 years, research demonstrates that many PPI effects are small and difficult to sustain over time (Bolier et al., 2013). Rather, developing WBL is a longer-term capability that requires deeper learning experiences and sustained personal adaptation. While this chapter does not have scope for a full review of WBL and its challenges and potential in the field of coaching, we argue that coaching is an appropriate vehicle for developing WBL.

WBL promotes the idea of capabilities – what we can *be* and *do* to increase wellbeing and how we can communicate about wellbeing. Thus, WBL is concerned with the language individuals use to improve or maintain wellbeing (Oades et al., 2021). Similarly, evidence-based coaching (EBC) is a relationship that is language-based (Oades, 2024), and builds a sense of possibility and capability in the individual. An emphasis on WBL allows for the complexity and contextual aspect of coaching to be honoured (Oades, 2024).

This chapter proposes that WBL is and will increasingly become relevant to EBC practice. Secondly, it demonstrates the strong link between WBL and EBC; and finally, it argues that effective coaching requires an emphasis on developing WBL both for coaches and for coachees.

We believe this chapter is the first to examine the relevance and application of WBL within a coaching context. Additionally, we propose and recommend WBL as a key future coaching competency, bridging innovative research with actionable EBC practices for enhanced outcomes.

Background

What Is Evidence-Based Coaching?

EBC was originally defined by Stober and Grant (2006) as 'the intelligent and conscientious use of *best current knowledge* integrated with *practitioner expertise* in making decisions about how to deliver coaching' (p. 6, italics in original), with 'best current knowledge' defined as 'up-to-date information from relevant, valid research, theory and practice' (p. 6).

The evolution of EBC requires an important shift in moving the focus from coaching techniques and skills to a broader and deeper understanding of relevant science and knowledge (Grant & Stober, 2006), and the sustained and genuine transfer of that knowledge (Grant, 2017). Grant (2005) argued there are four key disciplines which inform coaching practice. These are (a) the behavioural sciences; (b) business and economic science; (c) adult education, including workplace learning and development; and (d) philosophy. We argue that wellbeing science falls under both (a) the behavioural sciences and (b) adult education.

Workplace coaching has evolved over the last three decades (Grant, 2017). Where first-generation coaching was concerned primarily with performance management, and second-generation coaching with facilitating leadership capability, third-generation coaching explicitly focuses on enhancing both performance and wellbeing of individuals and organisations in ways that are sustainable and meaningful (Grant, 2017). It is now well-established that both performance and wellbeing are critically linked for successful and sustainable outcomes (Grant, 2017; Peiró et al., 2019). Hence, the relevance and need for greater knowledge and application of wellbeing science and literacy are highlighted.

Coaching is a collaborative relationship between a coach and a coachee to attain valued outcomes, supported by sustained cognitive, emotional, and behavioural changes (Grant & Stober, 2006). Central to the coaching process is the clarification and articulation of goals set to stretch an individual's current capacities (Spence & Grant, 2007) and foster the ongoing learning and personal growth of the coachee (Grant & Stober, 2006).

Green and Spence (2014) argue that the use of simple process coaching models, such as the GROW Model (Goal, Reality, Options, Wrap-up; Whitmore, 1996), supports coachees to take ownership of their goal-striving and behaviour change. The GROW model is also an ongoing iterative process of goal-directed action across multiple coaching sessions, permitting modifications to goals or action plans, and thus, creates a 'cycle' of self-regulation that is important for successful behaviour change (Grant, 2003).

Research has shown that the identification and pursuit of personally meaningful, or self-concordant goals leads to increases in wellbeing (Sheldon & Elliot, 1999), regardless of the focus of such goals. We suggest that enhanced WBL in both coach and coachee may lead to setting and striving for more skilful and relevant self-concordant goals, thus improving associated wellbeing outcomes. However, further research is required to confirm or deny this hypothesis.

What Is Wellbeing Literacy?

Wellbeing and wellbeing science, as a focus for researchers, policy-makers and the general public, has expanded in recent decades, with remarkable advances and 'waves' of development towards 'global wellbeing scholarship' (Lomas, 2022, p. 257; Tov et al., 2022). New theories and constructs have emerged, including that of WBL. Before introducing the construct of 'wellbeing literacy', it is important to acknowledge there are many definitions of wellbeing and related concepts such as 'flourishing' and 'thriving' (Jarden & Roache, 2023). Differing from academic definitions, the lay understanding of wellbeing comprises mental health, feeling valued, work-life balance, and inner harmony (Jarden & Roache, 2023). The Centre for Wellbeing Science at the University of Melbourne locates WBL in an individual context, suggesting that 'Well-being can be understood as how people feel and how they function, both on a personal and a social level, and how they evaluate their lives as a whole' (Michaelson et al., 2012, p. 6). Nevertheless, Oades (2024) argues that both lay and expert concepts of wellbeing are relevant within the coaching context.

WBL is defined as the capability for mindful use of language for and about wellbeing (Oades et al., 2021). WBL focuses on how and why we use language in our everyday lives and specifically how this language use can be capitalised on for wellbeing (Hou et al., 2021). Furthermore, WBL is a relational ability and process between a person and their environment, facilitating options to transform available wellbeing 'opportunities' into wellbeing 'achievements' (Oades et al., 2021). A coach may consider what internal or external 'opportunities' exist for the coachee (what skills, attributes, resources, supports, freedoms, environmental or social conditions or choices they have) that they can convert into wellbeing 'achievements' (wellbeing goals as valued by the coachee) with the knowledge that the higher the coachee's WBL skills, the greater the likelihood for success (Oades et al., 2021).

Oades et al. (2020) argue that the related components of WBL provide increased language choices for individuals, either for their own wellbeing or that of others, and high WBL means a high language capability for wellbeing. Like coaching, WBL draws its focus to what we have capability for, shifting attention to what is possible and moving people towards growth and positive change (Hou et al., 2021). In attending to what coachees may gain and carry forward through the coaching process (i.e., WBL) rather than focusing on particular 'interventions' for wellbeing, attention is directed towards a discourse of learning and sustained growth. WBL provides a framework through which coaches and coachees can put elements of wellbeing theory into practice, intentionally using and adapting wellbeing language. Figure 21.1 shows the five components of WBL.

Both EBC and WBL are concerned with facilitating understanding and meaning-making of an individual's capabilities, focusing on possibility, and encouraging growth (Oades et al , 2021). In the section below, we outline some of the ways that WBL is a useful framework for EBC.

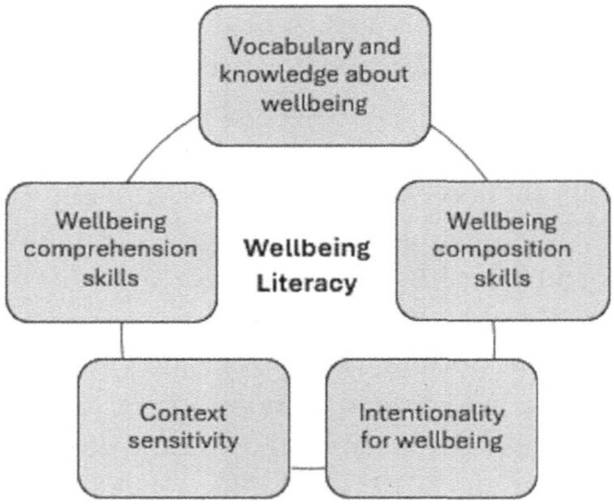

FIGURE 21.1 The wellbeing literacy capability model – how the five components interact to create wellbeing literacy.

Source: Oades et al. (2021).

The Relevance of WB Literacy in EB Coaching

In this section, we will utilise the WBL model as a framework to understand the relevance and rationale of WBL in EBC.

Knowledge and Vocabulary

To be wellbeing literate, a person requires knowledge and vocabulary about wellbeing (Oades et al., 2021). Does the coachee have the words and information to describe their own wellbeing, to enhance their functioning or that of others? The role of the coach here is to ascertain and/or build on the coachee's wellbeing vocabulary and knowledge. This may include providing information about concepts and frameworks from wellbeing science to build the coachee's knowledge and understanding of the different psychological, social, emotional, and physical elements of wellbeing. It may include asking the coachee to share how they believe they thrive in these areas of their lives to help them understand the multi-faceted nature of wellbeing. Many other areas of wellbeing science knowledge such as character strengths, gratitude, mindfulness, resilience and self-compassion could be drawn upon. The role of the coach here is to pay careful attention to the language used by the coachee when describing their own wellbeing, to become familiar with the coachee's wellbeing vocabulary and current strategies or preferences for wellbeing.

Comprehending & Composing Skills

Next, WBL involves skills of both comprehending and composing wellbeing language or 'texts' (Oades et al., 2021). This may be achieved through many modes, such as reading, listening or viewing. In our multimodal world, a wellbeing literate person may access comprehension and composition avenues/texts through wellbeing related books, internet sites, videos, YouTube clips, music, social media, the arts (performing or visual arts, craft, literature, cultural or digital art) and/or conversation. A coach may ask their coachee to think of avenues they use to increase their understanding of wellbeing (comprehension of texts), e.g., books or podcasts, and which of these modes work well for them? Also, in what ways does the coachee build on their wellbeing (composition of texts) – do they sing or dance to feel good? Can they write, draw, speak or create things that promote their own flourishing? As WBL is about knowing and accessing language and information both *about* and *for* wellbeing, that is of value to the individual (which may differ between the coach and coachee), facilitating awareness of which language, information and modes of communication will work for each person is important (Lyubomirsky & Layous, 2013).

Context Sensitivity

Theories, definitions and approaches to wellbeing are complex and contextual, and WBL requires consideration of one's context and the ability to change and adjust accordingly. Perhaps certain words, information or avenues of wellbeing communication exist or are relevant between professional and personal settings, for example, or between different groups of people or under varying circumstances. Language and available modes of communication change within various contexts (including cultural contexts) thus, a wellbeing literate person demonstrates the capacity to adapt to these different contexts.

The role of the coach here is to identify and understand the coachee's internal and external context and to support the individualisation of wellbeing concepts to this context. For example, what are the coachees strengths and values? What are some of the contextual considerations in a coachee's life or work and how do these impact the coachee's ability to enhance their own wellbeing? What is their intention (goal) around wellbeing and how might this need to adapt to different places, people, cultures or times? Can they use the same modes of communication at home or work? Is one mode of communication more suitable than another (e.g., writing versus texting; watching versus reading)?

Intentionality

Finally, WBL involves intentionality – a habit of intentionally using language to maintain or improve wellbeing (Oades et al., 2021). A wellbeing literate person demonstrates a desire to prioritise wellbeing and mindfully adapts their wellbeing language and communication modes not only to the context, but

TABLE 21.1 WBL informed GROW structure for both coaches and coachees

Grow coaching model	*Wellbeing literacy model*
GOAL	**Intentionality** How does the coach plan and reflect on the coaching process? What is the coachee's goal and how does it relate to wellbeing? Is wellbeing implicit or explicit? How can a habit of intention be built to support wellbeing strategies?
REALITY	**Knowledge and Vocabulary** What wellbeing language and knowledge do the coachee and coach possess? What language and knowledge is shared or needs to be communicated? **Context sensitivity** What is the current context for wellbeing? What adaptations need to be made, i.e., cultural and language?
OPTIONS	**Composition and Comprehension** What modes of wellbeing language and communication are available to the coachee? How and what could they read, write, draw, create, view, speak, or listen to that may support their goals and build capacity? What multimodal ways does the coach have to support the coachee?
WRAP UP	**Underpinned by all – opportunities into achievements?** How can wellbeing intentions be articulated/built/supported and made habitual? What elements can be built further? What contextual considerations need to be made? What wellbeing knowledge and vocabulary can be accessed?

in service of their wellbeing (or that of others or the world). Coaching is key in promoting reflection and intentionality with clients – in fact, coaching has been referred to as 'making the implicit explicit' (Stober & Grant, 2006), and many coaching models and PPIs rely on developing a client's intentionality. Arguably, without a reflective space, comprehension and intentionality in the application of wellbeing science and WBL to everyday life remains limited. We suggest the GROW coaching model, and other structured coaching models, provide a framework to create a reflective space. In Table 21.1, we propose how the WBL model intersects with the popular and ubiquitous GROW coaching model.

Key Considerations

There are two key areas that are an essential consideration for the use of WBL in EBC. These are (1) Coach as Expert and (2) Coach Wellbeing Literacy. We acknowledge other key considerations that need to be addressed in future discussions, such as the limitations and challenges of implementing WBL in coaching contexts, and how coaches may expand their WBL knowledge, but these questions are beyond the scope of this chapter.

Coach as Expert

There are different considerations of how coach expert knowledge is used in coaching, and whether coaching should be non-directive or directive. Expert knowledge in coaching can be understood as highly specialised or technical knowledge held by the coach, where the coachee has less expertise than the coach, and where such knowledge is related to the coachee's goals. It is not necessarily the case that the coach may fall into the trap of 'expert advice-giver'. Grant and O'Connor (2010) delineated the ask/tell continuum (refer to Figure 21.2) to contrast coaching to other behaviour-change approaches like training and advice-giving. A skilful coach can move along the ask/tell continuum to maintain autonomy and engagement in their coachee and still allow for the genuine transfer of knowledge (Grant, 2005). Thus, a coach can intentionally develop the WBL capability of the coachee, for example, through the use of solution-focused questions, and strengths-based language.

More recently, Biswas-Diener (2020) questioned the degree to which a directive approach may be beneficial and concluded that directive support might be appropriate in instances characterised by a coachee's lack of critical skills or knowledge. We argue that WBL and knowledge is one such instance where coaches need to develop genuine expertise to share with coachees. In our experience as professional coaches (Green & Dulagil), we suggest that there are individual differences in coachee interest in understanding wellbeing. A solution-focused and strengths-based approach can be used to support a coachee's interest in wellbeing knowledge and science. For example, whilst a coachee may initially be cynical around the concept of gratitude, the coach may suggest that whilst gratitude interventions may not work for everyone (i.e., person-activity fit), research confirms that they enhance wellbeing and might be worth considering

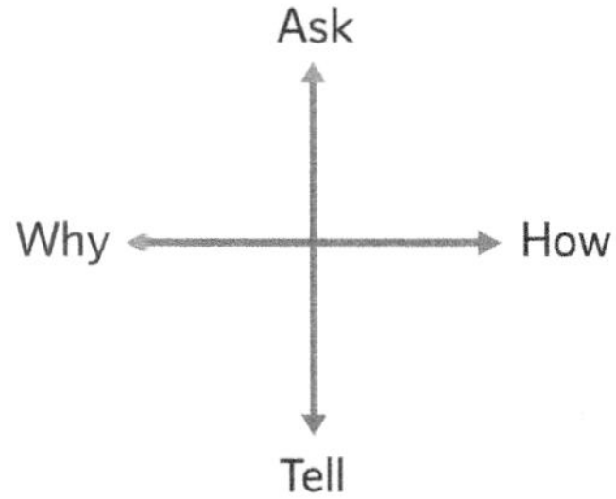

FIGURE 21.2 The ask-tell matrix.

Source: Grant and O'Connor (2010).

as a behavioural experiment. Hence, using the WBL framework may allow the coachee to consider their level of wellbeing knowledge. The use of specific WBL tools such as Well-Lit 6 (Hou et al., 2021) may support coachee's WBL and to allow the development of coaching conversations.

Coach Wellbeing Literacy

Coaches need not be an experts in the coachee's profession (e.g., law or education) to successfully enhance the coachee's performance or development. However, coaching accreditation bodies (e.g., ICF, AOC, EMCC) do require certain coach competencies (e.g., demonstrates ethical practice, embodies a coaching mindset; ICF, 2020). Currently, there is no requirement that coaches hold expert knowledge in wellbeing science, and we argue that it may soon need to enter the realm of key coach competencies. Recent publications by leading authorities in coaching have questioned the value of current coach competencies and called for an alternative curriculum for coach education that recognises the 'complex linguistic collaborative task' (Garvey et al., 2024) that is coaching and contributes to a deeper and more sustained way of being than merely behavioural competencies (Boyatzis et al., 2024). WBL fits under this linguistic conceptualisation of coaching and equips coaches with the tools to understand, interpret, and effectively communicate wellbeing strategies and wellbeing science.

Conclusion

We have argued that one of the areas of expert knowledge that coaches need to develop is that of WBL. In the same way that highly effective coaching has moved beyond conducting interventions with coachees to building capabilities within coachees, wellbeing science is moving away from wellbeing interventions to building wellbeing capabilities in individuals that are sustained during and beyond the duration of the coaching engagement. Therefore, EBC and WBL are deeply aligned as both emphasise an approach that focuses on 'building capabilities' (Oades et al., 2020, p. 696) rather than conducting interventions or simply imparting knowledge. We have further argued that EB coaches need to develop their own WBL to comprehensively identify and support their individual clients WBL. As the concept evolves, future research and discussion will help explore its application and how best to cultivate it to support both coach and coachee.

Reflection Questions for Coaches

- What areas of WBL do you already facilitate or develop in your coachees versus areas that may be beneficial to focus on more explicitly?
- How might you already be building coachee WBL in your current coaching practice?

- How could you more explicitly work towards building WBL in your coaching practice?
- What components of the WBL model are your strongest points as a coach? How can you dial up these strengths and/or work towards developing components/skills that may be beneficial to yourself and your coachees?

References

Australian Government. (2021). Work Health Sand Safety Act 2011. https://www.legislation.gov.au/C2011A00137/2018-07-01/text

Biswas-Diener, R. (2020). *Positive provocation: Radical interventions for meaningful change*. Berrett-Koehler Publishers.

Bolier, L., Haverman, M., Westerhof, G. J., Riper, H., Smit, F., & Bohlmeijer, E. (2013). Positive psychology interventions: A meta-analysis of randomized controlled studies. *BMC Public Health*, *13*, 119. https://doi.org/10.1186/1471-2458-13-119

Boyatzis, R., Liu, H., Smith, A., Zwygart, K., & Quinn, J. (2024). Competencies of coaches that predict client behavior change. *The Journal of Applied Behavioral Science*, *60*(1), 19–49.

Duijts, S. F., Kant, I., Van Den Brandt, P. A., & Swaen, G. M. (2008). Effectiveness of a preventive coaching intervention for employees at risk for sickness absence due to psychosocial health complaints: Results of a randomized controlled trial. *Journal of Occupational and Environmental Medicine*, *50*(7), 765–776.

Garvey, B., Clutterbuck, D., & Dierolf, K. (2024). Supposing everything we knew about coach education was wrong. *Organisations & People*, *29*(1), 6–8.

Grant, A. M. (2003). The impact of life coaching on goal attainment, metacognition, and mental health. *Social Behavior and Personality: An International Journal*, *31*(3), 253–263.

Grant, A. M. (2005). What is evidence-based executive, workplace and life coaching. *Evidence-Based Coaching*, *1*, 1–12.

Grant, A. M. (2017). *Coaching in the workplace: The role of the coach in enhancing employee performance*. In H. K. Kauffman & H. D. Becker (Eds.), *The Routledge companion to coaching* (pp. 189–199). Routledge.

Grant, A. M., Curtayne, L., & Burton, G. (2010). Executive coaching enhances goal attainment, metacognition and mental health. *Social Behavior and Personality*, *38*(3), 267–280.

Grant, A. M., & O'Connor, S. A. (2010). The differential effects of solution-focused and problem-focused coaching questions: A pilot study with implications for practice. *Industrial and Commercial Training*, *42*(2), 102–111. https://doi.org/10.1108/00197851011026090

Green, S., Jarden, A., & Leach, C. (2021). Coaching for workplace wellbeing. In W.-A. Smith, I. Boniwell, & S. Green (Eds.), *Positive psychology coaching in the workplace* (pp. 199–219). Springer Nature. https://doi.org/10.1007/978-3-030-79952-6_11

Green, S., & Spence, G. B. (2014). Evidence-based coaching as a positive psychological intervention. In A. C. Fields, J. L. R. Brown, & P. M. Franchetti (Eds.), *The Wiley Blackwell handbook of positive psychological interventions* (pp. 273–285). Wiley-Blackwell.

Harter, J. K., Schmidt, F. L., & Hayes, T. L. (2002). Business unit level outcomes between employee satisfaction, employee engagement and business outcomes: A meta-analysis. *Journal of Applied Psychology*, *87*, 268–279.

Hesketh, I., & Cooper, G. (2023). *Wellbeing at work: How to design, implement and evaluate an effective strategy*. Kogan Page.

Hou, H., Chin, T. C., Slemp, G. R., & Oades, L. G. (2021). Wellbeing literacy: Conceptualization, measurement, and preliminary empirical findings from students, parents and school staff. *International Journal of Environmental Research and Public Health*, *18*(4), Article: 1485.

International Coach Federation. (2020). *ICF core competencies.* https://coachingfederation.org/credentials-and-standards/core-competencies

Jarden, A., & Roache, A. (2023). What is wellbeing? *International Journal of Environmental Research and Public Health*, *20*, 5006. https://doi.org/10.3390/ijerph20065006

Langford, P. (2010). Benchmarking work practices and outcomes in Australian universities using an employee survey. *Journal of Higher Education Policy and Management*, *32*(1), 41–53.

Lomas, T. (2022). Making waves in the great ocean: A historical perspective on the emergence and evolution of wellbeing scholarship. *The Journal of Positive Psychology*, *17*(2), 257–270.

Lyubomirsky, S., & Layous, K. (2013). How do simple positive activities increase well-being? *Current Directions in Psychological Science*, *22*(1), 57–62.

McQuaid, M., Australian HR Institute., & Kern, P. (2020). Wellbeing Lab August 2020 workplace survey. Retrieved from https://www.michellemcquaid.com/thewellbeinglab/

Michaelson, J., Mahony, S., & Schifferes, J. (2012). *Measuring wellbeing: A guide for practitioners.* The New Economics Foundation (NEF).

Miller, L., Moore, D., & Ziguras, C. (2004). Learning at work: Workplace transformations and worker learning. *Work and Learning Journal*, *6*(2), 35–49.

Oades, L. G. (2024). The wellbeing coach: Dimensions, concepts, and language-use of wellbeing. In *The health and wellbeing Coaches' handbook* (pp. 10–19). Routledge.

Oades, L. G., Jarden, A., Hou, H., Ozturk, C., Williams, P., R. Slemp, G., & Huang, L. (2021). Wellbeing literacy: A capability model for wellbeing science and practice. *International Journal of Environmental Research and Public Health*, *18*(2), 719.

Oades, L. G., & Johnston, A. L. (2017). Wellbeing literacy: The necessary ingredient in positive education. *Psychology and Behavioral Science International Journal*, *3*(555621), 10–19080.

Oades, L. G., Ozturk, C., Hou, H., & Slemp, G. R. (2020). Wellbeing literacy: A language-use capability relevant to wellbeing outcomes of positive psychology intervention. *The Journal of Positive Psychology*, *15*(5), 696–700.

Peiró, J. M., Kozusznik, M. W., Rodríguez-Molina, I., & Tordera, N. (2019). The happy-productive worker model and beyond: Patterns of wellbeing and performance at work. *International Journal of Environmental Research and Public Health*, *16*, 479. https://doi.org/10.3390/ijerph16030479

Rasool, S. F., Wang, M., Tang, M., Saeed, A., & Iqbal, J. (2021). How toxic workplace environment effects the employee engagement: The mediating role of organizational support and employee wellbeing. *International Journal of Environmental Research and Public Health*, *18*(5), 2294.

Sheldon, K. M., & Elliot, A. J. (1999). Goal striving, need satisfaction, and longitudinal well-being: The self-concordance model. *Journal of Personality and Social Psychology*, 76, 482–497. https://doi.org/10.1037/0022-3514.76.3.482

Spence, G. B., & Grant, A. M. (2007). Professional and peer life coaching and the enhancement of goal striving and well-being: An exploratory study. *The Journal of Positive Psychology*, *2*(3), 185–194.

Stober, D. R., & Grant, A. M. (2006). Toward a contextual approach to coaching models. In D. R. Stober & A. M. Grant (Eds.), In *Evidence based coaching handbook: Putting best practices to work for your clients* (pp. 355–365). John Wiley & Sons, Inc.

Thach, E. C. (2002). The impact of executive coaching and 360 feedback on leadership effectiveness. *Leadership & Organization Development Journal*, *23*(4), 205–214. https://doi.org/10.1108/01437730210429070

Tov, W., Wirtz, D., Kushlev, K., Biswas-Diener, R., & Diener, E. (2022). Well-being science for teaching and the general public. *Perspectives on Psychological Science*, *17*(5), 1452–1471.

Whitmore, J. (1996). *Coaching for performance*. Nicholas Brealey Publishing.

22

WELLBEING LITERACY AS A SOCIALLY CONSTRUCTED, SOCIALLY DRIVEN, AND SOCIALLY SUPPORTED UNDERTAKING

Kelly-Ann Allen, Bonnie Bozorg, and Margaret L. Kern

Introduction

Jeffrey A. Greene, known for his work on epistemic cognition, once tweeted that critical thinking is inherently hard, but also inherently social. That is, individuals rely on others to help formulate critical thought (Greene & Yu, 2015). If social interaction is central to critical thinking, then it is also essential for acquiring and applying wellbeing knowledge. As we face rapid social change, global crises, and an ever-expanding landscape of information and misinformation, critical thinking becomes even more crucial for navigating the complexities of wellbeing. This chapter explores the social nature of wellbeing literacy, "the capability of comprehending and composing wellbeing languages, across various contexts, that may be intentionally used to maintain or improve the wellbeing of oneself, others or the world" (Oades et al., 2021, p. 719). We argue that wellbeing literacy is a socially constructed process, facilitated by our interactions, relationships, broader societal contexts, and social systems (Oades et al., 2017). This idea add to the Oades et al. (2021) capability model for wellbeing literacy. The model emphasises that individuals use language about wellbeing in ways that reflect both personal agency and the social context in which they learn. Social learning mechanisms are therefore central to the development of key literacy components outlined in the model: vocabulary, comprehension, composition, context awareness, and intentionality, where these elements interact dynamically with social processes and contexts.

The vocabulary and knowledge component enables individuals to articulate their wellbeing values while drawing from socially constructed evidence-based principles. Comprehension capabilities allow people to engage with wellbeing

DOI: 10.4324/9781003644293-22

information from multiple sources, ranging from traditional texts to digital media, reflecting how wellbeing knowledge is communicated in contemporary society. Composition skills empower individuals to express their wellbeing experiences through various channels that align with both personal values and social contexts, contributing to collective wellbeing discourse. Context awareness represents the metacognitive ability to adapt wellbeing language across different social environments, recognising that effective communication varies between settings such as workplaces, educational institutions, or online spaces. Intentionality, perhaps most significantly, reflects the deliberate orientation towards using language to enhance wellbeing both for oneself and within broader social systems. Oades et al. (2021) conceptualise these components within their capability model as mediating between environmental conditions (both internal and external) and wellbeing outcomes. This seemingly socially embedded framework shows how wellbeing literacy develops through collective processes rather than purely individual cognition, setting the foundation for understanding the social learning mechanisms and cognitive processes explored throughout this chapter. As we will examine in subsequent sections, these social dimensions occur across contexts, from geopolitical influences to epistemic foundations, revealing wellbeing literacy as something that is shared and socially constructed. At the heart of this process is the need to belong, which functions as both a context and conduit for wellbeing literacy to occur.

Social Validation and Striving to Belong

Given the dependence on social processes and learning, we suggest that wellbeing literacy is shaped by our fundamental human need to belong (Baumeister & Leary, 1995). As Baumeister and Leary (1995) posit in their seminal work, and complemented by self-determination theory (Deci & Ryan, 2001), the need to belong is a powerful, fundamental, and pervasive motivation in human beings. It drives much of human behaviour, whether conceivably positive or negative (cf. Allen et al., 2025 for a review of the belonging paradox). With respect to wellbeing literacy, it could be seen as profoundly shaping how individuals understand, communicate, and enact wellbeing knowledge. While the need to belong is considered universal, it is important to note that its intensity can vary significantly from person to person (Allen et al., 2024) and across cultures. Factors such as personality traits, cultural background, and individual experiences can influence how strongly one feels the need to belong and how they pursue social connections (Allen et al., 2021a, 2021b; Arslan et al., 2020; Palikara et al., 2021). Personal characteristics influence both the importance of and pathways towards the development of belonging. When such characteristics are supportive, wellbeing literacy is more likely to occur, whereas negative personal characteristics hinder the development of wellbeing literacy. That is, there is a mutually reinforcing relationship between belonging and wellbeing literacy, all of which occur within the context of personal characteristics and social structures.

Social groups play a crucial role in providing a sense of self-esteem (Leary & Allen, 2011). These social connections serve as both the medium through which wellbeing knowledge is transmitted and the context in which it is applied. The importance of social action in wellbeing literacy cannot be overstated. Leary and Baumeister (2000) argue that individuals use the feedback they receive from others as a type of "sociometer" to gauge their relational value and, by extension, their overall wellbeing. This social validation process could influence how individuals perceive their own wellbeing and also how they interpret and apply wellbeing-related information. Recent research by Allen et al. (2024) emphasises the importance of being socially valued within social groups. Their study found that the experience of feeling valued and respected by peers and teachers in the school environment was significantly associated with better mental health outcomes in young adulthood. It is possible that feeling socially valued can impact an individual's wellbeing literacy, either enhancing or undermining their ability to understand, communicate, and act upon wellbeing knowledge both during adolescence and adulthood.

Social comparisons influence an individual's understanding of what constitutes "good" wellbeing. A person might gauge their own emotional health against that of their peers or measure their stress management skills relative to societal norms. These comparisons, while not always accurate or helpful, play a significant role in shaping personal experiences of wellbeing.

The role of social validation in wellbeing literacy also impacts emotion regulation and expression. Sinatra and Seyranian (2016) argue that social identity and group membership can influence how individuals process information and regulate their emotions, particularly in contexts where their identity might be threatened. For wellbeing literacy, this suggests that individuals might modulate their emotional expressions or even their interpretations of wellbeing information based on social cues and group norms. For instance, in certain social contexts, individuals might feel compelled to withhold expressions of distress or uncertainty about their wellbeing to conform to group expectations of resilience or positivity. This social pressure to regulate emotions could create gaps between an individual's personal understanding of wellbeing and their public expression of it.

While social validation plays a crucial role in wellbeing literacy, it is important to recognise that excessive striving to *fit in* can be counterproductive. Frydenberg (2017) conceptualises this behaviour as a maladaptive coping strategy, one that can potentially undermine genuine wellbeing. This perspective aligns with the popularised work of Brené Brown (2017), who claims that adjusting oneself to fit in is antithetical to *true* belonging. Brown argues that authentic belonging requires the courage to be true to oneself even when it means diverging from group norms. In the context of wellbeing literacy, this suggests a considered and informed understanding is necessary. While social connections and validation are vital, an over-reliance on external validation or a compulsion to conform at the expense of authenticity could impede genuine experiences of wellbeing. Thus, a key component of wellbeing literacy may involve developing the discernment to navigate belonging with authenticity, and the skills to navigate the tension between *fitting in* and *standing out* when necessary (Gray et al., 2018).

Social Learning Mechanisms

The social construction of wellbeing literacy can also be considered to be rooted in various social learning mechanisms that occur within social systems (Kern et al., 2020), which provide the theoretical underpinning for understanding how individuals acquire, interpret, and apply knowledge about wellbeing within social contexts (Vilches, 2012). Wellbeing literacy, like other forms of learning, is socially learned and socially reinforced, beginning at birth and dynamically developing through childhood, adolescence, adulthood, and older age. Because wellbeing literacy impacts mental health and wellbeing, there are specific aspects of a socially constructed concept that go beyond general learning to apply uniquely to wellbeing literacy. This results in several social learning mechanisms that may enhance or hinder wellbeing literacy.

Bandura's Social Learning Theory (1977) offers a plausible basis for understanding how some facets of wellbeing literacy could develop through observation, imitation, and modelling. People may acquire wellbeing-related knowledge and practices by observing those around them. For example, an individual might learn to recognise signs of stress in others and adopt effective coping strategies by observing how others manage stress (Waters et al., 2014). Similarly, children might develop their initial understanding of emotional regulation by watching how their parents or caregivers handle challenging situations, mirroring the parents' responses (Paley & Hajal, 2022).

Wellbeing-related behaviours and attitudes can *spread* through social networks (Fowler & Christakis, 2008; Kramer et al., 2014). For example, research by Chi et al. (2019) found that both positive and negative aspects of wellbeing can be transmitted among family members. Similarly, Marx et al. (2024) demonstrated that susceptibility to emotional contagion can significantly impact interpersonal functioning and prosocial tendencies. For wellbeing literacy, this means that individuals surrounded by people with high wellbeing literacy may be more likely to develop or have a higher wellbeing literacy themselves, whereas being surrounded by others with low literacy will likely result in low wellbeing literacy.

Notably, social learning mechanisms are increasingly taking place online. Social media platforms, online communities, and various apps create spaces for observational learning, cultural transmission, and collaborative knowledge construction around wellbeing. For example, social media influencers focusing on mental health and wellbeing can serve as modern-day models for observational learning, potentially reaching millions with their wellbeing practices and insights (Raggatt et al., 2018). However, these digital environments also present significant challenges for wellbeing literacy. The spread of misinformation about health and wellbeing is a significant concern (Wang et al., 2019). Sensitive issues such as body image (Fardouly & Vartanian, 2016) and toxic masculinity (Gesser-Edelsburg & Hijazi, 2020) hinder the development of wellbeing literacy.

Cognitive Processes and Epistemic Foundations as Conditions and Beliefs Shaping Wellbeing Literacy

The cognitive processes and epistemic foundations intrinsically tied to social interactions, sense of belonging, and cultural contexts may also underpin wellbeing literacy. For instance, the concept of "chatter" (i.e., our inner voice and how we talk to ourselves) is deeply influenced by cultural norms, social experiences, and the systems in which we exist (Kross, 2021). For instance, research by Heine et al. (1999) found that Japanese participants engage in self-critical self-talk for group benefit, whereas US participants focus on self-enhancement. In Australia, the "tall poppy syndrome" can lead to modest self-talk despite high achievement (Feather, 1989). Markus and Kitayama (1991) noted American self-talk centres on personal goals, contrasting with East Asian cultures' focus on social harmony (Li et al., 2006).

Cognitive biases significantly influence how we process wellbeing information. The confirmation bias, where individuals seek information confirming their pre-existing beliefs about wellbeing (Nickerson, 1998), is amplified in group settings and on social media, where algorithms curate content based on user preferences and behaviours, creating echo chambers that reinforce existing beliefs, for better or for worse (Cinelli et al., 2021). In the context of wellbeing, this can lead to the rapid spread of unfounded "quick fixes" to mental health issues, which ultimately lead to psychological harm (van Prooijen & van Vugt, 2018).

Dechêne et al. (2009) explore the illusory truth effect, where repeated exposure increases the perceived truthfulness of information. These biases contribute to the social construction of reality (Berger & Luckmann, 1966), potentially internalising shared beliefs about wellbeing as "truth" within social groups. This is further strengthened by creating a sense of belonging to the community with shared beliefs, resulting in sub-groups with strongly held beliefs about reality, which may or may not reflect actual reality. For example, the persistent promotion of "positive thinking" as a cure-all for mental health issues in popular media has led many to believe that simply "thinking happy thoughts" is sufficient to overcome mental illness, despite this oversimplification contradicting clinical evidence (Ehrenreich, 2009), and results in the shaming of vulnerable individuals. Such socially constructed "truths" can significantly impact how individuals understand and approach their mental health, potentially discouraging them from seeking professional help when needed. It also can worsen mental health, as the individual feels like a failure when they cannot cure themselves through positive thinking alone. Alternatively, it can strengthen wellbeing within cliques, where people's ideas are validated and enhanced.

Epistemic beliefs may also significantly influence how we process wellbeing information (Greene et al., 2018). Epistemology research infers that information derived from authority figures, logical reasoning, or personal experience may powerfully shape wellbeing literacy (Chinn et al., 2011). Recent research by Kienhues et al. (2020) demonstrates how these epistemic stances affect the evaluation and integration of conflicting health information. Their study found that individuals with more sophisticated epistemic beliefs were better able to critically assess and synthesise contradictory health claims, highlighting the importance of epistemic cognition in navigating complex wellbeing information landscapes. Epistemology reminds us that the internal process of knowledge construction is set against the backdrop of social interactions, norms, groups one belongs to, and shared understandings. The social nature of these cognitive processes emphasises the need for environments that foster critical thinking and expose individuals to diverse viewpoints. Sinatra and Lombardi (2020) argue that such environments are crucial for developing critical thinking practices in an era of information overload; therefore, such as environments are crucial for wellbeing literacy.

Individual Factors and Motivations in Wellbeing Literacy

While this chapter emphasises the inherently social nature of wellbeing literacy, it is also essential to acknowledge the role of individual factors and context in shaping how people engage with and apply wellbeing knowledge. An individual's existing competencies play a role in their capacity to engage with the social dimensions of wellbeing literacy. Equally important is context. The ecological perspective challenges the notion of a one-size-fits-all approach to wellbeing and highlights the importance of culturally responsive and socially aware strategies for enhancing wellbeing literacy within a broader system (Bronfenbrenner, 1994). Similarly, the capability model of wellbeing literacy (Oades et al., 2021) emphasises that wellbeing literacy capabilities emerge through interaction between individual factors and environmental conditions, showing the importance of social context in wellbeing literacy development.

Conclusion

This chapter explored the social contexts and processes within which wellbeing literacy develops and exists, and therefore, has a potential link to our need to belong. Wellbeing literacy can dynamically evolve through social interactions, cultural influences, and opportunities and experiences of belonging. Social validation and learning from others are central to developing wellbeing literacy, which is shaped by cognitive processes and societal structures. This collective process is continuously influenced by the social environments in which individuals live and interact, which are influenced by and contribute to a sense of belonging, which in turn influence one's sense of wellbeing. As suggested by wellbeing literacy theory and application, wellbeing language and literacy are socially constructed, such that the communities to which we belong are crucial for our ultimate sense and experience of wellbeing.

References

Allen, K.-A., Counted, V., Bozorg, B., Crosby, S., Crawford, J., & Slaten, C. D. (2025). *Unseen intersections of trauma and belonging: The good, the bad, and the belonging-trauma paradox on university students.* Routledge.

Allen, K.-A., Gray, D., Baumeister, R., & Leary, M. (2021a). The need to belong: A deep dive into the origins, implications, and future of A foundational construct. *Educational Psychology Review, 34.* https://doi.org/10.1007/s10648-021-09633-6

Allen, K.-A., Greenwood, C. J., Berger, E., Patlamazoglou, L., Reupert, A., Wurf, G., May, F., O'Connor, M., Sanson, A., Olsson, C. A., & Letcher, P. (2024). Adolescent school belonging and mental health outcomes in young adulthood: Findings from a multi-wave prospective cohort study. *School Mental Health, 16*(1), 149–160. https://doi.org/10.1007/s12310-023-09626-6

Allen, K.-A., Kern, M., Rozek, C., McInerney, D., & Slavich, G. (2021b). Belonging: A review of conceptual issues, an integrative framework, and directions for future research. *Australian Journal of Psychology, 73,* 1–16. https://doi.org/10.1080/00049530.2021.1883409

Arslan, G., Allen, K. A., & Ryan, T. (2020). Exploring the impacts of school belonging on youth well-being and mental health among Turkish adolescents. *Child Indicators Research, 13*(5), 1619–1635. https://doi.org/10.1007/s12187-020-09721-z

Bandura, A. (1977). *Social learning theory.* Prentice-Hall.

Baumeister, R. F., & Leary, M. R. (1995). The need to belong: Desire for interpersonal attachments as a fundamental human motivation. *Psychological Bulletin, 117*(3), 497–529. https://doi.org/10.1037/0033-2909.117.3.497

Berger, P. L., & Luckmann, T. (1966). *The social construction of reality: A treatise in the sociology of knowledge.* Doubleday & Company.

Bronfenbrenner, U. (1994). Ecological models of human development. *International Encyclopedia of Education, 3*(2), 37–43.

Brown, B. (2017). *Braving the Wilderness: Reese's Book Club: The Quest for True Belonging and the Courage to Stand Alone.* Random House.

Chi, P., Du, H., King, R. B. et al. (2019). Well-Being Contagion in the Family: Transmission of Happiness and Distress Between Parents and Children. *Child Ind Res, 12,* 2189–2202. https://doi.org/10.1007/s12187-019-09636-4

Chinn, C. A., Buckland, L.A., & Samarapungavan, A. (2011). Expanding the Dimensions of Epistemic Cognition: Arguments From Philosophy and Psychology.

Educational Psychologist, 46(3), 141–167. https://doi.org/10.1080/00461520.2011.587722

Cinelli, M., Morales, G., Galeazzi, A., Quattrociocchi, W., & Starnini, M. (2021, 3/2). The echo chamber effect on social media. *Proceedings of the National Academy of Sciences, 118*, e2023301118. https://doi.org/10.1073/pnas.2023301118

Dechêne, A., Stahl, C., Hansen, J., & Wänke, M. (2009). The Truth About the Truth: A Meta-Analytic Review of the Truth Effect. *Personality and Social Psychology Review, 14*(2), 238–257. https://doi.org/10.1177/1088868309352251 (Original work published 2010)

Ehrenreich, B. (2009). *Bright-sided: How the relentless promotion of positive thinking has undermined America*. Metropolitan Books.

Fardouly, J., & Vartanian, L. R. (2016). Social media and body image concerns: Current research and future directions. *Current Opinion in Psychology, 9*, 1–5. https://doi.org/10.1016/j.copsyc.2015.09.005

Feather, N. T. (1989). Attitudes towards the high achiever: The fall of the tall poppy. *Australian Journal of Psychology, 41*(3), 239–267. https://doi.org/10.1080/00049538908260088

Fowler, J. H., & Christakis, N. A. (2008). Dynamic spread of happiness in a large social network: Longitudinal analysis over 20 years in the Framingham heart study. *BMJ (Clinical Research Ed.), 337*, a2338. https://doi.org/10.1136/bmj.a2338

Frydenberg, E. (2017). *Coping and the challenge of resilience*. Palgrave Macmillan/Springer Nature. https://doi.org/10.1057/978-1-137-56924-0

Gesser-Edelsburg, A., & Hijazi, R. (2020). When politics meets pandemic: How Prime Minister Netanyahu and a small team communicated health and risk information to the Israeli public during the early stages of COVID-19. *Risk Management and Healthcare Policy, 13*, 2985–3002. https://doi.org/10.2147/RMHP.S280952

Gray, D. L., Hope, E. C., & Matthews, J. S. (2018). Black and belonging at school: A case for interpersonal, instructional, and institutional opportunity structures. *Educational Psychologist, 53*(2), 97–113. https://doi.org/10.1080/00461520.2017.1421466

Greene, J., & Yu, S. (2015). Educating critical thinkers: The role of epistemic cognition. *Policy Insights from the Behavioral and Brain Sciences, 3*. https://doi.org/10.1177/2372732215622223

Greene, J. A., Cartiff, B. M., & Duke, R. F. (2018). A meta-analytic review of the relationship between epistemic cognition and academic achievement. *Journal of Educational Psychology, 110*(8), 1084–1111. https://doi.org/10.1037/edu0000263

Heine, S. J., Lehman, D. R., Markus, H. R., & Kitayama, S. (1999). Is there a universal need for positive self-regard? *Psychological Review, 106*(4), 766–794. https://doi.org/10.1037/0033-295X.106.4.766

Kern, M. L., Williams, P., Spong, C., Colla, R., Sharma, K., Downie, A., Kern, M. L., Williams, P., Spong, C., Colla, R., Sharma, K., Downie, A., Taylor, J. A., Sharp, S., Siokou, C., & Oades, L. G. (2020). Systems informed positive psychology. *The Journal of Positive Psychology, 15*(6), 705–715. https://doi.org/10.1080/17439760.2019.1639799

Kienhues, D., Jucks, R., & Bromme, R. (2020). Sealing the gateways for post-truthism: Reestablishing the epistemic authority of science. *Educational Psychologist, 55*(3), 144–154. https://doi.org/10.1080/00461520.2020.1784012

Kramer, A. D., Guillory, J. E., & Hancock, J. T. (2014). Experimental evidence of massive-scale emotional contagion through social networks. *Proceedings of the National Academy of Sciences of the United States of America, 111*(24), 8788–8790. https://doi.org/10.1073/pnas.1320040111

Kross, E. (2021). *Chatter: The voice in our head, why it matters, and how to harness it*. Crown.

Leary, M. R., & Allen, A. B. (2011). Belonging motivation: Establishing, maintaining, and repairing relational value. In D. Dunning (Ed.), *Social motivation* (pp. 37–55). Psychology Press.

Leary, M. R., & Baumeister, R. F. (2000). The nature and function of self-esteem: Sociometer theory. In M. P. Zanna (Ed.), *Advances in experimental social psychology* (Vol. 32, pp. 1–62). Academic Press. https://doi.org/10.1016/S0065-2601(00)80003-9

Li, H. Z., Zhang, Z., Bhatt, G., & Yum, Y. O. (2006). Rethinking culture and self-construal: China as a middle land. *The Journal of Social Psychology, 146*(5), 591–610. https://doi.org/10.3200/SOCP.146.5.591-610

Markus, H. R., & Kitayama, S. (1991). Culture and the self: Implications for cognition, emotion, and motivation. *Psychological Review, 98*(2), 224–253. https://doi.org/10.1037/0033-295X.98.2.224

Marx, A. K. G., Frenzel, A. C., Fiedler, D., & Reck, C. (2024). Susceptibility to positive versus negative emotional contagion: First evidence on their distinction using a balanced self-report measure. In *PLoS ONE* (Vol. 19, Issue 5). Public Library of Science. https://doi.org/10.1371/journal.pone.0302890

Nickerson, R. S. (1998). Confirmation bias: A ubiquitous phenomenon in many guises. *Review of General Psychology, 2*(2), 175–220. https://doi.org/10.1037/1089-2680.2.2.175

Oades, L. G., Jarden, A., Hou, H., Ozturk, C., Williams, P., Slemp, G. R., & Huang, L. (2021). Wellbeing literacy: A capability model for wellbeing science and practice. *International Journal of Environmental Research and Public Health, 18*(2), 719. https://doi.org/10.3390/ijerph18020719

Oades, L. G., & Johnston, A. L. (2017). Wellbeing literacy: The missing link in positive education. In L. G. Oades, L. M. Baker, J. J. Francis, & J. A. Taylor (Eds.), *The Palgrave handbook of positive education* (pp. 325–343). Palgrave Macmillan.

Paley, B., & Hajal, N. J. (2022). Conceptualizing emotion regulation and coregulation as family-level phenomena. *Clinical Child and Family Psychology Review, 25*(1), 19–43. https://doi.org/10.1007/s10567-022-00378-4

Palikara, O., Castro-Kemp, S., Gaona, C., & Eirinaki, V. (2021). The mediating role of school belonging in the relationship between socioemotional well-being and loneliness in primary school age children. *Australian Journal of Psychology, 73*(1), 24–34. https://doi.org/10.1080/00049530.2021.1882270

Raggatt, M., Wright, C. J. C., Carrotte, E., Jenkinson, R., Mulgrew, K., Prichard, I., & Lim, M. S. C. (2018). "I aspire to look and feel healthy like the posts convey": Engagement with fitness inspiration on social media and perceptions of its influence on health and wellbeing. *BMC Public Health, 18*(1), 1002. https://doi.org/10.1186/s12889-018-5930-7

Raggatt, M., Wright, C. J. C., Carrotte, E., Jenkinson, R., Mulgrew, K., Prichard, I., & Lim, M. S. C. (2018). "I aspire to look and feel healthy like the posts convey": Engagement with fitness inspiration on social media and perceptions of its influence on health and wellbeing. *BMC Public Health, 18*(1), 1002. https://doi.org/10.1186/s12889-018-5930-7

Sinatra, G. M., & Lombardi, D. (2020). Evaluating sources of scientific evidence and claims in the post-truth era may require reappraising plausibility judgments. *Educational Psychologist, 55*(3), 120–131. https://doi.org/10.1080/00461520.2020.1730181

Sinatra, G. M., & Seyranian, V. (2016). Encouraging transformative change in social identity and beliefs: The potential for epistemic cognition. In J. A. Greene, W. A. Sandoval, & I. Bråten (Eds.), *Handbook of epistemic cognition* (pp. 203–220). Routledge.

van Prooijen, J. W., & van Vugt, M. (2018). Conspiracy theories: Evolved functions and psychological mechanisms. *Perspectives on Psychological Science: a Journal of the Association for Psychological Science*, *13*(6), 770–788. https://doi.org/10.1177/1745691618774270

Vilches, S. P. (2012). Social construction of the well-being in young people. Unpublished master's thesis). Humak University of Applied Sciences, Finland. https://www.theseus.fi/bitstream/handle/10024/47252/Prudant_Sergio.pdf

Wang, Y., Mckee, M., Torbica, A., & Stuckler, D. (2019). Systematic literature review on the spread of health-related misinformation on social media. *Social Science & Medicine*, *240*, 112552. https://doi.org/10.1016/j.socscimed.2019.112552

Waters, S. F., West, T. V., & Mendes, W. B. (2014). Stress contagion: Physiological covariation between mothers and infants. *Psychological Science*, *25*(4), 934–942. http://dx.doi.org/10.1177/0956797613518352

23

DEVELOPMENT AND IMPLEMENTATION OF A WELLBEING LITERACY CAMPAIGN

Evaluation of the 'Take a Minute' Campaign in Tasmania, Australia

Matthew Iasiello, Joep van Agteren, Laura Cini, John McNamara, Amanda Aitken, Nick Sullivan, and Connie Digolis

Background of the Campaign

In response to the impacts of the COVID-19 pandemic on the mental health and wellbeing of Tasmanians, the Mental Health Council of Tasmania (MHCT) collected data for an 18-month period (starting March 2020) to monitor and review the impacts of COVID-19 on people with a known mental illness, on the community-based workforce providing services, and the population reaching out for support. Through these regular reports, it became apparent that situational distress was widespread and warranted a different response to that of an individual experiencing increased anxiety – that is, to seek professional support.

In an interest to address concerns regarding Tasmanians' mental health, the Tasmanian Government sought advice and acknowledged the need for a population-based response and subsequently funded the MHCT to design and deliver a campaign to promote mental wellbeing literacy in the community. The project was commissioned to (a) develop mental wellbeing literacy content and information, (b) whole-of-population Campaign, and (c) targeted community engagement. MHCT project staff partnered with researchers at the Be Well Co to assist in the design and evaluate the campaign.

Development of the Campaign

The resultant campaign was named 'Take a minute', which focused on empowering individuals and communities to develop wellbeing literacy by considering their unique resources and capabilities to maintain their own wellbeing. The campaign used the Intervention Mapping approach which supports the methodical design of theory-based interventions. The process involves (i) a needs

DOI: 10.4324/9781003644293-23

analysis, (ii) writing change objectives, (iii) selection of practical applications, (iv) developing the program, (v) implementation strategy, and (vi) evaluation (Fernandez et al., 2019). We describe the development, implementation, and initial evaluation of the 'Take a minute' campaign through the steps of the Intervention mapping process.

Step 1: Determine the Problem That Needs to Be Solved by the Intervention via a Thorough Needs Analysis

The first step of IM involves performing a needs analysis related to the problem that the program aims to solve, and subsequently defining the exact scope of the campaign. The needs analysis first drew on an extensive literature review on mental health and wellbeing literacy promotion, followed by consultation with mental health promotion stakeholders across Tasmania. The needs analysis identified four key themes which were relevant for the campaign.

THEME 1: THE NEED FOR CAMPAIGNS THAT FOCUS ON WELLBEING PROMOTION AND RESULTANT BENEFITS

Mental health campaigns have traditionally adopted a risk-reduction model, designed to target and prevent risk factors of mental illness (Barry, 2019). Recently, mental health campaigns have started shifting to the promotion of mental health and wellbeing (as opposed to solely reducing the risk of illness) as an alternative and potentially more effective strategy, in line with a parallel shift in focus that can be seen in mental health promotion in general (Slade, 2010). These modern campaigns adopt a competence/enhancement model focused on the promotion of competencies and positive mental health (Herrman & Jané-Llopis, 2005).

THEME 2: WELLBEING LITERACY MUST BE PERSONALLY DEFINED

Reflecting the paradigm shift to promote positive mental health, modern definitions of mental health literacy now include the promotion of mental wellbeing, in addition to recognising the symptoms of psychological distress and building knowledge on sources of mental health information and appropriate help-seeking (Sampaio et al., 2022). More suitable to a campaign based on empowerment and competency is the concept of wellbeing literacy (Oades et al., 2021). This refers to an individual's capability to comprehend and compose language around wellbeing, across different contexts, ultimately serving to help improve the wellbeing of individuals and the people around them.

Embedded within this approach to literacy lies a capability model: we can learn and use language to grow our capability to experience wellbeing in our own unique way. This understanding of wellbeing literacy argues that wellbeing a personal experience, and campaigns should empower individuals to define and identify what's important for their wellbeing within their contexts. Wellbeing literacy campaigns should avoid the 'top down' use of language, rather allow participants to share their own language to define wellbeing.

THEME 3: THE NEED FOR PUBLIC PARTICIPATION USING A DE-CENTRALISED, FLEXIBLE CAMPAIGN

The previous themes highlight the need for the freedom of campaign participants to express their unique wellbeing language and capacities, which might be considered a challenge for a universal campaign designed to reach a large population. Research has investigated mechanisms of de-centralised public participation in health promotion campaigns. Examples such as the ALS ice-bucket challenge reflect campaigns that can be de-centralised, allowing participants to customise the messaging and ensure the language is contextually appropriate.

Similarly, other successful campaigns have used partnership models which provide partners with campaign collateral and guidelines, with flexibility for co-branding and modification required by the partner (Donovan et al., 2006)

THEME 4: BUILDING WELLBEING LITERACY REQUIRES MOTIVATION, CAPABILITY AND OPPORTUNITY

The success of a wellbeing literacy campaign ultimately should be reflected in real behaviour change as a consequence of improving literacy. It is for this reason that the campaign uses Intervention Mapping as a framework, which uses behaviour change principles to help guide the design of initiatives to improve health. The Theoretical Domain Framework is a model that outlines evidence-based determinants that we can use to evaluate behaviour change as well as implementation (Atkins et al., 2017). The determinants can be clustered under three headings: motivation, capability, and opportunity, see Table 23.1.

Stakeholder Feedback on Needs Analysis Themes

Following focus groups with mental health stakeholders in Tasmania in March 2023, many concerns for 'what will not work' were expressed, with an endorsement for many of the themes identified in the needs analysis (summarised in Table 23.2).

TABLE 23.1 Examples of how motivation, opportunity, and capability can be considered at the wider campaign level as well as the individual level

	Campaign	*Individual*
Motivation	Does the person want to engage with the campaign?	Does the person want to work on their wellbeing?
Opportunity	Do we create an environment where we can reach a person?	Are the circumstances right for the person to make positive changes to their wellbeing?
Capability	Is the person able to engage with the content?	Do we provide the tools to improve literacy and work on their wellbeing

TABLE 23.2 Themes identified from stakeholder consultation regarding needs analysis

Design aspects	*Description*
To Avoid:	
One-size-fits all	The consensus was against employing a one-size-fits-all message and approach, emphasising the need for tailored strategies in promoting wellbeing.
Top-down approach	Participants rejected a top-down approach, advocating for community involvement and not imposing solutions from above.
Not giving agency to individuals	The group stressed the importance of empowering individuals, highlighting the need for initiatives that allow people to take control of their own wellbeing.
Boring engagement methods	The session identified a strong aversion to dull and uninspiring methods, emphasising the necessity of creative and engaging approaches to promote wellbeing.
Endorsed:	
Equitable access	The need for equitable access to wellbeing initiatives was emphasised, with considerations for both online and hard copy resources to cater to diverse preferences and situations.
Health literacy considerations	There was concern for consideration of low health literacy across Tasmania, such that intervention instructions should be simple and clear.
Tasmanians are local	Recognising the local identity of Tasmanians, participants stressed the importance of incorporating local elements and a variety of meeting places to enhance community engagement.
Community driven	Participants favoured initiatives led by locals, expressing a preference for authentic community-driven programs over external interventions.
Mental health by stealth	Advocacy for a subtle approach to mental health promotion – becoming creative in the way we use language and focusing on flow-on effects or drivers of mental health to increase its relevance. This would be combined with directly asking individuals about their needs, was highlighted, along with the importance of engaging reflection exercises to make the process interesting, enjoyable, and impactful.

The result of Step 1 is a logic model of change that summarises the problem, the outcomes and the determinants using the PRECEDE-PROCEED model (Gielen et al., 2008), which will be used to underpin the intervention. Simply, the model requires a clear rationale for (1) the key problems that the needs analysis identified, (2) the overarching behavioural and environmental outcomes (or targets) one needs to meet to improve the problem, and (3) the underlying determinants of those behavioural and environmental outcomes (here using the Theoretical Domain Framework mentioned above). The final logic model is displayed in Figure 23.1.

Step 2: Define the Objectives the Intervention Needs to Meet and What the Intervention Needs to Change to Meet Those Objectives

After determining the problem that needs to be addressed, IM continues to delineate what needs to change to solve the problem. Firstly, each target area identified in the needs analysis was rewritten into desired behavioural and environmental outcomes. Secondly, these outcomes were subsequently broken into sub-objectives called performance objectives. Finally, these performance objectives were broken down further into change objectives. A change objective links a performance objective with determinants from the Theoretical Domains Framework (e.g., knowledge, skill, and beliefs about capabilities). The final output of Step 2 was a collection of matrices, depicting each change objective per performance objective (placed in the rows) and determinant (placed in the columns), which are attached in Supplementary Materials (available at: www.bewellco.io/take-a-minute-suppl).

Step 3: Select Behaviour Change Techniques and Practical Applications of Those Techniques That Will Be Used to Achieve the Change Objectives

In Step 3, a new table is created by placing the change objectives on individual rows and matching them with evidence-based behaviour change techniques (Kok et al., 2016). Behaviour change techniques are theoretical strategies (e.g., goal setting, modelling, and active learning) that have been empirically demonstrated to be able to change individual behaviour. The IM framework comes with an extensive summary of behaviour change techniques and how they can be used to create impactful interventions. By matching change objectives with individual behaviour change techniques, IM aims to improve the chance that actual behaviour and environmental change in line with the change objective will be achieved. The final part of Step 3 is translating the theoretical behaviour change techniques into 'practical applications', referring to the proposed real-world application of each behaviour change technique (Supplementary

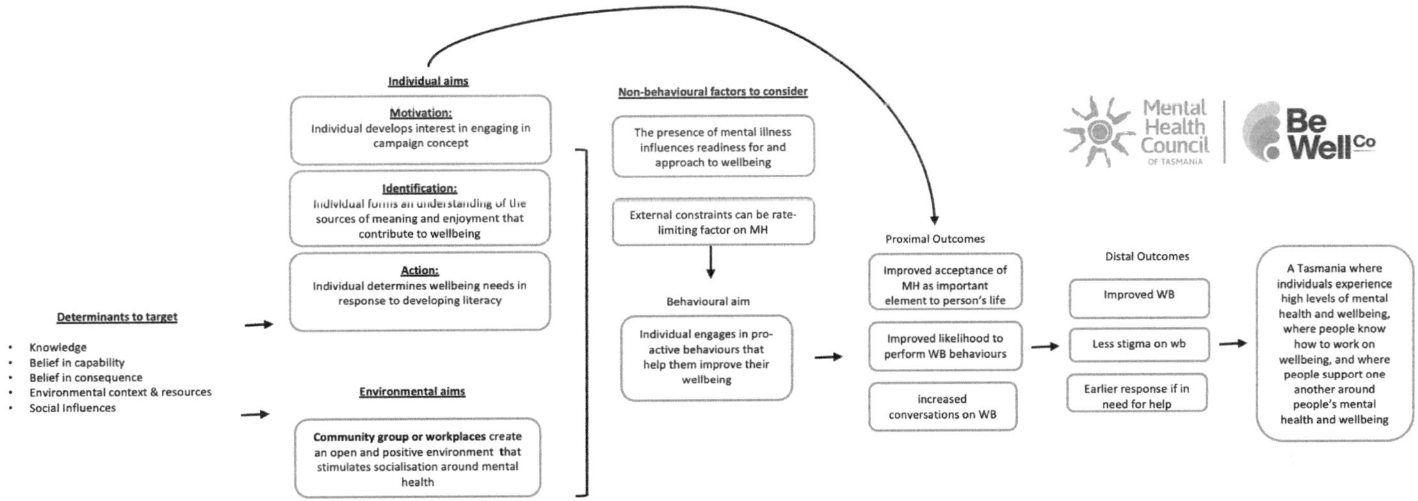

FIGURE 23.1 PRECEDE-PROCEDE logical model describing the determinants, individual aims, considerations, and proximal and distal outcomes of the 'Take a minute' campaign.

Materials). The result is a line-by-line itemised list (or blueprint) of practical applications that need to be incorporated into the programme design in Step 4.

Step 4: Design and Develop the Actual Intervention Components Based of the Practical Applications Identified in the Previous Step

In Step 4, the authors created the campaign based on the blueprint established in Step 3. This process was guided via project team meetings with creative partners, followed by focus groups with project stakeholders. The practical application of the 'Take a minute' campaign was centred on empowering individuals to develop the language and understanding of their unique resources and capacities to maintain good mental wellbeing.

Paradoxically, the campaign aimed to develop this reflection on wellbeing language without relying on the use of explicit language itself. The campaign used a technique called photovoice (Sutton-Brown, 2014), whereby participants are empowered to use their own unique non-verbal language to 'describe' difficult-to-explain concepts. It is a qualitative research method used in community-based participatory research, where participants are instructed to take photos that represent their experiences of a certain topic. For example, researchers focused on 'meaning in life' and used photography to help participants 'explain' what sources of meaning exist in their lives (Steger et al., 2013). Meaning in life, like wellbeing, is a difficult concept to convey to another person, and often we don't have the language to describe it. However, through self-reflection and photography, people are able to construct language of capabilities and resources available for their own wellbeing, which allows participants to compose their own wellbeing language for their context (Oades et al., 2021).

Photovoice has been used around the world, across the life course (for example in children; Waters et al., 2022) and in many vulnerable populations (Gaboardi et al., 2022), and aligns closely with empowerment in mental wellbeing promotion (Barry, 2019), as photovoice helps participants acquire new knowledge, develop critical awareness of their community, transformed their self-perception, and allowed them to expand their social networks (Budig et al., 2018).

Building on the notion of 'meaningful pictures', the 7-minute challenge was developed as a concept to invite participants to reflect on six themes across the week, with the seventh day used to summarise their reflections into a 'wellbeing literacy statement'; the opportunity to formalise their language about wellbeing literacy. The prompts across the six days included finding pictures that represent things, places, activities, or people that bring joy to your life, a person that is special to you, something that brings your life meaning and purpose, a place that you love to visit, something you do to de-stress,

TABLE 23.3 Themes identified from stakeholder consultation regarding practical applications

Theme	*Description*
Meaningful pictures	This activity received significant support as an enjoyable activity that promoted communication: Utilising visual aids and enjoyable activities was suggested as an effective means to facilitate meaningful discussions and support in the community.
Wellbeing is personal	Participants recognised the personal nature of wellbeing, emphasising the need for strategies that acknowledge and cater to individual preferences and needs.
Language that can be tailored	The importance of a universally adaptable language for discussing wellbeing emerged, ensuring that communication resonates with diverse Tasmanian communities.
Development of a wellbeing literacy statement	A proposed initiative involved creating a wellbeing literacy statement, guiding individuals to reflect on aspects important to their wellbeing and encouraging actionable steps.

and something related to self-development. Please find full instructions for the campaign in Supplementary Materials. The final 'wellbeing literacy statement' is designed to build and formalise intentional language to maintain or improve wellbeing of self or others (Oades et al., 2021). The 7-minute challenge was available to be conducted in groups or as individuals. Initial versions of the practical applications were presented to stakeholders in focus groups (summarised in Table 23.3).

Steps 5 and 6: Adoption, Implementation, and Evaluation Plans

After finishing the design and development of the intervention, IM concludes with two additional steps, the development of an adoption and implementation plan (Step 5) as well as an evaluation plan (Step 6).

This approach was implemented within a partnership model, whereby partner organisations are onboarded into the campaign, champions are identified to lead the campaign using language and approaches that were appropriate/tailored to the setting, and modelling the challenge by demonstrating their own examples. The project team included two project officers who could prioritise face-to-face engagement with stakeholders where possible (in addition to the usual email and telephone contact). When organisations join Take a minute as a campaign partner, they receive ongoing support from their Project Officer. The aim of this place-based approach was to address digital inequity (reaching people less likely to engage online) and support community groups and organisations to tailor campaign activities to suit their target audience.

Evaluation of the campaign is ongoing, using a combination of focus groups, interviews, and online surveys. There has been consistent feedback from individual and group participants that the 7-minute challenge was enjoyable, simple, thought-provoking, flexible, and helped people reconnect with their interests. Campaign partners (including workplaces and community settings) have been content with the support that they have received from MHCT to deliver the campaign, and appreciated the collateral provided. Participants have reported that the 7-minute challenge has helped them to adopt new behaviours and more clearly express wellbeing literacy language (the aspects of life that are important to their wellbeing and activities to maintain them).

- *It has helped me realise things I am able to do to help myself feel better if I'm not feeling great*
- *It was good to have a week to reflect on positive mental health, and is a new train of thought that I aspire to continue*
- *It prompted me to think about different aspects of my wellbeing, and increase my awareness of things in my life that I already do to maintain my wellbeing*
- *Yes, it has inspired me to do more of the activities I love*
- *Confirmed existing ideas*
- *It has helped me bring together what matters to my health and wellbeing*

Participants expressed some of the enjoyable aspects of the campaign:

- *Reflecting on positive mental health I also thought it brought our group closer together*
- *I liked seeing the other responses that people did we shared photos of our cats and I thought that was cool*
- *It was like a mini check-in with myself*
- *It was fun and gave me a break from my work tasks*
- *Making me think about what makes me happy and how I can bring these back into my life*
- *Thought provoking on the everyday things that keep us going*
- *It was quick and easy to engage with, and I like taking time to take photos of things that bring me joy. I have saved the emails so I can reflect back on them*
- *Simple idea I could share with students*
- *It was quick and easy to do. It focuses on what makes us mentally happy rather than mentally ill*
- *Short and simple daily reminders*

Preliminary evaluation indicates support wellbeing literacy as a priority in the community. MHCT has undertaken extensive outreach, engaging with over 230 stakeholders throughout Tasmania. Feedback consistently highlights mental health and wellbeing as significant concerns among Tasmanians. While recognising that wellbeing literacy isn't a standalone solution or treatment for mental illness, stakeholders agree on the value of empowering individuals to identify actionable steps for self-care. MHCT's outreach efforts have yielded broad interest and support across diverse sectors in Tasmania. From local government councils, non-profit organisations, state government departments, and private businesses, child and family centres, community centres, neighbourhood houses, private businesses, psychologists, sporting clubs, peak bodies, and stakeholders from all walks of life have shown enthusiasm and engagement. This widespread support underscores the community's recognition of mental health's relevance and importance. It reflects a collective commitment to addressing mental health challenges and promoting wellbeing throughout Tasmania. This broad stakeholder support is also a testament to a unique aspect of Take a minute: the two Community Capacity Building Project Officers, who cover the state as the campaign's 'boots-on-the-ground'. This unique and personal approach has resulted in very high stakeholder engagement with the campaign and multiple organisations signing on to be campaign partners.

Stakeholders responded to the initial campaign ideas as exciting and novel, with many organisations volunteering to partner with MHCT to deliver the campaign with their staff or communities. There have been more than 4000 hits to the campaign website, with more than 1200 requests for the campaign collateral since November 2023. The campaign's delivery has demonstrated flexibility across various partners, adapting to different settings both online and offline. Utilising platforms such as WhatsApp groups, Teams, email, and Facebook, as well as physical prompts in cafes and face-to-face group meetings, has allowed for widespread participation in the campaign. The final evaluation of the campaign will focus on acceptability and behavioural change outcomes of the brief 7-minute challenge.

Conclusion

The 'Take a minute' campaign is among the first campaigns specifically designed to promote wellbeing literacy. It was rigorously developed using the Intervention Mapping framework, with multiple rounds of stakeholder engagement. Ongoing evaluation indicates a positive result for the project design, which aimed to create a campaign which was broadly applicable and attractive across the state of Tasmania. Consensus across the state has endorsed the importance of mental wellbeing promotion and the valuable role wellbeing literacy can play.

References

Atkins, L., Francis, J., Islam, R., O'Connor, D., Patey, A., Ivers, N., Foy, R., Duncan, E. M., Colquhoun, H , Grimshaw, J. M., Lawton, R., & Michie, S. (2017). A guide to using the theoretical domains framework of behaviour change to investigate implementation problems. *Implementation Science: IS*, *12*(1), 77. https://doi.org/10.1186/s13012-017-0605-9

Barry, M. M. (2019). Concepts and principles of mental health promotion. In M. M. Barry, A. M. Clarke, I. Petersen, & R. Jenkins (Eds.), *Implementing mental health promotion*. Springer. https://doi.org/10.1007/978-3-030-23455-3_1

Budig, K., Diez, J., Conde, P., Sastre, M., Hernán, M., & Franco, M. (2018). Photovoice and empowerment: Evaluating the transformative potential of a participatory action research project. *BMC Public Health*, *18*(1), 432. https://doi.org/10.1186/s12889-018-5335-7

Donovan, R. J., James, R., Jalleh, G., & Sidebottom, C. (2006). Implementing mental health promotion: The *act-belong-commit* mentally healthy WA campaign in Western Australia. *International Journal of Mental Health Promotion*, *8*(1), 33–42. https://doi.org/10.1080/14623730.2006.9721899

Fernandez, M. E., Ruiter, R. A. C., Markham, C. M., & Kok, G. (2019). Intervention mapping: Theory- and evidence-based health promotion program planning: Perspective and examples. *Frontiers in Public Health*, *7*, 209. https://doi.org/10.3389/fpubh.2019.00209

Gaboardi, M., Santinello, M., Lenzi, M., Disperati, F., Ornelas, J., & Shinn, M. (2022). Using a modified version of photovoice in a European cross-national study on homelessness. *American Journal of Community Psychology*, *70*(1–2), 139–152. https://doi.org/10.1002/ajcp.12586

Gielen, A. C., McDonald, E. M., Gary, T. L., & Bone, L. R. (2008). Using the precede-proceed model to apply health behavior theories. In K. Glanz, B. K. Rimer, & K. Viswanath (Eds.), *Health behavior and health education: Theory, research, and practice* (4th ed., pp. 407–433). Jossey-Bass.

Herrman, H., & Jané-Llopis, E. (2005). Mental health promotion in public health. *Promotion & Education*, Suppl 2, 42–69. https://doi.org/10.1177/10253823050120020107

Kok, G., Gottlieb, N. H., Peters, G.-J. Y., Mullen, P. D., Parcel, G. S., Ruiter, R. A. C. Fernández, M. E., Markham, C., & Kay Bartholomew, L. (2016). A taxonomy of behaviour change methods: An intervention mapping approach. *Health Psychology Review*, *10*, 297–312. https://doi.org/10.1080/17437199.2015.1077155

Oades, L. G., Jarden, A., Hou, H., Ozturk, C., Williams, P., R Slemp, G., & Huang, L. (2021). Wellbeing literacy: A capability model for wellbeing science and practice. *International Journal of Environmental Research and Public Health*, *18*(2), 719. https://doi.org/10.3390/ijerph18020719

Sampaio, F., Gonçalves, P., & Sequeira, C. (2022). Mental health literacy: It is now time to put knowledge into practice. *International Journal of Environmental Research and Public Health*, *19*(12), 7030. https://doi.org/10.3390/ijerph19127030

Slade, M. (2010). Mental illness and well-being: The Central importance of positive psychology and recovery approaches. *BMC Health Services Research*, *10*, 26. https://doi.org/10.1186/1472-6963-10-26

Steger, M. F., Shim, Y., Rush, B. R., Brueske, L. A., Shin, J. Y., & Merriman, L. A. (2013). The mind's eye: A photographic method for understanding meaning in people's lives. *The Journal of Positive Psychology*, *8*(6), 530–542. https://doi.org/10.1080/17439760.2013.830760

Sutton-Brown, C. A. (2014). Photovoice: A methodological guide. *Photography and Culture*, *7*(2), 169–185. https://doi.org/10.2752/175145214X13999922103165

Waters, L., Dussert, D., & Loton, D. (2022). How do young children understand and action their own well-being? Positive psychology, student voice, and well-being literacy in early childhood. *International Journal of Applied Positive Psychology*, *7*, 91–117. https://doi.org/10.1007/s41042-021-00056-w

24

EXPLORING WELLBEING LITERACY AMONG JAVANESE UNDERGRADUATES

Siti Nuzulia, Fatma Kusuma Mahanani, Muhammad Nazil Iqdami, and Wulan Aulia Azizah

Introduction

Wellbeing literacy is a burgeoning concept focused on the ability to understand, interpret, and use language to improve one's own and others' wellbeing, described as a transformative capability that enhances life value, freedom, and a deeper sense of wellbeing (Oades et al., 2020, 2021a, 2021b). This concept includes the necessary vocabulary, knowledge, and communication skills to promote wellbeing intentionally within cultural contexts, bridging wellbeing interventions and outcomes, crucial for integrating positive education into broader systems (Oades et al., 2020, 2021a, 2021b).

Wellbeing literacy, viewed as a sociocultural phenomenon (Gee & Gee, 2015), is influenced by cultural, social, historical, environmental, and economic factors. A key aspect is context sensitivity, as language meanings shift across contexts (Oades et al., 2022), requiring individuals to identify and adapt their language accordingly. Communication modes and word choices vary across domains like home, school, workplace, and interactions with grandparents, friends, or colleagues. In Indonesia, ethnic and cultural diversity demands a nuanced approach to wellbeing literacy, avoiding generalisations. Therefore, examining Javanese wellbeing literacy is crucial, given that Javanese are Indonesia's largest population group.

Javanese culture, rich in traditions and philosophies promoting harmony and balance, has seen limited scholarly exploration regarding its influence on wellbeing literacy (Subandi, 2015; Waston et al., 2024). Unlike Western paradigms that often separate science from spirituality (Mazzocchi, 2006), Javanese culture presents a distinct epistemology where spirituality is deeply integrated into daily life (Geertz, 1976). This integration influences ethics,

DOI: 10.4324/9781003644293-24

health, and the interaction between the physical and metaphysical realms, crucial for understanding wellbeing in the Javanese context. Javanese customs and religious practices are inseparably intertwined, with daily life rooted in rituals, values, and ceremonies reflecting spiritual devotion and cultural heritage. Over centuries, Javanese culture has blended elements from Hinduism, Buddhism, Islam, and animism, creating a harmonious fusion where cultural traditions carry spiritual significance, often making them indistinguishable.

Rooted in tradition, Javanese wellbeing practices offer a lens to compare generational perspectives, revealing their preservation or adaptation over time. Older generations serve as custodians of cultural wisdom (Alzahra et al., 2024; Khadafi & Harahap, 2024), while younger generations (i.e., undergraduates) may gravitate towards Western, globalised perspectives (Haniah et al., 2024). This contrast highlights the ongoing evolution of Javanese cultural identity, particularly in the context of discussions around wellbeing.

This chapter explores the significant impact of Javanese culture on the Indonesian psyche (Woodward, 2004) and its crucial role in understanding and enhancing wellbeing literacy. Drawing from a study of 360 Javanese undergraduate students aged 17–22, the research employed qualitative methods, including online open-ended interviews, a literature review of traditional wellbeing practices, and focus group discussions with Javanese scholars. The study examined students' understanding, practices, and expressions of wellbeing. The literature review offered historical and cultural context, highlighting intergenerational continuities and changes in wellbeing practices, while the focus group discussions provided expert insights into Javanese cultural values. Content analysis identified themes reflecting students' wellbeing concepts and expressions, closely linked to traditional Javanese values. The authors, of Javanese origin, acknowledge their subjective and culturally embedded perspective, which adds depth to the contextual connection between Javanese culture and wellbeing literacy and emphasises the importance of reflexivity in qualitative research.

Javanese Cultural Context

In Javanese culture, spirituality is the cornerstone that profoundly shapes the understanding, expression, and maintenance of wellbeing (Geertz, 1976). Central to this worldview is the concept of '*manunggaling kawula gusti*' (the unity of servant and God), which represents the ultimate spiritual goal (Damami, 2002). This pursuit is an aspirational ideal and a deeply ingrained practice within Javanese life. Spiritual practices emphasising self-reflection, harmony, respect, and tolerance are key to achieving this unity and represent the pinnacle of Javanese mysticism (Magnis-Suseno, 2001). These spiritual pursuits are intricately woven into the broader societal fabric, playing a crucial role in fostering peace, preventing conflict, and guiding individuals towards a balanced and fulfilling life (Yogiswari & Murtiningsih, 2019; Ysmailova et al., 2020).

A central tenet of Javanese spirituality, the concept of *suwung* (inner peace), vividly illustrates the intertwining of spiritual wellbeing with everyday life. *Suwung* reflects an individual's harmony with God, self, others, and nature, signifying peace, self-control, and a profound connection to the divine (Setiyowati, 2017). This state embodies Javanese cultural values, prioritising spiritual balance as the foundation for prosperity and peace. In Javanese culture, spirituality is not just a separate aspect of life but the foundation from which other cultural values – such as collectivism, social harmony, respect for hierarchy, and indirect communication – emerge (Nadar, 2007). These values are direct expressions of Javanese spirituality and collectively shape how wellbeing is understood and practised within the community (Maulana et al., 2018).

Collectivism and social harmony are central to this cultural framework, with the group's needs often taking precedence over individual desires. The Javanese concept of *rukun* (harmony) embodies this collectivist orientation, promoting peaceful and harmonious relationships as a societal imperative (Casmini, 2020). However, this cultural emphasis on harmony can sometimes suppress personal needs or emotions to avoid disrupting group cohesion, a phenomenon often referred to as *rasa* (feeling) (Nadar, 2007). While analysis of collectivist cultures highlights the benefits of group solidarity and social cohesion, it raises critical questions about the potential costs, particularly the sacrifice of individual expression and the internalisation of emotional conflict (Hofstede, 1986).

The respect for hierarchy in Javanese society further complicates the individual's role in maintaining personal wellbeing. The Javanese language, with its varying speech levels (*krama, madya, ngoko*), not only reflects social stratification but also reinforces it, dictating the terms of social interaction and ensuring that respect and deference are maintained (Nadar, 2007). In this context, an individual's wellbeing is closely tied to their social obligations, particularly the expectation to contribute to the wellbeing of others within this hierarchical structure. This dynamic creates a complex interplay between personal and communal wellbeing, where the lines between self-care and social duty are often blurred.

Indirect communication, another critical aspect of Javanese culture, is closely linked to the value placed on social harmony. In Javanese society, direct expression of feelings or desires is frequently avoided to prevent conflict and maintain smooth interpersonal relations. Instead, euphemisms, polite refusals, or even silence are employed, relying on the listener's ability to interpret the underlying meaning (Nadar, 2007). While this practice supports emotional equilibrium and social cohesion, it also introduces challenges, such as the potential for internal stress and a disconnect between one's internal experiences and outward expressions. The tension between preserving social harmony and expressing individual emotions highlights the cultural complexities that must be navigated to enhance wellbeing literacy in Javanese society (Nursanti et al., 2024).

In summary, spirituality in Javanese culture is deeply intertwined with the cultural values of collectivism, social harmony, respect for hierarchy, and indirect communication. These interwoven values create a cohesive yet complex cultural framework that profoundly influences how wellbeing is perceived and practised. As traditional values continue to exert a strong influence, the younger generation's shift towards personal emotional literacy and more transparent communication suggests an evolving interpretation of wellbeing literacy within this cultural context. This ongoing dialogue between cultural continuity and emerging changes provides a nuanced perspective on the dynamic nature of Javanese culture and its impact on wellbeing.

Understanding Javanese Undergraduates' Wellbeing

Exploring wellbeing literacy among Javanese undergraduate students uncovers a complex interaction between traditional Javanese values (i.e., collectivism, social harmony, respect for hierarchy, and indirect communication: Nadar, 2007) and modern values (i.e., individualism, equality and egalitarianism: Davis & Williamson, 2022; Geertz, 1976) shaping the understanding of wellbeing. Refined themes from the data and the frequency of specific words in their responses provide valuable insights into the priorities and concerns influencing their perceptions of wellbeing.

Terms like *bahagia* (happiness), *damai* (peace), and *tenang* (calm) were the most frequently mentioned in their responses. These terms highlight how deeply ingrained the values of emotional regulation and harmony are within the Javanese cultural context. The emphasis on emotional states such as happiness, peace, and calmness underscores these students' importance of maintaining emotional stability. These findings align with the cultural principle of *rukun*, which emphasises avoiding conflict and maintaining *suwung* as vital components of wellbeing (Casmini, 2020; Nadar, 2007). The pursuit of emotional balance reflects the broader cultural aspiration for a harmonious life, personally and within the wider community. This focus on emotional wellbeing reflects a cultural continuity where traditional values still play a critical role in shaping the younger generation's understanding of wellbeing.

Another key theme in understanding Javanese undergraduates' wellbeing literacy is the importance of *sehat* (health) and *mapan* (individual economic security). In Javanese culture, wellbeing is viewed as the balance between physical, mental, and spiritual health. The concept of *sehat* (health) often encompasses not just the absence of illness but also the state of overall balance and harmony in life. Physical health is seen as foundational for achieving this harmony, as it influences mental clarity and emotional stability. The body is considered a vessel through which spiritual balance can be achieved (Chan et al., 2014), making the care of one's physical self an important aspect of maintaining wellbeing. For example, practices like *puasa* (fasting) are believed to cleanse both body and soul. While traditionally, economic stability has been associated with fulfilling familial and communal responsibilities (Nadar, 2007), the students' emphasis on financial independence indicates a shift towards a more individualised understanding of wellbeing. This reflects the broader economic realities and uncertainties young people face today, where financial stability is increasingly seen as essential for personal wellbeing.

The concern with economic security among Javanese youth highlights a tension between traditional expectations of communal responsibility and modern aspirations for individual financial autonomy (Ardyansyah, 2024). This tension suggests that the students are negotiating a new understanding of wellbeing that balances these competing demands, integrating the need for personal economic security with the cultural importance of supporting one's family and community. Javanese culture emphasises communal responsibility, where supporting family and community is paramount (Jatmikowati, 2024).

While themes such as *penak* (environmental comfort) and *hormat* (interpersonal respect) were mentioned less frequently, their significance in the Javanese cultural context should not be underestimated. Environmental comfort, though not explicitly highlighted, plays a role in creating a sense of physical and emotional security, which is foundational to wellbeing (Otto et al., 2022). Similarly, interpersonal respect, a core value in Javanese culture, is often implicitly understood as crucial for maintaining social harmony and fostering peaceful relationships. The lower frequency of these themes in the students' responses may suggest that they are so deeply ingrained in the cultural fabric that they are taken for granted rather than consciously articulated as separate components of wellbeing. Respect for hierarchy and maintaining harmonious social interactions are embedded in the cultural norms that guide daily life (Nadar, 2007), reinforcing the importance of these values even when they are not overtly expressed.

The distribution of themes in the students' responses reveals a dialectical relationship between traditional Javanese values and contemporary understandings of wellbeing. While emotional wellbeing and social harmony remain central, reflecting enduring cultural values, there is also a growing recognition of economic security as a critical component of wellbeing. This suggests that Javanese youth are engaged in the process of negotiating between maintaining cultural traditions and adapting to globalisation.

Javanese Undergraduates' Wellbeing Practices

Expressing wellbeing is a key component of wellbeing literacy, as it reveals how individuals communicate their emotional and psychological states. This study found that Indonesian youth express their wellbeing in various ways: through emotional expressions like crying, laughing, and smiling; through positive attitudes such as gratitude and mindfulness; and through behavioural expressions like pursuing hobbies, practising self-care, helping others, engaging in charity, and participating in spiritual activities.

The wellbeing of Indonesian youth, encompassing these emotional, attitudinal, and behavioural expressions, is deeply influenced by cultural values, religious practices, and social expectations. These expressions reflect Indonesia's collective approach to wellbeing, where emotional expression plays a vital role in social interactions and personal identity (Sulistyo & Sunarmi, 2021). Crying, laughing, and smiling are valued in fostering social bonds within the collective culture. Additionally, gratitude and mindfulness, integral to Indonesian cultural and religious practices – especially in Islam and traditional Javanese spirituality – promote present-moment awareness and appreciation (Casmini, 2020). This is reflected in how the word '*alhamdulillah*' (all things are for the almighty God) is commonly uttered by Indonesians regardless of their religions (Hutabarat, 2023). These practices of contentment facilitate the enhancement of wellbeing by encouraging a positive outlook on life and aligning young people with teachings that advocate for contentment and emotional balance (Snodgrass et al., 2017).

Community-oriented behaviours, such as helping others, participating in charity, and engaging in spiritual activities, are encouraged by norms that emphasise communal welfare and spiritual connections. These behaviours are not merely personal choices but also reflections of societal expectations (Nadar, 2007), allowing individuals to express and enhance their wellbeing by fulfilling social and spiritual duties.

Moreover, Indonesian youth maintain wellbeing primarily through hobbies, self-care, *olahraga* (exercises), and *silaturahmi* (maintaining good social relationships). These younger generations, exposed to diverse influences, including Western mental health concepts, engage in fitness routines, mindfulness practices, or modern hobbies like video games and social media – activities that older generations might not have valued or accessed (Zhu, 2023). In contrast, Javanese elders often rely on traditional practices rooted in cultural and spiritual heritage, such as meditation, praying, or rituals, to maintain their wellbeing (Maulana et al., 2018). Collectively, these findings illustrate a holistic approach to wellbeing among Javanese youth, integrating emotional management, physical health, social connections, leisure, and a mindset of gratitude.

Moreover, a central tenet of this holistic approach is the role of the family unit, which emerges as the most frequent setting for expressing wellbeing. This research finding reveals that familial relationships are the most dominant category among respondents, underscoring the profound cultural significance of family ties in shaping wellbeing (Maulana et al., 2018). This strong sense of belonging, support, and identity within the family unit is complemented by the importance of friends and close social circles to express wellbeing. The value placed on these social support networks highlights the crucial role of interpersonal connections, both within and beyond the immediate family, in fostering emotional stability and a sense of community.

Interestingly, the inclusion of *Tuhan* (God) in the responses, even if mentioned by a smaller number of individuals, indicates that spiritual expression is an important dimension of their wellbeing for some. This reflects the role of faith and spiritual practices in providing comfort, purpose, and a sense of connection to something greater than oneself, contributing to overall wellbeing (Casmini, 2020; Maulana et al., 2018). Together, these findings illustrate a multifaceted approach to wellbeing, where family, social relationships, and spirituality play significant roles in how individuals perceive and maintain their wellbeing.

Further reinforcing these cultural values, the research highlights the significance of parental guidance, religious teachings, books and articles, and the internet as primary sources for maintaining wellbeing. These sources underscore the deep-rooted values of *guru* (teachers) and *ajaran* (teachings) in Javanese culture (Casmini, 2020). Parental advice is highly esteemed, with parents serving as primary educators and moral guides, transmitting wisdom and cultural values across generations. Religious teachings offer a spiritual framework that shapes moral conduct and wellbeing, while respect for written knowledge is evident in the role of books and articles. The internet provides access to diverse information, making it a valuable resource.

Additionally, moderately important sources such as observations, experiences, conversations with friends, and academic sources align with Javanese cultural practices. The value of *ngrasani* (discussing and reflecting) is seen in the role of conversations with friends in shaping wellbeing (Casmini, 2020). In a culture that favours indirect communication (Nadar, 2007), these discussions facilitate shared understanding and learning. Observations and personal experiences, embodying the concept of *niteni* (paying close attention), are crucial, where understanding derives from careful observation of life's events (Casmini, 2020). While academic sources are considered secondary, they offer a structured understanding that complements lived experiences.

In contrast, the lower emphasis on seminars, social media, and personal reflection underscores a traditional Javanese approach to learning. Seminars may seem too formal or disconnected from daily life, and social media is often perceived as transient and less reliable. Personal reflection, though valued, is less prioritised in a culture that favours collective wisdom over individual introspection. These findings indicate that in the Javanese context, wellbeing is anchored in culturally revered knowledge sources, where elder wisdom, religious teachings, and trusted written materials are paramount. At the same time, modern and individualistic methods are more cautiously adopted. The dynamics of Javanese wellbeing are described in Table 24.1.

TABLE 24.1 Wellbeing literacy among Javanese undergraduates

Core component of wellbeing	*How to express and maintain*	*With whom to express wellbeing*
• *Rukun* • *Suwung* • Communal financial responsibility • Respect for hierarchy	• Crying • Laughing • Smiling • Gratitude (Saying *Alhamdulillah*) • Mindfulness • Helping others • Engaging charity • Participating in spiritual activities	• Family • Friends and close circle • *Tuhan*
↓	↓	
Emergent themes • *Mapan*	**Emergent themes** • Hobbies • Self-care	

Conclusion

Several key insights emerge based on the detailed exploration of wellbeing literacy among Javanese youth. This chapter highlights the intricate interplay between traditional Javanese cultural values and modern influences, demonstrating how these factors shape the understanding and expression of wellbeing among younger generations. Happiness, emotional stability, and security are central components of wellbeing, deeply interconnected with Javanese cultural values such as *rukun* and *suwung*.

Furthermore, family and social relationships significantly shape emotional and psychological wellbeing. The strong emphasis on maintaining familial ties and close social networks reflects the collective nature of Javanese society, where wellbeing is a personal pursuit and a communal responsibility. Additionally, spirituality remains an important dimension of wellbeing, providing comfort, purpose, and a connection to something greater.

This chapter highlights a generational shift in wellbeing practices, with younger Javanese incorporating modern activities like fitness routines and mindfulness, influenced by global mental health trends. This shift shows an adaptation to contemporary challenges while maintaining traditional cultural values. Understanding wellbeing literacy among young Javanese is crucial for personal and societal growth, revealing how they blend traditional principles with contemporary influences. Examining younger versus older generations' wellbeing reveals evolving cultural norms, stress management techniques, and mental health awareness. These insights highlight generational divides and opportunities for cross-generational education, which can strengthen community bonds, improve mental health outcomes, and inform culturally sensitive policies that respect heritage and progress.

Understanding the wellbeing literacy of Javanese youth is essential for designing effective, culturally relevant educational and mental health programs. Incorporating Javanese values ensures these programs resonate with young people, fostering belonging and identity and making the programs meaningful. This literacy promotes social cohesion by encouraging cooperation and collective wellbeing, empowering youth to recognise their potential, build resilience, and navigate challenges. Additionally, it provides a foundation for community-based initiatives tailored to Javanese society's specific needs and values, leading to sustainable and impactful youth development and mental health outcomes.

References

Alzahra, S., Safitri, D., & Sujarwo (2024). Peran Tradisi Wetonan dalam Menjaga Identitas Budaya Masyarakat Adat Jawa. *Mutiara: Jurnal Ilmiah Multidisiplin Indonesia*, *2*(2), 92–101. https://doi.org/10.61404/jimi.v2i2.206

Ardyansyah, A. F. (2024). *Perception and Practices of Personal Financial Management Among Generation Z in Indonesia*. *3*(12). https://doi.org/10.59141/jrssem.v3i12.687

Casmini (2020). *Kepribadian sehat ala orang jawa*. Kurnia Kalam Semesta.

Chan, C., Ho, P. S. Y., & Chow, E. (2014, February). A body-mind-spirit model in health: An Eastern approach. In *Social Work Health and Mental Health: Practice, Research, and Programs* (pp. 261–282). https://doi.org/10.1093/oso/9780195168785.003.0045

Damami, M. (2002). *Makna Agama dalam Masyarakat Jawa*. LESFI.

Davis, L. S., & Williamson, C. R. (2022). Individualism and women's economic rights. *Journal of Economic Behavior & Organization*, *198*, 579–597. https://doi.org/10.1016/j.jebo.2022.04.011

Gee, J., & Gee, J. P. (2015). Social linguistics and literacies ideology in discourses fifth edition. In *Social linguistics and literacies ideology in discourses* (3rd ed.). Routledge. https://doi.org/10.4324/9780203944806

Geertz, C. (1976). *The religion of Java*. University of Chicago Press.

Haniah, S., Firdaus, F., & Amin, S. (2024). Cultural transformation in Indonesian urban society: A case study of the millennial generation. *Daengku: Journal of Humanities and Social Sciences Innovation*, *4*(3), 516–522. https://doi.org/10.35877/454ri.daengku2593

Hofstede, G. (1986). Cultural differences in teaching and learning. *International Journal of Intercultural Relations*, *10*(3), 301–320. https://doi.org/10.1016/0147-1767(86)90015-5

Hutabarat, F. (2023). Navigating diversity: Exploring religious pluralism and social harmony in Indonesian society. *European Journal of Theology and Philosophy*, *3*(6), 6–13. https://doi.org/10.24018/theology.2023.3.6.125

Jatmikowati, S. H. (2024). Unveiling the lived experiences of Western Indonesian students in Javan higher education Institutions: A phenomenological exploration. *Public Administration Journal*, *14*(1), 18–28. https://doi.org/10.31289/jap.v14i1.11358

Khadafi, W., & Harahap, R. H. (2024). Caring for sekaten traditions, caring for Indonesia: Preserving local cultural values in the midst of foreign cultural exposure. *Tradition and Modernity of Humanity*, *4*(2), 32–35. https://doi.org/10.32734/tmh.v4i2.17100

Magnis-Suseno, F. M. (2001). *Etika Jawa: Sebuah analisa falsafi tentang kebijaksanaan hidup Jawa* (2nd ed.). PT Gramedia Pustaka Utama.

Maulana, H., Obst, P., & Khawaja, N. (2018). Indonesian Perspective of wellbeing: A qualitative study. *Qualitative Report*, *23*(12), 3136–3152. https://doi.org/10.46743/2160-3715/2018.3508

Mazzocchi, F. (2006). Traditional knowledge and Western science. *EMBO Reports*, *7*, 463–466. https://doi.org/doi:10.1038/sj.embor.7400693

Nadar, F. (2007). The prominent characteristics of Javanese culture and their reflections in language use. *Humaniora*, *19*(2), 168–174. https://media.neliti.com/media/publications/11651-ID-the-prominent-characteristics-of-javanese-culture-and-their-reflections-in-langu.pdf

Nursanti, E., Arimi, S., & Wijayanti, N. (2024). Face and politeness in Javanese multilingual interaction. *Issues in Language Studies*, *13*(1), 181–197. https://doi.org/10.33736/ils.5690.2024

Oades, L. G., Baker, L. M., Francis, J. J., & Taylor, J. A. (2021a). Wellbeing literacy and positive education. In *The Palgrave handbook of positive education* (pp. 645–674). Palgrave Macmillan. https://doi.org/10.1007/978-3-030-64537-3_25

Oades, L. G., Hou, H., Francis, J. J., Baker, L. M., & Huang, L. (2022). Well-being literacy: Language use as a way to contextualize the process of positive education. *Handbook of positive psychology in schools: Supporting process and practice*, 91–103. https://doi.org/10.4324/9781003013778-9

Oades, L. G., Jarden, A., Hou, H., Ozturk, C., Williams, P., Slemp, G. R., & Huang, L. (2021b). Wellbeing literacy: A capability model for wellbeing science and practice. *International Journal of Environmental Research and Public Health*, *18*(2), 1–12. https://doi.org/10.3390/ijerph18020719

Oades, L. G., Ozturk, C., Hou, H., & Slemp, G. R. (2020). Wellbeing literacy: A language-use capability relevant to wellbeing outcomes of positive psychology interventions. *Journal of Positive Psychology*, *15*(5), 696–700. https://doi.org/10.1080/17439760.2020.1789711

Otto, O. V., Redkin, A. G., & Esimova, D. D. (2022). Ecological comfort of the urban environment on the example of the City of Barnaul. *Siberian Journal of Life Sciences and Agriculture*, *14*(2), 282–295. https://doi.org/10.12731/2658-6649-2022-14-2-282-295

Setiyowati, N. (2017). "Suwung": Pola Penyelesaian Masalah Kaum Sufi Suku Jawa Di Kota Malang. *Jurnal Psikologi Ulayat*, *3*(2), 109. https://doi.org/10.24854/jpu22016-66

Snodgrass, J. G., Lacy, M. G., & Upadhyay, C. (2017). Developing culturally sensitive affect scales for global mental health research and practice: Emotional balance, not named syndromes, in Indian Adivasi subjective well-being. *Social Science & Medicine*, *187*, 174–183. https://doi.org/10.1016/j.socscimed.2017.06.037

Subandi, M. A. (2015). Bangkit: The processes of recovery from first episode psychosis in Java. *Culture, Medicine, and Psychiatry*, *39*(4), 597–613. https://doi.org/10.1007/s11013-015-9427-x

Sulistyo, E. T., & Sunarmi (2021). Emotional intelligence and balanced personality in Javanese cultural understanding. *Palarch's Journal Of Archaeology Of Egypt/*

Egyptology, *18*(4), 3344–3359. https://archives.palarch.nl/index.php/jae/article/view/6827

Waston, W., Maksum, M. N. R., Shobahiya, M., Wiranto, E. B., Rizka, R., & Ali, M. (2024). Culture, religion, and harmony: The struggle for roles in diversity in Indonesia. *Revista De Gestão Social e Ambiental*, *18*(3), e05225. https://doi.org/10.24857/rgsa.v18n3-099

Woodward, M. R. (2004). *Islam Jawa ; Kesalehan Normatif versus Kebatinan*. LKiS.

Yogiswari, K., & Murtiningsih, S (2019). Tinjauan Metafisika Anton Bakker Dalam Prinsip Hidup Orang Jawa Kawruh Begja. *Jurnal Filsafat Indonesia*, *1*(3), 112. https://doi.org/10.23887/jfi.v1i3.16135

Ysmailova, R., Kedeybayeva, Z., Barynbaeva, A., Seidaliyeva, M., & Yrazakov, D. (2020). The role of spirituality in the development of society. *E3S Web of Conferences*, *210*. https://doi.org/10.1051/e3sconf/202021017035

Zhu, A. (2023). Shaping the future: Navigating youth ideology and mental health in a digital age. *International Journal of Education and Humanities*, *11*(3), 24–27. https://doi.org/10.54097/ijeh.v11i3.14445

25

CULTIVATING REGENERATIVE SYSTEMS OF WELLBEING AND WELLBEING LITERACY

Jessica A. Taylor and Cass Spong

Introduction

Cultivating a System of Wellbeing (SoW) is introduced as an emergent, regenerative framework for understanding and implementing approaches to wellbeing in our organisations and schools. It provides an alternative lens for co-creating environments that support systemic wellbeing, which goes beyond individual-level wellbeing approaches that simply target health or happiness. An SoW focuses on cultivating collective action and activating regenerative capabilities – systems awareness and wellbeing literacy – and in the context of this practical example, the currently identified regenerative conditions – shared higher purpose, reciprocity, authentic relationships, and response-ability – with the intention of co-creating thriving, regenerative systems. Workplace and educational wellbeing have become key priorities in recent years, with numerous initiatives focused on mental health, resilience, and organisational culture. Wellbeing science offers valuable insights into how emotions, values, circumstances, and strengths influence people's ability to thrive in these environments (Alexandrova, 2017; Curren et al., 2024). However, while the field offers a variety of programs, models and tools for understanding wellbeing, many approaches tend to prioritise individual-level applications, and isolate specific components, such as stress management or leadership development. This individualistic and fragmented view neglects the interconnectedness of components within systems, and the way systems then interact, shape and influence the emergence of wellbeing in more holistic and systemic ways (Kern & Taylor, 2021; Kern et al., 2020). We believe this narrowed focus misses the broader dynamics in workplaces and schools – dynamics that can't be solved by individual-level interventions alone.

Meanwhile, traditional industrial-era thinking continues to influence organisational structures and individual behaviours, often reducing organisations and

DOI: 10.4324/9781003644293-25

schools to mechanistic, linear systems. Wellbeing in such contexts is treated as a series of isolated interventions, placing responsibility on individuals rather than addressing systemic and structural forces that shape collective wellbeing (Steger, 2024). While such initiatives may yield short-term improvements, they often fail to address the deeper structural conditions that are necessary for long-term flourishing (Boell et al., 2025; McLeod, 2019; Senge, 1997; Senge et al., 2012). With increasing disengagement, burnout, and ill-being, it becomes apparent that industrial-era structures may unintentionally foster environments that undermine wellbeing (Gallup, 2024; Lemon & Turner, 2024). To address this complexity, this chapter advocates for a change in thinking, viewing organisations and schools as living, dynamic systems capable of supporting collective systemic wellbeing when intentionally cultivated.

Through a practice-oriented reimagining, we introduce the emerging theoretical framework of an SoW, alongside the proposed regenerative capabilities and conditions essential for its cultivation. Drawing on our work as *Systems-Awareness* researchers, educators, and practitioners, we explore a lived example of fostering an SoW within an Australian school context. Using an adapted World Café format – a Wellbeing Café – we show how the regenerative capability of wellbeing literacy, supported by systems awareness, can activate towards the creation of thriving regenerative environments. We further highlight how activating these capabilities synergistically fosters the proposed regenerative conditions. Through this process, we explore how regenerative structures rooted in reciprocity, authentic relationships, shared purpose, response-ability, wellbeing literacy, and systems awareness, can replace outdated mechanistic models. Together, these capabilities and conditions nurture the collective systemic wellbeing necessary for cultivating an SoW in our organisations, schools, and beyond.

A System of Wellbeing

Many of today's challenges – especially those related to the wellbeing of people and the planet – are rooted in complex, interconnected ecological and social systems (Bateson, 2000; Capra, 1996; Meadows, 2008; Senge et al., 2019). However, in addressing these challenges, we often fall back on outdated Industrial Revolution-era paradigms that treat problems as isolated and controllable, rather than part of a larger, dynamic whole. This mechanical, linear mindset limits our ability to navigate the complexity of these issues (Capra, 2014; Scharmer, 2016; Senge, 1997). An SoW offers a paradigm shift, replacing fragmented, individualistic models with a holistic vision of wellbeing that values interconnectedness, interdependence, and regeneration (Bateson, 2000; Meadows, 2008; Senge et al., 2015; Steger, 2024).

An SoW, as an integrative, regenerative framework, focuses on cultivating capabilities and conditions that enable thriving – not just for individuals but also for the broader communities and organisations they are part of. It does this by activating and holding space for the dynamics of these capabilities and conditions, which become the "currency" of a "gift-ecosystem," generating renewable resources that grow with each interaction (Kimmerer, 2024). By nurturing these capabilities and conditions, an SoW seeks to optimise wellbeing across all system aspects – people, practice, policy, and place – while ensuring regeneration and vitality for both current and future generations. Wellbeing, within this framework, is seen as an evolving process rather than a fixed outcome, activated through the regenerative capabilities, wellbeing literacy and systems awareness, and the regenerative conditions - authentic relationships, reciprocity, response-ability, and shared higher purpose. The regenerative aspect refers to the system's ability to adapt, evolve, and restore balance and vitality, in ways that meet the needs of the system to thrive (Allen, 2019; Kimmerer, 2024). In this context, wellbeing emerges as a dynamic, relational process – shaped by the interaction of regenerative capabilities and conditions that work synergistically, continuously adapting to changing circumstances through ongoing collective engagement (Gibbons, 2020).

Regenerative Capabilities and Conditions to Support an SoW

Cultivating an SoW requires more than implementing specific programs; it demands a shift in the collective consciousness and the development of key capabilities and conditions that enable long-term transformation (Spong & O'Keefe, 2022). By integrating a regenerative lens, we can challenge industrial-era mindsets and embrace a process of continuous renewal and adaptation (Gibbons, 2020). This ensures that wellbeing is not a fixed outcome but an emergent quality, evolving with the system's changing needs (Bateson, 2022; Quinn, 2015; Senge et al., 2015). Drawing from regenerative agriculture, regeneration goes beyond maintaining status quo or replenishing what is lost; it focuses on enhancing systems for ongoing resilience and growth (Gibbons, 2020; Giller et al., 2021). This principle mirrors human systems, suggesting that regenerative practices in organisations and schools reflect the same natural processes (Steger, 2024; Winton, 2010). In an SoW, regeneration occurs through small, accumulative interactions – how we show up, relate, co-create meaning, and respond to the system's evolving needs (Winton, 2010).

Regenerative capabilities and conditions lay the foundation for nurturing an SoW that transcends industrial-era limitations. When activated together, these regenerative elements work synergistically enhancing each other's effectiveness in creating dynamic interactions that support adaptive systems and foster collective flourishing (Allen, 2019; Gibbons, 2020; Kimmerer, 2024). In the context of an SoW, this means that regenerative capabilities – wellbeing literacy and systems awareness – and conditions – reciprocity, authentic relationships, response-ability, and shared higher purpose – work in tandem, amplifying each other to produce a more holistic and impactful flourishing of the SoW. The following section explores these regenerative capabilities and conditions in detail, and highlights how their interconnectedness enables the cultivation of an SoW, as illustrated in Figure 25.1.

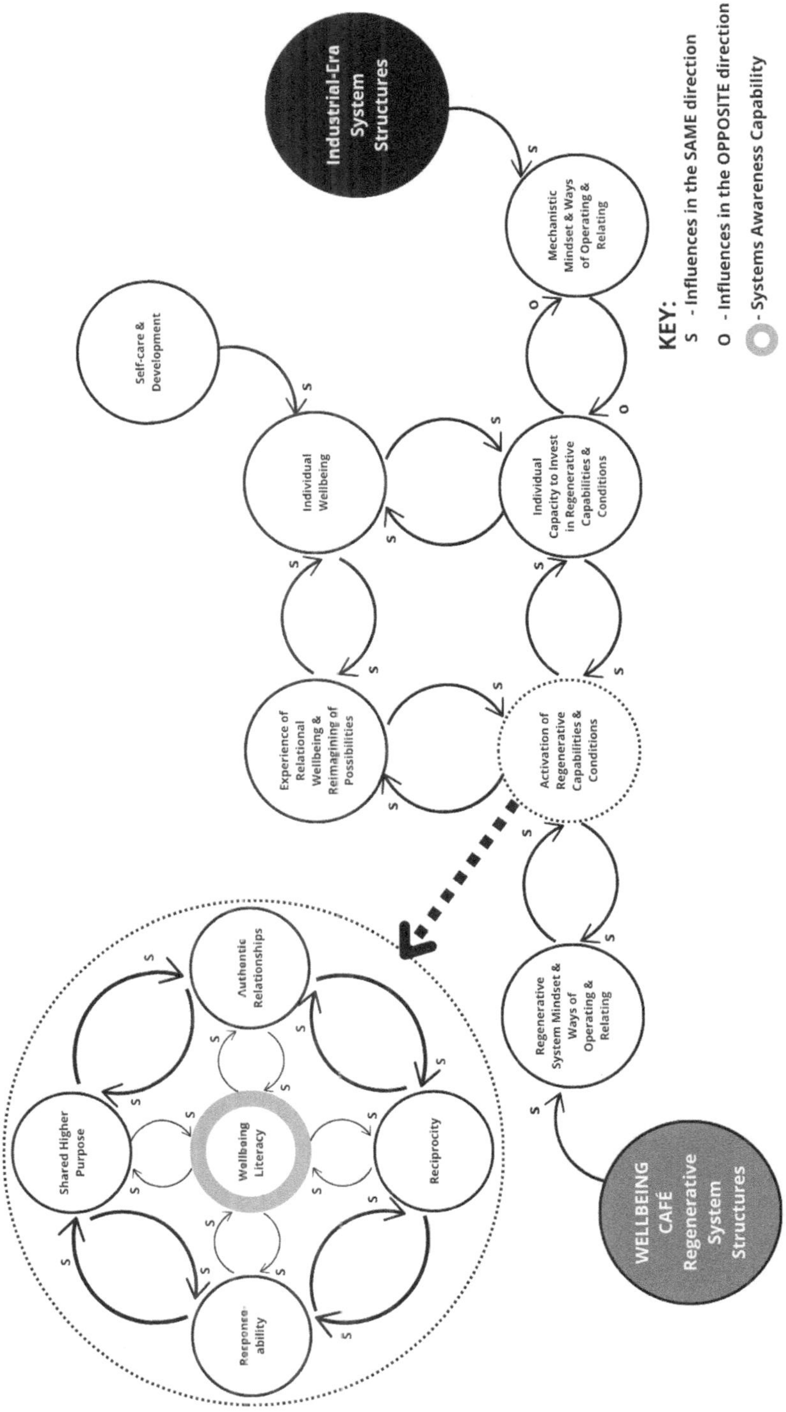

FIGURE 25.1 Activation of regenerative capabilities and conditions to enable a system of wellbeing.

Regenerative Capabilities

Regenerative capabilities – a blend of skills, knowledge, attitudes, behaviours, and capacity – are key to cultivating a SoW, enabling individuals and organisations to adapt and thrive in dynamic environments (Oades et al., 2021). These capabilities support resilience, self-renewal, and long-term vitality by creating conditions for continuous growth and transformation (Allen, 2019; Capra, 2014; Meadows, 2008; Scharmer, 2016). In the context of the SoW framework, key regenerative capabilities include Wellbeing Literacy, the intentional use of language *about* and *for* wellbeing (Oades et al., 2021) and Systems Awareness, the ability to perceive and respond to the interconnectedness of the systems we inhabit (Senge et al., 2015; Senge et al., 2019). Together, these capabilities empower individuals and communities to become agents of positive change, working within adaptive, resilient systems that align with regeneration and collective systemic wellbeing.

Systems Awareness as a Regenerative Capability

Systems awareness enables individuals and groups to perceive the interconnections and interdependencies within a system (Senge et al., 2019), helping to navigate and respond to complex challenges in adaptive, regenerative ways. By building awareness of interconnections, systems awareness helps address complex challenges and shift beyond the narrow perspectives that contribute to these problems (Fullan, 2011; Meadows, 2008; Senge, 1997). Systems thinking, as a way to enhance the practice of systems awareness, offers a powerful lens to understand how elements within an organisation or community are interconnected and interdependent. This combined perspective helps us see the patterns and dynamics that emerge from these interactions, revealing opportunities to address systemic issues in more holistic and regenerative ways (Lawrence, 2021; Meadows, 2008; Senge et al., 2019). Key concepts from systems thinking, such as the dynamic nature of living systems, and tools for "seeing" in systems, are vital for cultivating an SoW. They allow us to move beyond isolated actions, recognising broader patterns that shape the wellbeing of individuals and groups across workplaces and schools (Boell et al., 2025; Senge et al., 2012). Systems thinking and systems awareness foster deeper insight into nurturing wellbeing across all parts of the system, including the dynamics that can shape and influence the emergence of wellbeing.

By activating systems awareness, we deepen engagement with systems from an embodied and relational perspective. A practice of systems awareness integrates systems thinking with a heightened awareness of our perceptions, somatic awareness, and relational dynamics within the system (Senge et al., 2019). This practice strengthens the capacity for focused attention, groundedness, compassion, and adaptive response (Bateson, 2022; Senge et al., 2019). Through enabling us to perceive the interconnections and interdependencies within a system, this practice can unfurl new insights from somatic and relational sensing to help better navigate complexity and respond to challenges in more regenerative ways (Boell et al., 2025). As a regenerative capability, systems awareness fosters understanding of how actions ripple through the system, ensuring wellbeing practices align with overall system health and include diverse perspectives. At its heart, systems awareness emphasises the importance of mutual contribution – the idea that the wellbeing of a system is nurtured through ongoing learning, collective engagement, and interconnectedness, rather than isolated efforts (Bateson, 2022; Winton, 2010). By developing systems awareness, individuals and groups within schools and organisations are better equipped to adapt to changing circumstances and engage with the complexity of the system, while remaining open to emergent possibilities.

Wellbeing Literacy as a Regenerative Capability

Wellbeing Literacy as a regenerative capability involves the mindful and intentional use of language to shape, transform, and nurture experiences of wellbeing both individually and collectively (Oades et al., 2021). Language plays a central role in creating meaning and influencing how we engage with ourselves, others, and our environments. It impacts not only our perceptions and actions but also the very emergence of wellbeing within systems such as workplaces and schools (Oades et al., 2021). Through language, we can consciously foster a culture of wellbeing, as it facilitates deeper connections between mind, body, and environment, making it a powerful tool in the cultivation of regenerative, thriving systems (Brooks et al., 2017). Wellbeing literacy consists of five key components (Oades et al., 2021):

- **Words and vocabulary:** The ability to understand and describe experiences of wellbeing through appropriate language.
- **Comprehension:** Comprehending and engaging with wellbeing-related texts and ideas in a meaningful way.
- **Composition:** The creation and application of language to enact wellbeing values, beliefs, and actions within an enabling environment.

- **Context Sensitivity:** Adapting language to diverse contexts and being attuned to emerging relational dynamics, signalling when intervention or action is needed to promote wellbeing.
- **Intentional Action:** The conscious choice to align language, knowledge, and behaviour to support the emergence of individual, collective, and planetary wellbeing.

In the context of an SoW, when wellbeing literacy engages synergistically alongside systems awareness, it moves beyond merely the cognitive skills required to engage in language. Here, wellbeing literacy becomes a relational and embodied practice that uses language to foster adaptive, regenerative actions, generating systems that both shape, and support wellbeing. It shapes how individuals engage in and respond to subtle cues within the system – whether these cues are interpersonal, somatic, or environmental (Brooks et al., 2017; Senge et al., 2019). For example, a regenerative leader with strong wellbeing literacy might sense, even before a colleague articulates a concern, the relational and somatic dynamics at play and respond with empathy and intention. Therefore, as a regenerative capability, wellbeing literacy supports the real-time cultivation of wellbeing by enabling dynamic, interconnected interactions between language, communication, and meaning-making. When paired with systems awareness, wellbeing literacy evolves from a cognitive tool into a regenerative practice that nurtures and sustains a thriving SoW. It is through this continuous interplay of language, awareness, and relational dynamics that wellbeing literacy can also amplify the regenerative conditions.

Regenerative Conditions

Regenerative conditions are the environmental, relational, and organisational qualities that create fertile ground for the emergence and ongoing cultivation of wellbeing (Kimmerer, 2024). These conditions are dynamic, not static, and foster regeneration at every level – from individuals to communities to the broader ecological context. When activated, they enable thriving, resilient systems that evolve in response to changing circumstances (Capra, 1996; Kimmerer, 2024). The regenerative conditions of reciprocity, response-ability, authentic relationships, and shared higher purpose are identified as foundational elements within this emergent framework for nurturing an SoW. These conditions catalyse a regenerative approach to human and organisational systems, facilitating environments where adaptation, collaboration, and continuous renewal can occur (Allen, 2019; Stengel, 2023). When activated, they enable systems to evolve and thrive, supporting collective and mutual flourishing (Kimmerer, 2024). Table 25.1 further elaborates on each regenerative condition, outlining its key attributes and illustrating regenerative processes and practices associated with each.

TABLE 25.1 Proposed regenerative conditions in cultivating a system of wellbeing

Regenerative condition	*Description*	*Examples of conditions in regenerative ecosystems*
Shared Higher Purpose	Shared higher purpose plays a vital role as a unifying force helping to create a regenerative social field of consciousness that nurtures cohesion, motivation, and belonging for the people in an organisation (Allen, 2019; Boell et al., 2025). Connecting the tasks we do in our roles to the purpose and value we are collectively contributing towards, helps people organise around and align with an organisation's goals (Senge et al., 2012). The work of cultivating the condition of shared higher purpose requires an ongoing process of shared cultural meaning-making which happens through our shared conversations and continuous awareness of, and participation in influencing the visible, and invisible dynamics (Winton, 2010). For a shared higher purpose to be effective it must resonate deeply with members of the organisation, and in doing so can shift human energy into life-giving energy (Allen, 2019).	A shared higher purpose creates synergy, where the actions of individuals working towards a common goal are more powerful than the sum of individual efforts (Allen, 2019; Meadows, 2008; Senge, 1997). This is akin to the idea of synergistic relationships in regenerative ecosystems, where collaboration across different elements enhances the whole (Gibbons, 2020).
Authentic Relationships	Cultivating authentic relationships is enabled through creating space for people to feel safe to show up as their authentic selves. This means inviting diversity and sameness, and creating conditions for all people to feel seen, heard, and valued. When people show up in their organisational roles and hierarchical positions, they often feel pressure to take on an in-authentic persona, which acts as a survival strategy to feel safe (Allen, 2019). This is not to say that authority and hierarchy are inherently bad, but instead their usefulness in our systems needs to be integrated so the system has balance, and the culture is not dominated by a "power-over" dynamic (Winton, 2010). When people are treated as unique individuals with unique value to contribute, it becomes possible to mitigate and transcend a limiting "power over" dynamic. Instead, authentic relationships recognise the value of "power-with" others, bringing a positive energy to the organisation (Allen, 2019; Lencioni, 2012; Quinn, 2015).	Just as regenerative ecosystems rely on diverse and interconnected relationships between plants, animals, and the environment to maintain their resilience, human wellbeing is strengthened by authentic connections that support individual and collective regeneration (Capra, 1996). In regenerative ecosystems, vitality and resilience stem from interdependence – the relationship between components sustains and nourishes the whole (Gibbons, 2020). In human systems, authentic relationships foster psychological and emotional vitality, enabling individuals and communities to exercise resilience in time of challenge and adapt to changes (Allen, 2019).

(*Continued*)

TABLE 25.1 (Continued)

Regenerative condition	*Description*	*Examples of conditions in regenerative ecosystems*
Reciprocity	Reciprocity between people in organisations builds both respect and trust, enabling organisational collaboration and innovation. Playing a key role in the development and continuation of relationships, reciprocity is the ongoing and intentional practice of mutual and beneficial exchange of things with other people, non-human beings, and our planet (Karisto, 2017; Kimmerer, 2024). Responding to positive actions with another's positive actions creates a reinforcing, regenerative cycle of social harmony (Allen, 2019; Karisto, 2017). Creating reciprocal spaces for people to contribute in a way that has mutual benefit unleashes both positive energy and creativity, transforming our organisational work to productive and enjoyable experiences, sowing, supplementing, and nourishing beneficial ripple effects across the organisational culture (Allen, 2019).	Regenerative ecosystems are often cyclical, with inputs and outputs flowing in a balanced way (Gibbons, 2020; Giller et al., 2021). Reciprocity in human systems mirrors this flow, ensuring that support is reciprocal, not one-sided. This creates a continuous loop of regeneration – each participant gives and receives in ways that benefit the whole. In nature, mutualistic relationships like those between pollinators and plants, represent reciprocity. These relationships allow for mutual flourishing, much as reciprocal human relationships sustain psychological and emotional health in wellbeing systems (Allen, 2019; Kimmerer, 2024).
Response-ability	Response-ability acknowledges living as an interconnected being and is an activation of our ability to respond in ways that promote flourishing for all (Stengel, 2023). As such, response-ability is linked to our relational interactions, group functioning, decision-making, and supports the creation of our institutional structures (Stengel, 2023). Response-ability is the process of sensing into our ability of being and becoming better at responding to situations in a way that creates a regenerative space for future response and responsiveness. When people can exercise response-ability in recognising their own role as a self-aware participant in the emergence of change, we are creating pathways to greater flourishing in our organisations (Lawrence, 2021; Stengel, 2023).	Regenerative ecosystems rely on the ability to respond to change. They are not static but evolve in response to environmental shifts, disturbances, and feedback (Capra, 2014; Meadows, 2008). Response-ability mirrors this, as it requires individuals and systems to adapt, learn, and act in ways that restore balance when faced with disruptions. Just as regenerative ecosystems can self-heal in response to damage, response-ability allows humans to act with foresight, learn from mistakes, and take corrective action that leads to restoration and renewal (Kimmerer, 2024; Stengel, 2023).

Wellbeing Café – Real-Life Examples of Cultivating a System of Wellbeing

Exploring a case study from an Australian school setting, the following sections illustrate how wellbeing literacy as a regenerative capability, supports the activation and development of other regenerative conditions, bringing the SoW framework to life in practice. The Wellbeing Café is a practical application of this framework. It activates regenerative capabilities and conditions by engaging participants in meaningful conversations that foster individual and collective wellbeing. Through regenerative practices, the Wellbeing Café creates conditions where wellbeing can emerge, counteracting the mechanistic, fragmented approaches typical of traditional organisational systems (Brown, 2010; Oades et al., 2021). Figure 25.1 is a causal loop diagram illustrating how the design and hosting of the Wellbeing Café activates the regenerative capabilities and conditions, helping to cultivate a shared higher purpose that strengthens relationships, reciprocity, and response-ability. When wellbeing literacy is developed alongside the regenerative conditions, it contributes to a culture of collective responsibility, where individuals and communities co-create environments that nurture the wellbeing of all. This interconnectedness forms a regenerative cycle that supports the dynamic, ongoing emergence of wellbeing within organisations and schools. By understanding these conditions in relation to regenerative practice, we can create environments conducive to collective systemic wellbeing.

The Wellbeing Café Experience

The Wellbeing Café was designed and hosted for a regional co-educational school in Victoria, Australia, encompassing Early Learning (ELC) to Year 12 students. The school's mixed-age structure made it an ideal setting for the case study, involving a diverse group of participants, from teaching staff to business operations personnel. By engaging all staff, the initiative emphasised the collective responsibility in co-creating an SoW. The Wellbeing Café used participatory conversations to bring out collective wisdom for problem-solving and idea generation (Löhr et al., 2020). Participants – 160 staff members – discussed how to cultivate wellbeing, identify barriers, and envision changes to support a regenerative, holistic school environment. This process highlighted wellbeing as a system-wide responsibility, extending beyond the classroom to include all school members.

Wellbeing literacy was key to enabling intentional and mindful language use through this regenerative process (Oades et al., 2021). The structure allowed participants to expand their wellbeing vocabulary, strengthening their understanding of wellbeing as a collective process. Through shared language, staff co-created meaning, identified systemic barriers, and reimagined organisational practices. The conversational rounds facilitated exploration of what a

SoW might look like within the school. Through storytelling and creative idea-sharing, participants not only sparked hope but also began aligning around a shared vision for a thriving, regenerative community. The Wellbeing Café activated the potential for system-wide wellbeing, reinforcing the interconnectedness of individuals and their shared responsibility in nurturing thriving communities (Oades et al., 2020; Senge et al., 2019).

Intentionally Designing for Regenerative Capabilities and Conditions

Intentional design and invitation are critical to the success of any World Café process (Löhr et al., 2020). The Wellbeing Café was intentionally crafted with regenerative system structures that activated the capabilities and conditions, fostering a regenerative mindset and associated ways of operating. These structures, illustrated in Figure 25.1, created the necessary conditions for participants to engage in co-creating a system that nurtures wellbeing for all. Unlike mechanistic systems designed for efficiency, regenerative systems recognise human beings as relational and adaptive, capable of tending to, and enabling flourishing and wellbeing (Allen, 2019; Kimmerer, 2024). Therefore, careful attention was given to the design of the Wellbeing Café's regenerative structures, including the invitation process, space curation, and the integration of wellbeing literacy's five components. Table 25.2 outlines the key design components of the Wellbeing Café. By thoughtfully designing the space, interaction norms, and structures to invite collective wisdom, the Wellbeing Café created a platform for transformative conversations that united participants around a shared higher purpose of wellbeing for all.

Integration of Wellbeing Literacy Five Component Model in the Wellbeing Café Process

The Wellbeing Café highlighted the role of wellbeing literacy in activating and reinforcing regenerative conditions. Over 4500 qualitative data points were collected through open-ended questions which explored what can help or hinder wellbeing in the school context. Participants identified the Wellbeing Café as crucial for recognising existing wellbeing-supportive practices and uncovering future opportunities for collective systemic wellbeing. Many expressed a desire for more regenerative relational practices. A central focus was observing how wellbeing literacy integrated with systems awareness was activated, and how it reinforced the regenerative conditions. Table 25.3 demonstrates the five-component model of wellbeing literacy showing how the regenerative conditions emerged through the Wellbeing Café process.

Through this experience, participants shifted from viewing wellbeing as an isolated program for students to recognising wellbeing as a collective, relational process nurtured by everyone within the system. Qualitative data drawn from focus

TABLE 25.2 Wellbeing café design elements and insights

Table Host Invitation and Initiation	A key element of the Wellbeing Café's success was the careful selection of 32 table hosts, drawn from the school's Wellbeing Executive and open to all staff wishing to play this role. Some participants, such as Business Operations staff, were intentionally invited to ensure diverse participation. Table hosts were asked to embody wellbeing literacy, guiding participants through modified World Café etiquette, rebranded as "Ways of Being." These principles encouraged participants to step outside traditional roles and engage in regenerative patterns of interaction. Hosts played a vital role in nurturing generative conversations and surfacing emerging insights.
Wellbeing Café Ways of Being	The invitation in this design element emphasised connection, deep listening, and meaningful dialogue. Participants and table hosts were encouraged to experiment with "Ways of Being" – a set of behaviours fostering curiosity, safety, and openness. By shifting from professional roles to personal expression, participants engaged more authentically, leading to greater collective awareness and mutual respect. This experimental approach also promoted creativity and collaboration, essential for regenerative dialogue (Allen, 2019).
Space Design and Curation	Recognising the influence of physical space, the Wellbeing Café was intentionally designed to foster authentic connection. Drawing from World Café principles, we moved beyond hierarchical, boardroom settings towards a café-style environment that promoted intimacy, equality, and curiosity. The school's meeting hall was transformed into a warm, inviting space, complete with natural light, wattle flowers on the tables, and uplifting background music. Forty small tables encouraged intimate conversations, with paper tablecloths and markers for notetaking and drawing. The space also featured "Ways of Being" guidelines and identified each table with a specific character strength. These design elements empowered participants to express themselves and engage in meaningful dialogue. Additionally, the design encouraged self-organisation as participants moved between tables, ensuring continuous idea weaving.
Conversation Harvesting	A critical component of the Wellbeing Café was conversation harvesting, which allowed participants to capture and build on each other's insights. Participants recorded key points on post-it notes, which were then placed on a "harvesting wall." This process ensured all voices were heard and allowed collective wisdom to emerge. The post-it notes provided qualitative data that captured key insights and shared ideas, creating an ongoing record of the dialogue.

TABLE 25.3 Five component model of wellbeing literacy integrated with regenerative conditions in the wellbeing café process

	Wellbeing literacy five component model				
	Words and vocabulary	*Comprehending*	*Composing*	*Context sensitivity*	*Intentionality*
Shared Higher Purpose	Through conversation and documentation, the shared language of words associated with wellbeing were surfaced in creating a unifying language and force that nurtures cohesion, motivation and belonging.	Through personal stories of experiences of wellbeing in the system, varied perspectives revealed an array of ways to comprehend experiences of wellbeing. These stories helped connect people's understanding of each other's tasks and roles in co-creation towards the desired future.	A shared meaning making process occurred through inviting imagination and meaningful dialogue which helped surface and make conscious the shared higher purpose of the school as a System of Wellbeing.	By drawing upon the ways of being invitation to "focus on what matters" participants were gently nudged to pay attention to what best serves the group given the context and purpose of each conversation round.	The whole process of the Wellbeing Café was intentionally designed to ignite hope and unite participants in the shared purpose through engagement of everyone in co-creating the desired future.
Authentic Relationships	Encouraging participants to draw upon words and vocabulary that nurture authentic relationships with others.	By drawing upon the Ways of Being invitation to "appreciate diversity of perspective," in listening and understanding each other participants created a container for inclusion that helped build relational wellbeing.	Engaging with the Ways of Being invitation to "speak from both mind and heart" and to "play, doodle, draw - write on tablecloths" participants engaged in playful activity that honoured what was in their minds and hearts, creating a safe environment to show up authentically.	Designing the Wellbeing Café space to look and feel like a café environment (small tables, flowers, snacks, music), people were encouraged to show up as their personal selves and not in an organisational role.	The intentionality of coming together not in an organisational role, and by embracing the Ways of Being created an invitation to have fun and play with new ways of showing up together that strengthens relational connectedness.

(*Continued*)

TABLE 25.3 (Continued)

	Wellbeing literacy five component model				
	Words and vocabulary	*Comprehending*	*Composing*	*Context sensitivity*	*Intentionality*
Reciprocity	Words such as trust, creativity and innovation as ways of describing wellbeing, contributed to building reciprocal exchanges in conversation.	Through listening to the different stories, and in the process of collective meaning making, participants were able to comprehend the different ways that wellbeing shows up and the ways that we can each support our own and others' wellbeing.	In linking and connecting in an exchange of ideas, deeper understanding of the desired future enabled the collective intelligence to be surfaced, thus composing a narrative that belongs to the whole and not just individuals.	In bringing together business operation staff and teaching staff, realisation of the value that each mutual exchange offers towards the benefit of how the whole system functions were made conscious across multiple contexts.	By intentionally honouring all contributions and individual perspectives, greater trust was cultivated through people knowing their individual unique contributions unitedly contribute to the greater whole.
Response-ability	Using words and vocabulary in ways that nurture response-ability for the purpose of collective wellbeing.	Through listening together for insights and deeper questions, participants engaged in a process of shared meaning-making and were better equipped to comprehend and develop responsive approaches that support collective wellbeing and thriving.	Through the Wellbeing Café process, contributions of ideas supported comprehension of group functioning, relational interactions and decision-making, leading to greater comprehension of the co-creation of the ways our interactions shape our culture.	The process of conversational rounds and listening to each other revealed participants' greater capacity to embrace their roles and responsibilities beyond operational roles towards embracing their relational roles in the co-creation of a System of Wellbeing.	Participants developed relational awareness in becoming more adaptable and responsive in how they show up, inviting in an intentional way of being around letting go of rigid agendas that aren't serving, towards following and trusting in the collective wisdom of the group.

groups, interviews, and the Wellbeing Café process indicated that positive social interactions and connections were key factors in enabling wellbeing to emerge, reinforcing the importance of wellbeing literacy in transforming organisational culture. The insights gathered through this qualitative data not only validate the theoretical framework for cultivating an SoW but also provide concrete examples of how regenerative capabilities and conditions can be activated in real-world settings in the promotion of an SoW. While the table includes just a few examples, it illustrates the transformative potential of wellbeing literacy and regenerative conditions in creating experiences of regenerative, relational wellbeing.

Concluding Remarks

At its core, this chapter invites individuals and organisations to reconnect with their humanness and relational intelligence through the activation of regenerative capabilities and conditions to co-create a gift ecosystem and generate renewable and regenerative resources that multiply with each exchange and interaction (Kimmerer, 2024). In a world dominated by command-and-control leadership and culture, conditions in organisations, schools, and communities often foster competition, isolation, inequity, anxiety, burnout, and fear – factors that undermine both individual and organisational wellbeing (Senge et al., 2012). We propose that overcoming these degenerative patterns hinges on our capacity to nurture regenerative structures and mindsets and relational wellbeing. By recognising the value of our relational capacity in building shared understanding of the systems we occupy, and activating regenerative capabilities of wellbeing literacy and systems awareness, and the regenerative conditions, we can take small, intentional steps to curiously, compassionately, and courageously develop new ways of showing up and co-creating systems where everyone thrives. As society becomes increasingly mechanistic and technology-driven, there is a pressing need for spaces that inspire meaning-making, new possibilities, and new ways of being. The premise of this chapter is to move beyond limiting mechanistic worldviews by activating regenerative practices and structures that support collective systemic wellbeing. Through valuing regenerative and relational capabilities and conditions, we can collectively build systems that promote shared understanding and create thriving communities, schools, and workplaces – *Systems of Wellbeing* where everyone can flourish.

References

Alexandrova, A. (2017). *A philosophy for the science of well-being*. Oxford University Press.

Allen, K. E. (2019). *Leading from the roots: Nature-inspired leadership lessons for Today's world*. Morgan James Publishing.

Bateson, G. (2000). *Steps to an ecology of mind: Collected essays in anthropology, psychiatry, evolution, and epistemology*. University of Chicago Press.

Bateson, N. (2022). An essay on ready-ing: Tending the prelude to change. *Systems Research and Behavioural Science*, *39*(5), 990–1004.

Boell, M, M., Herrmann, L., Cook, L. (2025). Towards a methodology for living systems change. [White paper]. *MIT Systems Awareness Lab.*

Brooks, J. A., Shablack, H., Gendron, M., Satpute, A. B., Parrish, M. H., & Lindquist, K. A. (2017). The role of language in the experience and perception of emotion: A neuroimaging meta-analysis. *Social Cognitive and Affective Neuroscience*, *12*(2), 169–183.

Brown, J. (2010). *The world café: Shaping our futures through conversations that matter.* Berrett-Koehler Publishers.

Capra, F. (1996). *The web of life. A new scientific understanding of living systems.* Anchor Books.

Capra, F. (2014). *The systems view of life: A unifying vision.* Cambridge University Press.

Curren, R., Boniwell, I., Ryan, R. M., Oades, L., Brighouse, H., Unterhalter, E., Kristjánsson, K., de Ruyter, D., Macleod, C., Morris, I., & White, M., (2024). Finding consensus on well-being in education. *Theory and Research in Education*, *22*(2), 117–157.

Fullan, M. (2011). *Change leader: Learning to do what matters most.* John Wiley & Sons.

Gallup (2024). *State of the global workplace.* Gallup.

Gibbons, L. V. (2020). Regenerative—The new sustainable? *Sustainability*, *12*(13), 5483

Giller, K. E., Hijbeek, R., Andersson, J. A., & Sumberg, J. (2021). Regenerative agriculture: An agronomic perspective. *Outlook on Agriculture*, *50*(1), 13–25.

Karisto, A. (2017). Reciprocity and well-being. In M. Törrönen, C. Munn-Giddings, & L. Tarkiainen (Eds.), *Reciprocal relationships and well-being* (pp. 9–25). Routledge.

Kern, M. L., & Taylor, J. A. (2021). Systems informed positive education. In M. L. Kern & M. L. Wehmeyer (Eds.), *The Palgrave handbook of positive education* (pp. 109–135). Springer International Publishing.

Kern, M. L., Williams, P., Spong, C., Colla, R., Sharma, K., Downie, A., Taylor, J. A., Sharp, S., Siokou, C., & Oades, L. G. (2020). Systems informed positive psychology. *The Journal of Positive Psychology*, *15*(6), 705–715.

Kimmerer, R. W. (2024). *The Serviceberry: Abundance and reciprocity in the natural world.* Scribner.

Lawrence, P. (2021). *Coaching systemically: Five ways of thinking about systems.* Routledge.

Lemon, N., & Turner, K. (2024). Unravelling the wellbeing needs of Australian teachers: A qualitative inquiry. *The Australian Educational Researcher*, 1–21.

Lencioni, P. M. (2012). *The advantage: Why organizational health trumps everything else in business.* John Wiley & Sons.

Löhr, K., Weinhardt, M., & Sieber, S. (2020). The "World Café" as a participatory method for collecting qualitative data. *International Journal of Qualitative Methods*, *19*.

McLeod, J. (2019). Reframing responsibility in an era of responsibilisation: Education, feminist ethics. In C. Halse, C. Hartung, & J. Wright (Eds.), *Responsibility and responsibilisation in education* (pp. 43–56). Routledge.

Meadows, D. H. (2008). *Thinking in systems: A primer.* Chelsea green publishing.

Oades, L. G., Ozturk, C., Hou, H., & Slemp, G. R. (2020). Wellbeing literacy: A language-use capability relevant to wellbeing outcomes of positive psychology intervention. *The Journal of Positive Psychology*, *15*(5), 696–700.

Oades, L. G., Baker, L. M., Francis, J. J., & Taylor, J. A. (2021). Wellbeing literacy and positive education. In M. L. Kern & M. L. Wehmeyer (Eds.), *The Palgrave handbook of positive education* (pp. 325–343). Cham: Springer International Publishing.

Oades, L. G., Taylor, J. A., Francis, J., & Baker, L. M. (2021). Wellbeing literacy as an emancipatory and transformative capability. In M. A. White & F. McCallum (Eds.), *Wellbeing and resilience education* (pp. 209–231). Routledge.

Quinn, R. E. (2015). *The positive organization: Breaking free from conventional cultures, constraints, and beliefs*. Berrett-Koehler Publishers.

Scharmer, C. O. (2016). *Theory U: Leading from the future as it emerges*. Berrett-Koehler Publishers.

Senge, P., Boell, M., Cook, L., Martin, J., Lynn, K., Haygaru, T., Gruen, S., & Urrea, C., (2019). Introduction to compassionate systems framework in schools. *The Center for Systems Awareness. Available at JWEL Compassionate Systems Report, 3*, p. 19.

Senge, P., Hamilton, H., & Kania, J. (2015). The dawn of system leadership. *Stanford Social Innovation Review, 13*(1), 27–33.

Senge, P. M. (1997). The fifth discipline. *Measuring Business Excellence, 1*(3), 46–51.

Senge, P. M., Cambron-McCabe, N., Lucas, T., Smith, B., & Dutton, J. (2012). *Schools that learn (updated and revised): A fifth discipline field book for educators, parents, and everyone who cares about education*. Crown Currency.

Spong, C., & O'Keefe, K. (2022). *Wellbeing – Taking a new perspective*. Medium. https://medium.com/@cassspong/wellbeing-taking-a-new-perspective-46e3620d1884

Steger, M. F. (2024). Regenerative positive psychology: A call to reorient wellbeing science to meet the realities of our world. *The Journal of Positive Psychology, 20*(3), 373–396.

Stengel, B. S. (2023). *Responsibility: Philosophy of education in practice*. Bloomsbury Publishing.

Winton, T. (2010). Flocks not clocks: Learning the principles of self-organisation. *The Systems Thinker, 21*(4), 1–5.

26

EXAMINING THE INTERFACE OF INCLUSIVE LANGUAGE AND WELLBEING LITERACY

Lisa McKay-Brown

Introduction

In an era where human rights are central to the ways that society interacts, fostering cultures where all people are valued, respected, and recognised for their unique talents and perspectives is integral to fostering wellbeing. Language and language use have critical roles in building inclusion and inclusive environments. Language influences the way individuals feel and interact with one another and can reflect societal attitudes and biases (Stuckings & McKay-Brown, 2024, Inclusive language guide). Inclusive language increases awareness of the ways that expressions and words can marginalise and exclude individuals and groups of people. To consider language to be inclusive, it "needs to be respectful, accurate, [and] unbiased", with its use led by people with lived experience of diverse backgrounds (Likis, 2021, p. 7). However, it also needs to be acknowledged that language, and certainly inclusive language does not always free individuals as it is inherently linked with power-knowledge relations of dominant cultures (Godley & Minnici, 2008) and entrenched histories of oppression and marginalisation.

This chapter will examine inclusive language and inclusive language guides as examples of wellbeing literacy. It will explore the ways that inclusive language can promote wellbeing using language that is respectful of diversity. The chapter will also describe the ways that inclusive language and associated guides can provide examples of inclusive language as it is used in relation to specific attributes (such as age, gender identity, sexual identity, socioeconomic status, disability and race) and identified groups with shared cultural experiences or backgrounds (such as Aboriginal and Torres Strait Islander peoples, people with disability). Acknowledging language that is representative of

DOI: 10.4324/9781003644293-26

diverse groups can uplift and empower which, in turn, promotes wellbeing. Viewing inclusive language through the lens of wellbeing literacy will add an additional dimension that further emphasises the links between inclusion and wellbeing.

Inclusion and Inclusive Language

Inclusion

Inclusion is a global construct and situated within a broad social justice agenda supported by United Nations declarations and conventions (e.g., the *Universal Declaration on Human Rights, 1948; the United Nations Convention on the Rights of the Child, 1989; the United Nations Conventions on the Rights of Persons with Disabilities 2007; the UNESCO Salamanca Statement, 1994*). These declarations and conventions recognise the need for a global commitment to combating discrimination and rising inequalities within and between individuals, groups and countries (United Nations System Chief Executives Board for Coordination, 2017) and have led to the development of the Sustainable Development Goals (United Nations, 2015). While all goals are centred in the human rights of all people, Sustainable Development Goal 10 has a specific focus on inclusion and aims to "empower and promote the social, economic and political inclusion of all, irrespective of age, sex, disability, race, ethnicity, origin, religion or economic or other status" by 2030 (United Nations, 2015, para 10.2). Inclusion is both a process and a goal and to achieve this the United Nations have created a conceptual framework that focuses on three related yet distinct concepts: equality, non-discrimination and equity (United Nations System Chief Executives Board for Coordination, 2017). Equality refers to ensuring that all individuals and groups have access to opportunities and outcomes. Non-discrimination focuses on the "prohibition of discrimination against individuals and groups on the grounds identified in international human rights treaties", and equity is the "fair treatment of all population groups in society and fairness in the distribution of costs, benefits and opportunities" (United Nations System Chief Executives Board for Coordination, 2017, p. 32). This framework provides a common approach to addressing equality, non-discrimination and equity at country, regional and global levels.

But how do we get there? How do we create environments that promote equality, non-discrimination and equity? Language and language use are examples of inclusive practices that can create conditions that are capable of influencing these concepts. Language misuse can increase stigmatising attitudes and negative stereotypes for individuals and groups and have a profound impact on the self-worth and wellbeing of individuals and groups (Lynn & Lennon-Dearing, 2024). Conversely, language that is supportive and empowering can "enhance the wellbeing of individuals, groups and communities by communicating inclusivity and acceptance" (Lynn & Lennon-Dearing, 2024, p. 3). Let's explore now how inclusive language can enhance wellbeing, raise awareness and support the creation of respectful relationships and environments.

Inclusive Language

Inclusive language is a key determinant in creating environments of support where the identities of individuals and groups from diverse backgrounds and lived experiences are affirmed and respected. Inclusive language is characterised by informed, deliberate and mindful word choices that respect the diverse values, cultures and experiences of individuals or groups (Stuckings & McKay-Brown, 2024, Inclusive language guide). Inclusive language can support people to feel safe, seen, respected and empowered and can provide representation and visibility to individuals and groups who have experienced discrimination and been historically marginalised and silenced (Stuckings & McKay-Brown, 2024, Inclusive language guide). The use of inclusive language demonstrates respect, acceptance, and care. Proactively engaging with, learning about, and using inclusive language can reduce the onus on individuals and/or groups who share attributes, experiences, or culture to "explain" their identity or lived experience (Stuckings & McKay-Brown, 2024, Inclusive language guide).

Language that is not inclusive can cause harm to individuals and groups. Certainly, language can be used to exclude and reinforce negative attitudes and stereotypes. Microaggressions which are the "experience of a slight or putdown, a violation based on a person's identity" (Smith & Griffiths, 2022, p. 287) and can be verbal, behavioural and/or systemic (Adedeji et al., 2023). McLean et al. (2021) suggest that the use of microaggressions may be unintentional as those using them may be unaware of the impact of their language, nor may they understand their own implicit bias. Examples of microaggressions include misgendering and mispronouncing trans individuals, asking someone where they were born, a security guard following a person of colour around a shopping centre, using the term "you guys" to refer to a mixed gender group, saying that someone "suffers from" a disability or using a phrase like "you people". Microaggressions can become normalised language and actions within society and identifying and calling these out often become the responsibility of the person who is the receiver of the message.

There is extensive research on the ways that microaggressions can impact wellbeing for individuals and groups from diverse backgrounds. Researchers have found that exposures to microaggressions may lead to social emotional distress, anxiety and depression, suicidal ideation, substance use and social-emotional wellbeing (Adedeji et al., 2023; DeSon & Andover, 2024; Gonzales et al., 2023; McLean et al., 2021; Perales et al., 2022; Smith & Griffiths,

2022). Avoiding microaggressions is more complex than simply avoiding words and phrases or actions. Rather it is important to understand that microaggressions entrench power relations and discrimination between and within individuals and groups. Inclusive language goes beyond avoiding discriminatory practices, rather its aim is to promote communication that acknowledges societal power structures and embraces diversity, while building environments where individuals feel safe to be their true, authentic selves (Andoh, 2024).

However, inclusive language is not just about the words that are used; it is the intent behind their use. Social justice issues cannot be fixed by just using inclusive language, rather it needs to be understood how and why inclusive language needs to be used. The terminologies used in inclusive language constantly evolve and change to better suit their useability for specific groups and support self-determination by being "contextual and fluid rather than static and fixed" (Mirabella et al., 2024, p. 10). Self-determination is a component of a rights-based approach with choice and autonomy being linked to advancing social justice outcomes (Jorgensen et al., 2023). Self-determination supports an individual's right to identify the language and terminology they choose for themselves and for others to use. Graham et al. (2023) state that when deciding the terminology to be used that "the person or group of people should remain present in the terminology" (p. 76), and once this has occurred then there are two positions, person-first (or person-centred) language and identity-first language (see Table 26.1). Person-first language puts the person before their attributes (gender, sexuality, ethnicity, disability, socioeconomic status), background or lived experience. It is used in the *Conventions on the Rights of Persons with Disabilities 2007* and can support intersectional identification. Identity-first language puts the aspect of difference before the person (Graham et al., 2023) and is used when a person or group sees their diversity as central to their identity or to show their cultural connection to a particular group. As with all inclusive language use, respecting the choices of the person is central to its use. Generally, in writing and research person-first language is used. Identity-first language is more commonly used by individuals with lived experience. It is recommended to

TABLE 26.1 Examples of person-first and identity-first language

Person-first (person-centred) language	*Identity-first language (using capital letters refers to the community)*
Person with disability	I am Autistic
Student who uses alternative communication	I'm Deaf
Individual with intersex variations	I am Queer
Children with diabetes	A disabled person

confirm a person's preference before using identity-first language when referring to individuals or groups.

Wellbeing Literacy and Inclusive Language

Wellbeing Literacy

Wellbeing literacy involves the intentional use of language about and for wellbeing (Oades, 2017) and is an umbrella term that incorporates emotional literacy, health literacy and mental health literacy (Oades et al., 2021). The authors go on to note that having the "language, knowledge, and language skills" (p. 327) related to wellbeing enables purposeful communication that supports the wellbeing of individuals and groups that is relational and, as with inclusive language, can create environments of support. Hou et al. (2021) assert that wellbeing literacy focuses on how and why language is used in the everyday as well as how it can be leveraged to produce wellbeing. Wellbeing literacy is also a language-based capability, rather than an intervention which uses "a repertoire of skills and options" to influence wellbeing (Hou et al., 2021, p. 3). This aligns with inclusive language use that requires a conscious decision that is contextually appropriate, with terminology carefully selected to promote respect and equity (Likis, 2021) to lead to positive outcomes for wellbeing. Wellbeing literacy and inclusive language can promote the human rights of equality, non-discrimination and equity by delivering empowering and transforming experiences through conscious language choices.

Wellbeing literacy has five components or dimensions that are used to operationalise this capability (Table 26.2). Hou et al. (2021) explain that wellbeing literacy requires an ability to use vocabulary to articulate or express understandings of wellbeing as well as a knowledge about wellbeing. Being literate about and for wellbeing requires individuals to be able to comprehend texts using multiple means of representation as well as compose wellbeing-related

TABLE 26.2 The five components of wellbeing literacy (Oades et al., 2021, p. 211)

Component	*Description*
Vocabulary and knowledge *about* wellbeing	Words and basic facts about wellbeing (i.e., content that is signified)
Comprehension of multimodal text related to wellbeing	Reading, listening, viewing about and for wellbeing
Composition of multimodal text related to wellbeing	Writing, speaking, creating about and for wellbeing
Context awareness and adaptability	Awareness of differences across contexts and adapting the use of language to fit the relevant context
Intentionality *for* wellbeing	Habit of intentionally using language to maintain or improve wellbeing of self or others

texts using multiple means of action and expression. Wellbeing literacy is context specific meaning that language changes and adapts depending on where and how it is being used. Finally, wellbeing literacy is intentional and requires a "desire to deliberately use language to improve the wellbeing of oneself, others or the world" (Hou et al., 2021, p. 3).

Wellbeing Literacy and Inclusive Language

Inclusive language aligns with the five conditions of wellbeing literacy proposed in Oades et al. (2020). Inclusive language uses specific vocabulary and requires knowledge about its importance in supporting the wellbeing of individuals and groups. The comprehension and composition of multimodal text can be seen in the use of inclusive language guides as tools to make language visible and support people to access it, to see it written but also to speak it when interacting with others. There are many resources available on the internet that include stories of the power of inclusive language that speak directly to wellbeing comprehension. Creating meeting and event guides that use inclusive language and prioritise digital and physical accessibility are examples of wellbeing composition (e.g., see Inclusion Australia, 2023).

Inclusive language is context-dependent. Its use needs to be adapted depending on who is using it and in what context. Inclusive language is not just about replacing words. Rather understanding the context is important in order to ascertain whether an alternative is more appropriate (Likis, 2021). Its use is also dependent on the preferences of the people to whom you are referring – that is do they use identity first or person first language (explained earlier), which is turn supports wellbeing. For example, a person might choose to say "I am autistic" when introducing themselves to others but prefers that when someone else is introducing them at a formal event that they are identified as a person with autism. When using gender-inclusive language, a person might ask that others use one pronoun in public and a different one in private situations. Using "black" when referring to Aboriginal and Torres Strait Islander peoples is considered an offensive and reductive term and should be avoided. Being aware of an individual's choice in specific contexts and using it correctly identifies a person who has context awareness. Inclusive language, inclusive language guides and other resources, are just that, guides and need to be used with care and consent. If you are unsure, ask but also realise that individuals and groups have a right to keep their identities private (Nee & MacFarlane Smith, n.d.).

Inclusive language is intentional and requires the person using it to have an awareness of the importance of its use and how it creates opportunities for wellbeing and respect. A recent Australian study examined the use of trans-inclusive language in the workplace and found that the intentional use of trans-inclusive language had positive effects on trans-gender individuals' wellbeing (Perales et al., 2022). The results also indicated that trans people's feelings of belonging and inclusion at work can be positively influenced by efforts to foster inclusive language (Perales et al., 2022). While this is but one example, it highlights the ways that an informed use of inclusive language can improve the wellbeing outcomes for people.

Inclusive Language Guides as Enactments of Wellbeing Literacy

Inclusive language guides are documents created by organisations to operationalise the use of inclusive language. With the increasing awareness about the harms associated with non-inclusive or discriminatory language, there has been a movement within organisations, publishers, government departments and professional associations to create guidance about inclusive language. These groups have developed policy statements, frameworks and language guides to encourage the respectful and inclusive use of language in a range of activities including research, writing communications, and referencing (Fernandez-Sanchez et al., 2024). When considering the importance of vocabulary, knowledge, comprehension, composition, context and intentionality in developing the capability of wellbeing literacy, inclusive language guides are well-placed to support the enactment of these components.

However, while these commitments to inclusion and inclusive language are positive, an environmental scan of web-based documents undertaken by Fernandez-Sanchez et al. (2024) found that there were conflicting and controversial terms that suggested an unawareness of the impact of language on diverse populations. Examples of this included the use of general terms such as "vulnerable, marginalized, oppressed, hard to reach, underprivileged, and underserved" (Fernandez-Sanchez et al., 2024, p. 9) rather than specific terms such as "populations made vulnerable" or "communities marginalized by systemic equalities" (p. 9). When developing guides for inclusive language and selecting language to be included, it is necessary to acknowledge that language can give power to some while silencing and marginalising others (Drill et al., 2019) and requires engagement with people with lived experience. Language also shifts and changes, so any guides created need to be living documents that are revised regularly.

When using inclusive language and inclusive language guides as an enactment of wellbeing literacy, I posit the following figure to consider their intersectional nature (Figure 26.1). The inner three circles show the connection between these components. The outer two circles encompass the inner circles because you cannot have inclusive language nor use inclusive language guides effectively without context or intentionality. The following paragraphs explain this conceptualisation further.

At the heart of using inclusive language guides to improve the wellbeing outcomes of all people but particularly individuals with lived experience is intentionality. There is an intentional want to promote equality, non-discrimination

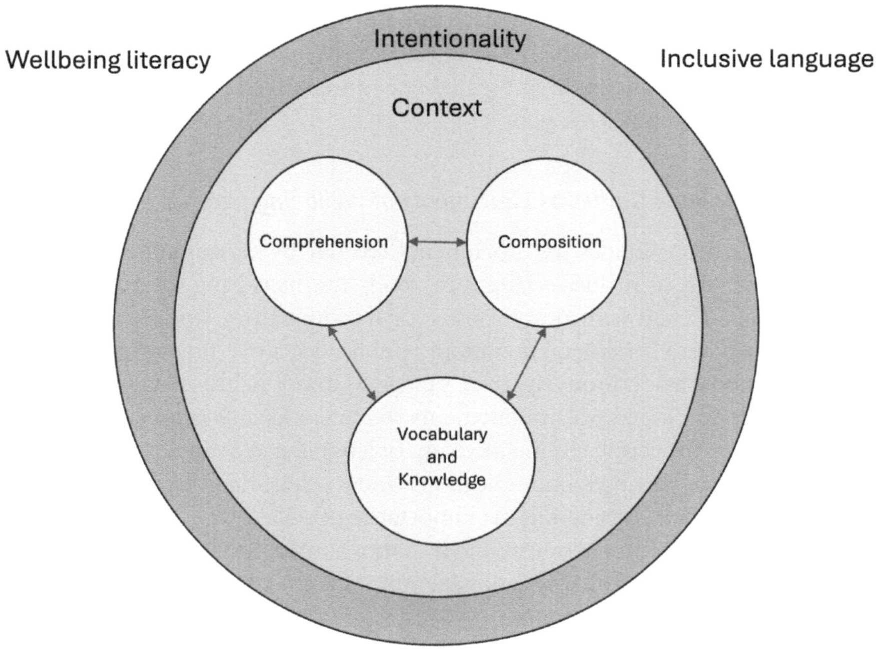

FIGURE 26.1 Intersection of wellbeing literacy and inclusive language.

and equity through respectful and thoughtful use of language in all of its modalities. Inside of intentionality is context and the intentional use of language to align with the context in which is it being used. Context sensitivity enables decisions to be made about language use that is appropriate, indicates ways to adapt language and gives guidance around communication modes. Context specific use of inclusive language is seen when language and communication modes are selected that meet different situations and the communication needs of the context (Oades et al., 2022).

In the centre circle are the components of vocabulary and knowledge, comprehension and composition. These are interrelated components that need to work together to support the intentional and contextually sensitive use of language. Inclusive language guides provide the vocabulary that can be used to support inclusion. However, this vocabulary cannot be used without knowledge, and inclusive language guides will often provide a range of guiding principles or recommendations to build knowledge of understanding diversity and inclusion and ways to use the vocabulary. Examples include, avoid language with harmful associations, honour how people identify themselves, consider intersectionality, and distinguish between borrowing and appropriating terms and work with others (Nee & MacFarlane Smith, n.d.). While inclusive language guides are often text-based documents, they are used to both comprehend and compose in multimodal ways. Inclusive language guides may include links to a range of resources to support their use. These include videos, podcasts and online web resources that individuals can access to build their comprehension about an aspect of inclusion that when put into action might increase their confidence in responding to diversity. Composing for wellbeing using inclusive language guides can be seen when an individual uses a person's pronouns when introducing them as a speaker. Another example might be using inclusive language when developing a research proposal, recruiting participants or writing a journal article. For example, if recruiting an Autistic population for a research study, depending on your own positioning and lived experience you might write "person with a lived experience of autism" or "Autistic person" but you would not write "individuals with symptoms of autism".

When all components are present and work together there is a greater possibility that an inclusive language guide can support the use of inclusive language and wellbeing literacy. As noted earlier in the chapter, non-inclusive and discriminatory language can have significant effects on physical and mental wellbeing for people with diverse attributes, backgrounds and lived experiences. It can reinforce positions of power and privilege in society and hinder efforts towards the universal human rights of equality, non-discrimination and equity.

Conclusion

In conclusion, the significance of inclusive language and inclusive language use to create environments that are equitable, non-discriminatory and promote equity cannot be overstated. However, inclusive language use alone cannot address the complexities of systemic inequalities, power dynamics and historical marginalisation of people with diverse attributes, backgrounds and lived experience. This chapter posits that by bringing together wellbeing literacy as a capability with inclusive language that there can be a move towards an intentional and contextually specific positioning that uses vocabulary and knowledge, comprehension and composition to engage with inclusive language and language use. This is a foundational step in advancing an approach to operationalise the use of inclusive language to promote wellbeing outcomes using a defined, conceptual model.

References

Adedeji, A., Olonisakin, T. T., Metzner, F., Buchcik, J., Tsabedze, W., Boehnke, K., & Idemudia, E. S. (2023). Interpreting microaggression as a determinant of wellbeing. *Journal of Racial & Ethnic Health Disparities*, *10*(5), 2470–2481. https://doi.org/10.1007/s40615-022-01426-z

Andoh, E. (2024, January 31). *Why inclusive language matters.* American Psychological Association. Retrieved September 9 from https://www.apa.org/ed/precollege/psn/2022/09/inclusive-language

DeSon, J. J., & Andover, M. S. (2024). Microaggressions toward sexual and gender minority emerging adults: An updated systematic review of psychological correlates and outcomes and the role of intersectionality. *LGBT Health, 11*(4), 249–268. https://doi.org/10.1089/lgbt.2023.0032

Drill, R., Malone, J., Flouton-Barnes, M., Cotton, L., Keyes, S., Wasserman, R., Wilson, K., Young, M., Laws, H., & Beinashowitz, J. (2019). Inclusive language regarding gender, sexual orientation, and relationship status: The ongoing process and outcome of revising psychiatric materials. *The Journal of Mental Health Training, Education, and Practice, 14*(6), 385–398. https://doi.org/10.1108/JMHTEP-02-2018-0009

Fernandez-Sanchez, H., Marfo, E. A., Santa Maria, D., & Mumba, M. (2024). Language matters: Exploring preferred terms for diverse populations. *Global Qualitative Nursing Research, 11*, 23333936241275266. https://doi.org/10.1177/23333936241275266

Godley, A. J., & Minnici, A. (2008). Critical language pedagogy in an urban high school English class. *Urban Education, 43*(3), 319–346. Retrieved June 12, 2010, from http://uex.sagepub.com/content/43/3/319

Gonzales, H. M., Chai, K. N., & King, D. M. (2023). Racial microaggressions: Experiences among international students in Australia and its impact on stress and psychological wellbeing. *Journal of Comparative and International Higher Education, 15*(1), 148–168. https://research.ebsco.com/linkprocessor/plink?id=a671fb86-f205-3412-bf12-c726414d5c04

Graham, L. J., Medhurst, M., Tancredi, H., Spandagou, I., & Walton, E. (2023). Fundamental concepts of inclusive education. In L. J. Graham (Ed.), *Inclusive education for the 21st century: Theory, policy and practice* (2nd ed., pp. 60–80). Routledge. https://research.ebsco.com/linkprocessor/plink?id=02550687-db9e-3982-8ccc-5466d5452bef

Hou, H., Chin, T. C., Slemp, G. R., & Oades, L. G. (2021). Wellbeing literacy: Conceptualization, measurement, and preliminary empirical findings from students, parents and school staff. *International Journal of Environmental Research and Public Health, 18*(4). https://doi.org/10.3390/ijerph18041485

Inclusion Australia. (2023). *A guide to running inclusive meetings*. Inclusion Australia. Retrieved February 10, 2025, from https://www.inclusionaustralia.org.au/wp-content/uploads/2023/04/A-Guide-to-Running-Inclusive-Meetings.pdf

Jorgensen, M., Nankervis, K., & Chan, J. (2023). 'Environments of concern': Reframing challenging behaviour within a human rights approach. *International Journal of Developmental Disabilities, 69*(1), 95–100. https://doi.org/10.1080/20473869.2022.2118513

Likis, F. E. (2021). Inclusive language promotes equity: The power of words. *Journal of Midwifery & Women's Health, 66*, 7–9. https://doi.org/10.1111/jmwh.13225

Lynn, V. A., & Lennon-Dearing, R. (2024). Putting people first: The power of inclusive language. *Journal of HIV/AIDS & Social Services*, 1–6. https://doi.org/10.1080/15381501.2024.2390923

McLean, M., Roche Jennifer, M., Audet, L., Stribling, D., & Kaufman, R. (2021). Explicit and implicit cognitive processes associated with microaggression endorsement. *Perspectives of the ASHA Special Interest Groups, 6*(6), 1719–1728. https://doi.org/10.1044/2021_PERSP-21-00005

Mirabella, M., Mazzuca, C., Livio, C. D., Giannantonio, B. D., Rosati, F., Lorusso, M. M., Lingiardi, V., Borghi, A. M., & Giovanardi, G. (2024). The role of language in nonbinary identity construction: Gender words matter. *Psychology of Sexual Orientation and Gender Diversity*. https://doi.org/10.1037/sgd0000729

Nee, J., & MacFarlane Smith, G. (n.d.). *Understanding inclusive language: A framework*. BerkleyHass. https://haas.berkeley.edu/wp-content/uploads/Understanding-IL-Playbook-3.pdf

Oades, L. G. (2017). Wellbeing literacy: The missing link in positive education. In M. A. White, G. R. Slemp, & A. S. Murray (Eds.), *Future directions in well-being: Education, organizations and policy* (pp. 169–173). Springer International Publishing/Springer Nature. https://doi.org/10.1007/978-3-319-56889-8_29

Oades, L. G., Baker, L. M., Francis, J. J., & Taylor, J. A. (2021). Wellbeing literacy and positive education. In M. L. Kern & M. L. Wehmeyer (Eds.), *The Palgrave handbook of positive education* (pp. 325–343). Springer International Publishing. https://doi.org/10.1007/978-3-030-64537-3_13

Oades, L. G., Hou, H., Francis, J. J., Baker, L. M., & Huang, L. (2022). Well-being literacy: Language use as a way to contextualize the process of positive education. In K. A. Allen, M. J. Furlong, D. Vella-Brodrick, & S. Suldo (Eds.), *Handbook of positive psychology in schools* (pp. 91–103). Routledge.

Oades, L. G., Ozturk, C., Hou, H., & Slemp, G. R. (2020). Wellbeing literacy: A language-use capability relevant to wellbeing outcomes of positive psychology intervention. *The Journal of Positive Psychology*, *15*(5), 696–700. https://doi.org/10.1080/17439760.2020.1789711

Oades, L. G., Taylor, J. A., Francis, J., & Baker, L. M. (2021). Wellbeing literacy as an emancipatory and transformative capability. In M. A. White & F. McCallum (Eds.), *Wellbeing and resilience education: COVID-19 and its impact on education* (pp. 209–231). Routledge.

Perales, F., Ablaza, C., & Elkin, N. (2022). Exposure to inclusive language and well-being at work among transgender employees in Australia, 2020. *American Journal of Public Health*, *112*(3), 482–490. https://doi.org/10.2105/ajph.2021.306602

Smith, I. A., & Griffiths, A. (2022). Microaggressions, everyday discrimination, workplace incivilities, and other subtle slights at work: A meta-synthesis. *Human Resource Development Review*, *21*(3), 275–299. https://doi.org/10.1177/15344843221098756

Stuckings, C., & McKay-Brown, L. (2024). *Inclusive language guide*. Faculty of Education, The University of Melbourne.

United Nations. (2015). Transforming our world: The 2030 agenda for sustainable development. https://www.un.org/en/development/desa/population/migration/generalassembly/docs/globalcompact/A_RES_70_1_E.pdf

United Nations System Chief Executives Board for Coordination. (2017). *Leaving no one behind: Equality and non-discrimination at the heart of sustainable development.* United Nations. https://unsceb.org/sites/default/files/imported_files/CEB%20equality%20framework-A4-web-rev3.pdf

INDEX

Note: Page references in *italics* denote figures, in **bold** tables and with "n" endnotes.